MW00605011

DEAD, BUT NOT GONE

Are You Part of the Soul-Bridge
to Guide Them Home?

TOBY EVANS

Toby Evans is also author of:

Keeper of the Circles: Answering the Call to Wholeness, an autobiographical journey into the mysteries of the labyrinth and the life of a "Keeper of the Circles."
Call to Wholeness, a CD of 11 original songs.

Chakra Labyrinth Cards, a 55-card deck with an instructional booklet and embossed Chakra Labyrinth finger-tracing pattern. A self-reflective tool that promotes awareness, facilitates change, and inspires inner peace. The pattern can be used as a portal to assist with 'soul crossings.'
Available at www.sagebrushexchange.com and Amazon.

Archived Radio Shows:

Dead, But Not Gone, boldbravemedia.com/dead-but-not-gone/

Live Soul Crossing Sessions, empirebroadcastinggroupcom/toby-evans-spiritual-counselor

Blog Talk Radio Interview, blogtalkradio.com/closeuptalkradio/2015/08/20/cutv-news-radio-spotlights-toby-evans-of-sagebrush-exchange

DEDICATION

To Dad, "Lefty" Green, and my brother Chris Green—In the 'wake' of your deaths, a deeper awakening began to wash over me.

To Mary K Barge, Debbie Maxey, Della Heese, Nicole Christine, Rowena Pattee Kryder, Gary Langston, James (Diego) Braddock, Don Fuerney, Brad Collins, Jack Bartholomew, Jana Hawkins, Graeme Gibson, Carol House, Betsy Wenzel, Therese Becker, Clarinda Sayre, Dan Holland, Dave Runions, Dolores Cannon and Dr. Michael Newton—You each served as a navigational buoy, an inspirational beacon for me and others, guiding us toward the shores of a 'New Earth.' Thank you for 'stirring the waters' in your unique ways while being anchors of grounded goodness.

To my 'Dog Pack,' the experts on living and dying—Daisy, Kia, Sparky, Cowboy, Butch, Neesa, Lexus, Donut, Chief and Lady. As protectors, you guarded the gateway of my heart. No matter how badly I wanted to slam it shut, you showed me that my most valuable contribution as a human, depends on keeping it open.

To Yukon and Rusty, our living sentinels who are still on 'heart duty' and Sunny the stray cat, who reminds me that having a place to belong is true freedom.

Copyright © 2018 by Toby Evans. All Rights Reserved.

No part of this work covered by the copyright hereon may be reproduced or used in any form or by any means—graphic, electronic, or mechanical, including photocopying, recording, taping, Web distribution, or information storage and retrieval systems—without the prior written permission of the publisher.

ISBN-13: 978-0-9762728-2-3
ISBN-10: 0-9762728-2-2

Published by Putman Productions LLC in the United States of America.
PO Box 85, Bellevue, IA 52031

First edition: February 2018. Second printing: April 2018

Credits:

Cover photo—"Architecture of a Single Breath" by Paul Rudy.
Background photo for the portal patterns insert—"Star Fish Solar System" by Paul Rudy.
Graphic Design—Pamela Hawkins, Indigo Creative Space, Kansas City, Missouri.
Editing with expert loving eyes—Haley Phillips, Lidia Young, and Jean Kilquist.

ACKNOWLEDGMENTS

To those who were gracious enough to relive, share, or allow me to tell your stories—my deepest appreciation: Nikkea Walkker, Marilyn Larson, Jo Ann Mast, Jean Kilquist, Dan Fagan, Teresa Scott, Cindy Welch, Paul Rudy, Jennifer Martin, Gloria Squitiro, Athena Zae, Steve Merritt, Julie Gosney McCutheon, Jelaila Starr, Angela Blare, Kristen Wolf, Julie Kellogg, and Kate Sinnett.

Poems by Vickie Putman and Therese Becker.

Gratitude to Vickie Putman for walking beside me on the big soul adventures that require deeper commitment. As a midwife extraordinaire, you are always there when I most need you—at the beginning and at the end of the birth canal.

To my husband, Bruce—Thank you for being the Earth Steward you are, caring for the land as well as our needs. In spite of having no interest in my beliefs or the work I do, you provide the support and love to make it all possible.

To my son, Adam—I acknowledge your leadership skills, not by what you achieve, accomplish, or accumulate, but by how you accept responsibility, tempering your power with compassion, and using your strengths to empower others.

To Pamela Hawkins—The 'siddhi' of your inherent genius shines through your artistic expressions. Infinite gratitude for giving the spirit of this book its 'skin,' bringing it into its final living form.

TABLE OF CONTENTS

INTRODUCTION

The late Dolores Cannon, engrossed in her own personal journey of discovery, perfectly described my life, circa 2013.

"Mainly because there were no instructions," she wrote, *"I felt I had been thrust into something new and exciting."*

This was part of my struggle in 2013, as I was learning remarkable truths about myself and about the natural physical and spiritual processes of our Earth. I thought I must really be special to be tasked with helping so many masses of earthbound spirits to find the light. Although I knew there were multitudes of other spiritual individuals being initiated into the ways of light workers, the path down which I was being guided was so foreign and so strange, I was convinced I was alone in the daunting task of learning how to guide lost souls home out of the prison that our Earth had become for them. I knew I was chosen for this and it made me excited and afraid, and filled with self-doubt, all at the same time.

I didn't know Toby Evans in 2013, but if I had I would have realized I wasn't so special or alone, after all. No matter how unique and important is our work, in reading this beautiful book *Dead, But Not Gone* Toby has taught me that there is always someone else who has done it first and done it better.

"I have never done this kind of thing before, but not having any rules makes it less daunting," Toby writes herein, echoing Dolores Cannon, but also suggesting a unique ability to self-realize the direction of her sacred work

guiding lost and trapped spirits to the higher astral densities.

"I trust that inner directions will come and all we have to do is follow them."

The amazing, groundbreaking work Toby describes in these pages has opened the gates that have been closed for centuries to trapped *earthbounds*. From the rocky landscape and ancient temples of Malta, to the mystical, cobblestone architecture of Michelangelo in Rome; from a transcendental journey through Incan ruins in Peru, to developing her own sacred and spiritual place on the Mid-Western prairie, Toby has blazed a remarkable path, seemingly with none of the existential angst I dragged along my own path.

"There must be some kind of cosmic rule that states: Taking on a 'soul assignment' means you will be always be given the 'tools' you need to carry it out," Toby writes.

One of the 'tools' I was given is Toby Evans. Not only did she come first, the importance of her work is far more fundamental than that. Without Toby Evans walking before me, my own work would not have been possible. Neither would the work of a host of other helpers of lost souls scattered throughout the planet.

Early in my own sojourn, a very gifted psychic friend of mine related a story of how she met a young man during one of her light worker experiences.

"Don't you recognize me?" he asked my friend.

"No," she assured him, you and I have never met before."

"But how could you not? I'm the Chosen One!" he exclaimed.

When my friend told me the story of her encounter, I had to laugh.

"Chosen for what?" I mused. "And what makes you think you're the only Chosen One?"

But isn't this the danger that so many of us face in the unfamiliarity of the ascension of our planet into a lighter and brighter density? This is something new for all of us. Our unique experiences elicit strange, euphoric, and even dangerous feelings. In our newfound freedom in the light, there is always peril of losing the humility that keeps us grounded along our path. For me, I am grounded in the constant knowledge that each one of the lost souls, the earthbound spirits, is equally valued and important—as I am—in any divine plan. Toby Evans, perhaps uniquely in my experience, understands how her work ripples through time and the Cosmos. She has opened portals closed for thousands of years, allowing healing energy to penetrate even to the darkest depths of the lower densities of our existence.

I was thrilled to read how Toby shares two of my greatest guides and influences that have helped us both along our somewhat parallel paths. Sai Baba is one of the ascended masters that has walked with me from the beginning. He has also worked with Toby and helped her through a particularly harrowing spiritual experience at the Sacsayhuaman ruins outside of Cuzco, Peru, the exact place where I had a lesser spiritual epiphany many years before. Toby also recognizes the special place of the Divine Feminine Energy in our work, epitomized for both of us in the person of Mother Mary. This Divine Feminine Energy gives life and direction to all mortal and spiritual transitions on this plane.

Dead, But Not Gone is both a practical guide to grounding and preparing yourself to be open to the light, and a preparation to offer aid to the souls and fragments of souls (including earthbound aspects of yourself from past lives) that can impede your own self-realization. It is also a richly hewn, touching and exciting account of the journey of one of the most important spiritual influences of our time.

~ Joe Lofgreen

Author of *Spirit Voices, Spirit Crossings*
Verde Valley, Arizona
Webmaster of Lightchannelers.com

PREFACE

Dodge and weave—with your guard up. As a former south-paw, 'Golden Glove' boxing champion, it is my father's instinct to doggedly fight his battle with lymphoma, deflecting the humiliating knock-out punch of death. His pride keeps me and my nine siblings in the spectator section outside his shadow-boxing ring at a safe physical and emotional distance. That is, until my sister, Gail, boards a plane and flies home, taking on the management of his care. In Dad's defended world, accepting help is as good as 'throwing in the towel.'

Gail's calm presence helps him face the reality of his final days. Although her training and work experience is as a dental technician, it is obvious to the procession of family and friends who are coming to say their goodbyes, that she is made for this role. Her innate caregiver abilities transfer into natural nursing skills. I don't arrive until three days before Dad dies, feeling that my part is less defined and more obscure. I'm not consciously aware that I have a soul-contract with him to be a spiritual midwife, giving him permission and support to go to the other side. My attention is focused on the 'big screen of death' where all the physical details are being monitored and rapidly progressing. But there is also a non-ordinary transmission—it runs like subtitles beneath the main plot, providing me with an invisible interpreter as I go deeper into the foreign territory of death.

When I sit alone with him at his bedside, I manage to say, "Dad, you are doing the hardest thing. None of us know how to die. You are showing us how to do that."

Matter-of-factly, he replies, "It's not so hard."

But in just a short 24-hour period I watch him pivot from the steep precipice of denial, stretched between terror and resistance, to find hand holds on the narrow ledge of surrender. Here he lands in a net of relief, touching down in the sacred ground called 'acceptance.'

Even though Dad's death is profound for all of us, the impact that it has on Gail and me is different. Being by his side in those final days forever changes us, re-directing our lives. This out-pictures for Gail immediately by altering her profession. Her calling to assist others is laid out in a straight line, leading her to a position with a large elder care facility where she is in charge of hiring and training entry level personnel. This eventually dissolves, but has prepared her for her soul's intended work: a job with hospice.

I, like Gail, know that Dad's death is a trigger-event, beckoning me to a path of service that involves the dying process, but my linear world expectations blind me from seeing the circuitous path with its spun thread that has been reeling me into the center of my calling all along. My work is not to help individuals prepare to die ... because my 'real' clients are already dead. Dead—but not gone. They stay connected to their old lives, their old loves, their known routines or dysfunctional patterns, remaining 'earthbound' for their own individual reasons.

I write this book to explore a perspective that typically is not considered, accepted, or even talked about: that someone that you know that has died may still be here, that large numbers of souls throughout the ages may have unintentionally run-aground. Like hitting a submerged sandbar, many remain marooned, caught 'in-between' on an emotional barrier. I hope to shed light on their reasons for remaining, and the impact that their staying may be having on your life. With expanded awareness, intentional focus, and a leap of faith, you may be part of a growing soul-bridge, learning to use the compass of your compassion to guide them home.

PREFACE

This book is presented in three parts.

Part 1: The personal experiences that opened me to the world of earthbound souls, with contributing authors sharing how this phenomenon has impacted them.

Part 2: A defining journey to Malta, illustrating a global picture of what is occurring with earthbound spirits due to the planet's current evolution.

Part 3. The influence that detrimental (dark) energies have on this issue, catalyzing us to acknowledge and heal our shadow sides in order to reclaim the Earth and our sovereign selves.

The * symbol preceding a word or phrase indicates that more information can be found in the Reference section at the back of the book.

PART

1

The only teacher better than our first-hand experiences
is the additional understanding that occurs
when we are willing to recount them.
Telling our stories offers us the gift of the Soul's perspective.
Through focused self-reflection,
we're given the opportunity to learn twice.

Is Death the last sleep?
No, it is the final awakening.

~ **Walter Scott** ~

1

PRECURSOR

The wreckage looks more like the aftermath of a tornado than a four-car accident. Millions of fiberglass pieces from a sheered RV are strewn for miles down the center median of the highway. En route to Denver, I am traveling across Kansas at dusk with my friend Alyse when we come upon this surreal scene. The cars move like a solemn funeral procession as the traffic opens back up to a one-lane crawl, flanked by the tending ambulances and the blinding strobe lights of the police cars.

Subdued by the tragedy, I am grateful that Alyse is driving so I can lie down in the back seat. Almost immediately, three distinct beings are pulled into my awareness. They are confused and shaken up. Two are men and one is a woman. Calm beyond my own comprehension, I allow the barrage of thoughts that are coming into my mind to flow out to them.

"It's going to be okay. You have all been in an accident. I am not certain if you are dead or just out of your bodies, but I want you to know you have some choices. You can remain near your body if it is injured and follow along as they take you to the hospital and then, if it is right for you, reenter when the pain subsides and you feel safe enough. You will know without any doubt and have assistance."

After transmitting this to them, one of the men disappears. Continuing, I tell the other two, "If the silver cord that connects back into your body has been severed and you have completed your time here on the Earth, you do not need to stay here. You can be anywhere you choose. If you have loved ones that you want to be with, go to them—tell them goodbye or reassure them when they find out the news. Just think of them and instantly you will be there. You are free to move into this light that is all around you. It's your true nature, and you can trust where it takes you."

The other man flickers away from my inner sight, leaving only the woman. I sense her anguish as she hesitates to impress her concerns into my mind.

"I am a single mother with an eight-year old son. We moved back to live with my father a short time ago after my mother died and now this happens! I can't leave my son and do this to my father!"

Close to hysterics, she firmly adds. *"I have to go and stay with them. I can't go anywhere else."*

My window of insight further expands, allowing me to respond. "What if your soul knew that you would die today, guiding you to already set everything into motion for both your father and son's highest good? What if you moved to be with your father because he is the perfect caretaker for your son, and your son is the perfect answer to fill the hole in your father's heart since your mother died? Raising him may give your father renewed direction and purpose. Your son may be small, but his soul is wise. He chose you as his mother knowing he would not have you long. Dealing with your absence will teach him the things that his soul wants to know. You need to trust both of them and not hold them back with your doubts and resistance to letting go. Go to them and fill them with your love, but then find the peace in the light that can set all of you free."

She withdraws her energy and is gone. Sitting up in the back seat slightly dazed, I relay this to Alyse, wondering if I made up the whole thing.

A month later I am traveling with my husband, returning from a weekend environmental conference when a motorcycle in front of our car wobbles and then careens across the highway, coming to a dusty heap on the edge of the road.

I shout at my husband, "We have to stop!"

He pulls over, doubtful that there is anything that we can do. I get out of the car and run toward the scene. Right behind us another vehicle stops. The woman getting out tells us she is an off-duty paramedic. Assessing the situation, she calls for help and tells me to keep the man from moving. I take his hand that is scraped and uncontrollably flailing and try to calm him. He is a big, gruff looking guy with long red hair held back by a dirty blue bandana. He is not wearing a helmet. Making grunting sounds, he is trying to talk, but he is incoherent. It is obvious that he is in a lot of pain. Shaken up, I am not getting anything telepathically from him and feel completely blocked. His keys are lying in the middle of the road so I run to retrieve them and return to kneel by his side. Smoothing his shoulder and arms, I wait for any non-verbal communication that might come, but none does. Within minutes an ambulance arrives and I return to our car, wondering if the reason I can't pick anything up is because he is still in his body. We resume our drive, and about ten minutes later an inner explanation is dropped into my mind like a 'thought-ball' that begins to unwind.

"You were too emotionally close to the situation. Because you were touching him, you were locked into the physical realm of the shock and disbelief that his body was experiencing. Even though he was attempting to speak—his soul was not in his body."

With this new understanding, it feels like a switch is flipped and I can clearly 'hear' his panicked thoughts. *"I don't know what is happening to me. I don't want to be in a handicapped body. I don't think I can handle that. How do I get out of here?"*

Telepathically, I think my response back to him: "You can stay close to your body as you go to the hospital, and then you will have time to decide what you want to do. If it is your time to go, an opening will occur and all you have to do is go through it. But consider that you may have set this challenge up and planned for your body to recover from this—giving you a whole new perspective on life. Whatever happens, you will have the strength to deal with it. Your spirit is greater than the fear you are feeling right now."

No response comes back from him and he fades away.

Up to this point, although I have adjusted to communicating telepathically with discarnate individuals and feel comfortable with nudging them towards a bigger perspective, I have not been directly involved with the actual 'crossing over' process. I am not sure what that even entails, but I realize, I have embarked on my own 'crash-course' to finding out.

Death is often our last opportunity to live.

~ Unknown ~

2

UN-DEAD INITIATION

In the early 1990's, I am working as a co-director of a youth education program at a Unity church with a woman named Debbie. Her mother, Della, has been instrumental in helping us with art projects and implementing creative ideas that we are using with the children in our Sunday school program. My relationship with Della is one of mutual respect, perhaps because of our common experience as both artist and teacher. Della is hospitalized, in her last days with cancer when I come to the hospital to see her.

As Debbie leaves the room for a needed break, I bluntly ask Della, "Are you ready to go?"

She answers with a heavy sigh, *"No."*

"What is holding you back?"

Pausing she replies, *"My relationship with George."*

George is her husband and I know their communication has been non-existent. He has been sick for a long time and she has had little tolerance or patience for his child-like, mental state and demanding care. I sense that she is now filled with guilt and regret, realizing that she no longer has the time to do this differently.

"Well, Della," I begin, knowing that she is not likely to ever leave the hospital, "Maybe this is something you are going to have to finish from the other side." I can tell by her silence that this answer is not what she wants to hear.

Della begins slipping away over the next couple of days going in and out of a consciousness and having restless dreams that seem real to her.

One fitful night, she wakes to insistently tell Debbie, *"The young woman with the scissors has to cut the cord."*

Debbie later asks me perplexed, "Does this mean that you or I should cut her silver cord—energetically—to help her get out of her body?"

I immediately back away from the idea, rationalizing that if this is to be done, then Debbie, as her daughter, should be the one to do it—after she dies. Being new to the death process, I do not know then that cleansing and balancing the chakras (explained in detail in Chapter 50, "Death Rites") could be helpful and I don't want to interfere in any way or do something that might be harmful.

Later in the week I return to find she has lapsed into a coma-like state. Debbie has asked me to bring my guitar and to sing to her while we wait for the arrival of a minister from our church that is coming to pray with us.

I sit on a chair at the foot of Della's bed and begin plucking the strings, tuning the guitar while tuning myself into her energy. Immediately I see her at a garden party, surrounded by many of her old friends and acquaintances. They are all wearing big hats and dresses, like a scene from the movie *The Great Gatsby*. I can hear raucous laughter, sensing the wonderful time they are having catching up.

Della suddenly lifts her head looking startled and silences all of them with a finger pressed to her pursed lips. *"Shhhh! Listen. Do you hear that music?"*

They all pause and start bustling their way toward the gate ... toward me. It dawns on me then that the music she is referring to, is me singing with the guitar. Unsure if I should continue, I begin bringing the song to a close when the door opens and the minister walks into the room. He moves to the head of her bed and stands off to one side as we tell him she is in a coma.

Closing his eyes to concentrate, he announces to us, "Well, she isn't even in her body."

I venture, what seems like a feeble explanation, "She is at a garden party with friends."

He then asks Debbie to come and stand on the other side of the bed across from him. I put my guitar down and stand at the foot of the bed. We hold hands encircling her while he silently prays, calling her back to her body. In my mind's eye, I can now see Della and the garden party ladies straight above me, as if they are behind an iron gate, peering down through a hole in the ceiling. They are completely enraptured by watching us. Within seconds, Della appears to drop into her body and opens her eyes, greeting the minister by name, even though she has never met him before. Later that evening she tells Debbie that she was at a party that she hated to leave.

It takes another week for Della to finally release her physical body. It feels as if her *spirit* is already gone, but the body is going through the physiological motions of shutting down her strong heart.

The morning of her memorial service, on the drive to the funeral home, I become aware that Della is sitting beside me in the passenger seat of the car.

In my mind, I hear her state in a matter-of-fact tone, *"Toby, I want you to look at the way they have the flowers arranged when you get in there. They are all wrong."*

I don't know what to make of this. I know Della has done flower arrangements, but I question if I am really hearing her or making this up, even though I would never come up with a concern about the flowers on my own. I'm involved with singing a part of the service so the flowers are not high on my priority list. Walking into the area, I stop to inspect the flowers and shrug my shoulders. They look fine to me. When Debbie comes into the room, I tell her of my 'conversation' on the way there with Della.

She laughs telling me, "Minutes before you arrived, a woman who works here came walking to the front of the room and rearranged all the flowers. No one told her to do this. Leave it to Mom to oversee the details."

I muse to myself that Della was always good at getting people to do what she wanted.

A couple of months after Della's service, Debbie phones to share a dream in which Della comes to her and asks if she can *be* her for a while. Debbie doesn't understand what she means by this.

Within the dream, Della explains to her, *"It would be like wearing your clothes for a while."*

"You know I will help you in any way that I can." Debbie replies.

Shortly afterward, I watch Debbie gain weight and take on new aches and pains that she did not have before. Physically, she is looking more and more like Della. She cleans out her father's house, puts it on the market, and moves him in with her. For several years, she rearranges every aspect of her life around his care. Because our paths are going in different directions, there is a long period without any contact.

Years later as it draws closer to Mother's Day, I follow an impulse to call her, finding out that she recently moved her father into a care facility and is making plans to relocate to another state. Debbie asks me the question that has been on her mind.

"Do you think it is possible to take on someone else's karma, because I suspect that I did that with my Mother?"

When I hang up the phone, I am aware again of Della's presence. I listen to her explanation.

"I joined my energy with Debbie's because I needed to work out the unfinished business I had with George. I had to be there and care for him in a way that I couldn't do when I was alive, but I didn't do this against Debbie's free will. She agreed to this."

Della indicates that the work is complete and she is ready to move on while encouraging Debbie to pursue her own life dreams. She doesn't think of herself as trapped between two worlds, but she is aware that she has grown attached to Debbie's body and knows that in order to release it completely, she is going to need some in-body assistance.

After I share this with Debbie, we decide to create a ceremony to move Della on. I have never done this kind of thing before, but not having any rules makes it less daunting. I trust that inner directions will come and all we have to do is follow them.

Days before we meet, instructions begin to 'download' in my mind directing me to gather certain required items. They consist of a woven cloth and ribbons that belonged to Della and an Owl wing that belongs to Debbie.

This is significant. When my partnership with Debbie began, working as co-directors, we also started offering Shamanic Journeying workshops. On the long drive to facilitate the first one, we saw a dead Great Horned Owl in the middle of the highway. Its wing raised up in the breeze—as if flagging us down.

We went back and retrieved its body, treating it in a sacred manner. Later, we asked permission to remove the wings, with each of us taking one.

Owl was a significant totem for both of us so receiving this gift seemed to signify the protection provided for the work we were brought together to do. When our time with the church was over, with Debbie taking care of her father and me pursuing my art, I received the inner guidance to bury my wing. This did not come as an isolated incident, but was accompanied by the death of my beloved Himalayan cat, Rainbow, who was hit by a car. (Rainbow, who would climb trees in spite of having no claws, always reminded me of a wise Owl.) In trying to console my 7-year-old son, Adam, and deal with the grief myself, I attempted to create some kind of ceremony to say our goodbyes. Adam held Rainbow's stiff body while I dug a hole under the big cedar tree, next to my Medicine Wheel.

As I was carefully lowering Rainbow into the hole, an inner voice suddenly sprang to life, informing me, *"Go get your Owl wing and place it over his body. This is the time to let go of your partnership with Debbie—accepting that it has come to completion."*

For me, this triggered a whole new level of grief as I cherished our friendship and the work we had done. I later told Debbie what I was instructed to do and asked if she was ready to release her half of the wing. She understood the symbolism, but the wing remained in her closet.

Now here it was, almost a year later and fittingly, we have chosen to do this work on Mother's Day. Debbie lies down on the floor of my art studio with a tall, wooden stepladder opened over her body. At the top of the ladder I place the woven cloth with the Owl wing on top of it. Unwinding the ribbon, I am shown the areas on Debbie's physical body where Della's energy is most infused. Ceremoniously, I tie one colored ribbon at a time around her wrists, ankles, hips, solar plexus, chest/heart area, throat, and forehead. From each of these areas, the ribbon is stretched skyward by climbing the ladder, going up and down until all of the ribbons are attached to the wing of the Owl that is perched on top of the cloth.

With everything in place, I turn on a CD of *Fairy* music that Della loved and begin coaxing her out of Debbie's body. At first nothing seems to be happening. Circling Debbie, I internally call for help, asking for Della's guides and angels to assist.

Minutes later, I have the impression of Della's spirit sitting straight up out of Debbie's mid-section calling out, *"Ruth! Ruth! You have to help me."*

Debbie clarifies for me that Ruth is Della's deceased sister. Instantly, she is there as well as other helpers. I watch them support her on all sides. In unison, we assure Della that it is time to leave. Slowly, she begins to lift out of Debbie's solar plexus. Her nebulous form appears to be following the ribbons skyward, moving up the ladder, rung by rung.

When Della arrives at the Owl wing, she whispers to me, *"It is harder for me to let go now than it was when I died."*

She pauses before giving me the final command, *"Take the scissors and cut the cords."*

I can't help but think of the dream she had before she died. I move all around Debbie's body cutting each ribbon, which clearly represents severing the cords that served as the energetic connecting wires that were tied into her chakras. All of the cut ribbons are removed and tucked into the cloth beneath the Owl wing before I tend to Debbie.

Etheric helpers seem to be wrapping her like a mummy, spinning energy from the top of her head to the bottom of her feet, squeezing out any last residue of Della's energy. This process is followed by an infusion of light helping her body recalibrate back to its own energy signature. Debbie then joins me as we tuck the wing with all the ribbon into the cloth and move outside to bury it at the East gate of the Medicine Wheel.

When we finish, we can feel that Della is no longer attached to Debbie or bound by this Earth. Owl's energy serves as the carrier, crossing the divide, while reminding us that as his wings are reunited, our work can now go forward in its own directions.

Because I personally know and care about Della and Debbie, I'm led to reexamine the view I have held about 'ghosts' and especially what it means to be 'possessed' by a spirit attachment. I see this as an initiating experience, making room for the awareness of other spirits who might follow.

Still feeling unsure of my role in all of this, I want to believe that there is some kind of cosmic law that states: *Taking on a 'soul assignment' means you will always be given the tools you need to carry it out.* As my situation unfolds, I realize this is true, but with a slight adjustment which requires me to take responsibility.

Taking on a 'soul assignment' means **you are here to develop** *the tools you will need to carry it out. And yes, that means you will bumble your way through it, but that is a key part of the learning.*

Ancient Egyptians believed that upon death
they would be asked two questions and their answers
would determine whether they could continue
their journey in the afterlife.
The first question was, "Did you bring joy?"
The second was, "Did you find joy?"

~ **Leo Buscaglia** ~

3

DOG/GOD

Developing yourself (in any area) is a lifelong process. I didn't come in knowing how to deal with death or the feelings that accompany loss. Like photographic paper that has to first be immersed in a chemical developer in order to become a print, this was a step I couldn't skip while taking on a soul assignment to help earthbound spirits. In hindsight, I can see that a 'team' was sent in, setting up an ongoing course that would run concurrently with the work I was here to do with others. Their job was to dismantle the 'hardware' around my heart and provide me with first-hand experience in facing death. The 'team members' didn't have my skewed vision of what dying was, so they lined up as beloved pets, more than willing to 'teach me the ropes.' *Rainbow* would only be the first of many volunteers buried beneath the big cedar tree by my Medicine Wheel.

While living in the city, we never had dogs. The idea of keeping an animal tied in the backyard all day while at work seemed cruel and pointless. I would smile at the saying that "Dog is God spelled backwards", but I had no personal experience with that kind of love. I found out when we moved to the country in 1987 that back roads are a dumping ground for unwanted pets: the perfect set-up for the Universe to hand-select each four-legged drop-off and guide them to our door.

The first one came just months after we moved in, when one of my husband's co-workers could no longer keep a dog in her apartment. *Donut's* job was to break us in, introducing us to Dog's highest kind of unconditional love. He dashed in, opened us up, and dashed out a few months later, run over by a tractor right before our eyes in front of our house. This was our first experience of sudden death, feeling helpless with our hearts ripped open, realizing that the country could be a hard teacher and a cruel place to live. He died in my arms on the frantic trip to rush him to the vet. I felt his spirit escape from his body like a deflating balloon, but immediately, I was aware of him licking my face, and assuring me that he was right there in the seat beside us.

Months later, the first stray showed up, answering my silent plea for protection after our house had been broken into. *Kia* was clearly an Alpha dog, regal in his carriage and demeanor, winning me over with his fierce loyalty and ancient wisdom. Within months, a neighbor brought us a puppy who had been dropped off and followed him home while jogging. He was a smaller version of Kia's same Irish setter and Collie mix. The man had called him *Sparky*, and we kept the name. Our dog-pack quickly grew to include two more strays coming a year apart. *Neesa*—a kind, black Lab who had to grow into her deep, loud bark—mothered all of us, and then came *Lexus*, a magical, elemental sprite who was some kind of a cattle dog breed called a Catahoula. Complete with herding instincts, she could see things no one else could. She would jump for long periods in the tall, prairie grass like a kangaroo. Kia took Lexus under his tutelage, as if passing down his knowledge and grooming her to take his place— somehow knowing his time had come to an end. He died shortly thereafter, just before I was to take a trip out of the country to Peru. Ironically, it seemed that this was his intention—to be able to travel unencumbered, by my side. In coping with his death, I was being trained to see life from a new perspective, being prepared for the continuous cycle of opening up and letting go. I didn't know then that the hole that is created in the letting go process actually makes room for more love to enter.

Neesa was eight-years-old when she was diagnosed with liver cancer. One week later, she insisted on dragging herself outside to be on the frozen earth to die. As hard as it was to sit beside her day and night, under a make-shift tent, in a death vigil, we at least had time to grieve, to tell her how much we loved her and give her permission to go. Of course, she waited until it was the middle of the night and she was alone, not having to worry about the ropes of our feelings trying to hold her here. This was in stark contrast to the shocking and unexpected loss of Lexus, who broke her neck in pursuit of a feral cat when getting her head stuck in a rusted auger pipe. I was submerged in guilt, blaming myself for not going to look for her when I heard her distant barking, but had assumed she was just off playing, doing her own dog thing. The "If only I had..." scenarios haunted me for a long time.

On the heels of one dog's death, another would arrive—inviting me to open more to Love, instead of the pain. The part of me that would want to say "NO—go away," trying to protect myself from any future hurt and loss, would dissolve in the furry face of the new arrival's unique personality.

Our son, Adam was responsible for bringing the dogs to us that were not strays. *Butch*, was the runt of his dog's litter, full of mange and blind in one eye. But Adam, who always wanted a Pit Bull, took him into the bachelor pad where he was then living. When the neighbor's complaints of Butch's incessant barking required action, Adam brought him to us. We were to be a short term holding ground, but that wasn't the case. Instead, Adam moved back home temporarily, bringing a new Boxer puppy named *Daisy* with him. His intention was to take her and Butch when he moved into his own place. At eight-weeks old, Daisy instantly established herself as the Alpha dog over Butch and Sparky and quickly became my shadow. When Adam was ready to move out, I was bonded to Daisy and Daisy was bonded to Butch ... so they stayed.

Sparky, with his easy-going and passive personality, welcomed the new arrivals and remained with us for 20 years before his time came to leave. A truck rolled over him backing out of our driveway. Trying to save him, I reached under the tire to protect his head from being crushed, and was badly bitten. The searing pain enveloping my hand was so excruciating that it numbed me to the horror that was unfolding when the men decided the only humane way to release him was to shoot him in the head. I sat in shock in the emergency room, waiting for my Tetanus shot, split between the emotional and physical suffering that ensues when we hang on longer than we should, refusing to let go. Like all the others before him, Sparky was buried under the huge cedar tree in the back yard—which had become our pet cemetery.

On a New Year's Eve, while waiting for the ball to drop in Time's Square,

Butch died in our living room. His body was ravaged with little bumps, indicating cancer, and by that time he was also recovering from having his 'blind' eye removed. Although he never showed any signs of being in pain, it still seemed that once again, we held on too long, trying to postpone the loss of another family member. Daisy especially missed him. She was reserved and not quite her spunky self for many months following his death.

Then, during a rainy stretch in the spring, my husband looked out the front door to see a stray walking down the road. His exposed ribs told us he was starving. We poured some food for him—even though we knew what feeding a dog means. He was a young Pit-Bull and Boxer mix. I was convinced that he had a little bit of each of our other dogs in him—along with some 'horse'—because of his proud carriage and prancing gait. The marking across his white back looked like a cowhide, so I called him *Cowboy*, although the name "Outlaw" would have been more fitting because of his over-zealous, mischievous spirit.

He quickly took Butch's place in accompanying Daisy wherever she went. He was an incredible exercise buddy for her, reviving her 8-year-old spirit as they would disappear into the fields chasing and exploring together. One Saturday morning they left on their run and an hour later, only Cowboy returned. I knew something was wrong. I found Daisy at the far end of our property lying in the dense grasses. She had been shot in the left front paw by a shot gun and was close to going into shock. We were not expecting the vet to tell us her leg needed to be amputated, but realized quickly that her survival depended upon taking this action.

It took about two weeks for Cowboy to return to wanting to roughhouse with her. It was clear that he didn't see Daisy as disabled or handicapped. His attitude finally transferred to her and to us. It helped her reclaim who she was— the Alpha dog, still in charge. Because of his challenging nature, she adapted quicker, growing stronger every day, able to do all the same things she used to do, including running up the stairs, jumping in the truck, greeting clients, and digging for moles with only one front paw— all while managing to keep Cowboy at bay from her claimed territory.

The more comfortable Cowboy became with the idea that he 'belonged' to us, the more protective and aggressive he became. He began to take up his post lying crouched like a jaguar by the mail box waiting for worthy opponents (loud vehicles) to go by so he could race them. His grey hound speed was a wonder to behold, but each time we held our breath, knowing country roads are not safe for dogs that chase cars. We attempted to keep him inside when we knew the mail was coming, as he could easily jump the fence. And he had resurrected the bad habit that had been passed down from the head of the pack—from Kia to Sparky and then Butch—of routinely flattening the mail car's tires by puncturing them with one bite. It happened so many times that they made us move our mail box to the very edge of the property.

On an unusually warm January day, two friends who appreciated and loved Cowboy's exuberance came to walk the labyrinth on our land. Cowboy accompanied them to the center and then bolted to the yard upon hearing the approaching mail truck. It was an hour early, and no one could stop Cowboy from meeting his destiny. In attempting to bite the tires, he was pulled under and run over by the new and impatient driver. Daisy was in close pursuit, but came back into the yard, yelping for me to come. Cowboy waited until I reached his side before taking his last breath. There was no holding him back from the finish line across the 'Rainbow Bridge.' I've never heard a dog grieve as much as Daisy did in losing him. She tried to get up into the back of the truck where his body was placed, howling for him in desperation. While digging the hole, she laid on the mound of dirt and remained there for some time afterwards, seemingly lost in her own conversation with Cowboy's spirit.

Daisy lived three more years, before joining him on the other side. The night before she died, I had the distinct impression that the entire dog-pack was standing by my bedside. Kia took the lead in informing me that they were all waiting for her. Three years of pushing hard on 3-legs had stressed her hips and there was a building weakness in her pancreas. There were signs that she was struggling, but I had no idea that the very next day when she accompanied me to go out to start the stove in the art studio, that this would be her last walk by my side. She gave a long, wolf-like howl and fell to the ground. She was gone instantly. In agony, my screams matched hers as I rocked and held her close to me. She had become my constant companion, apprenticing me in the fine art of authenticity, unconditional love and acceptance, diplomacy, standing my ground, reading energy, living in the NOW ... and appreciating the gift of being with every person I met. Her passing was telling me that after twelve years of learning from the best, I had finally graduated to doing this work without her oversight.

Every one of these dogs came to stretch our souls, teaching us how to be better humans and, ultimately, how to remain open—while letting go. They taught me firsthand that Dog is the perfect reflection of God.

You are a divine being. You matter, you count.
You come from realms of unimaginable power and light
and you will return to those realms.

~ Terence McKenna ~

4

SOUL CONTRACT OF SUPERHERO

There is no such thing as an isolated event. One experience builds on the next, tempering our characters and refining our spirits. The loss of our beloved 'pets' demands that I feel what is occurring inside of me without shutting down. Each loss allows me to practice what I will have to apply in dealing with the most dreaded situation—that of losing a human family member. Helping Debbie to release her mother is a preview of the 'soul-crossing' work to come. It also gives me the opportunity to dip into the complex process of death from a more detached point of view. Within the year, that neutral perspective comes zooming in to impact me on a personal level.

Overnight, I have to accept that my Dad is dying. At least we have time to prepare, unlike with the sudden loss of my brother Chris who, at age 34, will follow him in death six-months later in a freak electrocution accident. There is no greater pain or feeling of helplessness than losing someone unexpectedly when they are ripped without warning from our midst.

We all make 'soul contracts' with specific people in our pre-birth plans. But when the contract is a major one, needing extra assurance that we won't miss or avoid it, we often agree to marry the individual, or be born into their midst as a sibling, or choose them as a parent.

My father has always been larger than life with an outgoing, gregarious personality that impresses people while he 'works the crowd.' In a positive light, he is people-oriented, generous, and self-assured. I, like my other nine siblings, have him on a pedestal, dazzled by the mask of his 'superhero' image. As we grow older, the mask and cape fall away to reveal his imperfections and core wounds. It is hard for him to really be present with any of us because he is always juggling work demands with his own desires and sometimes unscrupulous agendas. He is a functioning alcoholic who lives a double life. He has the best excuses to explain away the slew of broken promises, and in the end his lies had caught up with him and his world crumbled—ending in a divorce with my mother. We each experience our own litany of disappointments, betrayals, and let-downs from him and I remember spewing my grievances to a counselor on numerous occasions.

Having a professional diagnose him as 'narcissistic' helps my mind accept what I cannot change, but the longing for approval and love is still there, stuffed deep down in the empty hole of my heart. Not having his attention and validation always leaves me feeling that I am not good enough. I am propelled by a subconscious drive to prove myself worthy—to prove I don't need him and that I can make it without him. But all of that changes when cancer enters the picture.

He tells us he has lymphoma, but keeps his armor up for the year-long assault of treatments, waging his own isolated battle. He is as determined as any trained warrior—to beat it.

Somewhere in this timeframe, I hear *Neale Donald Walsch, author of *Conversations with God*, speak. Near the end of his lecture he shares a fable about what it must have been like when God decided to send aspects of Himself, as tiny flames of light, down to explore the beautiful blue ball called 'Earth.' Paraphrasing to get to the heart of the story, he tells us that when God asked for volunteers for special missions, all of the tiny flames began jumping up and down excitedly exclaiming, *"OOH, OHH, Pick me! Pick me! I want to go! I can do it. I can be your representative!"*

And God cautioned them, saying, *"I am looking for very special lights to play very difficult roles. This is not for the faint of heart. Can you be a light that goes down, forgetting you have any light to share? Can you be a light that will betray, harm, and cause others great sorrow and anguish—all as a way to challenge them, to help them refine and find their own light? Can you play your convincing part, getting lost in your role, and still find your way back home? Only the strongest among you can do this."*

In that moment, I see my dad with new eyes. It does not excuse any of his failings. It just gives me compassion for the role he is playing, for the contracts he made with so many. I am able to admit and acknowledge that, because of what I did NOT get from him, I had to develop my own internal muscles, building my self-confidence and self-acceptance. I had to learn how to believe in myself and trust my intuitive knowing instead of relying on his or anyone else's approval. For the first time, I see what a gift he has given me by playing his self-absorbed role. The anger and blame fall away.

In the last days before his death, I have time to be with him alone. He is lying on his side in the bed and I assume he is unconscious. Here it is—my chance to get off my chest any last things that I need to express ... and there is nothing to discharge. Searching my heart, I am surprised to find there is no hole, no emptiness that I need him to fill up. I sit on the bed behind him, massaging his back to release the pockets of pain he carries while I sing a song I wrote. It is the song I will sing at his funeral.

When I finish singing I lie down behind him and, with my hand on his shoulder, I whisper, "I love you Dad."

"I love you too," he quietly replies. This is the first time I have ever heard him say these words aloud.

I am at his head when he dies, able to steer him toward the next world, giving him permission and encouragement to go, and fulfilling the soul contract I unknowingly have with him. I know that Dad had a soul contract with each of us kids. He was doing the best he could. The difficult part he agreed to play has given us the opportunity to grow and stretch, making our own mistakes, becoming responsible for the choices and actions that we will have to live with. Because of his example, I am more willing to see beyond the black and white world where judgments about myself and others hold everyone hostage.

We are all imbued with imperfections that are perfectly matched to serve as catalysts for change. In this way, we assist the greater evolution of our souls. I cherish the gift of my Dad's influence, learning more from his failings than from his accomplishments because, ultimately, he helped me to open my heart, to forgive, and to accept that being human is the real 'power' behind any superhero.

Coping with the loss of Dad and my brother was a process. It isn't until two years after their deaths, in an Incan Medicine Wheel training, that I realize that I am still carrying Chris with me. I never allowed myself to grieve when he died. Part of this is because I believe I have to be the strong one, helping everyone else through the shock. But it is also because I am having conversations with him that began the day of his death. The verbal connection keeps the loss from hitting me in the same way that it does everyone else. At the funeral service, I am aware of Chris coming up the aisle in the church with my father behind him. They sit down in the empty pew next to the rest of the family. I can feel both of their silly antics taking in everyone who is there.

I want to scream to the congregation, *"Why are you all so sad? They are right here beside us!"* I intellectually know that death is not the end, and don't want to FEEL the separation, the pain, the anger, the futility … so I don't. Not until it comes back up in the Medicine Wheel training when we are doing the 'Work of the West' that involves death and our ancestry.

In an exercise where we are getting information through muscle checking, Chris' presence is registering in all of my chakras. I cannot hold the tears back—buckling under the full force of the love and loss that is present. I don't think I will ever stop crying. How could I not have known that Chris was earthbound? Of course he has motivation to stay here. He has a young son who adores him and his wife was pregnant when the accident occurred, providing even more reason for him to remain with them. Yet, the concept of being earthbound is still too foreign to grasp. I surmise that when he was out of his body and saw Dad standing before him, he made his choice to be with him, but I did not think that it meant he remained HERE.

We are told that a fire ceremony will be held that evening to honor all the people in our lives who have died. We are to find a stick representing our 'Life Arrow' and decorate it for the legacy that has been passed down to each of us. The stick will hold the energy of our loved ones and the intention is to feed it to the fire while releasing the people in our lineage.

I am still trying to adjust to the fact that Chris is right here with me while knowing that I have to willingly let him go. I feel like a mother who just gave birth to her child, seeing him for the first time, and minutes later am told that he doesn't belong with me and I have to give him up. Feelings of intense joy and pain are wrapped together in a tight bundle waiting to be attached to my Life Arrow.

When it is time to prepare the legacy stick that will be used for this purpose, I go to a spot in the woods where an old tree has been uprooted, leaving a large hole. Earlier that day I had placed in the hole particular medicine stones that I am using to represent the people in my lineage who had died. There is a stone for both my grandmothers, one for my father, and one for Chris. In the process of retrieving the stones, I begin to clear away the leaves and then stop abruptly. My hands have uncovered a dead bird who was not there earlier in the day when I first placed the rocks. It has a triggering effect. I hold the bird and sob and sob. Through the bird, I am able to hold Chris. I am able to hold my own child self. I am able to hold the babies and loved ones I lost from this and countless other lifetimes. The bird has a black hood over its head like a nuthatch, but there are yellow streaks above each eye. It makes me think of Shamans with yellow paint above their eyes—indicating that they are seers into other worlds. I know I am to release the bird with my Life Arrow. This 'totem,' acting as a guide, is here to lead them through the Golden Door of Spirit.

At the fire ceremony, I sense both of my grandmothers sitting side by side, finding all of this interesting. Dad is there with two of his older brothers who have preceded him in death, but they are more in the background. Chris stands beside me. He asks if he can play my drum through me. I hesitate, but then allow him the pounding sensation that vibrates through both of us.

When it is my turn to offer my stick, I see many 'awakened' ancestors creating a light bridge for those ready to join them. In crossing over, they will be reclaiming their luminescent selves.

The bird's physical body is wrapped in a cloth, but his spirit is sitting on my shoulder ready to fly. I hold his body close to me in thanks, sprinkling sacred cornmeal over it as I release it into the flames. It disappears immediately. Offering my Life Arrow to the fire, I embrace each of my ancestors in my mind. They nod their gratitude before parting. With Chris, it is different. For precious seconds I am held in the strong embrace of his gentle spirit. For someone who looked like Hulk Hogan when he was alive, tender-hearted is his true nature. He makes his way toward Dad and the others—ready to join them on the other side of the bridge.

"May you touch the sweet dew of birth
and the sweet wine of death to your lips
entwined beyond time as you both climb and climb
back to the Father.

You've traveled through the dark blue hue of pain
to the richest, reddest vein
where Golden Spirit eternal remains."

~ Vickie Putman-1994

Traveling the River

The night watches, the dreamers
collapse into sleep in their solitary tents,
and the tethered rafts of their bodies
begin to open and drift into a song
that awakens only in dream. There,
they enter the river of unknowing —
a river that waited and moved within them
even as they fought each changing current,
each imagined separate self
in the day's violent sun. Here,
adrift inside each breath, each deep
letting-go, the river of dreams
begins to weave them back into the river
that birthed them, the river that will
now deliver them to a new shore
upon which when they awaken,
their faces will surely no longer
resemble their names.

~ Therese Becker ~
www.mandalapress.com

You can never cross the ocean
unless you have the courage
to lose sight of the shore.

~ Christopher Columbus ~

5

THE CHANGING CURRENT

I did not simply wake up one morning and make a decision to pursue a career dealing with earthbound spirits. Helping souls 'cross over' isn't exactly a recognized, mainstream vocation. Even though the role has long been documented, this specialized field is not acknowledged by the general population. If you have no awareness of discarnate spirits, then there is no reason to be concerned about them. One who knows not, cares not. My perception of their presence had to be awakened many times before I could consider that they might want or need my help. It was an awareness that was accelerated because of my personal losses.

Given the crazy times we are now living in, the awakening process is no longer a gently, sloping pool giving you the chance to wade down to the deep end. For those paying attention, there are only two choices—jump or be pushed. Why is that? In these unprecedented times of carrying more light, everyday people are beginning to see, sense, hear and feel things from multidimensional levels that they can't control or easily explain. This includes the awareness of souls who have not yet crossed over. Assisting them is a valuable service intended for the good of all beings, a service that many will have reason to investigate or become involved in as time goes forward.

The main stream (mainstream) is being re-directed by a fast-moving current of intensifying light patterns and energies. Incoming waves of higher vibrations are uprooting the conditioned, dominating beliefs that are the bed rock of our linear, third dimensional reality and splitting open the fault-lines of our collective misperceptions. You could say, we are all going through an up-leveling that is affecting our physical, emotional, and mental wellbeing—redefining our consciousness, and even our DNA. Life as we know it is changing, and every particle of matter is being accelerated—anointed as an agent of change.

Even though it doesn't feel like it, the awakening process is very much self-determined. Standing on the banks overlooking the swirling current, you can choose to back away and build a containment wall, but the rising 'frequencies' are making it harder and more agitating for those staying rooted on lower ground. If you are willing to get into the water and allow the current to take you, there are 'check points' that routinely show up. We arrive at these independently by following the inner blueprint of our soul's journey.

Growing up on the Mississippi River in Dubuque, Iowa, gives me a reference to understand these check points. When we were young, my mother used to draw pictures of the big boats she saw through binoculars from our kitchen window that went up and down the river. One in particular stands out to me. This was the *Delta Queen Riverboat*, a sternwheel steamboat that is a U.S. National Historic Landmark. Spotting the Delta Queen was a rare, but joyous occasion and one that inspired Mom to pile all of us into her 1956 Chevy to race down to the riverfront docking area where we could get a closer look at the Queen's big, red paddlewheel. Dubuque was her turn-around point. Originating from several Southern ports, this riverboat from another era slowly churned up the river, providing a relaxing, scenic cruise for all of her passengers.

The other more modern boats and barges were not as interesting looking, but they got our undivided attention whenever we happened to be at *Eagle Point Park* with its 164 acres of land, renovated during the depression and located on rock outcroppings, high up on the Northeastern bluffs overlooking the Mississippi river. The park is lined with walkways leading to overlook points with a panoramic view of three states—Iowa, Wisconsin and Illinois. From these lookout towers, one can see below to the Lock and Dam System #11.

Traveling from New Orleans to St. Paul, the barges and shipping boats moved much faster than riverboats. Adhering to their own checkpoints, they passed through our town using the lock and dam system to make their way to the next Northern port. Watching these huge boats transition from one level of water to another always impressed me. All locks & dams operate the same way. By moving through a section of locks, the vessels are stepped up or stepped down, allowing them to adjust to the new water level they are entering.

An important consideration when engineers design and create lock and dam systems is that all the structures must be built to withstand the incredible forces of water pushing on them. This is an interesting concept when we apply it to what is happening to us in our human evolution. Following our own internal schedules, we make our way to the 'locks' where we are 'stepped up' from the ebbing tide of an old energy platform to the steady, swelling heights of a seismic sea wave that continues to build. We instinctively move (when it's our time) into the 'deeper channels' where the contained situation of the 'locks' sets up the right conditions to receive and handle optimum impact. The states we are going through require concentrated immersion, allowing the inpouring of the Creational forces to act upon us. This is expedient growth.

Can you accept that you are designed to withstand whatever it is you are going through—even though pressure is being applied to every one of your systems when you begin to change levels of consciousness? The pressure inside the 'locks' affects all of us differently. Some fight it, trying to make sense of the odd and sometimes uncomfortable things that are occurring; some buckle-under with the overwhelm and may even self-destruct or sink. Some back out and chose to remain at the old level (like the Riverboat whose route ended at our town), unprepared to go past a certain point. The ones who fare the best are those who are able to let go, surrendering to the inpouring forces, using the transition points as periods to rest, reflect, and regenerate, buoyantly rising to the new level.

As *Ronna Herman tells us, through Archangel Michael, *"There are great pulsations of new, higher, Cosmic Ray vibrational patterns bombarding the Earth, with quiet times in-between so as not to create an overload situation. Ascension is not a steady, forward-motion process. It is an insurgence of energy and new information, and then a time of assimilation, integration and manifestation. Your immediate goal for this round of Ascension is for all of your Soul Fragments to be reintegrated within the first sub-level of the Fifth*

Dimension."

In other words, we pull into the 'locks' preparing to be hit with the rapid up-leveling that is pouring in, and then have to adjust to the shift before being released into an even faster moving (5D) stream. The 'locks' are strategically placed throughout our lives by our soul's plan which challenges us to adjust to our new roles, preparing us for the parts that we've come to play in the higher consciousness. Keeping our heads above water and acclimating to these transcendent depths means going forward—at increasingly higher levels. We can't go back to where we were before—as much as we may pine for the 'good ole days' of moving at the leisurely pace of the old Riverboat excursions. That world is gone, and along with it is the comfort zones we had settled into at the 'sea level' that defined our old shores.

The survivalist mentality of 'battening down the hatches' instructs us to shut down, buckle up, and weather the storm in a mode of struggle that reinforces the isolating concept of 'every man for himself.' In these turbulent times of increasing chaos, each of us must choose how to navigate the uncharted waters that the Earth is passing through. We can cling to the tangled net of separation that keeps us fragmented—caught in the lower vibrational undertow of 3D mistrust, victimization and blame—or we can lean into the upward-tilting momentum, adapting to a lighter, catamaran style of interconnected cooperation. The infinite nature of our being is waiting to know itself beyond the barrier-reef of our small, ego limitations.

Prominent writer, *Anais Nin tells us, *"We do not see things as they are, but as WE are."* This means we see what we expect rather than what is possible. We cannot notice the new world emerging if we have no reference for it. This is the same premise that was used to explain the many versions of the story, attributed to different explorers (Magellan, Christopher Columbus, and Captain Cook) when the indigenous people could not see the ships of the explorers anchored off shore. Only the Shaman was able to perceive them. When the ships appeared before him, he pointed them out to others until everyone could see them. He was able to do this because the imaginal inner realms were already real to him, opening him to the possibility of strange things from other worlds. This reminds us that the solutions to all our current challenges are already here—sitting in the harbor of our closed minds, waiting to 'set sail' when the answers become visible to us.

With the present, incoming energies, the bandwidth with its old fear-based programming, is slowly becoming obsolete. Coming on line and functioning in our DNA are the 4D/5D towers of new cellular awareness, upgrading all of our systems, changing the 'system' from within. Studies show that major changes in our DNA lead to major changes in our thinking; as humans evolve, it seems that the walls between the conscious and subconscious are thinning, making our 'bubbles' of reality more permeable.

On a personal level, the most noticeable shift point occurred for me in 1982 when I began hearing the voice of my Higher Self. It expanded into sessions with other dimensional beings that I recorded through a process called 'automatic writing.' After five years of receiving these private consultations, the inner voice I associated with my Higher Self informed me I was done with this format. It was taking too much time and keeping me in isolation. By then, I was aware, even while operating in my every day waking mode (Beta and light Alpha), that there was a steady stream of guidance just under the surface. Flowing and available, like a freshwater spring, it was inviting me to dip down into it.

When we are in an expanded or altered state (Theta, Delta or Gamma wave consciousness) our filter naturally dissipates—and we step out of time. People who practice meditation or yoga, or those engaged in creative pursuits, can more easily access this state. It's possible that some who are addicted to drugs have touched this state and keep going back, trying to relive or reach it again. Far more impressive and reliable than using mind altering substances to achieve the state of timelessness, are the countless, documented cases of people who have had Out of Body (OBE) experiences, Near Death Encounters (NDE), Past Life (PLR) and Life Between Lives (LBL) spiritual regressions, as well as those who practice mindful Meditation, participate in focused breath work, or embark on Shamanic journeys. These pioneers of expanded consciousness have contributed valuable information and insights to broaden our understanding of how we operate in higher vibrational fields, including the afterlife and the passageway beyond.

As we steadily move into the higher dimensions, energy surges will continue to increase and intensify. Your physical surroundings may be altered— if that is what is needed to redefine your inner landscape. The rising energy impacts each of us in very individual ways.

For me, it resulted in leaving my hometown of 35 years, my friends, my family, my reliable job with the school system, and all my comfortable routines that provided stability, safety, and security. In one big WHOOSH, my old life was swept away. With it went my identity and any idea of the person I believed myself to be. As much as I wanted to cling to the old familiar 'water level' and go back into teaching, or at least subbing just to bring in some money, the incoming wave of energy" said, *"NO!"* Re-location put me into the 'locks' where I had to adjust to being in containment, emptying out everything that used to define me.

From discomfort and loneliness came the gift of silence, which allowed me to tap the subtle signals of my Higher Self as it came bubbling up, closer to the surface. The physical move to a city eight hours away was instigated by my husband, who took a job there. He, too, was responding to the energy which gave us both a choice: stay at the old 'sea level' or surrender to the 'current' and let it take us to meet the next soul assignment waiting around the bend.

The boundaries between the worlds are softly blurring for all of us, resulting in a bleed-through of sensory awareness, intuitive insights, and connected communications which are becoming more widespread and common place. Without orientation, picking up frequency overlays may be disconcerting and chaotic. With awareness, higher transmissions can be empowering, and inform, educate, and serve us. Being of service at this time of galactic realignment requires us to simultaneously function in two or more worlds. This is much easier if we recognize and accept that our role might be as a bridge between them.

One such role documented throughout history by religion, psychology, and mythology is that of the *Psychopomp*. This sacred bridge role has been captured in works of art, real life stories, and film. (Remember the TV series *Touched by an Angel*?) The term *psychopomp* comes from the Greek words *pompos* (conductor or guide) and *psyche* (soul, breath, life, or mind), referring to someone who is a 'guide of souls.'

I first became aware of the concept during Incan Medicine Wheel training. It is natural to associate a Shaman with being a soul guide, as Shamans have historically filled this role in indigenous cultures all over the world. Although the word 'psychopomp' may sound a bit off-putting, the work one does is invaluable. Typically, a soul guide refers to someone in spirit form who greets a soul when it separates from its body and then serves as an escort, accompanying the soul to the other side. Psychopomps are mediators between the unconscious and conscious realms who provide safe passage by calming the possible panic and distraction of death. How a guide appears is compatible with a person's comfort and belief system, providing world-wide varieties of archetypal forms such as angels, deities, orbs of light, mystical creatures or well-known spiritual figures that represent every religion. More commonly, they show up as a personal guide or in the form of a deceased relative, loved one, or friend, or possibly an animal totem or beloved pet. (I look forward to being greeted by my dog-pack when it's my time to go.)

You would think that aid from other-world helpers would be sufficient to ensure that the newly departed arrives successfully in the afterlife, but there are times when the soul is unaware of or overrides the assistance, bound by a strong desire to remain here. When this happens, a soul guide may need additional help from a living, human psychopomp—someone who has the innate or trained ability to help a person cross over after death, or provide assistance when it becomes clear a transition is not complete.

Sacred psychopomp work, once sanctioned by the Shaman, is now taught in Shamanic training preparing soul-helpers to serve on multidimensional levels. But you do not need to traverse the 'lower, middle, and upper worlds' to help those who are dying or those who have not completed their transition. There are Soul Midwife classes, Soul Rescuer courses, Transitional Team trainings, *Soul Detective classes (which include certification), and Conscious Dying workshops offered around the world, not to mention the extensive information available from books, videos, and the internet. This is an unfolding, spiritual ministry not limited to members of the clergy.

Psychopomp work usually chooses you before you choose it, creating an undeniable draw to investigate it further. If it is a *calling* meant for you, this work will seek you out in the form of some unexpected experience which slips right past the 3D barrier of your logical mind. Once it pries open a higher dimensional door, you—try as you might—will not be able to close that door.

Basic attributes needed to do this work are:

1. An open, objective, and non-judgmental attitude.
2. Enough spiritual maturity and sensitivity to listen to, trust, and focus your intuition and intention.
3. A willingness to help, with a fearless, open heart.

Above all else, you need to develop strong enough boundaries to remain grounded and maintain your own center, as discarnate energy can and will affect you. Psychopomps have a tendency to learn this the hard way.

The week before my father's death, I woke up hearing a strange word being repeated in my head. Phonetically, it sounded like "Waken Nelay" or (A wak'a Nilay).

Perplexed, I wondered aloud, "What does that mean?"

Immediately there was a response impressed upon my mind. *"It refers to the Ones who walk beyond illusion."*

In the South American Quechua language, a *huaca* or, a *wak'a* is an object that represents something revered and can also refer to the state of being after death or the spirit of something sacred. The name *Nilay* is of Hindi origin meaning 'home, heaven or deep blue.'

As I got into the shower minutes later, I sensed a shadow falling across the glass door and I inadvertently recoiled, gasping under my breath, "Oh no, the 'Angel of Death' is here."

A female voice startled me by answering, *"You have no reason to be afraid of me. You are an angel of death too. I am A'wak'a Nilay'. This is not my name, but a title that refers to many who walk beyond the 3D illusion of death. It is our job to guide others there."*

At the time, I had no context for this encounter, but now as I look back I realize that she was an otherworld psychopomp, a *'walker between the worlds'* activating a novice, human psychopomp, preparing me to be a 'soul-bridge' for the work to come.

The ultimate crucible for making human beings
is not success, growth, or happiness.
It is Death.

~ Stephen Jenkinson ~
"Grief Walker"

6

THE SHADOW OF DEATH

The concept of 'soul guides', although well documented, has been largely overlooked, forgotten or chalked up to wishful thinking—especially in our death phobia culture where we are prone to fear, deny, or view death as an inevitable, solo tragedy. This was the impression death made on me as a second grader when an 8-year-old boy in my sister's class, suddenly died. Up to then, death was something reserved for the 'old' people and it was not supposed to come this close to my age. It didn't make any difference that the boy was quiet and a good student; he was even 'laid to rest' in his altar boy outfit. Death still broke into their house at night while everyone was sleeping and took him from this world. Fear was injected into my system with the feeling that no one was safe from death's random choosing. For a few months, I was on my 'best behavior'—just in case Judgment Day was around the corner.

If the thought of death is morbid, frightening, or unbearable we will avoid talking about it, just as everyone did when the young boy died—except to reinforce that it was 'God's will' to take him. The idea that God is the 'hand of death' gives us good reason to stick our heads in the proverbial sand—to keep what we dread away from us. If we have no real understanding of death—what happens in the death process or in the afterlife—then it stays in the shadow realms of our collective consciousness, leaving much of the population (as it did me) anxious, overwhelmed, or, at best, unprepared to take the final journey to the great beyond.

In a discussion about death, a friend shares with me a simple revelation that came to her through a dream.

The Power of the Fear of Death

"I dreamt that a white-haired man dressed in black came to teach me about the shadow. I saw black kites tethered to people as they walked along streets and roads. He described these kites as personal shadows. As the kites rose they came together as if magnetized into a great, dark cloud. He said that this mass is known as the 'collective shadow' and as a person pulls their own shadow to them, the collective shadow comes closer as well.

He said, 'The fear of death sustains the collective shadow and has to be overcome before one can regain their own personal shadow/power.' Carl Jung tells us that 80% of the gold is in the shadow.

Upon waking from this dream, yet not opening my eyes, I heard the dresser drawers opening and closing. I knew I was home alone. The door next to me began to rattle and slam. Air moved over my face. I dared not open my eyes. I repeated this mental request over and over ...

'Let any energy of anger, fear, resentment, envy, jealousy or hatred that comes to me, be transformed to loving energy and returned to its source.'

I fell into sleep again and woke to sunlight streaming into the room. The air was clear and silent. The day felt fresh. Memory carried the gift of night-knowledge to this page. My sense was that the 'collective shadow' did not want to be exposed and tried to scare me out of this newly acquired knowledge. I suspect that the personal shadow is at the mercy of the collective shadow's bidding... until the fear of death is overcome."

~ Marilyn Larson

Can it be that the fear of death keeps us tethered to the black cloud of the 'collective shadow?' If, as astrologer *Lilan Laishley describes it, "'The Shadow' is the reservoir for human darkness that lies deep within ourselves," then the fear of death is certainly a major, behind-the-scenes contributor. Lilan suggests that the toxic, fearfulness of death buried deep in the Root Chakra of our unconscious needs to be excavated, cleaned up and brought into the light.

To pull our individual 'kites' free, we must change our relationship with death. Behind every addiction, there is an attempt to by-pass or numb the 'dark' feelings—like death—that stalk us. Craving and aversion both create separation. The more we are dead inside, the more we reach outward for some kind of sensory stimulation to feel alive. For many, this is an attempt to not feel at all. Lilan reminds us that there is a soul-sized hole in each of us. Until we have the courage to put our fingers into the wound, it can't begin to heal. This includes what author *Kim Gould so poignantly says is occurring at this time.

"Everything that has been shamed or made invisible or unimportant, misunderstood, buried and forgotten ... is coming back from the dead zone where we shoved it and then became too afraid to look. Because, you know, death is to be avoided, even all those parts of ourselves we made dead over the years in our best attempts to survive."

Resistance is a powerful force that keeps us in bondage. Any resistance we are unable to voice, we will find ourselves acting out. Pushing against death or our negative feelings as a threatening enemy, keeps us in a paralyzed state, handcuffed to the adversarial shadow from which we flee.

From the shadow's perspective, dying is the annihilation of life. It is synonymous with failure. "Game Over," you lose. Seen as a potentially punishing passage, it is often marinated in fear or worry that the life we lived was not quite good enough, subject to being judged by a conditional 'god' with the possibility of being condemned to suffer 'eternally.' Being 'perfect' was never the goal of taking on a human body, but this misunderstood ideal is very effective in subduing and controlling the psyche of the masses.

A new relationship with death requires a different perspective—one that goes beyond the belief that death is the end of our existence. To eliminate the fear of death, we have to accept it as part of the continuum of life that forever evolves—with or without the impressive 'uniform' of the body. The only part of us that really dies is the illusion of the temporary self.

We are each imprinted by the family we are born into and its ascribed religious beliefs—or lack of—some with vague and some with very set ideas about what happens when we die. These ideas become the default program that shapes both our shadow perceptions and our acceptance about the dying process. Even though our belief systems vary, most agree that at the time of death, the soul separates from the body. And what is the soul? Some call it our *immortal essence*, our *innermost being*, our *divine blueprint*, our *core consciousness*, the *recorder*, or our *Innate*.

Others might say that these words describe our *spirit*. The words *soul* and *spirit* are often used interchangeably, yet some religions (including Christianity) consider that we are composed of three parts; the physical or the *body*, the *soul* and the *spirit*. At the time of death, our *luminous body*—also called the *Astral body* (made up of both our *soul* and *spirit*)—detaches from the physical body. The *spirit* portion would be considered our *God consciousness*. This is our Higher Self connection that includes our intuition and conscience. This part of us has never been under the illusion that it is separate from Source, so it is ready to return and does so without delay. The *soul* portion is our *self-consciousness* which includes our *mind* with all its thoughts, our *will* with our ego desires, and our *emotions* related to everything we are feeling. It is the *soul* portion that remains like an echo, or shell of the *spirit* when a crossing is not complete. The *soul* is the portion that makes us unique, but lying just beneath that is the universality of our *spirit*. It is easy to become identified with and cling to our uniqueness, believing this is what sets us apart or makes us special.

Analogies are useful to help us grasp how this occurs. One with which I resonate refers to the body as being a garage where we park our soul. When we die, some souls head out of the garage ready to take to the open road. With these individuals, the *soul* and *spirit* are aligned as driver and passenger. They leave as one unit, exiting onto the wide open *freeway*. Yet, there are other souls who back out of the garage and come to a halt in the driveway. Instead of willingly accelerating with their *spirit*, the *soul* puts on the brakes and a split occurs, resulting in a soul fracture of sorts. The misalignment creates a parting of ways, with the soul portion now in a mere shell of the original 'vehicle.' Attached to its 'earthly house' which is jam-packed full of relationship thoughts, desires, and emotions, the 'soul shell' is not ready to leave, so it sits idling outside the garage for an indeterminate time.

Another way to view the body is seeing it as a wetsuit you wear while on 'active duty' swimming in the waters of *Earth school*. Taking off the wetsuit doesn't dissolve or end who you really are, but it does release your luminous body, as if unzipping it from the inside out. No longer restricted to stay behind the 'barrier reef,' you suddenly have unlimited access to this world and beyond. Just as it was when you were in your 'wetsuit,' your very presence adds to either the illumination or the turbulence that animates the vast ocean of possible realities.

To *die consciously* is to remain aware of what is happening when you slip out of your restricted life-jacket (body) and realize that 'drowning' is just a convincing illusion. Everyone survives the death process, but knowing this beforehand is the ultimate freedom. Staying 'land-locked' is usually an unconscious option taken by default, rather than an eyes wide-open, informed choice. Awareness of our own death is a powerful, first awakening.

When the collective can see death as a graduation passage, and anticipate a celebratory homecoming with one's reunited soul-family, the *soul* portion will no longer be detained or imprisoned by the 'shadow of death.' We will welcome the healing debriefing that enables us to reexamine the whole gamut of growing experiences that were part of our volunteer assignment on the Earth playground.

On the **Dying Consciously* website, it states that 9 out of 10 'light bodies' return naturally—leaving 5-10% that may choose to remain. Although uncertain of how they arrived at these numbers, I accept that, upon death, the larger part of ourselves—our Higher Self/*spirit* portion—immediately heads home, constantly calling our souls to accompany it into the flow. For some, this doesn't happen. What do those souls who remain here have in common? *Dynamic* or *negative resistance*.

In electronics, dynamic or negative resistance means that when the voltage is increased, the current may not increase proportionally and, in some cases, it may even decrease. With some souls, resistance to the 'high voltage' event called 'Death' occurs, activating their iron clad willpower to hold on like a superglue bonding agent. Resistance to the unknown (which is really the natural flow) slows down the return process. When you buck the stream, it creates enough interference to disrupt the 'signal' that continues being broadcast from the 'homing device' sent out by the Higher Self. Choosing to remain here is choosing a lower frequency. The result can be a 'dropped signal.' The Higher Self/*spirit* portion transmitting from the higher astral planes, appears to be 'out of range.'

Before earthbound souls became a blip on my screen of reality, I used to think that, whenever and however someone died, they automatically crossed-over. After a period of review and rest, it seems logical that they would then continue their soul exploration with renewed purpose, applying what they learned. I know I am not the only one who assumed this, including afterlife investigator and author, *Bob Olsen, who is convinced that earthbound souls are nothing but a myth.

He explains, *"Our souls are connected to our Higher Selves like an elastic band that can be stretched as far as you want without breaking it and if you let go of one side, it's always going to find itself. You can't break the connection between your spirit and your soul so the elastic band is never going to break. But when you leave your body, it (the soul) goes back to the (spirit). It's still connected to it so it returns to the spirit without effort. It's automatic. It's not a process where anything can go wrong."* And he adds, *"It is human arrogance to suggest that God, who can create all this, can get a soul to go into a body and have a lifetime, but when that body ceases to exist, is then unable to get his children home."*

As much as I too believe that eventually our souls all go where we are intended to go in the afterlife (guided back like a retractable rubber band to the original loop of our Higher Self/*spirit*), Mr. Olsen's closed-circuit analogy needs a little more 'elastic' in it to take into account the God-given gift of free will.

Source does not interfere with each soul having its own experience. According to the Universal Law of Attraction and the Law of Resonance, it is possible for a soul, or a soul fragment, to remain with a person, place, or thing, magnetized through the attraction of their matching resonance. The decision to slow down the process or delay the departure is allowed—even if it 'flies in the face' of getting us home in a *snap*—which is our human attempt to apply the limiting concepts of 'time' and 'success' to the all-expansive God principle. 'Time' is an agreed-upon 3rd and 4th dimensional construct that is used as a teaching tool so we can learn and grow, but it doesn't exist in the same way outside the body. So, why would we assume that a soul's desire to move at its own vibrational pace wouldn't be honored? Choosing to remain earthbound does not indicate that something went wrong. It is a feedback loop or direct reflection of a person's present state, including their desires, longings, and perceptions about the afterlife.

If there is a charged attachment to staying *here*, it may or may not be coupled with fear, disorientation, or resistance of going *there*. The 'brakes on' approach is primarily due to the inertia of unresolved thoughts and emotions which keep the soul in a lower frequency state of separation, possibly feeling unsupported in its new predicament. A vibrational shift can lead to healing and transcending this illusion, but it often requires assistance.

The word 'earthbound' carries a negative connotation, implying that spirits are being held/bound against their own will. This is something we will explore when talking about the influence of intrusive astral entities and detrimental energies in Part 3. Rather than being trapped against their will, earthbound souls often choose to remain, bound by the vibration of their own longings or regrets. Intense, unresolved feelings or desires may make moving on feel like an imposed sentence that they strongly resist.

From my involvement with many forms of energy work and shamanism, I was peripherally familiar with 'ghosts' and the general references to 'entities.' They can leave an energy imprint and sometimes attach themselves to individuals, objects, or locations. This was not something I was looking for or commonly dealing with in my early practice with others. It sounded like a lot of drama causing unnecessary angst, and I wanted to steer clear of it.

When I heard other energy-workers talk about 'removing entities' attached to their clients, I had my own charged reaction. It was hard not to conjure up images of black, negative, vaporous forms, imprinted by the movie *Ghost*. Hollywood's portrayal of impersonal, dark, parasite-like beings, were images I didn't want to entertain. It was easy to discard as fictional the thought of 'energy vampires' attempting to drain one's life force, by causing some kind of ailment or disruption. However, as I listened to others share their experiences, I found myself asking two questions:

1. *How did the entities get there?*
2. *Where do you put them once you remove them?*

"Sending them to the light" sounded good, but seemed pretty vague to me. The idea of dispersing them like fleas leaves the chance that they may jump to a new host—a real possibility that did not appeal to me.

From a shamanic perspective, intrusive energies can be removed, whether they are *entities* or *thoughtforms.* Thoughtforms are the combination of our thoughts and emotions. When packaged together, they begin creating our reality. The frequency of the thoughts and emotions must be in synch in order for a thoughtform to fully develop. If you are in a state of higher frequency, feeling happy, trusting, and loving, and encounter a lower frequency thought like fear, your emotions and thoughts will not be in synch long enough to create a fearful thoughtform. If you are already in the emotion of fear and then have a fearful thought, a feedback loop begins to form with the fearful emotion feeding the arising, fearful thoughtform. *Mort Nicholson, a long-time energy professional, helps us understand this concept:

"Each thoughtform is a temporary entity—like a battery, waiting to discharge. Normally, it will discharge and disappear in a short period of time. But if we repeatedly think the same or similar thought, or others think the same thought, fueled by matching emotions, then the thoughtform, rather than discharging, becomes strengthened."

This applies to both negative and positive thoughtforms. Becoming aware of the energy patterns around you can help you make adjustments to this powerful operating system which affects your daily life.

Negative or obsessive thoughts directed at another person can become embedded in their energy fields, creating psychic dents that bind both the sender and the receiver. Thoughts can sometimes be extremely strong and last for many years—especially if they are heavy, dense and dark, giving them the appearance and powers of an entity. The prolonged intensity may literally attract an entity that matches this frequency. You become susceptible to darker energies when your energy field is lowered with heavy emotions. Negative emotions are highly charged and bond magnetically to all other thoughts like them in the lower frequency band resulting in drawing detrimental energies to you like fly paper. This is a good example of the black, tangled 'kites' of the collective shadow.

In my early practice, I used some basic shamanic tools like smudging with sage and cedar bundles, drumming or using a rattle, holy water, and essential oils. The intent was to 'ward off' the entity as if I were dealing with a flu virus. When I began having my own experiences with earthbound individuals, the 'dead' who were caught betwixt and between two worlds suddenly became very alive.

The clinical approach of sweeping entities into someone else's space or removing them like ticks belonged to an old-energy tool box that needed to be dumped out, updated, and revised. When I began seeing the impersonal, scary 'entities' as beings who had personal connections to living people who loved them and were concerned about them, I was suddenly on new ground, engaged and motivated to figure out a way to help them *off the ground*. Situations I had previously seen as 'black and white' began morphing into infinite hues of complex colors simply because the ingredient called compassion was now stirred into the mix.

(Note: When a negative thoughtform escalates to a 'dark entity,' the protocol is different and will be covered in Part 3.)

The Labyrinth is an archetype of transformation.
Its transcendent nature knows no boundaries,
crossing time and cultures with ease.
The Labyrinth serves as a bridge
from the mundane to the divine.

~ Kimberly Saward ~

7

THE LABYRINTH PORTAL

My introduction to the Labyrinth comes at an American Dowser's convention in Las Cruses, New Mexico in 1994. I have no way of knowing that this ancient, meandering pathway will become the foundational backbone for my life's work, but there are clues. From the first presentation, I am overcome with continuous waves of emotion. Some part of me knows I have entered another 'check point' which, when I leave, will rearrange my world. My soul recognizes the significance of this 'Master' spiritual tool long before my mind can begin to comprehend it. Irrationally captivated, my fascination quickly turns into a full-blown obsession which takes over my waking hours. Returning home, I don't hesitate to put my limited dowsing skills to the test. With the kinesthetic awareness of a creative friend, Mary K Barge, we lay out *The Prairie Labyrinth* on five acres of native prairie grasses.

Right from the start, people coming to walk the paths begin having their own experiences with spirits although the 'spirit-attracting' possibility was never mentioned by any of the initial Labyrinth presenters. The pattern is described by *The Labyrinth Society as *"a unicursal* (single-path) *tool for personal, psychological and spiritual transformation."* Imagine, just by walking in circles, we have at our fingertips—or more accurately, at the tips of our toes—a down-to-earth instrument, calibrated for transformation.

I was completely unaware that I was really setting up a 'locks' system on my land, giving others a convenient way to wind through a land-ocean of blowing grass while acclimating to the higher waves of the incoming frequencies.

The earliest labyrinths can be traced back 4,000 years to the Neolithic and Bronze Age periods. Throughout their long history, they have been found worldwide, but the purpose of the labyrinth has remained an enigma. These transcendent forms may have contributed more than we know to the Earth's energetic infrastructure. The goal area of the labyrinth functions like a lightning rod while the connected paths serve as a conductive grid. Lightning rods are known to provide a low resistance path to ground. In the case of the labyrinth, it is not about grounding electricity, but grounding and conducting much higher frequencies, adding to the stabilization and up-leveling of the earth's grid system. According to *Kryon (channeled through Lee Carroll), the magnetic grid was intended to be a DNA delivery engine.

Those who work with labyrinths (designing, building, maintaining or just walking them) may not think of themselves as 'grid workers,' but labyrinth patterns serve as present day *earth to sky antennas*, plugging us into the incoming waves of crystalline energy acting on our DNA. Labyrinths are 5D SELF towers providing uninterrupted service to Higher Self awareness, helping us reestablish our sovereign connection to Source.

The resurgence of the modern day 'Labyrinth Movement' is a concentrated/ *consecrated* effort that is energetically and spiritually guided to assist the quantum leap that humanity is going through. In just the last 25 years, there have been an estimated 10,000 labyrinths constructed in both populated and remote areas throughout the world. That number continues to multiply and spread at a grassroots level, calling forth more individuals who possess the obsessive urge as well as the skills to organize resources and the labor needed to create them.

How can an unassuming walk in-and-out of these patterns contribute to the shift in human consciousness? Labyrinths are like camouflaged 'seed banks' hidden in plain sight. The 'seeds' are stored within you, but visiting a labyrinth 'repository' enlivens them, giving you access to your own innate 'light codes' of higher consciousness.

Labyrinths, as physical locations, can be compared to 'hotspots' providing access points where people can connect with Source energy and receive the 'downloads' intended for humanity's evolvement. Found all over the globe, labyrinths are ubiquitous, full-service, recalibration stations. When your frequency has dropped and you find yourself caught up in the lower 3D dramas (serving as initiations), simply walking a labyrinth can plug you directly into the only 'power station' you will ever need: the one that radiates from your own sacred center.

Some have observed that labyrinths act as time machines. The patterns are certainly right brain enhancers or 'time out' sanctuaries, transporting you beyond the ever-demanding concerns that consume you, to reconnect with your own timeless wisdom.

My friend Marilyn Larson, who shared her *Shadow of Death* dream with us (Chapter 6), also had an insight about 'time' that came to her early one morning when she was waking up: *"Time is a sonic membrane."* Later, while walking a Chartres-style labyrinth, more information was added.

"In the beginning, was the word. The so called 'beginning' was when the commencement of time began, and the word was a sound. A sonic membrane was created which became containment for what we call reality. This structure ... this reality ... shares walls with other dimensions beyond their walls or veils. Time is the veil ... (the fourth dimension) the edge. Timelessness is the center."

Returning to the center of the labyrinth, we circumnavigate through those veils (walls) to return to our own center where our real answers lie. It is a safe place to practice and assimilate inner and outer changes. You may think you walk a labyrinth to find your balance within the world but, in the stillness, you allow the world to find its balance within the Self. If *"time is elastic"* as Einstein tells us, then in that elasticity, time can contain many realities. Walking labyrinths may be a way to ground the fluctuating timelines. We are tasked in our walking to clear and release the lower timeline potentials by planting seed thoughts which will grow the most optimal temporal reality we can envision.

Labyrinths appear to be stationary, yet are actually multidimensional portals serving to remind us that we are mobile, human portals with direct access to an ever-expanding, flexible network of Light. Recalibrating allows us to release whatever dross we have accumulated while coming back into alignment with the planet's rising vibrations.

In the first year after opening the Prairie Labyrinth (1995), many individuals come prepared for a self-reflective meditation but emerge from the grasses relaying that they felt, smelled, heard, sensed, or were energetically touched by someone close to them who had died. Until then, the idea that some of these spirits might actually be earthbound has not previously registered with me, but I become convinced early-on that all labyrinths, with their circuitous pathways, create a magnetic field revolving around the goal area which acts as a central vortex.

Walking the pattern stirs or spins the energy through its counter-rotating, sacred geometry ratio, creating an opening which acts like a hole-punch, penetrating the 'time veil.' It has the effect of reaching out like an invisible, airport beacon, naturally drawing energy to it like moths to a flame. The 'beacon' serves as a conduit for inspiration and present-moment awareness, including subtle contact. I conclude that it creates a two-way flow cycle, bringing energy in and moving energy out. Although my focus is on identifying and releasing destructive, habitual patterns or thoughtforms, the spirits seem to already know that the labyrinth can be used to assist them in crossing over.

Trying to understand what is occurring in my own backyard, I research ancient labyrinth sites and find that approximately 300 have been preserved in the world. Among some of the best are the 13-14 Neolithic stone settings on a small island called *Bolshoi Zayatsky*, which is part of the Solovetsky Islands in Russia. Throughout the islands, 35 labyrinths were found on terrain covered with boulders, moss, and large bushes. The labyrinths were created using the local boulders.

The purpose of these stone settings and those found at other ancient labyrinths sites is not clear, but one intriguing theory suggests that they symbolize a border (the edge) between our world and the underworld and that they were used for specific rituals to help the souls of the deceased travel to another world. Another perspective of this concept is held by the Hopi of the American Southwest who see the labyrinth as a point of emergence, believing that their ancestors used the counter-rotating paths to enter this world. Both versions—whether entering or exiting—suggest a potent portal.

The seven concentric rings and serpentine, meandering paths of a

Classical seven-circuit or Cretan-style labyrinth are reminiscent of the seven celestial gates or halls that *Ascension researcher William Henry describes as *"stellar tollbooths that the soul goes through after death."*

What if moving through the circuitous pathways somehow imitates the winding 'serpent rope' of the Milky Way, connecting the soul to the tunnel of light? What if the center of the labyrinth, which represented 'New Jerusalem' to the medieval pilgrims, acts as a 'stargate' or wormhole that delivers them to the Galactic Center or the 'world to come?'

My far-fetched train of thought is reinforced by my friend and fellow labyrinth builder, Marilyn Larson, who shares an interesting conversation that takes place in a Unitarian Church in Minnesota.

Marilyn is using the floor space of the church to draw a seven-circuit labyrinth on a piece of canvas. She carries the canvas in a rolling suitcase and with the help of the janitor, clears the chairs so she can spread it out to work. Sometime later when he is on his break, the janitor comes back in and sits down watching her draw the design. He tells Marilyn that he was a Tibetan monk living in a monastery in Katmandu, Nepal before relocating to this country. He then shares that he is familiar with the seven-circuit labyrinth because it was used in the monastery as part of his training. They walked it as a daily morning ritual with the intent to commit the pattern to memory so, when they were released from their bodies at death, they would know how to cross over. I am amazed to hear there are places where instructions are given on how to successfully cross over, but even more amazed that these instructions involve the Labyrinth.

Spiritual Masters teach that the dimensional levels are separated by 90 degrees and a particular wavelength. The 3rd dimension has a wavelength of 7.3 cm. How do we access other dimensions that are right next to ours? It is done through 90-degree turns. It doesn't matter if it is a right turn or a left turn as long as it is at a 90-degree angle. It seems that the monks are imprinting the 90-degree turns into their cellular structure—laying down an internal 'breadcrumb trail' which their spirits would automatically follow when released. This starts making more sense when I read an excerpt by *Drunvalo Melchizedek, a well-respected spiritual teacher, who explains:

"Beings such as angels are able to disappear at will, merely by tuning

into, and then out of, our dimension of reality. Devas, faeries, and UFOs can be similarly explained. You may have heard stories of UFOs streaking across the sky, taking a 90-degree turn, and disappearing. The beings on this UFO have linked together their consciousness, and made a specific change inside of themselves, which happens to be related to 90 degrees. When they do so through their breathing and their connection, they can make the entire ship disappear, and move into the dimensional level that they are tuned to."

Is it a coincidence that labyrinths utilize a steady progression of counter-rotating, 90-degree turns to reach the center? Whether I was conscious of it or not, my ordinary reality and the way I viewed it were subtly being altered ... simply by moving through the paths.

Spirits are not part of my everyday life until the labyrinth is installed, afterwhich a gradual increase in incidents occur. I do not *see* them until I *hear* them: then their telepathic communication is accompanied by vague, visual impressions. I don't walk the labyrinth looking for spirits; they usually come to my attention through a concerned or grieving loved one. It's then that I find that using the labyrinth is a viable way to assist them. Unlike mediums who can see, sense, or communicate with spirits wherever they go, only when I am asked to help by a concerned human or nudged by the earthbound spirit, do I turn the dial to the 'station' where they exist.

In the beginning when I am called to assist, I feel incompetent and unsure of what to do, but, without set instructions to follow, I feel I have permission to let my heart guide the process. Getting my left-brain out of the way becomes easier as I surrender to my Higher Self which nudges and prods me, providing the assurance that I can't do it wrong. 'Trusting' becomes the primary art form that plugs me into the ever-present relay-system of multidimensional communication.

Hollywood's portrayal of earthbound spirits moving on is much more dramatic than in real life. In my experience thus far, individuals have not shown up with the displayed injuries of their death, as shown in the movie *The Sixth Sense*. The early season of the show *Ghost Whisperer* accurately portrays those who remain here as staying until they complete some unfinished business, but the later seasons seem caught up in the 'dark side' of things featuring plots with dark entity attachments. The general public might watch this type of show or movie for intrigue or a thrill. However, because of sensational or dramatic overlay, people don't consider the possibility that their own loved ones might be nearby; nor do they realize their daily lives might be impacted by an earthbound spirit.

After 15 years of investigating the afterlife, and serving as the host of *Afterlife TV*, one of Bob Olsen's criticisms of those who believe in earthbound spirits is this:

"Too many of the bereaved are suffering in their fear that their deceased loved ones are lost or stuck between worlds—commonly known as earthbound spirits. To me, this is a sad and unfortunate tragedy for the grieving because I have not seen any evidence of this belief."

My observation in working with earthbound spirits since the mid 1990's has been that bereaved survivors are NOT suffering over the fear that their loved ones may be earthbound. Most of them have never even given this a consideration. Instead, I have seen many individuals who suffer because their loved ones *are*, in fact, still attached, and *because* those still living are unaware of this connection. Ironically, these people receive relief from a host of symptoms, as well as comfort and closure, when they become open to this possibility and feel empowered to assist their loved ones in crossing over.

This can be done in countless ways, but my portal of preference is using the labyrinth. This means one can physically walk a labyrinth, or 'finger-walk' a labyrinth pattern, with intent and focus. Any pattern will do, although the image of the Chakra Labyrinth works best for me. There is an embossed design on the inside cover of the *Chakra Labyrinth Cards* meant to be finger-traced (and that image has been included at the back of this book on a perforated sheet for easy removal). Why does this work? My logical mind has struggled with this from the beginning. The pattern creates a containment vessel for the earthbound spirits. As with the real labyrinth, the enclosed design places them into their own kind of 'lock system.' Once inside, the rotating circuits produce a rapid stepping-up of their energy while damming off the lower vibrations that have been holding them back.

I did not create the *Chakra Labyrinth Cards* to be used specifically for assisting earthbound spirits, yet have found that they work beautifully as a releasing tool. I have also used the *Chakra Labyrinth Cards* in combination with the Eden Energy Medicine technique of *Clearing and Balancing the Chakras* (described in Chapter 50 "Death Rites"), as a way to assist someone who is dying. Identifying and releasing feelings which hold a dying person's soul back, can be of great benefit.

I have an opportunity to use this method in a phone session with great success when a client (June) tells me about her friend (Frank), who she's known over 40 years. He's now racked with cancer and remains in a coma, reluctant to die. She wants to know if there is anything we can do to help him. Clearing and balancing the chakras comes to my mind immediately.

We prepare by mentally constructing the image of a golden *octahedron*. I have heard it said that the original photon is an octahedron. This geometric shape, with a total of eight sides, is one of the three-dimensional shapes known as the Platonic Solids. Through the power of your imagination (which should never be underestimated), you visualize yourself in the center of a four-sided pyramid that extends above you with another matching pyramid below you. The bases are joined, forming a square on the level of the floor where you are standing. It may help you to visualize this by aligning it with the four walls of the room you are in, but it can be any size as long as it completely surrounds you. By envisioning yourself inside a geometric shape like this, you are increasing the vibration. Like the labyrinth, the octahedron can also serve as a 'lock system' because it provides contained protection and a rapid way to level-up.

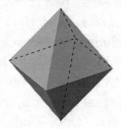

(The Octahedron is also explained in Chapter 50 "Death Rites.")

We set our intent to create the octahedron in three separate places:
1. Where I am sitting in the center of the Prairie Labyrinth in Missouri.
2. Where June is sitting in her sunroom in Oregon.
3. Where Frank is lying unconscious under hospice care, in a skilled nursing facility in California.

June knows Frank doesn't have any belief in the afterlife or much to do with anything spiritual in nature. She senses Frank's resistance to moving on, primarily due to his concern for his wife, but she is also aware of his volatile nature which has affected several of his key relationships. Through this process, I know we will address the futility he may be feeling around making amends with his troubling relationships when it seems, at this last stage of the game, that those opportunities are lost to him.

Using a table as a portable altar, June prepares her space, laying out her own *Chakra Labyrinth Cards* and a Chakra finger-labyrinth that was collaboratively created on my land to be a representation and extension of the Prairie Labyrinth.

Tuning into Frank, June easily brings her 'remote presence' into his private hospital room. The fact that Frank's body is in a coma allows his soul to be fully aware of her 'entrance' (albeit surprised by June's metaphysical ability to so easily communicate and transfer her energy to be with him). He is a bit confused about who I am, so I introduce myself with a brief overview of our intentions to help him.

Because June and I have worked together before, we are able to move as a coordinated team into our defined and clear roles. My job is to guide June, leading her through the step-by-step process, while offering Frank additional understanding about his issues. June's long-term relationship with Frank, along with her own developed psychic abilities, enable her to easily establish and maintain the flow of the session. Like a symphony conductor, she sets the tempo, shapes the phrasing, and even has to monitor the entry of other members joining the 'ensemble.' Specifically, this means his wife, who comes in to check on him, momentarily flustering Frank. As June reassures him, he calms down, and his wife too becomes settled, reading a book in a chair a few feet away from the bed, unaware of what is going on in the ethers around Frank.

Guided in this process, the 'score' is spontaneously given to me and passed along to June who embraces her 'directing' role, assessing and translating how Frank is responding energetically to what is occurring. She is his advocate, making any adjustments needed on his behalf.

I relay to Frank that we are going to open a portal of light to assist him. This is achieved by my literal walking of *The Prairie Labyrinth* to its center with the intention of connecting the central axis to both June and Frank's location. June is going to re-activate the portal where she is by finger-walking her labyrinth pattern. In combination with the *Chakra Clearing and Balancing* technique, the portals will merge together and come into Frank's awareness.

At the beginning of each chakra path, June randomly selects a Chakra Labyrinth card, guided by the 'unseen helpers' who understand Frank's issues. The cards are designed with a *Release* statement (intended to be read on the finger-walk in) and a *Renew* statement (to be read as you finger-walk your way out). Instead of doing this, we use the cards to personalize the chakra balancing technique for Frank. June begins by tracing the first pathway, the Root Chakra, and then reads the *Release* statement on the card she has selected for him.

"I acknowledge and bless my core wounds, old patterns and limiting beliefs." She mentally positions herself, sitting off to the side of Frank's body and uses her hand to make counterclockwise rotations over his Root Chakra. She repeats the statement over and over as she slowly makes the rotations, while we discuss impressions that we are receiving so he can review how the statement applies to him. He is very receptive. When June feels a shift, she shakes the energy from her hands, mentally seeing it being transmuted in a violet flame. Proceeding, she reads the *Renew* portion.

"I have the courage to face my issues and make the changes I desire."

While saying this, June resets Frank's Root Chakra by tracing clockwise circles with her right hand in the air above it. This process (tracing the path, reading a corresponding card while cleansing and balancing the chakra) continues all the way to the Crown Chakra. As we work, June senses deeply held anguish, anger and remorse being released, especially with the bottom chakras (Root, Sacral, and Solar Plexus). With the higher chakras (Heart, Throat, Third Eye and Crown) June becomes aware of doors beginning to open which have been blocked Frank's entire life.

Arriving at the center of the Labyrinth, I explain to Frank about the opening of the portal occurring here and the presence of his Higher Self/*spirit* body that will serve as his soul's escort (when he is ready) to accompany him all the way to the World of Light. We encourage Frank to visit, in his Light body, those family members whom he is agonizing over, and we impress upon him that he can easily impart to them whatever he needs to express. He is relieved to know he can do this.

Two days later, I feel Frank in the Prairie Labyrinth when I am on my morning walk. I assure him that the portal is wide open and he can leave whenever he chooses. Several hours later, June calls to tell me that Frank has made a peaceful transition and she can feel his gratitude coming back to her. She is left with an open heart and a clear mind, able to finger-walk the labyrinth back out, affirming the *Renew* statements one more time before dismantling her altar area and closing the portal.

Chakra Labyrinth Cards used while finger-tracing the Labyrinth pattern.

Life is the childhood of our immortality.

~ Johann Wolfgang von Goethe ~

8

THE THIN PLACE

In 1995 *Rev. Lauren Artress founded Veriditas, a non-profit organization born from her own profound experiences with the Labyrinth. The word Veriditas originated with Hildegard of Bingen and means *"The greening power of life."* In 1997, Lauren began offering the Veriditas Labyrinth Facilitator Training as a way to prepare people to introduce others to the labyrinth experience. To date, Veriditas has trained more than 3,000 labyrinth facilitators.

As a master teacher and a long-time certified Labyrinth facilitator, Jo Ann Mast was very familiar with using this powerful tool as a personal practice for healing and growth, but that did not include using it to assist earthbound spirits in crossing over ... until it became a very personal matter.

MOTHER
Jeanne Gertrude, Ashton, Mast, Ryan
Born November 19, 1926
Died September 2, 1998
Crossed Over November 15, 2010

"My mother died in 1998 of a brain aneurism. She lived three days on life support, remaining in a coma in the hospital. That first day I washed her body, combed her hair and talked with her making my peace and wishing her peace. I rubbed her feet and looked up to see her ashen face begin to radiate

a warm peach-pink glow. Wrinkles slowly disappeared; her mouth offered a slight smile. For a brief moment, she was the young girl I never knew. As quickly and silently as it appeared the blush and smile were gone. My heart filled with tender, beautiful love in the life between mother and daughter, a forever moment of gratitude and grief.

Her husband could not let her go. When she was removed from life support there was nothing, only silence as we stood around her bed holding hands—holding space for her transition. One by one family members left quietly, including her husband. I said one last silent prayer. A nurse came and held me. I cried a silent cry and left the room. We buried her with the usual memorial service and mass including Gregorian chants. As I write this it feels like yesterday.

It is 2010. I am attending the 12th Annual Labyrinth Society Gathering at New Harmony, Indiana. A utopian town of 900 people located on the Wabash River, known by some as 'The Thin Place,' hovering between the earth and sky. New Harmony understands its national role in labyrinth culture, opening its doors with beautiful venues and meeting spaces, a perfect spot for both thoughtful work and engaging downtime. It wasn't until the last day of the Gathering that I am walking their lovely pink and gray stone labyrinth, nestled in a garden surrounded with flowering trees. Complete with three days of labyrinths, stories, learning and experiences, I begin my walk in richness and wonder. Suddenly I recall a conversation with Toby Evans from the first evening of the Gathering. She had asked about my mother who she sensed was around me while I was talking with her. How can that be? Mom's been dead for years. Toby is a gifted and talented wise woman and I learn she helps souls complete their crossing or transition to the other world. She believes my mother is still here, and tells me I might experience her presence during the days at the Gathering. She indicates that the Labyrinth can be used to help free her.

I continue walking, placing one foot in front of the other, following the ancient path. Gently I feel my mother's energy. I am aware of her words, her fear, and her urgency. She pleads with me for help, such as I had often provided throughout her earthly life.

I take her hand. We walk toward the labyrinth center. Along the way, I console her with words and loving energy. The labyrinth is safe, nothing to fear, she is protected in this sacred pattern. I leave her in the center with instruction to remain in this beautiful loving labyrinth.

Three days later, I am home sorting through conference materials and discover a picture of the labyrinth, which I took when saying goodbye to Mom. Shockingly, there in the labyrinth center is a bright white sphere.

"'Oh my God, it must be Mom," and I remember my promise to help her get 'unstuck.'

Granite labyrinth in New Harmony, IN with the 'white sphere' of her Mother's presence. Photo by Jo Ann Mast

Not sure what to do, I am guided to create an altar for her using my wooden finger labyrinth. The only photograph I have of her is placed in the center. Around and on the labyrinth are photos of her husband and grandchildren, her rosary, a Mother Mary picture and several of her favorite

Mary prayers.

My best friend Lisa agrees to assist. We gather around Mom's altar in Lisa's beautiful, safe meditation room. I call Michael, my brother, who was recently visited by mom while on a hunting trip. He joins us on speakerphone. The process takes about 30 minutes. We invite spirits of the four directions. We acknowledge Mom, assuring her that it is now safe to complete her transition and be with Mother Mary where there is no pain. There is nothing to fear, only joy and incredible love. We all love her very much (my brother's voice can be heard saying this). Lisa reads the 149 steps from the Buddhist Book of the Dead.

All is quiet. I feel Mom's energy shift, and encourage her to reach for Mother Mary's hand. All three of us wait and pray, quietly supporting her movement. Little by little, Mom tentatively reaches up for Mary's hand. There is silence. We hold loving sacred space until she has crossed over.

Collectively, without words, we know it is complete. Mom's energy is gone, each of us uniquely experiencing the moment of her crossing. Involuntary tears mingle with giggles, laughter, and gratitude and thanks to all present—seen and unseen. From the speakerphone, I hear my brother blowing his nose and jokingly saying, "Mom, I know you are happier than you could ever imagine."

~ Jo Ann Mast

A vortex by nature acts as a transformational portal
to other dimensions.

~ David Cowan and Erina Cowan ~
"Dowsing Beyond Duality"

9

SACRED GEOMETRY AS PORTALS

In the early summer of 2001, a neighbor down the road put his home up for sale. Friends who come to walk the labyrinth ask if they can see his property. I accompany them to his door and receive a tour of the house and land. Upon leaving, I remark to my friends, "There's no way that his house is going to sell." I make this statement because, as wonderful as the land seems, I can't wait to get out of the stifling energy in the house. He calls me the next day to find out if my friends are interested in buying. Struggling with how to tell him that he is going to have a hard time selling it to anyone, I end up blurting out, "Before this house will sell, it needs an energetic cleaning that goes beyond the carpets and drapes."

Undaunted by my remark he asks, "Is this something you can do?" I stammer, "Yesss, but what I do may seem kind of weird to you." There is a long pause before he responds, "Be here tomorrow morning. I don't care how weird it is, just do it."

I show up with a sage stick, my eagle feather, and rattle intending to move and release the stuck energy. I am not really thinking in terms of an earthbound spirit ... more like stuck energy of negative, accumulated thoughtforms. Walking into his office, I feel a heavy presence. I know he lives here alone since he recently put his father, who has a diagnosis of Alzheimer's, into a care facility. He tells me his mother died five years earlier. We talk briefly about her in the living room when he makes an offhand comment about never sitting in the recliner because that is his mother's favorite chair. On the stoop of his front door I smudge him from head to toe with the lit sage bundle and prepare to leave. He comments on how bizarre this is as he actually sees black, soot-like energy leaving from the bottoms of his feet. I don't see anything through the smoking sage, but on the walk back home I feel like I am drugged. I assume this is due to the fact that he is a heavy smoker and I was in his enclosed space for a while. When I still can't shake the feeling of brain fog days later, I email an energy healer and ask if he will work on me. He writes back saying I have a tear in my aura, and the 'entity' that was attached to my neighbor is now attached to me. His sense is this is a woman, possibly my neighbor's wife.

I read this, knowing my neighbor is not married, while grasping the reality that it's his mother whose presence I feel in my energy field. Doing nothing more than acknowledging this, I feel her energy pulling up and out of me. The relief in my body is immediate. I quickly send her a mental message:

"Do not go back and reattach to your son. I can help you move on." There is silence before I begin receiving her explanation.

"I stayed around because I wanted to make sure my husband was cared for properly, but he doesn't need me anymore and now I don't know what to do."

I attempt to reassure her. "I believe I can help you cross over by walking the labyrinth."

She is quick to cut me off, *"I'm not going anywhere unless my son is a part of this. I need him to agree to this."*

I don't know how I am going to break this unconventional news to her son without sounding like a lunatic, but I don't have much choice. To my surprise when I broach the subject with him the next day, he only asks me one question:

"Will this help to sell my house?"

In that moment, he refrains from telling me all the strange occurrences he has experienced over the years since his mother died, such as hearing his father in his room at night having conversations with her. He dismissed this as part of his father's dementia, but he also heard muffled voices at night, disturbing enough for him to knock on the ceiling with a broom handle to silence them. He witnessed a can of Coca-Cola move unassisted across his desk and, more dramatically, he was once physically restrained with the wind knocked out of him when he moved angrily toward his father. He'd lost his temper when he found his kitchen floor flooded with overflowing water as his father continued to feed broken glass into the garbage disposal. He doesn't tell me any of this until much later, so I am amazed that he is agreeing to come.

With the date set for three days later, his mother seems satisfied to remain in the labyrinth, but is curious about the process of crossing-over. When I explain that we will be using the center of the labyrinth as the portal to release her, she innocently inquires, *"Do you think we can use your garden space? I like that statue of Mother Mary that you have in the center."*

She is referring to a 55-foot circular garden of flowers and herbs connected by sand paths that are outlined with base quartz crystal. The sacred geometry installation designed by Earth Symbol artist *Alex Champion is called *"Chante Ishta"* (pronounced *shawn-tay eesh-ta*) associated with both Eastern Cherokee and Lakota Sioux languages. It means "Single Eye of the Heart." The pattern is made up of nine overlapping vesical-shaped pathways that form a continuous walking path that many people use before or after walking the labyrinth to quiet and center themselves. The paths wind around a raised bed of earth in the shape of a 9-pointed star. At any point, you can step into the raised area, intended to bring you into the single-eye focus of returning to your heart.

A *vesica* is an almond shape created from overlapping or intersecting spheres. The configuration of two overlapping circles is referred to as the Vesica Piscis. Circles create natural portals. Interpenetrating circles connect dimensions. The overlapping circles represent the two worlds—the physical world of matter and time, and the spiritual world of the eternal and divine. The intersecting portion (the vesica) symbolizes the bridge between heaven and earth or the union of cause and effect.

*Vesica Piscis is a Latin phrase meaning "bladder" or *vessel of the fish*. The symbol appears frequently in medieval art and architecture and is considered the basis of all sacred geometry and the base of creation used in both ancient and modern times. As a birthing platform, the Vesica Piscis is made up of opposing forces that come together to create a gateway capable of holding our purest intentions. This symbol is on the cover of the Chalice Well in Glastonbury, England, depicting a place where worlds overlap and is a universal symbol of the womb of the Divine Feminine.

The statue of Mother Mary in the center of Chante Ishta is another representation of the Divine Feminine that honors my own Catholic upbringing.

I respond to her question by saying, "I have never used this walking path to move people on, but I will think about it. Why does it appeal to you?"

"I loved gardening, and I was named "Marion" for Mother Mary."

The next morning, before I am out of bed, my husband—who knows nothing about the spirit-moving events of the day—stands at our bedroom window and suddenly announces, "You need to get up and look outside."

I don't budge or open my eyes, but mumble, "Why? What do you want me to see?"

His reply jolts me out of bed. "The sky is completely overcast with one ray of light coming down and hitting that statue you have in the middle of the garden."

I pull myself up to the window-sill in wonder, taking this brilliant light shaft illuminating Mother Mary as visual confirmation that the nine-pointed star center of Chante with its nine overlapping 'worlds' can also be used as a portal.

The morning of Marion's departure, she greets me with an unusual request.

"Will you make bacon and eggs for breakfast?"

I seldom have bacon in the house, but this is one time that I do. "Why bacon and eggs?"

"The smell reminds me of happy times with my family."

I am glad that I can grant her this simple wish.

By 10:30 her son is standing in my yard with a no-nonsense, let's get down to business attitude. I give him the download of directions that has started to come into my mind, combining them with Marion's requests.

"Your mother wants you to walk the labyrinth with her first. At each of the seven turns, there is a fence post with a wind chime attached to it. Stop at each post, ring the wind chime, close your eyes and let a memory that you have shared with your mother come into your mind. Reflect on it as you walk to the next post and continue this process all the way into the center. In the middle, sit on one of the benches and say whatever you want to her. Then come back out and I will meet you in Chante where we will move her on."

He sputters, "What? You are not going to go in there with me? What if I get lost? I don't know how to do this."

"You can't do it wrong. This is not a maze. You only have to follow the same path in and out while paying attention to what thoughts and feelings come up."

He leaves uneasy, wanting the whole weird ordeal over with. Forty minutes later, he glides into the yard, peaceful and softened. I ask if he wants to share what happened.

"When I got to the first post, I rang the bell and then closed my eyes. I couldn't believe that I remembered when I was in kindergarten and did not want to go to school one day so I pretended that I was sick. My mom knew I was fine, but she said I could play *hooky* and have a day off with her. She took me to the A&W where we had root beer and fries. It was a great day. I haven't thought about this in ages."

After sharing his additional memories, I am convinced that a transformation is already occurring. He is not the same impatient person who walked into the field. Giving him the next part of the instructions, I explain how we are going to use the 9-petal, vesica star design to move her on.

Standing on a large flat crystal that is placed at the entrance of the design, we pause as I am guided to invite Marion's Higher Self to come in and meet her. Taking the immediate path towards the right side, we spin through each vesica in a counterclockwise manner. When we arrive back at the beginning, I check in with Marion to see if I can sense her Higher Self. She appears to be 'melting' into an all-loving energy field and her fear and resistance are evaporating. We walk the whole pattern again, this time taking the outer-most path towards the left in a clockwise fashion before stepping up into the raised, center section in the shape of a 9-pointed star. I play a song on my guitar that feels appropriate and then relay her final words to her son as she seems to lift up and evaporate above the statue of Mary.

Although this feels both natural and unreal, I am still bombarded with the doubts of my critical mind that question it all. However dubious I am about what happened, my neighbor's house sells two weeks later.

Only those who have dared to let go-can dare to re-enter.

~ **Meister Eckhart** ~

10

BOUND BY LOWER EMOTIONS

I don't have to wait long before Chante Ishta is used again as a portal. Within a month, a friend from England emails me to ask for assistance. At his advertising firm, one of his secretaries was driving with her boyfriend when they were involved in a car accident. Although she was unharmed, her boyfriend did not survive. Unnderstandably distraught and traumatized, she confided in her boss a week later.

"I am worried about Geoffrey. I can feel him and I think he is refusing to move across." Aware of my other experiences with earthbound souls, my friend decides to contact me to see if I can help. While sitting at the computer reading his words, I am flooded with tears, deeply saddened and frustrated by the situation. Another part of me calmly steps back and questions, *Why am I this upset? My reaction is way out of proportion. I don't even know these people.*

Because of my recent experience with Marion, I suspect the secretary's boyfriend, Geoffrey, is enmeshed in my energy field. Mentally, I pull him up and out of me, as if I am taking off a tight-fitting T-shirt. Immediately, I feel a subtle release as I hear him sputter, *"Where the hell am I? How did I get here and who are you?"*

"You are in the United States, outside of Kansas City, Missouri. I think you got here through the power of thought transference, via fiber optics using the internet. I know you are confused and want to leave, but hear me out ..."

He cuts me off, angrily shouting, *"I want to go home and be with my*

79

girlfriend. I want to be back in my own body. This can't be happening to me!"

Trying to calm him down, I ask him to tell me what he remembers. Instantly, I am swept into his story, watching the scenes unfold in my mind. It's as if I am in the back seat of the car, looking over his shoulder as we speed down a narrow road. He is in a heated argument with his girlfriend with one hand on the wheel and the other waving wildly in her face. He is not watching the road, intent only on making his point.

In a burst of anger, he jerks the wheel and the car flips over, crashing into some kind of fencing structure. Geoffrey is out of his body instantly, not having a clue that this accident resulted in his death.

I realize that he needs this explained to him. "Geoffrey, you are no longer in that physical body. The emotions you were experiencing just before the accident are still with you, continuing to be replayed ... as if caught in a loop. Because you haven't crossed over, all whom you cling to—your girlfriend, family, friends—struggle not only to process their own shock and grief, but their feelings are all mixed up with your unresolved anger, blame, frustration, confusion, and sadness."

I can tell he is struggling to take this in. "Moving on doesn't mean you will never have contact with the people you love again. There are no barriers to Love. When they think of you or you think of them, the circuit is complete. Crossing over means you will join with your Higher Self, giving you a bigger-picture perspective with full understanding of why you left the Earth so young. Right now, you are just angry that you can't get back in your body and none of this makes any sense to you. If you cross over, you will see how this is part of a bigger plan which you helped design, and you will understand how it fits in with your entire soul journey. Crossing over means returning to others who love you and can connect with you. They can help you clear up the confusion and pain you are feeling right now. You won't feel so alone and isolated. A new light body waits for you when you start your healing process, and your healing will free your family to begin theirs."

He wants to believe me, but I can feel his skepticism and doubt, overwhelmed with this disorienting situation. I move to the back yard and tell him I am going to walk the 9-petal, vesica star pattern with him and call in his Higher Self. Then he can decide if he wants to go. Around and around I walk, only getting as far as the first set of counterclockwise rotations when a friend pulls up into my driveway. The friend is familiar with the work I do, so I pause, reasoning that having his added energy will help me support Geoffrey's challenging spirit.

Stepping out of the pattern, I give Geoffrey telepathic instructions to wait in the nine-pointed star center (with the statue of Mary) while I bring my friend up to speed. Patience is obviously not a virtue Geoffrey had time to develop while he was in his body. Within seconds of coming back to resume the walk, one of my dogs (Lexus—who can see energy quite easily) is drawn to the center where she tentatively begins to sniff the area around the statue. We watch as Lexus suddenly jumps back just as the statue comes off its cement pedestal, crashing to the ground.

I can feel Geoffrey's anger rolling out at me, followed by an emotional outburst. *"You said you were going to help me and then you walk away! I don't need this. I don't want to be here. Screw you! I want to get out of here right now!"*

I am taken aback and shocked that his anger has enough force to tip over a heavy cement statue. I approach him like a stern mother dealing with a small child who is having a temper tantrum. I know his anger is his attempt to take control of a situation that feels out of his control, but I am also convinced that I am witnessing the same out-of-control pattern which ended his life. I have to collect myself before responding to him.

"I know you are confused and feel upset, but your anger is not going to help free you. It is going to keep you locked in your own in-between prison cell. Is that what you want? You are not going to be aware of the help that is already here unless you calm down and trust what is happening. We are here to help you, but you have a part to play in this. You have to let the anger go. You wear it like heavy armor, without realizing it is weighing you down. Only by letting it go can you become aware of the love that is waiting for you and feel light enough to join with it."

Picking up the statue, my friend and I reposition it and begin again at the entrance to Chante. This time, we are oriented to move through all the vesicas in a clockwise direction. The clockwise motion helps to spin off all the lower emotions dragging down Geoffrey's field. I sense ripples of energy coming off him which expand and rise with each vesica rotation. By the time we make our way through all the paths and return to the beginning, my body is tingling. This is my indication that Geoffrey is finally aware of his Higher Self. His frustration and resistance dissolve, evaporating with the morning dew. Without any more fanfare, he floats to the center and merges with the unconditional love surrounding him. Much to my relief—he is quietly gone.

To the well-organized mind,
death is but the next great adventure.

~ J.K. Rowling ~
"Harry Potter and the Sorcerer's Stone"

11

EDUCATION FROM BEYOND

Midsummer in the prairie is hot and dry, and not commonly a time people choose to walk the labyrinth. However, two close friends call to ask if they can bring a third woman (Barbara) who is unable to move beyond the grief of losing her husband a year earlier. I agree, and find myself looking into the eyes of a sad and depressed woman.

"Ron was ready to retire and we were going to finally travel in our RV and see the country and then he goes and has a heart attack! How could he do this to me?"

Ron was her whole life. She depended on him for everything and the thought of doing things now on her own is terrifying. As hard as it is to be in the grief and blame, it is harder for her to face the demanding world of decisions and choices … alone.

My friends have already talked to her about the necessity of letting go of Ron, encouraging her to move on with her life. Her polite resistance tells me that she thinks they brought her here to speed up this process, fearing that my intent is to 'take' Ron away from her. She isn't ready for that. I tell her to just walk the labyrinth and open herself to connect with him, sharing what she most needs to express in whatever way is right for her. My experience has been that, when people go in *expecting* to hear from or meet their loved ones, they usually don't, due to their idea of how this should look or feel.

When she comes out of the field, there is a slight shift in her demeanor, momentarily suspending the self-pity and fear. Curious, I ask if she wants to share anything about her experience.

"Well, it was peaceful enough, but," she hurriedly adds, "I am still not ready to say goodbye to Ron. When I was sitting in the center, a butterfly came and landed on the tip of my index finger. It stayed with me the entire walk. Can you believe that?"

Lifting her finger, she shows me that the tenacious creature is still poised there, stuck like glue. I smile at the obvious symbolism that I'm sure has also dawned on her. I can't refrain from asking, "Are you ready to let the butterfly go?"

"No! As long as it stays on my finger, I am going to keep it."

She thanks me for letting her walk and assures me that it is not the time for Ron to move on. She then asks if she can walk into Chante Ishta and create a small medicine wheel with tiny, polished stones that belonged to Ron, whose lineage was Cherokee. Choosing one of the outer sections planted with roses, she takes a few minutes to arrange the semi-precious stones in her own private ritual.

A month later, forgetting all about the stones, I am pulling weeds in Chante and inadvertently scattered the stones in several directions. When I realize what I have done, I 'think' an apology to Ron while attempting to reassemble his wheel. In that instant, Ron's thoughts come into my mind.

"Don't worry about it. You don't have to put them back into place, but I would like your help in crossing over." Surprised by this I have to ask, "Does this mean that Barbara is finally ready to let you go?"

He laughs, *"No! I thought if I stayed I could help her adjust, but I realize now that as long as I am here, she isn't going to get on with her life. The only way she is going to be able to move on is if I do first."*

Ron is head and shoulders above other earthbound souls I have encountered. His calm demeanor is a stark contrast to a younger soul like Geoffrey. Ron is not lost, agitated, confused, or resisting the idea of crossing over, and instead has great wisdom and poise that impress me. I ask if he would be willing to talk with me before he leaves to help me better understand why earthbound spirits remain here.

More than happy to oblige, he launches into a very logical explanation.

"There are three primary reasons why souls don't cross over when they die, along with other contributing factors:

1. ***They may not know they are dead.*** *If people die suddenly, they can be disoriented and have trouble accepting that they are dead. If they have a belief that death is the end and there should be nothing at all, confusion can stop the process or cause the soul to ignore, reject, or not even notice the opening of the light. Some stay around the area or location of their death.*

2. ***They may not be ready to go.*** *This can be due to unfinished business—like financial or survival concerns for the ones remaining, or wanting to make sure a certain deed is done—but unresolved emotions are the bond that binds them the most. At the top of the list are the two extremes—strong feelings of love or fear. They may be so identified with a particular person, their family, or their role, feeling either responsible for or dependent upon them, that they cannot conceive of letting them go. This can be coupled with fear. Fear of the unknown, fear of losing those they love, fear that the life they lived wasn't good enough, especially if they hold the ingrained belief in Heaven/Hell. Staying here is preferred to the possibility of the final judgment, just in case 'eternal damnation' is what is waiting for them. Fear may extend into guilt, holding onto regrets, longing to make amends or needing to forgive or be forgiven ... or the flip side of this: wanting revenge or justice.*

3. ***A surviving loved one is not ready to let them go.*** *The pull of the emotional bond from our loved ones creates a 'double bind' for the soul—as it did for me. I decided to stay, thinking I could comfort Barbara and help her adjust to life without me while still acting as her protector. I saw myself as her guardian angel trying to steer her toward things that could help her become more independent and happy, but this isn't what happened. My presence was only keeping us both in a limbo state where we remained locked in the same*

emotions, repeating the same old patterns."

Wanting to understand more, I interject, "Using the Labyrinth or Chante Ishta seems to create a portal to the other side. It also seems that holding the intention for the Higher Self helps with the crossing over process, but I don't understand how or why this really works. If the soul decides to stay around for one of your reasons, then why don't they just leave when they're finally ready or feel complete? And if the Higher Self is the primary escort, why doesn't it just come and get them? It seems like we, the human psychopomps, are just 'middle men' that don't really need to be in the equation."

Ron responds to me like a patient teacher. *"At the time of death, the portal or bridge between worlds is wide open and remains this way for around 24 hours, though sometimes up to several days."*

(Note: In some traditions, the body is not moved or touched for several hours to insure non-interference, allowing the light body to make the journey home. It is interesting that most cultures have some sort of wake, funeral or burial within 3 days to a week.)

"The magnificence of the Higher Self is always present, but the soul has free will. This means that if we have a strong desire or urgency to stay, that desire can override the process of moving on. When I died, I was aware of the 'passageway' and the All-Loving Presence that was with me, but the emotional pull to Barbara—including the guilt I felt in leaving her—ensured that I would cling to the Earth as well as to my old, co-dependent ways of trying to protect her. When the grid system around the portal seemed to close, my awareness of the Higher Self closed with it. I made my choice to stay, thinking I could change my mind whenever I wanted to. This was true, but it is not as easy as I thought it would be to detach from this lower vibration and find my way to a light bridge.

The Earth plane vibrates at a certain frequency. Being earthbound is choosing to stay here in a holding pattern between the third and fourth plane. It's the closest frequency to our loved ones on Earth. When you state your preference to remain here, it feels like the Higher Self leaves you, but that is only because of the limited perception we have at this level. The Higher Self, with its higher vibration fades from the forefront of our awareness. Clinging to the lower vibrations creates an energetic barrier. 'Crossing over' implies that you remove the barriers to the awareness of your Higher Self, where the complete life review takes place as well as understanding your entire soul's journey.

Upon death, many earthbound spirits return to the places that were part of their daily routines or go back to the place of their death—if they are confused or still in shock about what happened. This is in spite of having the freedom to move unrestricted to any place they desire.

If a loved one was their motivation for staying, they will remain with them. It is a safe, comfortable existence, but it's also empty without real contact with those we most want to communicate with. In reality, we just stay in the same patterned loop that we became accustomed to while in body, and often find or hang out with other earthbound souls who have a similar vibration. Eventually, some begin looking for a portal of light that hopefully will lead us back to Source. Because of coming here with Barbara, I knew when I was ready I would come back to ask for your assistance.

You might think of yourself as an unnecessary 'middle man' (woman), but human intervention makes this much easier for us. This is because a human's vibration serves as a conduit. Your willingness to focus on our behalf acts like a transducer. All of you participating in this work are valuable 'ground crew.' You are using your bodies as grounding rods, intending that the energy of the Higher Self steps down as our energy steps up to meet it—morph into it—and become aware of who we have always been. You don't have to figure out how to do this. Your willingness to serve as a bridge between the worlds causes the bridge to form. Focusing on the Higher Self acts like a satellite link-up, overriding the lower signal of the 3D fence, opening us to the higher planes. Your intent, combined with moving through any sacred geometry pattern (like the labyrinth or the 9-petal vesica) *helps us dissolve the barriers of our old resistance. By reinforcing the patterns of creation around us, you activate the patterns inherent in us. The illusion of separation creates a gap that can finally close when the vehicle of our Higher Self arrives (in our awareness) to take us home."*

I realize from this discussion that, until the frequency is high enough, the Higher Self is not visible to the earthbound soul. The 'arrival' may seem to be occurring in their outer awareness, like someone coming to meet them, but the Higher Self has always been there. It is simply revealed when the weight of the soul's resistance is removed.

Just as Michelangelo said, *"I saw the angel in the marble and carved until I set him free,"* each soul must go through the process of hewing away the rough excess imprisoning the core Self. When we remove the density of the surrounding 'negative space,' the only thing that remains is the true essence of our eternal Masterpiece.

Before Ron moves across, he thanks me, but I am the one filled with gratitude. I wonder if part of Ron's soul contract was to remain earthbound just to educate me. I am certainly the beneficiary of his delayed departure.

If we have no peace,
it is because we have forgotten
that we belong to each other.

~ **Mother Teresa** ~

12

UNFINISHED BUSINESS

Considering that unfinished business is one of the primary factors which can keep a soul from moving on, the following stories are two different experiences by the same woman. They exemplify the difference it can make to help someone release their burdens before dying and then a contrast situation is presented that resulted in an earthbound state due to unresolved issues and obligations.

On a conscious level, you aren't usually aware that you have a 'soul contract' to assist someone in their passing; yet if you are destined to play this significant role, you can bet that the Universe will conspire on your behalf, compelling you to fulfill your part.

Athena is one of twelve children brought up with all the complexities involved in a large family. A younger sister named Rebekka was considered schizophrenic, most likely caused by her mother taking free samples of a drug called Thalidomide in the later part of her pregnancy. Rebekka's unstable mental health created untold hardship in the family, eventually resulting in estrangement with Rebekka who moved from Denmark to Nova Scotia to distance herself from the rest of her family.

Leading up to this was an intervention that had occurred years earlier, arranged by some of the concerned family members. A social worker asked both her mother and father if they wanted Rebekka removed from the house.

Her mother said, "Yes" with her father nodding in agreement, because they had become afraid of her and what she might do. The social worker took Rebekka to a shelter, leaving her mother feeling guilty and blaming herself from that day forward for her decision.

It took several years for the family to find out where Rebbeka had moved to, and now that her mother was dying in a hospital from a brain tumor, the family sent a fax via the police department to notify her that her family was offering to pay for her to fly home so she could say goodbye to her mother. She declined the offer. With a heavy heart, Athena took it upon herself to break the news to her Mother.

Athena's description follows:

"I place my left hand above the tumor on the top of Mom's head, with my right hand over her heart. I lay my head on her mattress and feel her feelings. All that is left is the pain she feels because of Rebekka, still wanting forgiveness for sending her away.

I whisper to her, 'It was not your fault—you did all you could.'

I let her feel my heart, filled with frustration over all the family dynamics that are playing out between us. I wonder how Mom has managed mothering twelve children; what pain she has endured at our hands and thoughtlessness. I apologize for staying so far away and not fighting to have my time with her as an adult.

'I'm so sorry, Mom, that I have not been here for you. It was not even your fault. You loved the best way that you could and no one should judge you. All the remaining work will have to be done by the rest of us. We know we have work to do.'

Then I focus on Rebekka. I tell Mom that we have tried everything we could to contact her in order to bring her home to say good-bye. I tell her about everyone's efforts and how wonderful the police captain and officers have been. And though I dread telling her, I know she needs to know. I describe to Mom the details of the phone call I just received from the officer who had gone to Rebekka's apartment and, finally, that she had declined the offer to come home and closed the door.

I have no idea where the strength comes from to continue, but suddenly I hear myself say these words, 'Mom, it is not your fault. It is clear now that there was no way for you to repair your relationship with Rebekka. Even the officer said she wasn't in her right mind. You tried your best. We tried our best. None of us could reach her heart. You just need to let it go. Maybe you can work with her spirit in another realm, but your work here with her on this plane is done ... let it go, Mom... let it go.'

Suddenly, I am hit with the heaviest aching pain in my heart that I have ever felt—deep, penetrating agony that only a mother could hold.

She lets her pain go into me, and all I can think is, "Yes, that's right, let it go."

The pain is so vast and penetrating that I think I might die from its burden ... it feels like I was only ever here for this expressed purpose: to take it from her. I sob quietly with my head at her heart, my hands and arms the conduits and circuitry to receive her pain.

I lay there whispering between sobs, "Beautiful ... beautiful ... beautiful!!!" And when she is done, I have no energy to move. Two of my sisters come into the room and lift my upper body off the bed. They support me as we walk to the bathroom. They wash my face and neck while I run my hands and arms under cool water to release the energy I have taken in. When we go back into the room, I lie down on the adjacent hospital bed before feeling strong enough to sit in the chair.

Within one minute, Mom's breaths are very far apart. My sister Lena and I both come closer to listen and watch. We can feel it as she lets go, little by little, each breath smaller than the previous.

'Oh, Mom ... there you go ... you go now, go, go, go... go on, Mom, there is light for you. There is a place for you ...' I whispered in her ear.

Lena calls for Dad, who comes over and glances at Mom, then turns around to go gather everyone. But Lena and I call him back to us. He comes in and sits beside her for her last breath.

He says, 'Oh, Helene, that's beautiful ... oh, what a way to go. I love you.'

I add, 'Go, Mom ... you go, go, go—fly now to the light, run like the wind with your new legs ... you go, Mom ... Oh God, you take care of her!' I kiss her on the forehead. By the time the rest of the family comes in, she is almost all the way gone—all the color begins to drain out of her fingers, hands, arms, and her face. All that remains of her body is white and peaceful ... and still."

"One would think that by witnessing such a positive transition, there would be no regrets. But what proved to be the most difficult factor in my letting go was the accumulated intents that somehow never came to fruition. I had wanted to spend a day walking on the coastline with her, to cook a good steak on the grill and share it just with her; to be there for her mile markers, and I knew that I missed two big ones. It was 7 or 8 months later, and I was still trying to move forward.

I was in America visiting a friend in the Midwest. She became interested in my plight, and suggested that I visit the Prairie Labyrinth in Sibley, Missouri, with the intent to address any straggling issues from Mom's death at each chakra station within the Labyrinth.

Off I went. The Labyrinth is a huge one set in native grasses and wildflowers. I was admittedly in somewhat of a daze from the moment I arrived until nearly at the center of the labyrinth. Each chakra post was beautifully constructed. I wrote in my journal about what I was able to release, and what I'd gained at each chakra point.

At the sixth post, the third eye chakra, I began to feel a sense of urgency to get to the center. It did not feel like my mother, but there was definitely somebody waiting there, beckoning me. Nothing was dark or foreboding about it, but it did distract my attention.

As I entered the center and sat on the bench, I eased into a meditation, visualizing dolphins swimming. Gradually I became aware of a thought that wasn't my own.

'Don't look straight over here.' The thought was coming from the bench to my right.

I responded back, 'Okay, how about just a soft glance in your direction?' When I did, there were two little girls sitting on the bench, their feet dangling, and their arms straight down, gripping onto the edge of the bench seat. I didn't know what to do. Toby had told me that this was a portal between dimensions, and spirits sometimes came to be released. My focus had been on my Mom, not anyone else.

'Who are you?' I asked. Then I recognized the one with blond hair. She was Angela, the daughter of my husband's cousin, but I could not place the other child with dark hair. I forgot to ask what they wanted.

Instead, I said, 'Your lives here served their purpose and your work here is done. You need to go on ... the bright light will welcome you home.' They looked at each other in disappointment and expectation. I sensed that my Mom was fine and had no issues. When I thought again of the little girls, they were gone.

I had gained much guidance already, and as I left the center, I felt much lighter. Stopping at each post on the path out added to my appreciation of my own power and connection to the creator. But the closer I got to the entrance, the more I felt the gentle tugging, wanting me to go back in. The girls were still at the center.

Toby was waiting for me at the entrance. She sensed that something was unfinished. I told her about the two little girls still inside the center including the sad fact that Angela had been murdered by her father, and that I didn't know the other girl. Toby asked me to close my eyes and describe her. Amid that description, I realized that it looked like Sarah, who was Angela's 28-year-old mom, only now she appeared as a 3-year old. How could that be? Fourteen years earlier, she had also died by her husband David's hand. They were devout Christians and David had become involved with another woman and lost all perspective. He stabbed his wife with a hunting knife and had gone upstairs to the bedrooms and whispered to his children that they were going to be with Jesus. He then stabbed the girls, but his oldest daughter, Lisbeth didn't die, and he did not stab baby Monique due to Sarah's desperate pleas.

Toby suggested we go into Chante Ishta to release them. We stood on either side of a huge crystal embedded in the sand at the entry and visualized the energy of their Higher Selves coming to enfold them.

Toby turned to me and said, 'Sarah is telling me that the reason she took the appearance of a 3-year-old was that emotionally, she felt like a child, just as helpless as Angela to stop what had happened to her family. But they couldn't leave Lisbeth and Monique, and have stayed close by all these years *to watch them grow up in a safe setting.'*

We proceeded to walk Chante Ishta's paths. Once we arrived at the beginning point, we reversed the direction. Next, we went straight to the center where a statue of Mother Mary stood in the middle of the 9-pointed star. All the while, Toby shook a gourd rattle. As she shook it in the center area, she swirled the rattle in a spiral, moving from low to high in the air. I FELT the spiral of their release. An amazing shiver chilled up and down my spine and then all over my body.

Tearfully, I said to Sarah, 'You would be so proud of Lisbeth, and of Monique!'

Toby replied, 'She is—and because she knows they are fine, they can cross over.'

The spiral continued up, up, and away as the wind picked up, blowing leaves around the huge spiral, and ringing the chimes at the entrance. It was powerfully exuberant! I felt so relieved and happy for them. They showered me with golden sparkles as they left, and indicated that they would assist me in my future work."

~ Athena Zea

You were born a child of light's wonderful secret ~
you return to the beauty you have always been.

~ Aberjhani ~
"Visions of a Skylark Dressed in Black"

13

FEELINGS BURIED ALIVE...NEVER DIE

Behind all unfinished business lies the quicksand of unresolved feelings which can easily sink a newly departed spirit to an earthbound level. We don't usually associate children with the psychopomp role, but young children are naturally sensitive and more adept at picking up information while still connected to the larger workings of the unseen realms. These realms remain open to them until the outer-world conditioning sets in. Then it often gets shut down when the child feels they need to fit in to survive.

The following account is from a woman who, as a questioning adult, had to make peace with, and subsequently retrieve her childhood abilities to become a gifted, intuitive healer, working with subtle energies. But long before she understood and accepted her talent as a soul-guide assisting others, she was playing this role from her innocent but wise child perspective.

"Growing up was different for me than most children. One, because my father was a funeral director/undertaker (which for most children wouldn't be a problem), and Two, it was a problem for me, because I could see and hear the departed souls.

I can still vividly remember, at age four or five, waking up at dawn feeling that I needed to go outside. I quietly went out onto the front porch of our little house across the street from the funeral home, and saw an older man pacing back and forth on the sidewalk, looking very troubled. When he saw me, he stopped pacing and waited for me to come to the sidewalk. I asked him what was wrong and why he was so troubled and sad. He told me he was lost and did not know what to do. I noticed he was grayish and had no color to his skin and, as I looked around, everything looked gray.

I said, 'We can go find my dad. He will know what to do.'

He said, 'No, I already tried to talk to him, but he can't hear me!' He seemed angry about this. After more dialogue, with him sharing his frustration that everyone he loved was crying and nothing he said or did comforted them, his shoulders drooped and he began to fade from my sight.

I can still hear him explaining that he was sad because he had a heart attack (that's what he heard the doctor say), so he died suddenly, leaving his wife and two children behind. He was beside himself with worry that they would not have the means to support themselves, as his wife did not work outside the home. Then he began fretting over reasons why he could not go to Heaven, listing his poor decisions and choices, lies and unforgivable behavior. He believed he needed to 'stay' to make everything right before going to Heaven.

With his head hanging down on his chest he said, 'I finally gave up when the pastor—who could not see me or hear me—shut his bible and said, 'It is finished.'

He disappeared then; I waited a moment and then he was back. The more we talked, the more agitated he became, especially when he described the embalming process and how he screamed and flew away. His agitation increased when he was locked inside of the casket and when the vault was lowered into the earth and everyone was leaving the cemetery. I thought he might disappear again, and I also knew I had better get back inside before it was discovered that I was gone. I took his hand and walked to the end of the block and pointed to my family's little church. I told him that Jesus would help him. At that moment, the church seemed to glow with heavenly light and Mr. Glover (I recognized him after he told me the names of his children) let go of my hand, crossed the street, and Jesus met him, took his hand, and they both disappeared into light.

Through the years, I had many more experiences such as this, each one unique to the person. I got to the place where their stories bothered me, realizing at a very young age that almost everyone seemed to die with unresolved feelings, regrets, and pain, so I learned quickly to just walk them to the end of the block and wait for Jesus to welcome them into the light.

I was getting pretty good at this and found I wasn't shocked by what I saw or heard, until one day I walked to the end of the block and the church was dark. There was no light and Jesus did not come.

Puzzled and a bit terrified, I wondered, 'What am I going to do now?'

With a quick plea for help, light came—and though I did not see Jesus, the souls still went into the light.

Although I was just a kid, I recognized that our church was having revival services where the central theme was getting saved because Hell was waiting, with most of the emphasis being on Hell, fire, damnation, the devil, etc. I realized that God's love was now God's wrath. The light went out. I did not know what to do, or how to help, or who to talk to, although I tried ... which is when I might have gotten teased, and viewed as 'special' or 'weird.' I eventually stopped going outside to meet the departed; it just wasn't worth it, so instead I asked God and the angels to take care of them.

Now, in my adult years, I fully understand and know that, because feelings never really die, helping others cross through the veil to find their way is an important and invaluable service to humanity."

~ Teresa D. Scott
  Overland Park, KS
  teresa@regenesiscore.com

One does not become enlightened
by imagining figures of Light,
but by making the darkness conscious.

~ CG Jung ~

14

HARRY POTTER VS THE BIBLE

Having the ability to see or communicate with the dead is not an easy burden for anyone, but it may be especially rough on kids who just want to be accepted as normal. When the hard and fast rules of this life take hold, we get the undeniable message that our heightened abilities may be frightening, unnatural, unacceptable, and even interpreted as 'evil' by others. Unfortunately, because of the status quo programing, we shut down or talk ourselves out of the things we can't rationally explain. The following account is shared by a mother who brought her son to me when his proclivity to 'see dead people' began to adversely affect him, dredging up her own childhood memories.

"Because I am now menopausal, a situation that proves God is a man, I can no longer recall the first time a spirit came to my son. But I do remember my own first time.

I was probably around five years old when I woke up in the middle of the night and made my way to the bathroom, which was just around the corner from the bedroom I shared with my younger brother. The reason I remember this normal occurrence is because it was the first time I had ever ventured there alone in the dark. Typically, I had always shouted for one of my parents to accompany me. When I started back to my bedroom, I made sure not to glance in the mirror, as Italian superstition had already taught me that you'd better not do such a thing at night, lest you see a ghost staring back at you.

As I proudly entered my room again, what should I find standing against the wall between the twin beds but a man wearing a long overcoat and a Fedora tipped low over his brow. I was so terrified that I started screaming and ran to my parent's bedroom. Well, I thought I was doing that. Problem was, I couldn't get the sound to come out of my mouth, and my legs were fixed in place. And of course, not having control over my voice and reflexes made me even more afraid. When free will finally came back to me, I let out the biggest blood-curdling scream that anyone on Earth has ever let out, which brought my father into my room in a flash, certain that someone had broken into our home. Yet a thorough search beneath the beds and inside the closet proved no one was there. On any other night, I would've been in trouble for waking him over nothing, but not that night. Looking back, I'm certain he let me off the hook because he also had the ability to peek into another world. I assume that he guessed at what had happened to me, so all he did was bring me into his bed to finish the night out from there.

After that experience, I became afraid to be alone, afraid go to sleep, afraid to close my eyes, afraid to wake up in the dark, and afraid to open my eyes if I did. On the occasions where I found myself awake in the middle of the night, forget about going to the bathroom alone. I was too afraid to even peer around the room. Scary things happened anyway. Lying on my bed face down, I noticed my bed wasn't a bed anymore. It was the desert floor, with dried up animal skulls and other bones sprinkled about it. I still don't know if I was in the scene, or if it was only what I was seeing from my vantage point from who-knows-where.

I don't recall seeing a spirit again, not until I was much older. However, seeing that one spirit—and then all those bones—brought on a world of anxieties and phobias, although that settled down a bit after I had children.

When my kids were five and nine years old, we purchased a three-story shirtwaist home in Kansas City, MO. Of its many redeeming features, the one that I loved best was that it had a big stone front porch and was built by a Swedish family almost a hundred years before. My family was only the second owner, and I can't tell you how deliriously excited I was to finally get the keys and go inside after we closed on it ... which is what the kids and I did one steamy August evening when my husband was out of town. Opening the front door, we walked over the smashed-flat green carpeting and straight into the dining room.

Somehow you just knew the dining room had been the heart of the home for the previous family, and there were tangible clues to confirm that premise. It was the only place in the entire house that was ostentatious in any way. It had a built-in window seat with drawers beneath, a box-beamed ceiling with small light fixtures gracing each corner, and a center light fixture that had another 4 lights dangling two feet down from chains. It was the center light fixture that caught our attention. The minute we entered the room the chains began swaying ever so gently, almost too gently to notice. Yet when all four chains started going in different directions, notice we did. My children and I got a little creeped out, even if I wasn't too surprised by the happening. Just the week before, after I picked up the photographs that I took during the closing walk-through, I noticed each photo contained an outline of a person somewhere in the scene. One even had a shape looking into the kitchen from a window outside the house. Talk about skin crawling...mine sure did when I saw that. But remarkably I wasn't afraid like when I was younger. In fact, I felt a little reassured by it. Felt protected, for some reason. And curious.

Shortly after moving in is when my son started seeing people gathered in our new living room that most everyone else didn't see. In the beginning, the incidents weren't that big a deal for him. Since I didn't want him to be afraid of spirits like when I was small, I just nonchalantly accepted his comments as if they were just one more boring thing a five-year-old boy told his mother on any given day. He would describe the folks sitting on our couch—people that were clearly the previous owners. My new neighbor had given me many old photographs of the family as a welcoming gift, and Andrew was describing them to a T. While I was absolutely dying to know more, I didn't ask him the first question about it. I just let him say as much as he wanted to say, and passed his comments off as if we were having a normal conversation. My daughter didn't exactly gloss over it.

It was my practice to move to the rocker in the dining room once I was through eating dinner so that I could carry on the conversation from a more comfortable seat. One time, when my son asked me why there was a lady eating the leftover food from the plate I'd left sitting on the table, my daughter freaked.

'Andrew! Please! Stop saying that! You're really creeping me out!'

But even with that, my son didn't think anything about it, not until we sent him to Catholic school for seventh grade. Because that's when he was told for the first time that spirits existed, but were the work of the devil. And that anyone who saw such things was odd at best. And my son, wanting to fit into his new environment, realized after hearing all this that his special faculty would be a problem for him. A big problem. It seems Andrew had been seeing a lot of spirits, yet had only told us of a few. I guess the approach I took with him had worked, at least until he got to middle school.

It was of no matter that my son was able to poke holes in his teachers' theory. Or I should say, theories. Turns out, not only were spirits evil, but so was Harry Potter. And to a kid of high intelligence, that didn't make sense. In his mind, the Bible had more fantastical stories to share than Harry Potter books ever could. And it was no matter, either, what I countered in response: that spirits bore no ill will. My words couldn't compete with what his teachers, nuns, and the priest were teaching him. Because what did I know? I was just his mother. My son desperately wanted to stop seeing spirits before he got called out at school.

The spirits wishes superseded my son's. They weren't going anywhere, which is why I took my boy to see Toby at the Prairie Labyrinth. I called to make an appointment with her, explaining a little about myself, about my son, and then about the horror he was being taught at his new school. Toby understood at once and, hearing her reassuring voice, I knew that I'd found the right person to help me with this. Someone who would back me up that hanging with spirits would have no undesirable consequences, and that seeing them didn't make my son wicked, but actually just the opposite.

Pulling into her driveway, we were met first by her dog Daisy, and Toby quickly followed. After a few minutes of chitchatting in her driveway, we were welcomed into her home, where we got straight down to business.

Toby began by telling my son that the spirits no doubt realized he could see them and were aware of his light, hoping they'd finally found someone who could help them to cross over to the other side.

'Why are they still here?' my son wanted to know.

Toby explained there were many reasons, and whatever their initial reasons were at the time of their death, most of them were now moot. They had just become comfortable or accustomed to their surroundings with an attachment to the house itself, feeling this is where they belonged. It was possible that, when one family member died and then stayed around, the next one that followed would recognize them and stay with them, creating a nesting effect, drawing in other spirits. They didn't know how to leave or reach where they were supposed to be going.

Her explanation rang true, and she said she would teach my son how to help them. She gave him an image of her Chakra Labyrinth and instructed him on how to trace it so the spirits could cross over to the other side. And more, she told him how she had even enlisted a friend who had recently crossed over and indicated that she was willing to help him with the task. After all this, Toby got up from the table and came back with a photograph of her friend to show us.

But just as she was starting to explain her relationship to the woman, Andrew interrupted her and said, 'Yeah, I've seen her before.'

And although I had become braver when it came to spirits, well, I wasn't so brave after hearing my son say that. The flip my stomach took rivaled any terror-induced carnival ride! His ability far exceeded anything that had ever happened to me as a kid.

I can't remember how long we stayed at Toby's, but I do recall her parting instructions. The next time my son came upon a spirit, he was supposed to enlist the services of Toby's friend, and together they would cross the person over to the other side. She also provided him an escape clause. If Andrew didn't want to bother with it, he could simply direct them to Toby's place, and she would cross them over herself.

My son slept in the car for most of the 45-minute ride home, but I could tell he felt better. The rest of the day passed uneventfully. I cooked dinner for my family and we enjoyed the meal at the dining room table, after which we moved to the porch and chatted into the night about everyday normal things. Later in the evening, as was our custom, my children and I piled on top of my bed, each of us engrossed in a book of our own choosing. And since my husband and I also believed in the concept of a Family Bedroom, when it was time to turn off the lights, the kids just got off my bed and went down to their pallets on the floor, one on each side of a parent.

At this time, I was a doula and not yet menopausal, which means I slept well on any night that I knew I wouldn't be phoned to assist at a labor. Such was the case this night. Nevertheless, I woke up at 1:30 a.m., and only because I felt squished. Like really squished. It was as if every square inch of space inside my bedroom—from the bottom of the floor to the top of the ceiling, from corner-to-corner—was filled with people. It was like a spirit convention was being held inside my bedroom.

Coming to consciousness, I thought to myself, 'What have I gotten us into?'

'Ange, you awake?' I whispered to my son, just in case he wasn't.

'Yes,' came his immediate reply.

'What the ... ????'

'I know,' he said, although seemingly unafraid.

'Well?'

'Well what, Mom?'

'Aren't you going to cross them over?'

'I did already. More keep coming!'

Now what? I thought to myself. But then I came upon a swimming idea, and began shipping them off to Toby myself. Let her deal with this frigging mess! Serves her right for getting us involved in whatever this was. Surprisingly, after I said in my head to whoever was loitering around my bedroom that they needed to beat it over to Toby's place, the room instantly felt less crowded and I was able to fall back to sleep. That was a complete miracle in itself as, believe me, that wouldn't have happened ten years ago. No, if something like this had happened back then, I wouldn't have been able to close my eyes again in this century.

The next morning, I went into nonchalant mode with my son again. I acted as if the night before was just a real normal thing that sometimes happens. Got both kids to school, and then raced back home and phoned Toby.

'Toby, what did you do to my family!'

'Gloria?'

'Of course, it's me! Listen Toby, I brought my son to you to help him get rid of spirits, yet my bedroom was stuffed full of them last night!'

'Yes, I know,' Toby laughed, 'they came to me after they left you! I crossed them over. All 160 of them.'

Since I felt so at home with this woman, I treated her like any other of my intimate relations.

'Christ, Toby, what the hell have you gotten us involved with?'

Unnerved, she answered, 'I think it's because Andrew is calmer and more confident now that more came to him for help last night.'

'Oh great, that's just what he wanted,' I laughed a little, not quite so spooked.

'Well, what now? I don't want to wake up to a roomful of people in the middle of the night ever again.'

'If you do, Gloria, just send them to me again. They'll leave just as fast as they did last night, knowing they have a way to go home.'

'Lord, Toby,' I said, almost with a whine in my voice. 'Whatever—I really wish we didn't extend this invitation to them, but I'll deal.'

'It'll be fine, Gloria,' Toby said, not finding the situation at all dark, but more amusing ... as I was slowly beginning to, as well.

There is a lot more to this story, and it's mostly good. My son found a way to cope with spirits. However, the longer he stayed in that Catholic School, the more he wanted to stop seeing the spirits, and eventually he did. My guess is that he simply wouldn't allow himself to take notice anymore. The sad part is that, as time wore on, he convinced himself that he'd made the whole thing up.

Not me! I was there, and I witnessed some of his experiences for myself. The possibility of him peeking into another world is backed up from what occurred in my own childhood, so it will always remain very real to me.

~ Gloria Squitiro

By knowing yourself,
you change the world for the better,
and live your Higher Self.

~ Michael Teal ~

15

THE HIGHER SELF MATRIX

In my own childhood, I can't say I am able to look into the other realms, but I am fascinated and comforted by the notion that we each have a guardian angel who works overtime on our behalf. As part of my metaphysical exploration as an adult, I attend an Angel Therapy training with *Doreen Virtue who is a spiritual doctor of psychology and a metaphysician working with the angelic, elemental, and Ascended Master realms.

During the training, Doreen makes an off-hand comment stating that we each have two guardian angels. This concept deviates from my Catholic upbringing and the more accepted view that we each have *one*. It's not like I am trying to solve the famous riddle of *how many angels fit on the head of a pin*, but her statement makes me wonder how or where the extra angel fits in.

Around this time, Phyllis, who served as my spiritual and emotional counselor, makes her transition after a long illness. I attend her memorial service convinced she is not likely to need assistance in crossing over. Yet, when I go into the labyrinth later, I sense that she is there. She makes herself available to me while assuring me that she is not earthbound.

I jump at the opportunity to ask my silly question: "Phyllis, can you tell me if there is anything to the notion that we each have two guardian angels with us?"

She chuckles, *"I guess you could say that. The 'Higher Self' can be viewed as the sum of all your parts, and that includes both poles (genders) that your* *soul has experienced in all physical incarnations. A male and female 'light being' could be seen as symbolic representatives of all that you have been as you return to the unified field of your innate wholeness. It isn't that your 'Higher Self' exists as two parts that are above you (higher) or are out of reach, but when you are consumed with lower thoughts and emotions, this Divine <u>Inner</u> Awareness seems separate from you because it maintains a consistently higher vibrational field with access to All That Is. The moment of death dissolves the restrictive barriers that you've grown to accept as part of your limited identity, bringing your full potential back into your awareness, but you still have the choice to cling to the small-self amnesia or embrace the fullness of who you have always been."*

The idea of a male and female light being serving as overarching 'representatives' from our Divine Inner Awareness might sound simplistic, but it could also be comforting, allowing the soul that is transitioning, to be enfolded in reassurance with the inner voyage that is occurring.

Angels are universal archetypes accepted in almost all cultures and spiritual traditions. However, it is the *Seraphim* which we most associate with the task of guiding us home, as their mission on Earth is to instruct humans in the process of transformation. Their rainbow bodies of light possess the power to phase back and forth between the celestial and the physical realms. Their task is to assist us humans in fulfilling our destiny of each of us becoming a celestial being or morphing into our intended Higher Self light body. They have not been involved with our Ascension until now, but they assist us in direct service to the Mother principle.

According to the prophet Isaiah's vision, the Seraphim are described as *"golden, flaming angels with six wings on fire with the love of the Creator."* This description has been investigated by William Henry, a well-respected Ascension researcher who has dedicated his life's work to studying ancient texts and artwork portraying *Ascension of the Soul.* In an on-line healing retreat entitled "Path of Souls," William proposes a direct relationship between the Seraphim's six wings and the sacred geometry shape know as a star tetrahedron—or the *Merkaba.* We can easily envision how the swirling vortex-shaped body of a Seraph with its six wings could be seen as a six-pointed star (or Ascension vehicle) to take the departing soul home. His research indicates that the Seraphim play a vital role in showing us the way back to the 'Throne of God.'

The connection between the six wings of the Seraphim and the Merkaba is easily recognizable in the symbol of the Seraphim Wings that *Saxon Knight uses in her work with the Seraphim Angels. Saxon gives us an inspiring perspective on why they are here for us:

"The Seraphim Angels have come to be a bridge to connect you to Divine Grace so you can access your inner strength. They create this bridge of light connecting Heaven and Earth and become the gateway to allow us to join ourselves to the world of reality, our true selves, and the world of limitation and barriers contained in our beliefs about who we are. The energy of Divine Grace is carried through the streams of light and sounds that surround each of us. These beautiful Angels bring to us the knowledge of how to create oneness with our spiritual selves and our physical selves. In their love and devotion to us they come from this place of brilliance so we can shine, know, and feel the presence of love within us."

Basking in Love's awareness would surely dissolve all the boundaries which have kept the soul in a state of separation. Enveloped by a Seraphim escort, you would merge with your own highest light, returning to the sum of all your parts. Another way of saying this is that the Seraphim escort would deliver you to the awareness of your own OverSoul.

The term *OverSoul* was first coined by Ralph Waldo Emerson, meaning "over-abiding presence." Unable to define what is universal, but not uniform, he characterized the OverSoul as something beyond description only knowable through our intuition. The famous 'near death' account of *Melon Thomas Benedict, who was clinically dead for over an hour in 1982 before returning to his body to resume his life, beautifully captures the essence of the OverSoul/ Higher Self matrix. A portion of his detailed experience is below. The full account can be read online.

Insights from the Other Side

"There was this light shining. I turned toward the light. The light was very similar to what many other people have described in their near-death experiences. It is so magnificent. It is tangible; you can feel it. It is alluring; you want to go to it like you would want to go to your ideal mother's or father's arms. As I began to move toward the light, I knew intuitively that if I went to the light, I would be dead.

So, as I was moving toward the light I said, 'Please wait a minute, just hold on a second here. I want to think about this; I would like to talk to you before I go.'

To my surprise, the entire experience halted at that point. You are indeed in control of your near-death experience. You are not on a roller coaster ride. So, my request was honored and I had some conversations with the light. The light kept changing into different figures, like Jesus, Buddha, Krishna, mandalas, archetypal images and signs.

I asked the light, 'What is going on here? Please light, clarify yourself for me. I really want to know the reality of the situation.'

I cannot really say the exact words, because it was sort of telepathy. The light responded. The information transferred to me was that your beliefs shape the kind of feedback you are getting. If you were a Buddhist or Catholic or Fundamentalist, you get a feedback loop of your own stuff. You have a chance to look at it and examine it, but most people do not.

As the light revealed itself to me, I became aware that what I was really seeing was the Higher Self matrix. The only thing I can tell you is that it turned into a matrix, a mandala of human souls, and what I saw was that what we call our Higher Self in each of us, is a matrix. It's also a conduit to the Source; each one of us comes directly, as a direct experience from the Source. We all have a Higher Self, or an OverSoul part of our being. It revealed itself to me in its truest energy form. The only way I can really describe it is that the being of the Higher Self is more like a conduit. It did not look like that, but it is a direct connection to the Source that each and every one of us has. We are directly connected to the Source.

So, the light was showing me the Higher Self matrix. And it became very clear to me that all the Higher Selves are connected as one being, all humans are connected as one being. We are actually the same being—different aspects of the same being. I was not committed to one particular religion. So that is what was being fed back to me. And I saw this mandala of human souls. It was the most beautiful thing I have ever seen. I just went into it, and it was just overwhelming. It was like all the love you've ever wanted, and it was the kind of love that cures, heals, regenerates.

As I asked the light to keep explaining, I understood what the Higher Self matrix is. We have a grid around the planet where all the Higher Selves are connected. This is like a great company, a next subtle level of energy around us, the spirit level, you might say. Then, after a couple of minutes, I asked for more clarification. I really wanted to know what the universe is about, and I was ready to go at that time.

I said, 'I am ready, take me.'

Then the light turned into the most beautiful thing that I have ever seen—a mandala of human souls on this planet.

Now I came to this with my negative view of what has happened on the planet. So, as I asked the light to keep clarifying for me. I saw in this magnificent mandala how beautiful we all are in our essence, our core. We are the most beautiful creations. The human soul, the human matrix that we all make together is absolutely fantastic, elegant, exotic, everything. I just cannot say enough about how it changed my opinion of human beings in that instant.

I said, 'Oh, God, I did not know how beautiful we are.'

At any level, high or low, in whatever shape you are in, you are the most beautiful creation. I was astonished to find that there was no evil in any soul.

I said, 'How can this be?' The answer was that no soul was inherently evil. The terrible things that happened to people might make them do evil *things, but their souls were not evil.*

    'What all people seek, what sustains them, is love,' the light told me, 'what distorts people is the lack of love.'"

The architecture of our luminous body
is in the shape of a torus—
a tunnel moving us beyond death.
"Little death" is going through the axis of the torus
to resource ourselves
returning to Source.

~ **Alberto Villodo** ~

16

CALLING ALL ANGELS

A friend living overseas calls me in early August to tell me that he and his wife are about to liquidate property and sell a home that has been part of his mother-in-law's estate. As they prepare to put it on the market, his wife is overcome with fear, feeling her mother's disapproval and actually sensing her presence in the bedroom.

I ask, "When did her mother die, and is this the first time you have been aware of her?" He quickly hands the phone to his wife.

"My mother died ten years ago and yes, I am aware of her. I sometimes see her at the foot of the steps and especially in this house. It was her favorite property and I don't think she is pleased that we are going to sell it. My mother was a shrewd business woman and not many people ever dared to stand up to her. We've hung onto this house far too long and need to sell it, but I feel paralyzed by her. If there is anything you can do, we would appreciate it."

Gaining more information, I find out that when her mother, Maxine, was alive, she had an unhealthy habit of going on a drinking binge once a month. She would lock herself in her room, draw the curtains and remain inaccessible to everyone for three or more days. After her death, her daughter had begun to re-enact the same ritual, which is debilitating for all concerned. I hang up the phone calling Maxine into my space—which is a bit like summoning the 'Queen.' It is obvious that she is used to getting her way.

Annoyed, she informs me, *"I am not sure who you are, but I like my arrangement and have no intention of going anywhere. They have some nerve thinking they are going to sell my property to a bunch of strangers!"*

Internally, I am nudged by my inner guidance to get my rattle and eagle feather, but I hesitate because no 'tools' are usually needed to move someone on. I gather them up, anyway, and walk outside as Maxine continues to give me an ear-full, informing me of the 'authority' that she holds. With my inner eyes I 'see' that Maxine is corded into her daughter's chakras. With the overlay of Maxine's energy, her daughter's crown chakra looks like a gray, tight-fitting skullcap in the form of an octopus. Dangling tentacles are intertwined throughout the rest of her daughter's energy centers.

An energetic 'cord' is an ongoing, energetic attachment that can diminish the flow of life energy and put a drain on the person's entire system. When a soul is corded to someone still living, they will be bound by the gravitational pull of the earth—keeping them earthbound.

Maxine reads my disbelief and defensively states, *"My daughter is empty. She is nothing without me!"*

I re-adjust my resolve to help, and think my response to her: "Power is obviously something of great importance to you. Wouldn't you like to feel REAL power? I would imagine that everything on Earth pales compared to merging with the authority of your Higher Self. I don't know if you realize what you are doing to your daughter by staying here and using her body to carry out your old addiction, but it's not good for either one of you. I'm going to walk this pattern while calling in your Higher Self in the form of two angels. When you see them, you will feel this power for yourself and decide if you really want to stay here or go with them."

As I step between the two trees that create the entrance way into Chante's paths, she blurts out, *"STOP! You don't understand. I can't go across."*

She doesn't have to explain why. I can read it clearly from her energy. She knows that she has led a life in 'service to self' and fears that, if such a place called 'Hell' exists, there is a possibility that she could be going there. At least by staying here in her old routine, she remains the one in charge.

I begin heading toward the pathway, telepathically conveying my response, "You're in luck, Maxine. I don't believe in that version of Hell."

Stepping into the sand, I begin winding through each of the vesica-shaped paths when suddenly the largest yellow-banded bumble bee I have ever seen begins to aggressively dive toward my head. Holding the feather between its buzzing body and my scalp, I keep it at bay. Each time I move it away, it comes flying back at me more aggressively from another angle. I am aware that a discarnate spirit can re-direct the energy in living things with focused attention.

Shaking my rattle I continue to walk, saying aloud, "I know what you're doing, Maxine, and it isn't going to work."

With that, the bee disappears. I sense the sharp intake of Maxine's breath, knowing that she is now in the presence of two angelic beings—male and female—and they stand together, enfolding her.

She begins to softly sob, *"They are beautiful! I only wanted my daughter to be an extension of me. I wanted to feel power again through her. I never believed I would go to a place called 'Heaven' so I stayed here and tried to make this what I longed for. I didn't know what that was until now. This is the love I have always looked for. My daughter was the closest thing I could find to this. That's why I wanted to be with her. I didn't mean to hurt her. I'm ready to go now."*

Standing in the center, she composes herself before stating, *"I won't forget this. In case you don't know—I have friends in high places."*

We laugh together and I feel a whirling sensation as she disappears from my inner sight with the portal closing behind her.

Almost a month later on Sept. 4, 2001, I am lying on a massage table in my studio space receiving a 'Whole-Self Attunement.' This is an energy treatment outlined by *Dr. Eric Pearl in his book *The Reconnection*. A fellow energy worker is tracing the 'axiatonal lines' along the acupuncture meridians above my body. About half-way through the process, my quiet, meditative state is interrupted when I feel I am being watched.

Turning my focus inward to the 'watcher' I telepathically inquire, "Is there something I can help you with?"

There is an immediate response, *"Yes. Take us wherever you took Maxine."*

Fine-tuning my focus, I count that there are five earthbound spirits before me who apparently know Maxine. My assessment is that they either knew her while living and joined her as soon as they were out of their bodies, or they were drawn to her as a vibrational match and stayed around her as loyal, earthbound 'cronies.' Whatever the case, they now seem lost without her lead. I assure them that when I am finished I will be happy to walk them through the process of crossing-over. Time is not a relevant concept on the astral plane as they are immediately disgruntled, pressing me to do it NOW.

Instead of getting up, I decide to see what will happen if I just do the process in my head. It is easy to imagine myself lifting up and going through the trees into the sand paths of Chante Ishta. Spinning through the vesicas with ease, I call in the paired angels for each of them who make up their Higher Selves. Following the pattern seems to help the souls release whatever energy is keeping them attached to this realm. It also seems to be raising their vibration, helping them to bypass the 'frequency fence' that keeps them tethered between the third and fourth plane. Once I have finished going through the vesica rotations, the five earthbound souls stand in the center region surrounded by their whirling vortices of light. From this vantage point with my eyes closed, I am better able to observe that each spinning form resembles a three dimensional 'Star of David.'

This geometric shape, known as a *star tetrahedron*, is the one referred to as the *Merkaba* in early Egyptian texts. In Jewish mysticism, the *Merkabah/Merkavah* is known as the *Ark of the Covenant* or *Throne Chariot of Ezekiel*. From the universal language of proto-Sumerian times, *Me* is translated as Eye; *Re/Ra* refers to the light of God that rotates within itself; *Ka* refers to the essence of the human spirit; and *Ba* is defined as our human, physical body. Joined together, the Merkaba is our Light Spirit Body or *The Eye of God that brings ascended life to the human spirit and soul body.*

The Merkaba is described as a vehicle for interdimensional travel in both the ancient text of the *Kabbalah* and the channeled information of the *The Keys of Enoch*. The ancient knowledge of working with our human light bodies has been taught for years as a meditative breathing practice by *Drunvalo

Melchizedek and is shared in *The Ancient Secret of the Flower of Life*. It is seen as the joining of the divine masculine and divine feminine, creating two counter-rotating fields of spinning light in the same space. Drunvalo sees the activated field around our bodies as a disk that looks like a flying saucer, extending out 55 feet. This is the exact diameter of Chante Ishta.

Drunvalo explains, *"The Merkaba is a counter-rotating field of light that affects spirit and body simultaneously. It is a vehicle that can take spirit and body (or one's interpretation of reality) from one world or dimension into another. In fact, the Merkaba is much more than this, because it can create reality as well as move through realities."*

With my focus on the five souls, I witness the paired images of their male and female angelic beings morphing into geometric light patterns, encompassing the souls from head to toe. The male angel is now in the form of an upward pyramid of light and the female takes on the form of the pyramid pointing down. United, they resemble the spinning vortex bodies of the Seraphim—the cosmic conduits of the Higher Self Matrix.

In wonder, I observe the beauty of this moment, watching five spinning stars lift off like rockets. Instead of the portal closing as I am accustomed to seeing, there still seems to be activity stirring. I strain to get a better sense of what is going on as I observe a 'lighted' figure floating toward me.

My first response is to question, "What is going on here? This portal is used to help souls leave. It is not intended to bring souls in."

The light figure stops before me. Behind him there is a great flurry of rapid motion like a sea of starlings in murmuration (turning and flying in unison). They rush through the tunnel, sending a shockwave to my senses. I'm left with the impression that I'm standing at the mouth of a cave, shielding myself from an onslaught of whirling, winged bats bursting through the narrow opening, being funneled into the broad daylight of this third dimensional reality. Stunned, I try to make sense of what is happening.

The prominent light figure that has remained stationary whispers into my mind, *"Whenever someone dies, there are always angels to receive them. Lots of help will be needed."*

He turns and walks back into the opening of the portal.

As it closes I faintly hear Maxine's voice behind him saying, *"I told you I*

knew people in high places."
    The incoming angels don't make any sense to me until a week later when the planes hit the towers on 9/11/2001.

Our human compassion binds us
—one to the other—
not in pity or patronizingly,
but as human beings who have learned
how to turn our common suffering
into hope for the future.

~ Nelson Mandela ~

17

THE GRID OF COMPASSION

On 9/11 en route to a NIA class (Neuromuscular Integrative Action or Non-Impact Aerobics), my eyes are fixed on a circular vapor trail made by a skywriter's aborted attempt to draw a large 'happy face' over the Kansas City skyline. I never would have known that this was the intent, except that I see a completed version in the distance. Without the eyes and smiling mouth, the huge elliptical circle looks like a wispy halo, airbrushed on the powder-blue horizon. The angelic reminder hangs in the air accompanying me on the forty-minute drive to my destination.

Not having the radio on, I am unaware that the first tower has already been struck. Arriving at the Movement Center, the class is bombarded with reports of what is happening. Feeling stunned and helpless, we decide the best thing we can do for the souls involved is to continue the class, intending that our 'dance' will be our whole-body prayer. Moving in a meditative state to the stirring music of *Tim Wheater's CD *Heartland*, I mentally watch a large golden dome beginning to form in the sky above the twin towers. It seems to be serving as an etheric ER, filled with angelic beings ministering to the needs of all the incoming souls from both the World Trade Center and the Pentagon.

Suspended above the New York skyline, it remains in my mind's eye two weeks following the tragedy. I know that many healers, energy workers, and psychopomps from all areas of the world (in human and etheric forms) are doing what they can to assist, but the situation seems unusual and, admittedly, above my scope of understanding. I don't know why the crossing-over process seems to be suspended in time. I question, *What is different about this tragedy when there have been countless disasters around the world, with significantly more lives lost?* Yet, to my awareness, it seems that this event is being viewed differently from even the spiritual realm, and I silently wrestle with the impression I am receiving that some kind of 'dispensation' has been granted. I don't have a clue what that means.

Two weeks later, I open the Prairie Labyrinth to our spiritual community, to those who feel compelled to walk for all who have been impacted by the trauma. I assume that, as a group, we will make ourselves available to assist the remaining souls that still seem to be finding their way to the golden dome, and extend our help to the tending spirit-guides on board.

As we reach the center of the labyrinth, my guidance surprises me, giving me the directive to shift our focus from the victims of 9/11 to our own families, friends, and loved ones who are no longer in body—but still remain here. It seems that the way we can best help is to focus on those individuals who come to our minds, calling in their Higher Selves to escort them to the suspended golden dome. My understanding is that, by focusing on our own lineage and the individuals to whom we are each emotionally connected, the greater whole is being served. We are creating a wave of compassion that is reaching souls across many timelines. It is the unifying wave that is ushering them toward the 'superdome' portal. Their willingness to comply is releasing age-old agendas, creating a force-field that is being used as 'thrust' to uplift the newly deceased.

Immediately my thoughts go to the revolving door of war, with all the battles which have been, and are being, fought all over this planet and beyond. I realize with startling clarity that those who die in such an impassioned and polarized way may have trouble crossing over. Our state of consciousness when we die is a determining factor of where we go in the afterlife. Those blasted out of their bodies in battle may be blind or oblivious to the light of their own expanded presence holding the portal of return open to them. The adrenaline of fear, hatred, despair, and guilt—or even loyalty and righteous justification—can magnetically draw them to those who share the same feelings. Often this means the ones fighting right beside them, but they could also be drawn to others back home to whom they are emotionally connected. If they were consumed by their 'warring cause,' an energetic web is likely to adhere to the living as a sticky, recycled version of the same emotional upheaval that was coursing through the soldier's veins at the time of their death.

It is unsettling to consider the planet's long history of war and how common this 'attachment' scenario might be. Dark consciousness has a stake in perpetuating the unresolved, low-frequency emotions—using them as a secure noose around the necks of many generations to come.

*Greg McHugh CCHt, author of *The New Regression Therapy* (NRT), addresses the treatment of wartime veterans and describes a case involving a US military veteran who had returned from two tours in Iraq as a medic. He was having trouble functioning, finding himself battling chronic depression, bouts of anger, and constant anxiety. In therapy, he started becoming aware that there were other spirits around him. They were able to identify children who had died in the war as well as American and enemy soldiers who died in field hospitals where he worked. By using Greg's spirit releasement protocols from NRT, the client was cleared of the attachments in one session. A week later, he was free of all the symptoms.

Greg noted that attachments which happen in a wartime setting seem to come in clusters. It's not hard to imagine that a tight company of men and women, fighting side by side, would loyally stick together in death, but his example also shows that if they died at the same time, they have a tendency to remain linked. Who they attach to might be determined by the person's compassion or openness (as in the medic's case), by their authority (a higher-ranking officer), or their vulnerability, susceptible because of their matching emotional wounds. More commonly than you would think, after a period of time, one of the soul fractures may attach to an aspect of themselves who is presently in another incarnation and sometimes the entire group follows. They are not always aware that, ultimately, what they are seeking is a way to find resolution and a way back to their true home of Light.

Sitting in the center of the labyrinth in my meditative state, I use my imagination to begin 'skywriting' huge labyrinth patterns over the war-torn countries, and over New York and the Pentagon to create portals of compassion where departing souls can be intercepted by spiritual helpers and the awareness of their own Higher Self matrix. The energetics of the Labyrinth symbol descend like a cyclone, dipping below the dense fog of the lower vibrations that have kept the souls blinded in a stagnant return-loop of grief, hopelessness, confusion and suffering. The intent is to 'beam the souls up' like on *Star Trek*, collecting all of their scattered fragments to be reassembled and returned to the 'transporter platform' within the personal 'soul-ships' of their Merkaba.

Over a decade later, the significance of 9/11 is reinforced as I read multiple articles that indicate this act was initiated to start World War III. We stepped out of that reality and began to create a different one.

*On *The Nibiruan Council* website, Jelaila Starr states that 9/11 changed the 'time lines,' causing a ripple in the time/space continuum that impacted all of us. This would certainly qualify as a 'dispensation' from breaking out of the old order. Relevant sections from her articles are included below.

The 9D Compassion Grid: The Gift of 9/11

"We find ourselves asking, 'Is there any value in what appears to be a senseless tragedy?' The answer is yes, and it's a gift much greater than any we could have imagined. It is called the 9D Compassion Grid, a 9th dimensional electromagnetic grid. This type of grid is the foundation of all dimensions and realities of the highest frequency in the universe that now overlays our 3rd dimensional grid / frequency fence and gives us a way out of our prison.

Compassion (I'm talking about the multidimensional kind, not the 3D kind) has the highest frequency in the universe. That means that there is no frequency higher or more powerful than the frequency of compassion. As we know, everything is composed of energy and vibrates at a certain frequency. Love is a higher frequency than fear. Joy is a higher frequency than sorrow. Fear distorts our perception of reality, causing greater soul fragmentation, keeping us more polarized and separate. In quantum physics, a higher frequency will always pull a lower one up to meet it. So, compassion will always pull anything, in this case everything below it, up to its level. In the case of electromagnetic grids, this means that a grid composed of compassion will pull any grid composed of a lower frequency up to its level."

The number '9' is the number of completion and the number of the dimension in which the universal game of 'Polarity Integration' begins and ends. It is the number of Compassion.

*Sanat Kumara is considered an Ascended Master from Venus, an 'advanced being' at the ninth level of initiation who is regarded as the "Regent of Earth." In the Old Testament, he is referred to as the "Ancient of Days". He explains through Jalaila:

"We have a Compassion Grid. But how do we use this grid to free ourselves from our prison and create a new world in which to live? We use the Inner Technology held within our bodies ... the technology of Compassion. Compassion enables us to find the value in all things regardless of how they appear and become true masters of our reality. We step out of victimhood and into total godhood by taking responsibility for all that we consciously or unconsciously create. We look at people and events and see the higher purpose at work. We feel gratitude and appreciation for all the souls playing their roles in physical form to help us gain a gift of understanding. This ability to feel compassion is what recodes our DNA. In fact, compassion has been scientifically proven to be the one emotion that transforms DNA, changing it from carbon based to crystalline based where it holds more light, making us Light.

How did the events of 9/11 create the Compassion Grid? It only takes 144,000 people making the same choice at the same moment and with the same intention to create a new electromagnetic grid. On September 11, 2001, millions of individuals around the globe simultaneously chose compassion when they saw those planes hit the World Trade Center towers. They felt compassion for both the victims as well as for the terrorists."

According to *Patricia Diane Cota Robles: "Whenever there are hundreds of thousands of people focused on a particular event, a *Cup of Consciousness* is formed. That Cup creates an open portal through which the Company of Heaven can exponentially expand the Light of God flowing to Earth."

Jalaila *(The Nibiruan Council)* continues this thought: *"The way out is within. Like any new grid, this one must be energized. To energize it we must achieve compassion in all areas of our lives, both personally and nationally and send that energy by intention into the grid. This means we must achieve compassion for all the people and things we believe are bad and evil. We must integrate the Light and Dark within each of us. We do this by moving to a new level of personal integrity in our lives. To accomplish this requires rigorous honesty in our relationships. It entails expressing our dark feelings and emotions and telling the truth about them. We can do this when we truly understand the value of the dark, of anger and of pain.*

Compassion is the highest frequency in creation and with it you can create new realities or change existing ones. If you can achieve compassion, you can create a magnetic field of compassion. If you can create a magnetic field of compassion, you can create a grid from that field of any size you desire. To create one big enough to encompass a planet all you need is enough people (the magical 144,000?) *fueling that grid to expand it exponentially to the size you need."*

Corroborating input about the significance of 9/11 came from *Gregg Braden who was a guest on *Shifra Hendrie's *Quantum Healing, Consciousness and Soul* online series on February 20, 2013. Talking about the HeartMath Institute's *Global Coherence Initiative with Howard Martin, Gregg brought up the tragedy of 9/11, stating that it taught us the power of mass heart-based emotions and how they could influence the magnetic fields of the Earth. This was demonstrated by the geosynchronous satellites that send back signals every thirty minutes, informing scientists of the strength of the magnetic fields which connect and sustain all life. He reminded us that everything is linked to these fields. The scientists are accustomed to seeing an ebb and flow in a 24-hour period, but on 9/11 they saw a huge spike where the magnetic fields of the Earth were strengthened. The spike corresponded to the window of time when the media was broadcasting the horror of the images. Around the world, huge numbers of people were simultaneously seeing the images and responding from their hearts. It was spontaneous. He reminded us that the viewers were not trained in *heart/brain coherence*, but heart-based emotions were being registered. It was that spontaneous, simultaneous activation of the magnetic fields of hundreds of thousands—or millions of human hearts that were being coupled with the magnetic fields of the Earth that created such an incredible effect.

He also commented that, in the days just after 9/11, the world felt very different, noticing that people were more humane, with their guard down and hearts open, acting more like a global family. Scientists attributed much of that behavior to a spontaneous coherence that was created in response to the tragedy. A strong correlation exists between heart-based outpourings when they are coupled with the effect of the magnetic fields.

HeartMath asked the question, "Can we create that effect without a tragedy?" And the answer was "YES." The Global Coherence Initiative (GCI) project is training people to intentionally create coherence without having to respond to an external stimulus. We are learning to create it because we choose to. They are setting up the scientific network to tell us about our relationship to the Earth, when things are working and when they aren't.

Gregg ended by saying, *"The best science is leading us to validate some of the most cherished of our spiritual traditions, telling us that the way we learn to be inside of our hearts and our bodies plays a powerful role in the experience that we will have as we go through future transitions. It is no accident that it is happening just that way."*

*The Global Coherence Initiative is one of many ways to work together to energetically birth the new world.

There is no other teacher but your own soul.

~ Swami Vivekananda ~

18

TEMPLATE OF THE SOUL

Early on in my counseling sessions with Phyllis, she indicates that past lives are not exactly in the 'past' by asking me, *"Are you willing to heal the other parts of yourself that will come forward now?"* I have no idea what she is talking about.

She goes on to add, *"The soul sends out splinters or aspects of itself to simultaneously learn and experience life. We mistakenly call these splinters past lifetimes. When one aspect is doing good work, the other parts that are not learning or progressing may send their stuff to that aspect to get some resolution."*

Phyllis is not the first metaphysician to point out that it is more accurate to consider that everything is happening simultaneously. Earth operates on linear time so we naturally arrange past life memories along a timeline, believing that our soul progresses by building one lifetime on the next. But if everything is happening in the NOW, linear reality is only a truth when you are in a body.

*Robert Monroe, founder of the Monroe Institute, was a New York radio broadcasting executive before he became known for his research into altered consciousness. Born in 1915, he was a man far ahead of his time. In 1958, he spontaneously embarked on his first out-of-body experience (OBE). For the next thirty-seven years he explored the boundaries beyond the physical world, mapping the routes open to us when we leave our physical bodies. Recorded over three decades, the information in his classic trilogy of books blazed a trail in human consciousness that gives us a map of the 'Interstate' (his metaphor of its entry and exit ramps). In his last book, *Ultimate Journey*, he takes us further than he had ever previously been.

Unlike Melon Thomas Benedict, who encountered the infinite facets of the Higher Self matrix in one experience, Monroe was gradually introduced, over an extended period of time, to parts or aspects of himself which he had not known existed. Eventually, he realized that the wiser beings he encountered, who seemed to him to be mentors willing to assist him—as well as the distressed beings he was called upon to aid—were all aspects of his own 'OverSoul', from both past and future lifetimes. He referred to his Higher Self matrix as the *"I-There of me."*

Through Monroe's research, we begin to grasp that we each have a growing committee of vital parts who are assigned to gather experiences and knowledge with the intent to contribute to the whole of who we are.

Once out of the body, the soul is no longer bound by time and can move backwards or forwards to assist us. Everything that was ever encountered is stored in the vault of the Soul matrix. The major energy base or blueprint for our Higher Self template is the Love we have accumulated over countless lifetimes.

One of the Higher Self explanations that first stood out and still sticks with me comes from a published collection of the teachings of *Francie Steiger called *Reflections from an Angel's Eye*. Recounted in the book *The Star People*, co-authored with her husband Brad Steiger, Francie shares a vision she received of the Higher Self with its many incarnations.

The encounter takes place in a setting far out in space where she is shown a moving diagram. She understands there is a realm beyond ours, occupied by Source/God/All That Is. From that realm, a golden cord extends down to the Higher Self, which is represented as a glowing sphere of light. Francie interprets the golden cord as an umbilical cord, which intimately connects us each to Source. From the Higher Self, extending out in every direction, are many silver cords (also acting like umbilical cords) that connect each lifeform that the Higher Self / Soul enters into. Attached to each of these lifeforms are crystalline spheres, symbolic of each lifetime on Earth. Inside the spheres, embryos form that mature and gather knowledge. The knowledge is depicted by lights that sparkle around the sphere. Those lights produce corresponding lights that are incorporated back into the hub of the model or back to the Higher Self matrix. As each lifeform grows in awareness, the brilliance and vibratory intensity of the Higher Self/OverSoul is also increased. At the time of physical death, the lifeforms that had been vibrating at the same awareness as the Higher Self automatically become incorporated into the OverSoul, but she also notices that there are other lifeforms that just grow dark and do not return.

It is her understanding that this same process continues with all souls connected to their Higher Selves until their vibration is raised to such a degree that they radiate like a 'god.' When this occurs, the Higher Self ascends to be incorporated into Source—more splendid than when they were created, enriching the Whole. Her conclusion in observing the lifeforms that choose to remain dark, unable to return to the OverSoul, is that there must be another plan designed by Source to allow those that remain separate to someday return, but it was not clear to her what that plan is.

Combining my own past life explorations as well as those I have facilitated for others with Robert Monroe's findings, Phyllis's words, and Francie's vision, I've come to use a modified soul template to explain past lives and what happens to the lifeforms that don't return to the OverSoul.

I see the Higher Self / OverSoul as the hub of a wheel or, more organically speaking, I have heard it referred to as the stamen of a Lotus flower. Each lifetime (happening in the 'now') appears as one of the radiating spokes on the wheel or a petal of the Lotus flower. When the lifetime is productive and the soul grows from the experience, regardless of the difficulty, the radial energy is drawn back to the central axis at the conclusion of the life. Put another way, the soul crosses over (merging with the *spirit* portion we refer to as the Higher Self). It joins the OverSoul, able to incorporate its understanding of the life experience which enriches and expands the entire Higher Self matrix. If, on the other hand, the soul—or a fragment of the soul—becomes confused, disoriented, stuck in the illusion of the drama that is occurring, or is filled with great longing, fear, or a particular desire to remain, then it is likely to stay earthbound. This may also be the case if the soul has chosen an evolutionary path directed toward 'service to self.' Either way, there is a 'disconnect' from the essence of its own brilliant center. It's as if the soul has forgotten or is unaware that its own 'spoke' on the wheel forms a direct 'lifeline' back to the hub. Upon death, the silver cord of that lifeline dissolves, allowing this portion of the soul to wander at will. There is no 'statute of limitations' on the length of time a soul may be earthbound or choose to drift, since 'time' does not exist outside the body. Nor is the 'meandering' restricted or confined, meaning it can roam wherever it likes. However, logic tells me due to the vibratory match, a soul fragment would likely be attracted to and attach to one of the other 'spokes' sharing the nucleus of its own Higher Self / OverSoul.

On repetitive out-of-body missions, Monroe discovered that parts of his Higher Self matrix—his "*I-There of me*" group, were engaging and training him to help retrieve 'lost' aspects of his own OverSoul. Whenever the need arose, he also jumped in to redirect others not from his OverSoul.

Many of the so called 'past life flashes' or experiences which come up for examination may have a deeper purpose. It's as if we all have 'cold cases' stored in the basement of our deep unconscious, waiting for something in our daily lives to trigger the need for an investigation requiring us to gather clues of our own unsolved soul mysteries. As 'soul detectives' (a term coined by Dr. Barbara Stone and used to describe her work), we are here to uncover blocks or reversals which keep us stuck in a *Groundhog Day* movie type of repetitive loop, and ultimately free ourselves. We do this by raising our vibrational perception to a level of Compassion.

In an article by the Arcturians transmitted through *Dr. Suzanne Lie, we are offered this insight: *"Past lives are introductions to perceiving yourself from beyond the barrier of time, further loosening your attachment to third dimensional thinking. The first 'past lives' you choose to ponder will likely be those with unfinished business that you brought into this incarnation to finish. Hence, even your human history is beyond time, as it is stored in your unconscious mind. Once you release time to heal and complete unfinished lives, you gain the courage and wisdom to remember the past lives in which you completed your chosen mission and gained great insight and enlightenment.*

The acknowledgement of these lives activates the memory of your Multidimensional SELF. Very often your unconscious mind is the archive for old memories that you could not resolve when they occurred in that timeline. However, with the wisdom, power, and love of your Multidimensional SELF you have the ability to bring that experience into its conclusion."

This means that part of our soul's work while being in these bodies, is to first gather all incarnated versions of our human lives on Earth, with the intent to unify the conscious, unconscious, and super-conscious states of our Multidimensional Self. This does not require examining every past life, but instead is something which happens naturally when we raise our vibration.

While on my own spiritual path over a period of seven years, I became aware of three separate Native American lifetimes in which I was unable to cope with whatever disaster was occurring at the time of my death. After I had been internally working to accept and resolve the feelings involved, I found myself one morning standing at the East rock of my Medicine Wheel. Suddenly, I was aware of those three aspects of myself stepping into the Medicine Wheel to join me. One lined up in the South, one in the West and one in the North position. As I raised my hands from Earth to Sky, they each re-enacted the moment of their death scene in a synchronized fashion. This time, however, there was no energy of despair, hopelessness, or judgment. They snapped out of their separate stories where they had seemed locked in their isolated positions around the wheel and merged together, lifting into the ethers. Like a stirring breeze, I instantly felt lighter. I did not understand until later that, as a unit, they had just crossed over.

A powerful example of how it is possible to experience multi-dimensional levels was shared by beings from another world in *Sherry Wilde's groundbreaking story, *The Forgotten Promise: Rejoining Our Cosmic Family.* The beings gave her an image of a stack of thin, onion-skin papers that reached a height of 10-12 inches, and told her each paper represented a lifetime. They then took a pencil and stabbed it through the center of the stack. The pencil represents the core essence of each soul, or our all-pervasive connection to Source. Piercing the layers illustrates our ability to be present on many different levels in different dimensions and timelines, each existing in the now. The beings helped Sherry understand how each life being lived can potentially influence all the others. If something occurs that resonates on a deep soul level, it simultaneously registers in all the other dimensions, including parallel universes. Sherry tells us that we are moving toward the time when the timelines will be easily accessed. I believe many have already arrived at this fourth dimensional perception point where we are able to see our mis-creations and apply forgiveness, understanding, and compassion, as we prepare for existence in the fifth dimensional state of Unity consciousness. In a profound statement, Sherry eloquently summarizes the importance of doing our inner work from a higher perspective:

"It is our job at this juncture in humanity's development to bring all the aspects of our selves—all of those multi-dimensional selves—into alignment. It is time to awaken and time to bring all those many slivers of light together into a mighty beam of light and love. If you picture your core essence as a pillar of light, you would be close to the truth. But now, come in close to that ray of light and see parts of it where there is a disconnect, and other places where there are little chunks of matter blocking the light and keeping it from flowing freely. Those are the places where you are harboring grievances and carrying around pain from the mistaken belief that another has wronged you. When you realize how impossible that is, since there is nobody else out there (remember there is only one of us), see what that does to your feelings about being a victim. All that we believe has been done to us, we really did to ourselves. It cannot be otherwise. Now is the time to come into this awareness. Now is the time to open up that channel of light and let go of the blocks. It is time to let our light flow freely between the dimensions of our being and upward through the higher vibrations and home to Oneness ... home to God."

When we chose to bi-locate into a human vessel,
it was often because a version of our
Multidimensional SELF
was stuck in the paradigm of the third/fourth dimension.
Therefore, we took an earth vessel to assist that self.

~ Suzanne Lie ~

19

YOUR SOUL'S BEST ADVOCATE

Moving to the prairie land near Kansas City is the catalyst to awaken one of my own past life personalities, one of the three I mentioned earlier and recounted in detail in my book, *Keeper of the Circles: Answering the Call to Wholeness*. I am unknowingly, called back to the very land where I lived and died in another era. As an Indian girl, I lost my family in a massacre by Union soldiers and, in desperation and futility, took my own life. I am now challenged with resolving those feelings, which aspects of my soul still harbor. I have no doubt that this connection has drawn me to shamanism, leading me to study Native American and Incan Medicine Wheel teachings. This, in turn, introduces me to the concept of *soul retrievals*, in which I learn denser soul pieces can splinter off or become stuck in a past trauma. This rings true for me, so I undergo a soul retrieval with a local shaman. As impressive as this is, I return home afterwards—still in an altered state—to hear telepathic instructions coming from a future aspect of myself who had come forward toward the end of my session. She appears in my mind's eye as a very old grandmother. I think of her as "Owl Woman."

She tells me, *"Your work is to be doing a type of soul-retrieval with others, but it is not to be done in the traditional sense where you journey for the client who lies there passively while the shaman tracks down their lost soul pieces, gathers them up, and 'blows' them back into their energy field."*

When I question why this is not the path I am to follow, she continues,

"Individuals who have gone through traumatic experiences already feel powerless. Your role is that of a trail guide who is to there to empower them to retrieve their own pieces. Making the mental and emotional journey will help them step out of their victim role onto higher ground. The 'seeds' of healing are scattered everywhere and need to be gathered before they can be planted in their lives. The gathering is greatly assisted when they can actually see the scattered seeds from a bird's eye view."

Common sense tells me that the way to do this is through hypnotherapy. Over the next couple of years, I become certified with *Dr. Brian Weiss as a Past Life Regressionist, *Dolores Cannon as a Quantum Healing Hypnosis Technique (QHHT) Practitioner, and with *The Newton Institute as a Life Between Lives (LBL) Spiritual Integrationist. Why would anyone want to willingly examine a past life? Because going back (from a higher perspective) is one of the best ways to objectively view and clear the blocks you are presently dealing with. A spiritual regression allows one to set an intention to engage their super-consciousness mind to evaluate a past life. This higher frequency state enables us to understand, accept, and clear disruptions which occurred in a lower or denser vibration. Viewing the past from your multidimensional self helps you reframe your attitude toward your present challenges, bringing new appreciation, clarity, and resolve to align with your soul's current purpose.

For similar reasons, I also take the trainings to become an Akashic Record Consultant and shortly afterwards am introduced to Emotional Freedom Technique (EFT). I am a firm believer in EFT founder *Gary Craig's *Discovery Statement* which says, *"The cause of all negative emotion is a disruption in the body's energy system."* What this means is that our distressed memory of a past traumatic event is NOT the cause of the emotional upset. The real cause is an electrical disruption in the body's energy field (that occurs in response to the event) creating an imbalance in the whole system.

Ironically, I discover that it doesn't matter if the disruption happened yesterday or 5,000 years ago. Brain pathways holding the holographic event will register and start to run the imbalance if set off by similar triggers mimicing the original disruption. If a disruption is great enough, part of one's soul can fragment or detach (such as leaving the body) as a way to survive the incident.

Disruptions as energy imbalances can show up as anxiety, sickness, pain, panic attacks, phobias, depression, PTDS, or any number of physical, mental, or emotional problems.

I begin doing *Soul Integrations* to address my clients' current life problems, guiding them back to the original point of their disruptions. Before being aware of and applying EFT, I find one of the most effective ways to help a client is to enlist his or her current-age self to assist the part of his or her soul which went through an event at an earlier time. An example would be someone who went through sexual abuse at a young age. Instead of taking the client back to a painful and emotionally charged memory, I regress them to a point just prior to the incident. The client enters the situation, as the advocate they lacked as a child, tells the child what he or she most needs to hear, and does what the child most needs to happen. This can include holding the child, taking him or her to safety, assuring him or her that this is not their fault, etc. We can bring in a spirit guide or angel to help change the flow of disturbed energy, freeing it by re-framing or re-directing how it's being held. This is possible because the client has entered the scene at a higher vibration or energy frequency, and can hopefully see other factors which did not register when the event occurred. This could include the abuser's own history, the child's inherent resilience, qualities which developed as part of coping skills, and the possibility of a soul contract—which the client may have agreed to before coming into this life, in order to leap-frog his or her souls' learning and growth. This seems to fit in with Owl Woman's directive *"to empower their retrieval process."*

In helping others to track down their disruptions, in many cases I begin to find that the point of origination lies in another lifetime. Similar disruptions are set off in this life by circumstances their soul has agreed to as a way to ensure that they will finally deal with it. This is illustrated in one of *Echo Bodine's books, *What Happens When We Die?* in which she describes seeing the energy of a newborn baby who is holding onto nine suitcases, representing all the unfinished baggage (karma) he is coming in with to resolve.

Most clients are not consciously aware when booking a session that their intent is to help heal and complete unfinished business from another time, or help an aspect of their own soul find peace. Those who feel compelled to investigate past lives are usually motivated by more than curiosity or ego fulfillment. I notice that a parallel occurrence in a client's current life often becomes the catalyst which triggers past life disruption, and they are guided (most likely from their multidimensional self) to get to the bottom of it.

Over the years, as the past life sessions evolve, I notice an emerging pattern common to many. At the core of the energy disruption there often lies an aspect of the client from another lifetime who, in direct response to a past disruption, never crossed over. They are earthbound because the original energy disruption tied up their circuits. Now, that disruption is 'bleeding through', into the unsuspecting client's current life. Seemingly 'out of nowhere', a client begins struggling with a problem he or she can't manage to control. It is then that Phyllis's words make far more sense to me.

"Are you willing to heal the other parts of yourself that will come forward now? When one aspect is doing good work, the other parts that are not learning or progressing may send their stuff to that aspect to get some resolution."

While it may strike you as being intrusive, or interfering with your free will or happiness, to have a former (unsettled) aspect attach to you, it is actually a perfect plan that you agreed to on the soul level. You knew before coming into this body that this was a 'reconnaissance mission' designed to seek out and find your 'lost troops.' Your soul knew the truth of Albert Einstein's statement that *"No problem can be solved from the same level of consciousness that created it."* You agreed to come to this planet when the veils were lifting, and contribute to raising the vibration on the Earth by raising the frequency within your own soul matrix. You do this by bringing the fragmented aspects home. You enlisted as a compassionate, invested trail guide who will pull out all the stops to get resolution. You wholeheartedly took on their situation because, after all, it feels like it's yours ... because it IS yours. You ARE them. Your soul is the 'pencil piercing all the papers,' affecting both the layer you reside on and the layer where the original disturbance occurred. No one else is better equipped to help your past life aspects address the reversals and dissolve the disruptions. You are your soul's best advocate because there is no time (as timelines go) better suited for the multidimensional 'hookup' to occur.

Coming into the fifth dimension as Earth graduates to fourth density means we are converging at a cosmic round-about with access to the intersection of all timelines. The current you are riding (by being in body at this time) is flowing from a higher vibration than the earthbound part of you restlessly waiting to be lifted by your wave. By sanctioning your energy to become a 'soul-bridge,' you are helping displaced parts of yourself cross over into your *'I-There of me'* group, impacting and elevating all of us.

We are each of us angels with only one wing,
and we can only fly by embracing one another.

~ **Luciano de Crescenzo** ~

20

WORKING AS AN ANGELIC TEAM

The following story demonstrates how an unresolved aspect from someone's past life can suddenly intersect with and influence their present-day experiences. Nikkea first contacted me looking for answers to an unexplained condition. She had no idea her solitary problem would require conscious teamwork.

"I have been on a plane many times with no adverse reaction, but when I was pregnant with my twins, this all changed. Flying through a large thunderstorm, I had an anxiety attack and remembered thinking we were going to crash. Shocked by my reaction, I went to a therapist for help. My therapy led to uncovering a fear of flying or, as my counselor stated, it was more like a phobia. It started to affect my daily living, as the fear was constantly with me.

Using 'Guided Imagery,' my therapist led me through a situation imagining myself on a plane that was crashing, asking me what I was feeling as it went into a nose dive.

I was surprised by my response, 'I am not afraid to die or to feel the pain of crashing. The fear is in going down, descending, with the feeling of being out of control, helpless, hopeless, and not knowing what to do.'

The phobia reflected a definite parallel to what I was feeling in my life. Out of the three names given to me from my counselor, I chose Toby Evans to help me understand this better.

Upon calling Toby, I simply told her, 'I have a very new and big fear of flying.'

The minute she starts reading my Akashic Records, I begin to shake, feeling sick to my stomach and my palms become very sweaty. I do not realize that my body is responding to the memories, resonating deeply with the information that is coming.

She starts recounting a Past Life when my name was Nicholas (similar to Nikkea/Nichole). I was an overly confident, overly responsible Colonel in the Russian Air Force who prided himself on being in control at all times. I took two young men under my wing to train them, feeling intensely protective, as though they were my own sons. Because I was so ultra-responsible, I felt I could do anything, or fix anything, if I knew what to do. I did not listen to a fellow Colonel when he tried to tell me that the conditions were not stable enough to fly, and went up into the plane anyway with the two trainees on board. While flying through the storm, the plane went into a nose dive, leaving me with no sense of direction, no sense of control, and no orientation to guide me.

Toby tells me that the souls of these young men are back with me in my current life. She doesn't know I have children, let alone twins. I realize that these young men came back to me as my twins, this time as a boy and a girl.

Upon crashing, I was disoriented, unable to grasp that I was dead. This was compounded by the fact that the body was unrecognizable from the crash. I kept trying to pull everyone together, but the boys disappeared into the fog. The part of me that was Nicholas stayed behind, trying to figure it all out. Once the boys had transitioned, Toby mentioned that one of them (Jonathan in my current lifetime) wanted a 'spiritual' search party to go out after me and bring me through to the Spirit World.

When she tells me this, my mind flashes to when I had to leave Jonathan at the hospital for two months when he was a premature infant. This felt like I was abandoning him.

My cells were crying, 'You failed. You cannot leave him. What if he dies?'

In that moment, I knew just how Jonathan felt, trying to get a search party together to come and retrieve my stuck spirit. As Nicholas, I was completely out of control, helpless, and confused, not knowing where the boys went. As Nicholas, I was wandering as an earthbound spirit in a limbo setting for what felt like an eternity.

Nicholas was frustrated, trying to get my attention. Who knows how many lifetimes he had been trying to bring everything into wholeness? I experienced that frustration and helplessness when Jonathan began having seizures and none of the doctors knew what was going on with him. I pushed and pushed, feeling it was my sole responsibility to manage the situation, which activated my cellular memory as well as Jonathan's even further.

I remember thinking, 'I am responsible. I am not going to lose him! Why aren't these doctors listening to me? Can't they hear what I am saying?' I was trying to get things under control, just as I did when the plane was crashing.

As an Earthbound Spirit, Nicholas didn't know how to let go and cross over. In this current life, I hold the feelings of spinning out of control—confusion, anger, resentment, hopelessness, and helplessness—just as I had at the time of death. These are also the feelings that started to overtake me when getting on an airplane. I realize now that I drew these experiences into my life in order to find the connection so I could release the patterns and move on.

Toby helps me realize that I couldn't deal with the emotions I carried from the past life until I had the pieces to consciously integrate them. Because Nicholas was still earthbound, no amount of therapy, meditation, guided imagery, or breathing techniques were going to release this massive block, until I could help Nicholas cross over.

My soul was pushing me in this lifetime to consciously bring the pieces together. Jonathan's seizures were part of that pushing. Every time his little body shook, it activated my out-of-control feelings, but his seizures were ultimately a gift. And he was an angel supporting me in the highest way.

Toby walked me through a transforming Soul Retrieval, to help me gather the fragmented parts of Nicholas. There was both the male polarity / old patriarchal part that was traumatized and an old feminine aspect that was left reacting hysterically during the crash. I reunited them together in a sacred process, feeling it affect my entire being. The feminine part of Nicholas had been overridden by the macho male energy he carried. In this lifetime, I *gave birth to an extension of both my new inner male and female, with the intent to give all parts a voice to be heard.*

During the Soul Retrieval, I looked into the eyes of my pilot self, feeling the unconditional love he has for me. He was relieved to know the boys were safe now, living as Jonathan and Ella in my current lifetime. Toby guided me to call in his Higher Self matrix, his male/female polarity in the form of two angels. They came in a counterclockwise spiral above his head, moving down to enfold him in their angelic arms. I could feel this in my body, like I was coming Home to myself in a whole new way. I envisioned the male portion shifting over him as an upward facing pyramid of light while the female polarity interlocked around him as an upside-down pyramid. As one form, they started to lightly spin around and around, weaving light patterns within my physical body, lighting up the denseness and darkness. There was such gratitude streaming between Nicholas and me. The old anxiety, hopelessness, terror, and paralyzing fear that had been running through my system was spinning out of his soul as his matrix spun around him. I pictured myself walking into the center of the labyrinth where Nicholas was waiting for me. Through Toby's guidance, I allowed the Higher Self matrix to spin around me, and at the same time hugged him, feeling all the weight that he had been carrying being lifted off. As it lifted off of him, it lifted off me. We were working as an angelic team, supporting each other in the greatest way possible. Tears streamed down my face and the love in my heart exploded. I felt more confident, safe, and free to move in a very new way. This was the most powerful process of integration I had ever encountered.

After our session, I soaked in Epsom salts in the bathtub, trying to take in all that occurred. I felt like someone was shaking my shoulders every few minutes because of the trembling. My body was 'unwinding' and it felt like new neural pathways were opening up to flow the energy. I could finally breathe. The night after our session, I awoke suddenly, sensing someone standing over me.

Opening my eyes, I saw a male standing next to me, and heard a telepathic message echoing the words, 'Thank you.'

Recognizing him as Nicholas, I softly cried tears of joy, knowing that together we had reached a new level. A few weeks later I was able to get on a plane and fly to Mexico with my husband for our five-year anniversary."

~ Nikkea Walkker
  Mainville, OH

I will love the light for it shows me the way,
yet I will endure the darkness for it shows me the stars.

~ Og Mandino ~

21

GETTING UNSTUCK

Agreeing to be a soul-bridge to retrieve lost aspects of your *'I-There of Me'* group is a decision (soul contract) you make on a spiritual level before incarnating. Like all the other vital information you knew before arriving, as soon as you enter your body it is promptly forgotten. Earth is a carefully orchestrated 'blind-spot' where amnesia actually serves your soul's evolution. The 'contracts' you bring in with you are tattooed on your soul as indelible imprints that you might take notice of early on. They will remain with you, waiting to come to the forefront of your attention when you are 'activated' to take action and able to accept their encrypted significance.

A primary activation for me that served as a trigger was relocating to the same land where I had once lived in a past life. For Nikkea, being pregnant coupled with flying kicked her nervous system into 'active duty.' An unconscious part of her knew that she was bringing in 'reinforcements' that were meant to initiate the 'soul-rescue', sequence. When the activation or triggering occurs, it may feel unsettling and downright scary as some part of us knows that this is BIG, yet we have no clarification or logical box to put it in while we grapple with the feelings that begin to emerge.

For each of you, there will always be something serving as a catalyst to internally push you to complete your mission. You may find yourself inexplicably drawn (guided) to find people, information, or resources which your soul skillfully prearranges as clues to be placed in your path to assist you.

This is how it should be. We design the 'game' as an interconnected web where all paths eventually lead us back to our larger Self.

An initial hook serving as a common trigger for many often comes from reading a particular book. This was the case for Erik when he was compelled to do a *Life Between Lives* (LBL) spiritual regression after being ignited by the information in *Michael Newton's best seller, *Destiny of Souls*. Erik was hoping to find some of his missing pieces by looking into another lifetime, but he was also conflicted. As a lifelong practicing Christian, the issue of reincarnation challenged his beliefs. Conducting his own investigation, Erik found that the Emperor Constantine, at the Council of Nicaea in AD 325, ordered select passages of the Bible (including the ones referring to reincarnation). Resolving this in his own mind, he decided to contact me and set up a session.

A good candidate for an LBL is someone who has been hypnotized before and preferably has done a past life regression, or someone who has done guided visualizations successfully and is able to meditate or relax easily. Erik does not qualify in any of these areas, yet something prompts me to agree to see him.

At 73-years-old, Erik wants to make peace with his life and perhaps receive direction with regard to what he should do next. Sharing some of his personal history which he feels might be relevant to the session, he tells me of an incident that occurred when he was eight years old that still plagues him.

Erik was alone on a public bus, coming home as a latch-key kid, and it was already dark outside. Suddenly the darkness seemed to close in on him, making him feel like he was losing his mind.

With adrenaline shooting through his body, he stood up on the bus and pleaded, "Somebody, help me!"

Concerned that he was sick, they stopped the bus and let him stand outside, trying to calm the anxiety pouring through his veins. He was overwhelmed with the thought that he was going crazy. Eventually the panic subsided enough to get back on the bus and make it home. While relaying this to me, he was visibly shaken. He had never told anyone before what had happened to him because he was embarrassed, and he did not understand it himself.

Also during the intake interview he makes a point to share that his first love was a girl he described as *"way out of my league."* Asking what this means to him, he points out that, in contrast to his being dirt poor and primarily on his own, she came from a wealthy family who belonged to the country club and had the best that money could buy. After several years of dating her while they attended different colleges, he went to New York to meet her. Finding her surrounded by her Ivy-league friends, he painfully realized that their worlds were too far apart and decided it was best to stop seeing her.

Before we start the session, I explain to Erik that if he encounters anything emotionally difficult, that I may elect to use the Emotional Freedom Technique (EFT) with him. This is a simple process of using my fingers to tap near the end points of specific meridians. In a regular EFT session, the client would be doing the tapping themselves using all the points but, to be less intrusive during a regression, I would be taking one of his hands and tapping on specific wrist, hand, and finger points.

Since the cause of psychological reversals involves negative thinking, correction must start with acknowledging the problem or bluntly stating the persistent negative thought. Many people new to tapping, who are big on affirmations or trying to stay focused on the positive, resist this part. But telling yourself you shouldn't feel this way and to focus only on 'happy' thoughts is often the equivalent of putting whipped cream over poop (as *Debbie Ford so accurately described it). It is important to meet yourself where you are, before you can mine the 'gold' that lies within the shadow. Starting with what you are really feeling, you gradually diffuse or neutralize the negative emotions, while anchoring the person into the possibility of a positive outcome. This unblocks the restricted flow. I explain the points to Erik and ask him if he will give me permission to use tapping if it is needed. He agrees.

Starting into the portion of the regression where he is instructed to go to the most recent past life, Erik comes through the tunnel and tells me that it is night time and all he can see are the stars in the sky. He cannot see his body or give me any description of it. Hearing his frustration, I ask him to move ahead to another significant moment in that life. He begins to describe the sky from the same vantage point, but now it is daytime and the blue sky straight above him is filled with billowy clouds. Once again, there is no 'body' to describe and he is all alone.

He tells me, *"I am in a meadow, but there is nothing here but grass. I feel stuck, like I can't move from here."*

Asking him to rise above the ground and do a 360-degree rotation, he sees a bridge that jars a memory of one he has visited in France. Beyond it is a stone castle-like structure. I encourage him to find a way to go inside the castle and describe to me what he sees, reminding him that he doesn't have to be confined by the usual restrictions if he doesn't have a body. Immediately he passes through the wall, but then relays that he is filled with dread. He knows this place because he works here.

"What kind of work are you doing?" I prod, hoping I can finally anchor him into a body to understand who he is.

"I take care of the horses. I like the horses. I give them water and hay and help my father."

"How old are you as you work beside your father?"

"I am eight years old."

"Is there a name I can call you?"

"Anton."

Slowly his story unfolds: Anton lives in a small cottage on the land with his mother and father who work for the people in the castle. The land baron has a daughter close to his age. By the time he is sixteen, he has grown fond of her and they begin arranging time to be together, secretly meeting in the meadow. His father admonishes him, *"She is beyond your station in life, and no good will come of this."*

But Anton can't bear to be without her and they consider themselves in love. When I ask Anton to move to the next significant scene, he begins to describe the meadow and the sky again, telling me he believes he was buried in the meadow because it was so far away from the house. It is obvious that he does not want to go back to see how he died, fearing what will be revealed.

I assure him that he can view this from outside of his body. He does not need to be in it to understand what happened.

"Her father found us in the field. He's really angry. He puts me in chains and locks me in a cell in the dungeon of the castle. I am beaten repeatedly— not by him, but by one of the servants. The same servant comes over and over

again. I don't know how long I am there. I don't know when I died. I am just here in the meadow and my mother and father are gone. They had to leave."

I tell Anton, "You no longer have to stay here. You can cross over to the other side."

"I can't go. I have so much shame for what I did, and for the pain I caused my parents. My father was right. No good did come of this! I'd like to go, but I can't seem to move. It isn't so bad here. The meadow is peaceful."

Because Anton never crossed over, he attached to Erik, seeking his help. It's even possible that Anton's anguish was behind Erik's internal desire to do a regression. I ask Erik if he would like some help clearing feelings keeping him stuck, and he agrees to repeat statements I make as I tap on energy meridian points specifically designed to alleviate trauma.

He repeats each sentence after me as I tap.

"Even though I don't deserve to cross over, I deeply and completely love and accept myself.

Even though I have so much shame and guilt, I choose to love and accept myself.

I can still love and accept myself even if it is my fault that my parents lost their home and their livelihood.

My father told me no good would come of this and he was right.

I deserve to be punished. I deserve to be alone. I am afraid I don't belong anywhere and I have to stay here.

But what if I could be forgiven?

What if I could forgive myself?

What if I could start over again and not carry this pain anymore?

Even though I let my family down, I am safe now and I no longer have to suffer.

What if no one is judging me but myself?

I would like to believe that this is true.

I don't have to punish myself anymore. There are others here to help me and I want to accept their help.

I can calm down and accept that what happened in the past is now over.

I may have suffered enough and paid for what I have done.

This experience is over and I no longer need to stay here.
I can move into my light body now."

When Erik's breathing slows down and I begin to feel his body relax, I tell Anton, "I am placing a labyrinth in the meadow. The path will lead you into the center where a portal will open."

I finger-trace the path of the labyrinth in the air above Erik's body while describing the turns before telling Anton, "We are going to invite two angels in who represent your Higher Self. They will help you leave."

He quickly tells me, *"They are here. They are each holding onto my arms."*

The angels begin spinning spirals of light around him, helping him to dissolve the 'control grid' that's been reinforced by his constant companions of 'shame' and 'guilt.'

Erik offers, *"The weight that has been pressing down on my chest is letting up. I am starting to feel lighter and the black blob of fear that has been sitting in the back of my head is starting to dissolve. I can see it going down a drain."*

I watch he angels take the form of the star tetrahedron and surround him as they begin moving upward. His focus changes. He is able to relay to me that he is floating through a haze where he becomes aware of his deceased mother and father from his current life. He is happy to see them, but he also feels great sadness. He identifies the sadness as realizing that he can't go with them. His is still unable to fully forgive himself for what he perceives as a heinous wrong-doing.

The Higher Self team steers him into a waterfall of light identified as a healing chamber designed to cleanse and reset his agonized soul. Erik's guides tell him that, before going any further, he is here to reflect on all the pieces he has gathered.

Erik then sees that the incident on the bus when he was eight years old was a flashback from that lifetime as Anton, triggered by the darkness and feeling all alone. In the blackness of his prison cell, he felt he was going crazy with the physical, emotional, and mental pain closing in around him. Anton chose to escape, leaving his body before he finally died, but doing so was disorienting, causing confusion around the fact that he was dead. Erik then makes the connection that the high school sweetheart that was 'out of his league' was the same girl Anton loved in that life, but this time he had contact with her family and they accepted him. This time it was his decision to not pursue her. This realization helps him shift how he is holding the past, hopeful that, if they have already forgiven him, then it might be okay if he does the same.

When he tells me that he is ready to move into the full 'Life Between Lives' state, it indicates that Anton is finally ready to completely cross over. Angels escort him across the 'threshold.' Deeper understanding comes from his personal guide and council members who help him see that part of his present life mission as Erik was to help Anton face his issues. This happened through present-life situations Erik encountered and choices he had to make along the way, but it culminated in helping Anton get unstuck and bringing him home.

Not being ready to leave is one form of being stuck. But sometimes it is those most devastated by a loss who construct an emotional holding cell keeping their loved one(s) here. This is the story of a man who wasn't able to let go until he completely surrendered to the very love he was holding onto.

After 35 years of marriage, even cancer could not separate Betsy from her beloved husband, Paul. Every morning, after his boys left the house, he filled his travel mug with coffee and drove to a nearby lake to sit with Betsy, filling up with the love and support he needed to face his day. Their secret meeting time had become an integral part of his daily ritual over the previous four years, ever since Betsy had died.

Paul was not a spiritual seeker when Betsy was alive. He had plenty on his plate, managing a transportation business and co-parenting six kids. As a way to cope with his grief, he developed an insatiable desire to read whatever metaphysical material Betsy maneuvered into his path. The book that brought him to me, was *Michael Newton's *Journey of Souls*.

After he makes the four hour drive to meet with me, I ask him to describe the reason for his desire to do an LBL.

He replies, *"To find my way."*

He is lost without Betsy, even though he 'speaks' with her on a daily basis.

In a traditional LBL session, the client is regressed to the most recent past life, moving through significant memories to reach the last day. Going through the death sequence sets the person up to naturally proceed into their 'Life Between Lives' exploration.

In Paul's most recent past life, he is thrilled to find himself on a train, meeting the love of his life (Betsy). He is overcome with joy to know that in this other life, too, they get married. Two of his current children are recognized as being their children then. Moving to the end of this lifetime, Paul finds himself in a hospital bathrobe, dying of TB. When he draws his last breath and is out of the body, he is able to look back at the life. Immediately he states his regret that he did not love as much or as deeply as he could have.

Moving into the ascent away from Earth, he is pulled across a wide expanse of space, magnetized toward a waiting globe of light. That light breaks into countless lights which reorganize themselves into six figures who surround him as his own 'soul cluster.' When asked to focus on them one at a time, he easily recognizes them as individuals from his current life. Going around the semicircle, he describes each one, giving me feedback on how they look and feel to him. He hesitates when he gets to the person in the very center.

Excitedly he makes the connection, *"It's Betsy! Betsy is here!"*

His enthusiasm fades a bit as he adds, *"But she is not as distinct as the others. I almost didn't recognize her. She appears grey or almost wispy. She is fading in and out like she is not entirely here."*

I encourage him, "Ask her if she can explain this to you."

After listening to her response, he quietly tells me, *"Betsy is asking me to let her go so she can fully cross over. She knows now that our youngest boys will be okay and she wants me to move forward with my life. This is the reason she led me to come here today."*

Because he has just gone through the experience himself, he knows what it is to cross over. I suggest he might be able to help her. Without hesitating, Paul agrees to retrace his steps to return to the Earth plane to be her escort.

He holds her hand and with great pride and confidence brings her through the black expanse into the gateway like a seasoned explorer. Together they arrive back at the semi-circle, where now Betsy radiates brightly in the group's midst. Paul is able to participate in the homecoming celebration, feeling very different when it is time for him to leave.

The part of Betsy's spirit already in the afterlife made a lasting impression on both of us. It is hard to comprehend that the eternal matrix of our Higher Self remains on *the other side*, monitoring the aspects of energy that are still *out in the field*, but the reality of this can be of immense comfort. Just imagine that whenever a loved one dies before us, the essence of our True Self is already there to greet them as part of their welcoming committee. Betsy's faint imprint catalyzed Paul to go beyond his own personal grief to not only let her go, but to accompany her in her relocation process. Her return marked his turning point. He left feeling more grounded, and knowing that Love crosses all barriers. He was ready to return to live out the remainder of his life, vowing that this time there would be no regrets.

We only dream this bondage. Wake up and let it go.

~ Swami Vivekananda ~

22

DREAMTIME SOS

Many scientific theories exist about why we dream. Some say dreams express our repressed childhood longings. Others believe we are sorting through the garbage of our day-to-day existence or symbolically rehashing long-standing problems and issues connected to karmic patterns in our lives. Some scientists believe dreams are just random brain impulses. But no one seems to know *exactly* what they are. Although we often have trouble remembering our dreams, our dreaming selves have full access to our deep unconscious and that includes all that the soul has been through in our past.

The first brainwave stage that we enter when we are dreaming is called *Theta*. Theta brain waves are thought to be the subconscious. Governing the part of our mind which lies between the conscious and the unconscious, this state retains our memories and feelings, also directing our beliefs and behavior. With our dreamscape connected to the subconscious, it's not so hard to imagine that it could serve as a 'carrier wave' for an SOS signal coming from an earthbound spirit. If a past life aspect of yourself were sequestered in a walled off time-loop, the dream state could act like a drawbridge, allowing the call for help to be carried out across the 'moat,' reaching the shores of your waking self.

This was the case for Cindy, a woman who had a dream in her thirties which made no sense in her current life, yet it was so powerful she couldn't dismiss it. The dream continued to replay and 'haunt' her waking state over and over again until, in her early fifties, she came to me for a past life regression. Cindy had no idea, beyond looking for clarification to verify the dream, that she was also coming to meet the dream messenger from her deep unconscious, to finally release her.

The Dream

"I am standing in a line with many others in a big building that has a sickening sweet smell in the air and it is stifling hot. I am tired, hot, and very afraid. I do not know what is happening. Harsh looking women in German military uniforms are pushing drab dresses at us as we are shoved down the line. I am moving along with many others like cattle towards a tall SS officer. As I move closer I can see him motioning the people ahead of me to his right or left. He does it with a bored flick of his wrist. He barely looks at the people before him, but when he does he makes no attempt to hide his hatred and disgust. I wonder briefly why people are being sent in different directions. Then I see another officer enter the room behind him. He is shorter and stockier than the other. For a moment, we make eye contact. He looks at me intently—not with hatred or contempt, but with interest. I look away as the first officer points for me to go to my right.

I turn to go but stop startled when someone yells 'Halt!'

Looking back, I see the second officer speaking to the first and pointing at me. The tall officer is standing very straight at attention and I realize that the shorter officer outranks him. They point to me and motion for me to go to the left instead. I quickly do as I am directed, knowing something major has just occurred, but I have no idea what that is. What I do know for sure is I am a young Jewish girl that has just arrived in a concentration camp.

Time suddenly jumps, the way it does in dreams. It is horribly cold and I am more afraid than I had ever been since arriving here. I have survived thanks to the second officer. I found out that going to my right would have been a sentence into the gas chamber and immediate death, but going to the left meant going to the women's barracks and life. Most of the women around me have been sent to work long, tiring hours in different areas throughout the camps and many are starving, sick and before long—dead. I am one of the lucky ones—if there is such a thing in this place. I was sent to work for the officer who saved me. I am lucky in the fact that most of the women have lost weight to the point of being nothing more than walking skeletons. While I am thinner than when I first arrived, I am not starving. The others have been shaved bald while I keep my long, thick, dark hair. Their clothes are barely rags that cling to their emaciated bodies while mine are not. I see their suffering and feel ashamed that I do not have to suffer in the same way they do. My suffering is different. I try to help the others by bringing them food when I can, even though I would be punished severely if found out, but the other prisoners hate me for what I have become. I am a traitor in their eyes. I am hated by the German soldiers because I am Jewish and hated by the Jewish prisoners because I am a prostitute for a German.

Now I am back in the women's barracks and a group of angry women have me cornered. I know something has happened to the officer that was my savior. He is gone and he can't protect me. I have nowhere to go. I wish that I could make them understand that I hate myself more than they ever could. I have long ago given up trying to explain that I did not choose this life. They do not understand that I am simply trying to survive, same as them. I really do not think they would have done anything different if they were in my shoes. But they are so angry. They are saying very mean and ugly things—telling me that I should have been killed a long time ago, that good women died while someone like me still lives. I feel a deep aching sadness at it all. I have lost everything and everyone in what seemed an eternity ago and now what little protection I had is gone as well. The women before me want me dead. This is where the dream ends."

Research

"When I awoke, I was disoriented and shaken. The 'me' in the dream and the 'me' in the Now collided. Strong emotions ran through me. Once I realized it was a dream, my first thought was, *Where did that come from?* It made no sense. Nothing like that could have happened in the concentration camps during World War II—especially being a prostitute to an SS officer. Nothing

I had ever read, or seen on television, ever mentioned anything remotely like this. I rationalized that the Germans who hated and killed Jews would not have had sex with one. I decided that my mind made up the whole thing for some unknown reason and I would just forget about it and pretend it never happened. But that was not to be. The dream came back again and again and along with it were the vivid scenes and feelings. Each time I would say to myself that this could not have happened. At first I did not write it down. Why write down a wacky dream? But then I decided to see if writing it down would make it go away. It didn't.

Over many years, it would return and was just as strong. I went to the public library, because at that time the internet did not exist, and looked up what I could about the camps. But that only further confused me when I found pictures of Auschwitz. It was the camp in my dream, but the name did not match. At the time of the dream I really did not know much about the concentration camps. I thought there were only a few and that they were all in Germany. I knew some names such as Auschwitz, Bergen-Belson, and Buchenwald. But because none were the name in the dream, that was just further proof that my dream was just a figment of my imagination. I had seen the movie *Schindler's List and read some books about Josef Mengele, but otherwise the info I had contact with was meager at best. I still thought I must have heard or read this somewhere, but I sure could not find it.

Then one day I was at Hastings bookstore in Hutchinson, Kansas. I stopped to look at the clearance discount books. The collection included fiction and nonfiction of every kind and subject. As I scanned the assortment, one title jumped out at me. It was a thin black book with the title *House of Dolls and a strange number on the spine. To this day, I don't know why it caught my attention. Even as a child I did not like dolls, so why would this be of interest? I pulled it out and nearly dropped it. On the front was a picture of Auschwitz. I had seen this picture of Auschwitz many times through the years. It is probably the most famous picture of the camp. It shows the front with the train tracks that go right into the building. The hair stood up on the back of my neck when I read the words on the back cover. It was a diary written by a woman who had been a prostitute in a concentration camp. She chose to remain anonymous, and only used the prisoner number the Nazis tattooed on her wrist as her *nom de plume.*

I bought the book, took it home, and read it in one sitting. It turned out the only similarity between my story and hers was that we both were prostitutes for German officers. I had no proof her story was true. But it did make me wonder if what I had been calling a dream was, instead, a memory.

After the internet became a part of everyday life, I looked there to see what I could find out. I typed in 'Auschwitz' and soon I found a map of how the camp was laid out. To my surprise, it corresponded to my dream. I felt my heart pounding. The train track going right into the camp was an important part of my dream, but I had assumed this was the layout at all the camps. As I did more research I discovered this was unique to Auschwitz.

I had to ask myself, *'If the camp in my dream was Auschwitz, then why did I know it by a different name?'*

Finally, it became clear. By 1943 Auschwitz had expanded and a second camp was built there named 'Birkenau.' It gave me chills when I read that this became the women's camp. I searched and searched the internet for something about brothels in the camps but came up empty-handed.

In 2005, a much bigger confirmation came when a book was published by the name *Auschwitz. I bought it immediately and began reading the most complete gathering of information that had ever been compiled. The author had been able to interview Jewish survivors as well as German soldiers. They were in their eighties and decided that they needed to share their stories before they died—things they had never shared before, or that they had been too ashamed to admit to previously, all came out in this book. It was there that I found that brothels did exist in these camps and there were times when Nazi SS officers were attracted to some Jewish women. I found many things in the book that confirmed my dream, leaving me not knowing what to think. Was it a past life memory or was I tapping into memories from someone else during that time in history, or had I read or seen this somewhere before I dreamed it and simply did not remember?

It was very irritating to me at times because I felt there was something to be known here, but it was coming to me in little teasing morsels left on a trail through a forest of confusion. The truth is that the question of reincarnation had been in the back of my mind for many years. In the heart of Kansas where Christianity is the norm, reincarnation is not well accepted, so I did not find many who thought like I did. Eventually I read all of Dr. Weiss's books on reincarnation and it all made sense to me.

One day in 2013, I was watching an Oprah Winfrey show with Dr. Weiss as the guest and found myself reaching for my laptop and typing in *does anyone do past life regression hypnosis in Kansas?* This is how I found Toby Evans and booked my session.

On the day of my regression, I began telling her the story of my dream and, even though I tried to be stoic as we talked, I found myself breaking down in tears like I always did if I tried talking about the dream in any depth. I apologized for crying. Crying to me was a sign of weakness and something that I had learned to suppress in my thirty years as a paramedic, but when it came to this I could not hold back the tears. When it was time to start the session, I was a little apprehensive. Would I be able to do it? Could I be hypnotized? If so, would anything come through? What if it turned out that there wasn't anything to it and I was completely crazy? But then I thought, *Oh well, at least it was an adventure no matter what happens."*

The Session

"After the preliminary part to help me relax, the session began to deepen.

I see myself in an apartment over a violin shop in Poland. I know it's where I live with my mother and father. My father plays the violin and my mother and I play the piano. We are not rich but we have more than many people around us. We are happy and content until the war begins to make life harder and harder. My parents try to hide their fear of what is happening as Hitler and his army begin to destroy the world around us, but with each passing day I can see the fear growing in the eyes of everyone that I pass on the street, but especially in the eyes of my parents. I am young and have dreams of going to school, getting married someday and having children, but I have a growing feeling that that will not happen.

Moving forward, I stop at a time when German soldiers are rounding up everyone and telling us we are going to a work camp. It is complete chaos and we are all filled with fear. They say we can take with us whatever we can carry. We frantically shove anything of value into large brown suitcases. My parents and I try to stay together, but the panicked crowd pushes us apart as we are shoved into waiting train cars. The last thing I see is my mother looking back to find me. My suitcase is jerked from my hands in the shuffle as I scramble to find a way to keep from being crushed. The air is stifling hot and it is hard to breathe. The train begins moving. I am afraid, yet oddly detached, as though I cannot quite believe this is happening. The train continues on for what seems like forever. I can see light between the slats of the train car and have a sense that two days have passed. I wonder if anyone will survive. There is no food or water; only the stifling heat and the awful smell of human waste.

When the train comes to a stop we are ordered out. It is hard to stand, let alone walk after the long, cramped journey. I find out that some have not lived through the trip. Bodies are stepped over and stepped on as we scramble to do as we are told. One of the dead is a small child still in the grip of his mother who is being pulled from the train. I cannot comprehend how anything like this can be happening and can't imagine that it could get any worse.

Time moves forward again and now I am reliving the scene from my dream just after I have been directed to the left instead of the right. I am chosen by the second officer to be his housekeeper. His name is Heinrich. My name is Elaina. Along with the housekeeping it is clear that he expects sex. He is not mean, and often as time goes on he declares his love for me, promising that he will find a way for us to be together even after the war. I do not hate him, but I also do not know if I can completely trust him. At times he seems totally self-absorbed. He worries about how things are for him and does not recognize that I am in a worse situation. I find myself doing whatever he wants because I am afraid of what will happen if he turns me out. I see how bad it is for most of the other prisoners and I do not want to live like that. I try to bring food to some of the women in the barracks when I can, but they still hate and shun me. The only place I feel halfway safe is when I am with Heinrich—yet all the time I am with him, I hate myself for what I am doing to survive. He isn't completely evil and he even tried to find my parents several weeks after arriving in the camp, but there was no record of them. I know without being told that they are dead. I cry at night for them, but I am also glad that they are not suffering.

Then we move forward to a day when I am met by a guard as I try to enter Heinrich's quarters, just as I had done every day since I arrived. He tells me to go back to the barracks because Heinrich has been called back to Germany. Feeling abandoned and alone, I return to the barracks and am approached by the angry women. This time as the women surround me, saying their hateful words, the scene continues to unfold. They come at me. I back up and yell at them to stop as they begin to hit me with their fists. They are weak from starvation, illness, and hard work, but as a group they drive me backwards with force, causing me to fall. My head hits the edge of a wooden bunk bed, hard enough that I know then that this is how I die. It is January 1945 and I die at the hands of my fellow prisoners just before the camp is liberated by Russian soldiers.

I was surprised by this knowledge. I always thought I did not make it out of the camp alive, but I figured I died in the gas chamber or somehow by the hands of the Germans. I never imagined that it was by my own people. Yet, as it unfolded, I knew this is exactly what happened.

Once I am no longer in the body, Toby asks me if I want to check in on anyone before moving on. I know my parents are already gone, but I am curious to see what happened to Heinrich. I see that he has survived. When she asks me if I am able to now cross over completely, I hesitate and realize that this did not happen.

It slowly dawned on me that I, Cindy, born 15 years after Elaina died, agreed to work through her issues and help her find resolution, acceptance, and completion. It is likely Elaina did not even realize she was dead until now— when she could finally move beyond the 'closed loop' of the dream, taking in what had happened. I had been living my life in an attempt to re-pattern many of the ways she was still holding the things that she could not change.

As she finger-traces a labyrinth, Toby called in her Higher Self, asking that we visualize this as two angelic beings. We envisioned Elaina in the center. The angels lifted into a geometric shape surrounding Elaina in a three dimensional Jewish 'Star of David.' (This seemed appropriate.) She explained that this symbol is the vehicle that will take her across and help her find peace. I am hoping this will bring me peace, as well.

The crossing over of Elaina was the strangest part for me, sort of like saying goodbye to an old friend. Seeing her go was somewhat sad because I realized she was a part of me, but then again it felt right. Strangest of all was how, as she left, she turned back and smiled at me. It was in that moment that I knew this was as it should be. I was moved and could feel tears welling up. It reminded me of times when, as a paramedic, I had been touched by the profound knowledge that I had truly helped someone."

Afterthoughts

"After the regression, I decided to search for a list of SS officers who were at Auschwitz and I found Heinrich Oppelt. His title at the camp was 'Director of Labor.' This meant he would have had a say in who he wanted for work in the camp. Many officers were tried as war criminals, but under Heinrich it just said, *Fate unknown.*

Now that some time has passed, I am able to talk about the dream and this past life without the strong emotions which once plagued me. I no longer feel horribly sick when I think about it. It feels more like I am watching a movie instead of reliving it. I am much more of a believer in past lives, and see that unresolved aspects can have a big impact on your current life.

This was evident in my own life as I showed signs of fearing people almost from the day I was born. My parents noticed an abnormal startle reflex any time someone came near me—even at three days old. Relatives and friends of the family always described me as extremely shy. As far back as I can remember I found myself watching people very closely, trying to figure out what they wanted and if they were a threat. Going to school was hell. I had trouble learning because I was in a constant state of panic as I navigated through the day. By the time I reached middle school, I wondered if it wasn't better to end the suffering, although I never had an actual plan to do anything to end my life.

The anxiety carried over into my personal relationships. I have never been good at trusting people enough to really let them in, which was especially true with men. I have tried many times, but failed. I realize that I feel I am not worth their attention. 'Damaged goods' is what comes into my mind. It makes sense that this thought is linked to the camp, as the shame of what I did to survive was so deep that it colored this life as well.

As a way to survive in this life, I set a goal to find a career that I was really good at and could pour myself into. From this vantage point, I can see that my life in the concentration camp could have influenced my choice to become a paramedic. It was a way to help many people on what often is the worst day of their lives. I can see now that it has been a way to control or manage chaos (something I was incapable of doing in the camp). There I had no power, but here I do. I also became a Sheriff Deputy and SWAT officer/medic with the goal to yet again be in a position of power to help others. I discovered I have a fierce protective spirit when it comes to the suffering of innocent people, and have put my life on the line more than once. I also took Karate for twenty years. Could this be because I could not protect myself then? It makes me wonder if this life was solely about taking back my power. No longer afraid of everything, I have learned I am capable of navigating my way through just about anything.

Going through this experience has allowed me to deeply think about suffering and how much it can affect a person. I find myself looking at people around me in a new light. Sometimes I will see someone doing something that I don't understand and, instead of judging them, I consider that perhaps they are working through past lives and unresolved issues. I have had many opportunities, at the strangest times, to share my past life story. This is something I never thought I would do, but each time the response has been very good and it has helped the person whom I told.

Since the regression, I have not had problems with depression to the level I once did. I feel that it has brought me peace, understanding, compassion for myself, and deeper appreciation for all I have accomplished in this life. I think the regression—and crossing Elaina over—has made me stronger and freer as though a chapter of my life has come to an end. I am now open and ready to start a brand new one."

~ Cindy Welch
  McPherson, KS
  cindywelch32@att.net

In 2015, Cindy traveled to Poland with the intention of visiting Auschwitz and especially Birkenau. She arrived in rainy, drab weather conditions and noted that walking up to the famed 'Gate of Death' brought up a foreboding feeling in her, yet the tour and the wonderful guide helped neutralize that. At the end of the tour, when she had a moment to sit outside alone, she decided to ask the angels for their help in releasing any souls that still might be stuck there. In that instant, the sun suddenly broke through the clouds and a flock of white birds lifted up and took flight. The unexpected symbolism took Cindy by surprise. She walked through the Gate, feeling completely different. She was able to look back and perceive its looming, scary presence as just an old, worn out, tired energy that no longer held any power. It was all behind her.

People are like stained-glass windows.
They sparkle and shine when the sun is out,
but when the darkness sets in their true beauty is revealed
only if there is a light from within.

~ **Elizabeth Kübler-Ross** ~

23

RETURNING TO SUNSHINE

Helping an aspect of yourself cross over can make such a strong impression that it sets you on your own psychopomp path. This is exactly what happened for Nikkea. Because of her work with her earthbound pilot-self (Nicholas) recounted in Chapter 20, "Working As An Angelic Team," she was able to own her natural abilities and step fully into the role of a 'soul-guide.' A major contributor to this book, Nikkea has learned to apply her sensitivity and knowledge, building bridges of light for the stranded souls she continues to encounter.

Hearing that someone you know well has suddenly died may darken everything—it's as if the sun has been blotted out. A whole array of feelings might come up and some of them may not belong to you. The notion that you could be picking up what the deceased person is going through is something most people would never consider. Yet, as we go deeper into this work, it becomes a possibility which has to be examined in order to help both of you reclaim your inner light. Nikkea experienced this firsthand.

"I awake around 3:00 a.m. and cannot fall back asleep. I find out that my twins, Jon and Ella, can't sleep either. The past few months I have been sleeping very soundly so I am surprised at this sudden change. Lying there for two hours, I feel a strange, underlying anxiety, like something is 'off' or

that something unfamiliar is in the room.

Two days later, I find out that our neighbor died instantly in a head-on collision with another car on the local freeway. She was thirty-six years old, a very devoted mother of three young children—the oldest of which is friends with my son, Jonathan. I am shocked and really sad, as is everyone in our whole neighborhood. Another car was going the wrong way on the freeway and they collided. The other woman was also a mother of two young children, and a college student. As strange as it may seem, both of them have the same first name. I will refer to them using the alias Sarah to protect their privacy.

When I hear the news, I am sitting in the driveway, talking on my phone. I can't help but notice the shining reflection of the sun-spinning ornament on our front porch that is twisting in the wind. I've never seen it spin so quickly, nor noticed it reflect like that in the dark. It triggers my memory of talking with Sarah and seeing that this free-spirited loving mother also had a similar sun ornament hanging on her porch. It created an automatic connection between us. I always sensed her light and airy spirit. For this reason, I associate her with the symbol of the sun.

Sitting in my driveway, I wonder if it was Sarah's shocked and confused spirit I sensed the other night. I understand her feeling that she can't leave her kids, and know only too well the traumatic, death-accident nightmare from my own 'pilot' lifetime. I wonder if she is aware that I may be able to hold this space for her and offer what I have learned through my experience. I feel deep empathy and compassion for her situation as it brings up my old feelings. Perhaps they are inviting me to heal yet another layer.

I look up the accident online. Ten minutes before the crash there had been 911 calls stating that there was a car going down the wrong side of this small, winding freeway. The time of the accident was 3:05 a.m.—right around the time I awoke in my bedroom feeling uneasy. Shivering, I trust this is confirmation that I am not making this up in my head. I go to bed aware that the same energy is still around me. In the middle of the night I wake up at exactly 3:05 a.m. and understand the significance of the numbers.

The next day I take a deep breath and intentionally align with my Higher-Self energies in an attempt to talk to her spirit. Sarah is already here. I sense her saying, 'I didn't realize that you did things like this.'

I smile and explain, 'I am here to support you in whatever way I can.'

Sarah admits she is shocked and confused and not very clear about what happened. There is a frazzled feeling coming from her, even though at first I think it may be coming from my own feelings. When I ask whether this is her energy or my own, I am reassured that it is, in fact, hers. I have to trust my internal guidance because it is all a little surreal. I tell her I would be grateful to connect with her further, when she is ready.

I explain, 'When I receive the internal' signal from you, I will meet you outside my house.'

That happens the very next day. I begin by pulling cards from Toby's Chakra Labyrinth Cards. Each card has two sets of statements: one a statement of Release, and the other a positive affirmation that is a statement of Renewal. I do this as a way to help me to focus, asking her Higher Self to direct the process and to select what is most appropriate for her to hear.

The first card I pull says, 'I acknowledge and bless my difficulty staying focused or paying attention.' *I think back to the frazzled feeling I felt from her.*

The Renewal affirmation is this: 'I concentrate with ease, handling details and seeing the bigger picture.' *I can sense she intends to see the bigger picture.*

Next I choose 'I acknowledge and bless my blocked creative energy.' *I know Sarah feels blocked and stuck.*

The affirmation: 'I free my creative spirit to inspire, enliven, and direct me.' *I think of her life force flowing through her, the big sun ornament on her front porch and that free, light, airy feeling I associate with her. The last one is an Integration card. I am not surprised that it is the element of Air:*

'I connect with the spirit of Air to exhale what no longer serves me'.

Affirmation: 'I balance the Air of my being, breathing in my 'True Essence.' *I sit down and cry after that one.*

This makes perfect sense, I can feel Sarah almost smile, like 'Yes, that is me!' Her soul intent is to reconnect with her True Essence. I drum for a few minutes, focusing on the affirmations while saying them out loud. Then I go outside and face the area where we believe the portal resides (the future place for my rock labyrinth). I ask if she has anything she wants to share before moving through the labyrinth. I explain that crossing over does not mean she will be leaving her kids, and that I understand her feelings. I tell her she will be connected to them from a more expanded place within her spirit. I shed some tears while feeling such gratitude for our time together. I thank her for contacting me.

Finger-tracing the labyrinth, I imagine an etheric labyrinth positioned above it with the *tube torus of violet light running up through both of them like a fountain. It is a windy day. On our walk into the labyrinth the wind blows a little stronger, but seems to slow down once we reach the center where she transforms into her 'Merkaba.' It looks like a bright spinning vortex of energy patterns with the star tetrahedron spinning like the sun catcher on my porch.

When it is complete, I can't be sure that she has really crossed over, so I ask to receive some kind of confirmation when the time is right. Being still new to this, I really appreciate any kind of validation. I sleep much better that night and accept that this might just be my sign.

Later that week I am unable to attend the funeral, but Ella's ten-year old friend—who had Sarah as her baby sitter for several years—comes over afterward and tells us about it. She shares that something special happened during the husband's speech.

Their three young children were sitting in the front church pew when he concluded his talk by saying, 'Sarah will always be our ray of sunshine.'

At that exact moment, a ray of sunlight came beaming through the window, shining down on top of her daughter's head. What an incredible sign from her spirit, assuring all of us that she is still shining, but now it is from a much 'higher' place.

~ Nikkea Walkker

A reset of the solar Sun represents an initiation,
shifting from the current energy field into
a higher frequency energy field.

~ **Suzanne Lie** ~

24

SOLAR PORTAL

Human intervention can make all the difference in helping an earthbound soul cross over, but in certain situations there may be an outside force at work that we would never consider. A woman shared with me that her younger brother committed suicide, sending her family into a tailspin of depression, guilt, and sadness. This was ten years ago, but she still struggled with the grief every day—until something unexpected happened that changed everything. This was an X-class solar flare eruption. X-class solar flares are the strongest type of storms that explode on the sun, causing the magnetics of the sun to interfere with the magnetics of the Earth, creating two overlapping magnetic fields. The interaction may disrupt certain kinds of communication on Earth, but this state (called inductance) also triggers an amplified energy exchange of information.

Although she was not convinced that her brother was earthbound, she admitted that she experienced a huge release of her own tied-up energy, resetting her entire outlook on life after this occurred. Was there a connection between his release and the charged wave of particles bombarding our planet? I have no way of knowing, but if recalibration (readjusting reality) is the result of overlapping fields, then an X-class solar flare has all the makings of a supercharged portal. Thinking it was an interesting concept to consider, I shared it with my friend Nikkea who responded with her own story.

"My best friend committed suicide when I was 19. For nearly a year, I felt her close to me. The night she died, she came to me in a dream. I do not believe she ever left my energy field from then on. For that year, I was in a deep and constant depression, never leaving the grieving / depression stage of loss. I went through months of counseling, antidepressants, constantly sleeping, trying techniques for coping, but nothing helped. The evening of Sept. 16, 1996, I attempted suicide after feeling I would never get better. This was just not like 'me' at all.

Waking up in the hospital the next morning, my first realization was that my grandfather had been with me during the whole ordeal. This was a weird thought because I never had a chance to meet him; he had died of cancer the year before I was born. It made no sense why I would even think about him, but there was a strong sense of him in the realms during my sleep—as if he was acting as my protector. Coming back into full awareness, I felt completely different, like a huge darkness had been lifted off of me.

At the time, I thought it was because I had asked to understand why my friend committed suicide and, after walking in her shoes, I finally grasped what she had been feeling. My overnight recovery was still a shock to everyone around me. How could I be at rock bottom and the very next day arrive on a completely different level both emotionally and spiritually? I remember my mom trying to tell hospital personnel that I was not bipolar, although it certainly appeared that way. I was grateful my counselor knew me well at that point.

The first time I had a session with Toby, she mentioned that it was likely that my friend never moved on after her death, accounting for the way I felt. At the time, I didn't understand this, but it made sense somewhere inside of me. Even if it were true, it didn't explain how she just suddenly moved on and I wondered what occurred to make that happen.

Well, because of our conversation, I looked up what the sun was doing on that day, Sept. 16, 1996, and what do you know ... a huge X-class solar flare erupted after a very long period of time with no activity at all. Perhaps this was a piece to the puzzle I had been searching for.

Years later, after thinking I finally had all the pieces gathered, more revealed itself. My sister Beth called me, saying she could not get Jeff (my exboyfriend who died in a car accident in 1999) out of her mind. She had been doing a 21-day Reiki cleanse and was nearly sick over it. She thought maybe she was releasing old sadness, but she knew it felt different.

Jeff was like a part of our family for the five years we were together, and was especially close to Beth. He even met my husband after we were engaged and we remained like brother and sister. Beth now told me that she felt like Jeff hadn't crossed over. I was shocked, as it had never occurred to me. I did not sense that he was attached to me, either, but Beth was convinced. I looked back, remembering that when my mom was going through a challenging time she'd had a very strong sense of Jeff's hand on hers.

Through muscle checking it was confirmed that he was still here. I took him through the crossing-over process, surprised at how neutral I felt toward him as it was a very painful loss for me at the time. Being more emotionally detached allowed me to really hear what he was saying in my mind.

Just as he was crossing over, I saw him with a smile on his face as he said, 'Now we are even.'

At first, I didn't understand this. Then I remembered that he was the one who found me in his apartment bedroom overdosing on Ativan and had rushed me to the hospital. He had relayed that a 'force' told him to come back to his apartment sooner than he planned. At the time, he considered himself agnostic, but he could not ignore such a loud and insistent message. That clear message inspired him to get a tattoo of Archangel Michael years later.

After moving him across, I asked my sister, 'Have the intense feelings dissipated?'

And her response was, 'Yes, completely.' We were both amazed and in awe.

Jeff helped me to stay alive—pulling me back into the life that awaited me, while I was to help him release this life—propelling him forward to the eternal life that was waiting for him.

Reflecting on all of this, I had to question if my grandfather was also earthbound, using the solar flare as his exit passageway—or was he the insistent 'force' guiding Jeff back to the apartment that night? If he was there as my 'angel' protector, he could have also served as a soul guide (psychopomp) guiding my friend home using the transformative doorway of the fireball solar portal.

~ Nikkea Walkker

Give light and people will find the way.

~ **Ella Baker** ~

25

A GOOD RED ROAD

reating a portal to assist an earthbound spirit is much easier than waiting for an erupting solar flare. Any style of labyrinth or geometric pattern can be used. You can literally walk any labyrinth, but it also works to finger-trace an image of any pattern with intent. (Two portal patterns are included at the back of this book on a perforated sheet for easy removal.) If you are in nature, there are many settings that create natural portals. Trees or stones or rock caverns in circular formations combine with the wind to create whirling, energetic openings. In places like Cathedral Rock in Sedona, AZ there are no shortages of natural vortices. You could also just envision a staircase or mentally construct your own rainbow bridge of light. If you can imagine it, you can create it. Regardless of the portal you are using, it is important for you to be in a balanced state, willing to listen to and then follow your own inner guidance. Invite in angelic or spirit helpers who may have a connection to the souls involved, including the presence of their Higher Selves. Intention is everything.

The following story is co-authored by two colleagues, Jennifer Martin and Paul Rudy, who joined forces to create a ritual to assist many spirits that had waited a long time for their arrival. They partnered their intentions with the sacred element of fire ... one of the most ancient portals of release.

Jen's Story

"You're to help release the souls." That's the greeting I remember when I first met Toby Evans. I'd simply come to walk her labyrinth and have an Akashic Record reading and I didn't have a clue what she was talking about. Little did I know, now more than a decade later, that sentence would begin one of the most fascinating journeys of my life: the journey on a "Good Red Road."

Patterns of flow that escape awareness in the moment sometimes clarify in retrospect. As I reflect on the soul release ceremony of July 2010, I see that six distinct but ultimately interwoven paths led to the Road.

Six Paths

The first path began in 1968 when, for seven summers, I was a dancer in the company of *Unto these Hills*, the outdoor drama about the Cherokee who lived and died in the Great Smoky Mountains of North Carolina. During those summers, I was deeply touched by the Cherokee actors who shared their stories and by the healing wisdom of fellow cast member Amoneeta Sequoia, Medicine Man for the Eastern Band of the Cherokee Nation. My resonance with those mountains and the people who lived there was strong, and continued to call me over the years.

The second path was connected to healing practices. Thirty-five years ago my interest in healing shifted from healing in general to energetic forms of healing such as Polarity, Therapeutic Touch, and Reiki. Practice of these forms refined my ability to connect and direct energy in concrete and practical ways. Over time, I learned to trust what I could sense.

The third path was a long-anticipated trip to Machu Picchu about fifteen years ago to work with Incan shamans. During a cleansing ritual, I connected to the energy of a massive squaw who I called "Pachamama." At the time, I was energetically depleted and she brought a much-needed sense of clear, strongly-directed energy. While I thought about her and that experience from time to time, she did not reappear until February of 2010.

The fourth path began again in the North Carolina mountains. On an anniversary trip, my husband and I casually inquired about land without any intention to buy. An agent took us to a tree-covered mountain about an hour's drive from "Cherokee," the town where we'd spent summers thirty years before in the *Unto these Hills* drama. I charged into the buck-berry underbrush (just to get a feel for the land) and emerged a bit later with the words, "I think we should buy it." And we did. I still don't know what prompted my uncharacteristically impulsive and strong statement, but that land became the site of the soul release. In a session with Toby, it was revealed that within a five-mile radius of the land, many Cherokee were slaughtered by the British. Shortly after we bought the land and before we began to build a cabin, I built a fire pit "for ceremonies." I had no idea what that meant and for the next ten years it was used only to make s'mores.

The fifth path came in the person of Paul Rudy: composer, university colleague, and friend. Through classes that we team-taught, we discovered shared interests in healing, the power of resonance, and transformation. Paul's experience with indigenous ceremonies throughout the world—specifically his drumming, fire building, and ability to 'hold space'—proved central to our process. Plus, when I asked him if he'd be willing to help, he said "YES."

The sixth path. Paul and I had been guided in our preparation for the soul release by Toby through individual readings and her own experience. She helped us define our specific roles and encouraged us to be more playful as we tried to figure out just how to do it. Beckah Reed, a long-time friend and gifted healer, reconnected me to Pachamama and helped us to develop a framework to proceed.

The Process

Paul had a Vision Quest scheduled in New Mexico for late June, and I had folks arriving at the cabin the second week of July, so July 4th—8th was our window. Deadlines can be helpful. Once the date was set I wanted a "to do" list: stuff I needed to gather; personal preparation I needed to be doing (meditation is not my strong suit); "how to" books to read about soul release (there was not a whole lot written on this subject). I wanted concrete specifics. Beckah, through several sessions, guided me to a list of 'stuff' (metal bowl, gourds, medicine blanket, drums etc.) and a reconnection with Pachamama, who undertook the collection and organization of souls who were ready to move on the Good Red Road. Ultimately, Paul brought the medicine blanket he'd used in his Vision Quest, his drums and rattles and his knowledge of ceremonial fire building.

Paul's Story

A friend and colleague had asked me to go to her cabin in North Carolina. She knew she had work to do, and that I had a part to play in it. I had thought about it a lot leading up to my Vision Quest, and had even done ceremony during my quest that connected me to that upcoming task. I had purchased the Cherokee Basket Weaver blanket from Pendleton for her, and was certain that it, too, had a part to play. It was with me during the prep for the quest, during the quest, and for the decompression after the quest. I had prayed on, meditated on, performed with, slept on, and died a shamanic death under this blanket by the time we both arrived in North Carolina. This blanket was special...it was programmed...it was charged with the task it was to fulfill.

We were still looking for clues...information on how to release souls trapped on this physical plane after the sudden violent and tragic deaths of their bodies hundreds of years ago. It was not leftovers from the Trail of Tears. The ones here were from when the British callously went through the area burning towns, crops, and everything in their path. They had ruthlessly killed men, women, and children in 1760 and '61, and some were still waiting to move on 250 years later.

After nearly a decade of preparations being set into motion, we were here in North Carolina. The stage was set. We were gathering a few more props, but the cast was in place. We knew this was our task, and I suspected the blanket and my drum knew much more about the 'how' than Jen and I combined. We would have to trust these things like we trusted our security blankets as kids. We would also have to suspend our disbelief, like we naturally did as kids. We were excited and almost giddy—to "giddy up," like when we were kids. A 'type A' and a 'coyote' personality, we were the perfect combination to do what we knew we had to ... even though we didn't know how!

Jen told me the story about all of the tribulations of building the cabin: how the foundation washed out three times...the contractor was stealing their money and not paying the crew ... holes in the roof leaking all over the wood floors...The list went on. My first thought was that maybe they weren't really supposed to have this place. But after a while I began to see it as a test: *"We want to see if you are really up to the task, so we are going to put road blocks in your way so YOU can be sure you are up to this task."* My already high respect for Jen went through the roof (this time without causing any damage). So we gathered information in every way we could.

Jen: When Paul rides up the mountain on his motorcycle on July 4th, I've already sensed a gathering of souls who were ready to move on. We begin our joint preparation that evening by walking the land to 'get a feel for it.' The next day we expand our energetic connection with a hike up Whiteside Mountain, said to be one of the earth's oldest, and a visit to Dry Falls where I felt a strong resonance.

Paul: We go to Bridal Veil Falls so Jen can commune with tree roots and I hold space for her. There are many people, but they give a wide birth. They sense something larger than all of us going on, and so they stay away. This is the first of many experiences that I will have in creating and holding space. This, I will learn later, is one of my jobs...one of the reasons I am here. The second night we make a small fire in the ceremonial pit she had built four years prior. It is a perfect pit. A small hole sunk into a carefully laid circle of paving stones, rimmed on the south and north by huge flat boulders, perfect for sitting or lying on—perfect for releasing souls. The pit is lined in the east with a bed of lush green ferns and moss. It is all just right, and ripe with her intentions. She had built it well and I could tell she was excited to finally be using it for the purpose for which it was constructed. Our intention for this first fire is simple: to send out the call...the invitation to gather for anyone who was ready to move on. I sing a loud song with my drum, similar to the songs I had sung on the hill in New Mexico. Also similar to the ones that rang within my helmet as I rode my motorcycle 'Harmony' across Tennessee en route to this fire pit. I had a sense that these songs brought followers. I could not help singing at times on the beautiful road between Nashville and Knoxville. I also wonder if I was being called as much as doing any calling. This first fire is an official invitation—a whetting of the ceremonial whistle for the grand finale to come on the fourth night. Jen senses that they are waiting, so perhaps this mumbo jumbo is more for us to get clear on our intentions ... to piece by piece figure out how to release souls who should have travelled the Good Red Road two and a half centuries earlier. We have a lot to learn, but fortunately this school only requires one thing: quiet patience. Yes, all we have to do is sit and listen. And instructions come in that quiet space.

While sitting between songs, holding my drum, I notice that it feels like there are energies clambering against it. It is one of those feelings of movement in the body where the body is not actually moving. I get an image of people scrambling over each other to get at the drum. The drum gets very heavy, almost as if they are inside it. I am tempted to throw the drum in the fire. No, the fire does not get my drum. This drum is too special. Then I notice a spot lower down the mountain where Jen has buried some sacred items. She tells me it was to hold space for a future medicine wheel. This place is calling me, and my drum. This mini circle is delineated by three rocks buried deep and, like the fire pit, is open to the west. I drum and sing in this space. I invite the higher selves of these lagging souls to join our party. It is not for Jen and me to release these souls so much as it is to create a space where their higher selves can descend far enough back here on their thin tethers to join with them. We are merely space holders. So I drum to the sky, inviting them to the task. As I walk back to the fire pit, I feel the connection being made between these two spots as a metaphor for the connection being opened back up between these lost but not forgotten souls and their higher selves who are longing to be reunited. We have made progress this night. We have learned more about our job. We have good teachers ... and we are good students.

Jen: The next day we lay the foundation for a Medicine Wheel, spending quiet time tuning into each other's energy as Paul gathers wood for the second of our preparation fires. In the evening as Paul chants and drums, I attempt to use the owl rattles. I am uncomfortable with the rattles and at one point I accidently sit on one and break it. It is important to fix it in the moment, and the act of repair serves as a valuable lesson: that my task is not to do it right or well, but to do it with an open heart. This experience—with spirit's guidance—sets the stage for the whole process.

Paul: A broken instrument is a sign that something is out of balance...the flow is stopped up, something is not right. So, we both listen and sit still. I know that it is important to fix the rattle, to mend the break, and in so doing—heal the energy. The night before, when Jen awkwardly played them, I could feel her discomfort. She was 'rattle challenged,' but not because she could not play them in each hand, but rather because she felt like there was only one right way to do it. This is what needed to be healed. Too often creativity is stifled by what people think should be done, or because they think there is only one way to do it. As a composer, I have learned that the only rules are the ones we create, and those rules are often very arbitrary. So it is with the rattles. If they can't be played one in each hand ... big deal ... play them both in one hand. It is the same problem with ceremony whether Western religion, Buddhism, or Native American ritual. Rule-based ritual can get in the way of spirit. It is time for us to be free of rule-based doctrine. As my teacher Jim says: "Rules are here to serve us ... not the other way around." A rule is only as good as the amount of empowerment it engenders. A rule that shuts down energy is not only counterproductive, but damaging. And I think this is the lesson for both of us in the broken rattle. Instead of the owl rattles, we get the real thing—in the distance a barred owl hoots "Who ... who ... who wants to come on this adventure to the next realm?"

I am led down to the new medicine wheel again. This time I just sit and open up to the spirit of the west. I feel the presences of higher powers. They are eager to reconnect with their long-departed souls. They are grateful for what we are doing, and will be there when it is time. I slowly process up to the fire pit, and we both feel like the spaces are connected to serve their own function. Jen feels like the role of the medicine wheel is minimal because it is so new. I feel that it is the portal for higher selves. It is the doorway for them to enter the space where healing will take place. And that doorway is open. We both agree beyond a doubt that the blanket is the opposite doorway to this space. It is the threshold for those marooned on this plane. It is the comfort that they need to become un-marooned. Between the fire, the medicine wheel, the drum and the blanket, we feel more prepared with each ceremony we enter. I have a suspicion that this preparation is more for us than anything else. I think the other parties already know what is going down, and even how. We are the slow ones here ... the ones that need practice. It is a lesson on setting intention and then letting spirit take the rest. We are both learning how to create space with intention and to follow the flow of that space and its intention. The space is where the instruction manual is opened for us to read, but we do not have to search for instructions, only watch and listen, and follow the lead of spirit who reads to us from the instruction manual. It is actually quite fun. We end day three feeling ready. Still not so much knowing what we are going to do, or how we are going to do it, but aware of how to listen, and this sets the stage for the doing.

Jen: With important learnings from the previous night, on the day of the ceremony we set out to visit the Nikwasi Mound, site of Cherokee Council Houses which preserved the Sacred Fires. It's a four-sided grass mound with a flat top in a business district of Franklin, North Carolina.

Paul: Many mounds in that area had been flattened by the heavy feet of European invaders spreading civilization (the insane modern version), but this mound had been spared. Why? This was the place in the Cherokee Nation where the sacred fire was kept in an age long gone. And the fire is still burning.

Tonight is show time and we are with an anthropologist from Western Carolina University to gather what last information we might need. At lunch, when Jen mentions the Nikwasi Mound and that it is the place of the Cherokee Sacred Fire, I know this is the last piece for me. As I sit there experiencing the live Mound, thoughts and images roll through my mind. I feel a gathering of energies, asking for anyone who wants to participate to come along.

Knowing that Fire is a big part of the forthcoming ceremony, I ask for the sacred Cherokee Fire for use in the evening. I do not know what possessed me to ask for this sacred thing. Had I premeditated it, I would have talked myself out of it. I would not have felt worthy ... but I did not premeditate. I just asked.

My vision swirls ... and then suddenly it explodes into a golden-yellow solid and impenetrable wall of fire. *Holy shit ... I was just given the Sacred Fire from Nikwasi ... 13 Thank Yous!* This is a sacred task given in trust: to transfer this fire to Jen's fire pit that we had spent three days preparing. Tonight's fire will be special, powerful, and familiar to those we were helping. It was their Fire, not mine. It will be comforting to all involved.

Suddenly my role in the evening's ceremony is clear. I am the fire tender, and I will give this sacred fire back to the people who kept it burning down the roads of years ago, so that they could ride its comforting waves on the Good Red Road, and leave this place whose gravitational pull kept them here long after they should have departed. The sacred fire has the ability to purge violence and to transmute tears of sorrow into joyful laughter. It is a gift beyond measure that will bring peace to many. Tobacco is generously given to the seven directions on top of the Nikwasi Mound.

That night as I light the Fire, I give it all to our task, pouring it into the wood that will fuel the passage. And the fire burns strong. For such an honor, I have only humility and gratitude to offer in return for this sacred trust.

Jen: As the sun begins to set, we make our way from the cabin with drums, rattles, matches, bottled water and the medicine blanket. Paul stands a big three-foot log in the center of the fire pit and builds the fire around this pillar. In the 6+ hours of ceremony with intense heat and jutting flames, the center log never wavers. We begin in silence as I tune into Pachamama who is behind where I sit by the fire pit. She is holding space for all those who are waiting. I have a sense that there are hundreds, well-organized and standing close to each other, purposely waiting to begin. I also have the sense that they are ancient and have been waiting a long time.

With the fire at full flame, Paul begins drumming and chanting to hold space. I add the owl rattle and tone intermittently. I can feel the energy building and begin to sense a 'shaft,' roughly the diameter of the fire pit and extending from the center log upward into the sky. With Pachamamas's guidance, those who are waiting emerge from the woods behind me into the shaft and upward.

Their rising is like a canister in the tube of a drive-through bank. They *whoosh* skyward and out of sight. It is orderly and purposeful. I don't know precisely how long this takes—perhaps forty-five minutes in a steady flow. After the last one ascends, there is a marked shift in energy. Paul and I take a break to drink water and to share our experiences, not knowing that this is only the first group.

When Paul asks if he should add logs to the fire, my first impulse is "No," but then I look behind me and see that Pachamama has already amassed another group. This group is similar to the first in that they are orderly, standing close together, and also seem to have been waiting a long time. Their energy, however, is more youthful and there are fewer of them. For this group and the three that follow, the process of rebuilding the fire, restoring the energetic 'shaft,' Pachamama's directing of the group and Paul's holding space have only minor variations.

The third group has a youthful, celebratory energy. Instead of standing in an orderly mass, they individually hop, skip, and cart-wheel into the shaft, gleefully bouncing off the sides as they ascend. They are all different shapes and sizes and, while I cannot distinguish facial features, their delight in moving on is palpable.

The fourth group takes longer to gather. They are heavy, slow-moving, and separated from one another. They all stand with their arms extended low in front of them as if they might be feeling for obstacles in their path. I have the sense they are blind and need to find their way quite deliberately. Even though there are fewer of them than the previous group, it seems to take a long time. They need a sign in order to move. I have been instructed by Spirit to have a bowl of water for tears, and this has been placed at the beginning of the Ceremony in the West of the fire circle. When I verbalize this to Paul, he opens a bottle of wine that he'd felt led to take to the fire circle, and pours some in. This is the sign they needed to move onward. I expect them to be the last group, but when I check, Pachamama is still back there quite literally 'beating the bushes.'

The last group is the smallest in number, perhaps a couple dozen. Their bodies are in distorted positions as they crawl or back toward the fire with jerky movements. They don't seem to know how to approach the shaft. I have a sense that they are insane and, on some level, they have asked Pachamama to direct their passage because they can't do it for themselves. I am grateful for her presence. After a few minutes, I turn to check in with her and she is gone. I know we are finished.

Paul's role shifted throughout the four days we worked together. During our time gathering information and materials needed for the actual ceremony, he was getting information through many ways. For example, his ceremonial drum (made in the Taos Pueblo by Deer Snow Trail) would pull in different directions, or move in circular movements (or other patterns), suggesting things relevant to the inquiry at hand.

Information came in other ways too, such as visions, questions, and perceived movements, and it always flowed effortlessly during our research stage. However, the moment the ceremonial space was set and the ceremonial Fire started, this information stopped for Paul. It was as if the lights went out. It was not for him to witness this process, or even actively participate. It was his job to hold space, and to support me with whatever I needed, which he did. I would describe the energy or disposition of each group and then would ask for certain drum beats, tempos, or feelings ... and he would provide them.

Paul and I sat with the fire for some time in gratitude that we'd been gifted with the opportunity. We marveled at all we'd been given over the past four days. Spirit did, indeed, provide. The next morning the air was lighter and the sun brighter as the fog lifted from the valley. It's difficult even these years later to reduce this mystery to narrative. Perhaps that's best left to those who have traveled their own Good Red Road.

~ Jennifer Martin, PhD
    James C. Olson Professor
    Hall Family Foundation Professor of Theatre, Emerita
    Kansas City, MO 64110
    martinj@umkc.edu

~ Paul Rudy
    Music and Sound Alchemist
    rudyp@umkc.edu

The one you have been looking for
is the one doing the looking.

~ **James Twyman** ~

26

LINCHPIN SOULS

I n North America, there are particular locations where the native people died in large numbers due to battles, massacres, sickness or other atrocities. Those who have an emotional affinity to what occurred long ago may have participated firsthand. Even though your current identity might be unaware of any past life involvement, your soul could carry a karmic contract into the present time agreeing to return to readdress the old wounds in some kind of balancing interchange. There are even individuals in this current lifetime who have specific assignments that include gathering earthbound souls together from another era to facilitate what was impossible to do when the tragedies were initially occurring ... and that is to bring everyone home.

One such woman appeared at my table at a busy psychic fair. She was willing to wait for what seemed like a very long time to have an Akashic Record reading. I had never met her before.

Angela was a gifted medium and life coach who regularly worked with people, but she'd been increasingly feeling stuck and out of balance, like there was something she should be doing or needed to learn. She described it as a puzzle piece that was eluding her. As her Spirit guides began feeling distant, she found herself withdrawing and not wanting to tend to anyone else. On the Friday before the fair, she received a clear message from her primary spirit guide (her Great Granny) telling her that she needed to come and see me at the fair and that I could help her with that missing puzzle piece.

When I began by saying the Akashic prayer to open her records, the noise and commotion in the room seemed far away for Angela. She later described waves of fear, pain, and anger surfacing as she was flooded with lots of emotional destruction. In my head, I heard the words *"Trail of Tears"* and knew that Angela had died there in another lifetime. I asked her if she had any connection to this timeframe and she acknowledged that there were several Indian tribes in her family history. She had been told that she came from a long line of medicine women and that her great-grandmother (who was her primary guide) died on the Trail of Tears. She added that this part of history fascinated her and she had always wanted to learn more and explore the real story, but when she tried to read about it or watch a DVD documentary of what occurred she couldn't last more than fifteen minutes before becoming so upset that she had to turn it off.

I knew that Angela was the reincarnation of her beloved great grandmother—the medicine woman so dedicated to her people. When she died, she believed she had failed them and, out of desperation, tried to hold them together by staying with them. Because she remained, the numbers of the earthbound souls kept growing. Here she was in another body, in another time, guided by her own earthbound aspect to reunite them and this time bring them to safety.

We used the Chakra Labyrinth pattern as the portal to release them. She finger-traced the embossed design inside the cover of the *Chakra Labyrinth Cards.*

As the portal opened in the center and the mass exodus began, she described that she had helped souls cross over to the light many times in her own work, but this was different as these souls were partly in the light and also part of her own soul, like little parts that had been lost between worlds. She greeted each one as family and felt them pass through her as they crossed. This was not a lengthy process as the sessions at the fair were restricted to thirty minutes. As we closed, she felt thousands of small but intense pieces of her soul returning to her. She wrote me later and shared with me her continuing experience once she made her way out to her car.

"Going through this process, my emotions were indescribable. I felt an enormous weight was lifted. I sat in my car trying to gather my thoughts and clear my head, trying to clarify to myself what just happened, while at the same time still feeling many spirits around me. As I calmed myself, the parade started. I could see Indians (men, women, children, babies) only they weren't in rags and tatters as in history's recording. They were dressed in their finery. Men, some in beautiful war bonnets or full headdresses, some in turban-style head gear, some with painted faces. Women with beautiful doe-skin beaded outfits—many with beautiful colored shawls or skirts. Children and babies in soft skins or simply covered in red clay or mud. I realized that there were many different tribes besides the Cherokee from many different places all together on this final journey to meet and greet Great Spirit. As the parade continued, many simply nodded at me; others held up their hands and palms to me showing me their thanks. I was honored and blessed to be able to help them and myself.

It was hard, but I had to shut down and release the vision to drive home. However, the closer I got to home, the vision kept trying to creep back up. I kept getting glimpses of the great, happy occasion. The sun seemed to be shining extra hard and bright, directed right at me. When I came to a stop light, I tried to block the sun and the visions with my hand, but all I could see was the happy parade dancing into the sun so I snapped a picture with my cell phone. I wanted to hold this vision with me.

Later that evening I sent the picture to a fellow medium who is very talented at reading photos. She contacted me a bit upset after reviewing the pictures.

She said, 'Angela, why were you driving with half the Indian nation with you? And where were they all going in their finery?' We were able to validate each other's sights from the photo. This was truly a gift for me."

~ Angela C. Blare
   Kansas City, MO

It is not hard to think of individuals throughout our more recent history—those who rose to a position of leadership, or were seen as icons—standing out because they possessed a charismatic quality that spoke to the masses. Some of these souls were targeted when they were living because they didn't conform to the status quo of the *sheeple* mentality, or their influence was perceived as a threat to those who wanted to maintain control. Often they were maligned as an example to the rest of us, and their lives taken because the magnetic power of their influence was seen as a threat. People like Cochise, Geronimo, JFK, Martin Luther King, Bobby Kennedy, John Kennedy Jr., Princess Diana, John Lennon, Bob Marley, Michael Jackson, Prince, and countless others fit this category.

Does having them dead remove their influencing vibration? No, it doesn't, but if they stay here bound by their sense of obligation or longing to set things straight, it can be used against them, to keep them between the worlds acting as a magnet, pulling countless souls to them, who will remain with them in a holding pattern.

We, as the living mass consciousness, can contribute to their *binding* by our judgement, fear, anger, or grief with all of the lower emotions acting like glue, holding onto them, or we can contribute to their freedom with our directed thoughts of love, appreciation, and gratitude for the parts they have played. Offering prayers on their behalf can create an updraft for their release. By their willingness to cross over, they create an energy wave, bringing with them multitudes of souls who are released in their wake.

When large numbers of people die together from things like natural disasters, wars, or genocide, earthbound souls can remain, bonded by the trauma of their joined experience. With massive numbers, it is possible that a revered soul who stays might be serving as a 'linchpin,' holding the entire group together ... which also makes them instrumental in their collective release.

PART

2

The chapters in Part 2 relay my initiation
with one catalyzing 'linchpin' soul.
This encounter felt like a practicum for everything I had learned,
laying the foundation for the deeper work to come.

The Great Birthing

There was a time long ago—look just around the corner of time.

And there in a flash, the souls of all took shape as the Mother
moved within herself.
She moved and flashes of light took shape in every direction.
Each was a spark of the Mother, complete unto itself,
yet forever connected to Her.
And so your journey begins...

Long, long ago a star being, mighty and large, came down from the heavens.
He looked around and fell in love with the roundness of the Earth.
He placed his seeds into the fertile Earth and waited.
Sun and moon shone their light upon Her.
Mother Earth smiled and felt the stirrings within her womb.
She held and nurtured these seeds.
Her joy ran deep and colored the land with glory.
Her soft murmurs were heard in the depths of the sea.
She cradled and sang to these seeds.
And the seeds grew within her,
until a time came when they were ready to emerge.
The mountains shook, the rains came, and She knew the time was near.
She waited.
The great being from the heavens stood near her.
She rested, leaning into the rainbows.
A mist appeared and cloaked the land,
and herein she gathered her energy, preparing for the birth.
Thunder and lightning split the sky and shattered the stillness of the night.
And it seemed it would never end.
Exhausted, she surrendered and allowed the star children to be released into
the world.

A hush fell over all as the beautiful children breathed their first breath.

~ Victoria Putman ~
October 10, 2012 [in Malta]

Sometimes in order to keep moving forward,
you must be willing to look back.

~ G.K. Adams ~

27

THE CURSE AND VOW

While wandering the border between sleep and awake, my attention is drawn to a woman's voice whispering the words *"Sleeping Goddess"* into my ear. Aware that I am hearing this, I pull myself back into the present moment and stumble to the window to witness the rising sun as it stains the sky with the first blush of a long-awaited dawn. January 1, 2012 is here.

The words, still echoing in my head, may have caught me off guard, but they are not completely foreign. Vickie—one of my closest friends, and author of the preceding poem, *The Great Birthing*—has sent me the itinerary for a trip to Malta, home of the world-famous Hal Saflieni Hypogeum where an exquisite 5000-year-old representation of a woman called the 'Sleeping Goddess' was unearthed. A pilgrimage to the islands of Malta and Gozo, situated off the coast of Sicily, is planned for October under the competent leadership of Christine Page and her husband Leland through their organization, *'Frontiers for Health.'

Vickie, who has taken other sacred tours with them, sent the information to me three months earlier with a simple message that said, "What do you think?"

I had closed the email and put the idea aside in a noncommittal, mental folder. But now, with these words surfacing from somewhere in my deep unconscious, I am prompted to find the literal folder and give the information renewed consideration.

Tearing myself away from the red orb in my upper window view, I move to the computer to search my old email files for "The Sleeping Goddess." Within seconds I am reading Christine's enticing description of the trip.

"Why did our ancient ancestors build over fifty megalithic temples on these tiny islands south of mainland Italy? What is the purpose of the deep 'cart tracks' which still crisscross the land after 6500 years? Why are so many of the temples built in the shape of the female body? What is the meaning of the multiple references to bees and beehives? What will awaken the sleeping lady?

On the tiny Mediterranean islands of Malta and Gozo are some of the oldest megalithic sites in the world, most of which are precisely aligned to celestial bodies such as the sun and moon. Many of the buildings are rounded in honor of the feminine and her role as recipient and mother of universal consciousness. Mythology tells that, during the time of Atlantis, Malta was a major portal for divine inspiration to enter the Earth, being energetically transmitted around the globe via the cart tracks. The guardian of the door was known as the Queen Bee. However, prior to the fall of Atlantis, humanity misused their access to the multidimensional realms, causing the door to close and the Queen Bee to fall asleep. It is foretold that the door will only reopen when we meet together in such sacred sites with compassion, joy, and self-awareness. That time is now."

Reading her words, I realize I have just accepted a soul-invitation to be a part of this internal awakening, and my preoccupation with the 'Sleeping Goddess' begins. Seeing images of the oversized woman carved in terra cotta, dreaming on her side, I am compelled to paint her as a non-linear way to flesh out her underlying story.

Christine has already shared her findings, that the 'Sleeping Lady' who was the queen of Atlantis was known both as Astarte and the Queen Bee, residing on the mountains of Malta.

"Astarte acted as an intermediary between the worlds, giving birth to order out of chaos while holding open the door to humanity so it could explore the multi-dimensional universes. However, it became clear that humanity was not willing to be only a spiritual traveler, but wanted to possess the universal power for its own benefits. To prevent further abuse of her gifts, the queen bee

'fell asleep,' thereby closing the door on the flow of new inspiration reaching Earth as well as preventing us from interfering with the natural order of the Universe, until we reached a level of conscious maturity. It is believed that her withdrawal from the world eventually led to the downfall of Atlantis around 9600 BCE." ~ Christine Page

Painting her image is a curious process for me. I place her reclining body in a honeycombed cavern, exploring the 'hive' that supported her, but I also know early into the process that I will be adding something that is not part of the myth. Between the cleavage of her large breasts and from the deep creases in her pleated skirt, I paint golden, liquid light, pouring out of her, cascading down onto the pallet she is resting on and pooling beneath her as expanding ripples that form the paths of a labyrinth. Many of my paintings contain images of labyrinths so, at the time, this does not seem unusual to me. I am also compelled to glue the skin of a boa constrictor to the palate that she is lying on.

Incubating the Dream by Toby Evans—Sleeping Goddess of Malta

By mid-summer, Vickie contacts me, excited about a new energetic modality that she is certified in and offers me a *"Theta Healing' session over Skype. I have no preconceived ideas of what it will entail, knowing only that we will be using muscle testing for verification of my responses. I am mystified when my body responds to a line of statements completely the opposite of how my mind is answering them.

False Belief Statements:
(My body's response)
I have to fight constantly against the evil forces of the Universe—(Yes)
I have to fight the forces of evil—(Yes)
I know how to be safe—(No)
I understand what it feels like to be healthy—(No)
I understand what it feels like to be loved—(No)
I understand what it feels like to have joy—(No)
I understand the Creator's definition of love—(No)
I understand the Creator's definition of love for my human body—(No)
I understand what it feels like to allow someone to love me—(No)
I understand what it feels like to have discernment and love—(No)

When the majority of these statements do not clear using the given protocol, Vickie discovers that there is a 'curse' present, as well as a 'vow' that was made in some other timeframe.

Moving up seven levels to the Theta level of understanding, we ask to see the inception of the curse and the vow. A bizarre story begins to unfold in my mind that sounds more like a Sci-Fi film:

I am transported to an ancient time outside of this planet where the only home I know is aboard a vast, moving craft exploring other worlds. With a Draconian mother and a human father (who I never met, merely chosen for his genetics by my imposing mother), I am a male hybrid 'wanderer' named Zurell. My nomadic life aboard a ship changes paths when my mother arranges my marriage to a woman (Zephra) from Alpha Draconis. Because of her status, I am made a Draco commander in charge of a fleet of five smaller ships. The main objective of the Draconians is conquest—to colonize all planets and star systems by conquering the inhabitants and taking over their territory. In their ruthless pursuit, they begin rounding up humans and hybrids, placing them in designated imprisonment areas. Many bases are set up, with a particularly large one at Rigel, one of the Orion outposts.

Growing more uncomfortable with my expected duties of capturing and delivering the hybrids to the assigned camps, I convince my fleet over time to join a resistance movement. Much like the 'Underground Railroad,' we pick up the prisoners in the guise of transporting them to restricted work camps and deliver them instead into free zones, one of them being through the Sirian portal entering the Earth over the area we now call Malta.

On the day that everything goes sideways and our scheme is exposed, we are doing a routine transfer with prisoners that were housed on the main ship. The guards overhear something one of my men is saying and suspects what is really going on. Challenged to explain, my men fire on the guards. Knowing that everything is unraveling, I order the men to take my eight-year-old son to the exiting ship and go to my wife and teenage daughter telling them that we have to leave. My wife is enraged that I am involved in such treason, and she flat out refuses. In the escalation of the ensuing battle, I leave with my men, and she, along with my daughter, and everyone else aboard the Mothership ... are destroyed.

In the aftermath of this disaster, I make the 'vow' with many others to try to keep Earth sovereign. Because I have been taken into the inner echelon of the Draconians, I am 'corded' with their energy codes. (I'm still not sure what that means, except that it feels like my energy system was 'wired' in some way.) When the other Reptilian bases find out what happened and begin transmitting that I am a traitor, the 'curse' is delivered. They 'unplug' me, which I experience as a blow-out that disconnects my spinal cord. (All higher frequencies within our 'lightbody' are contained within our spinal cord.) I am effectively 'grounded.' I have betrayed and abandoned my Draconian wife and family, and many who trusted and depended on me, causing a schism and havoc in multiple worlds. The guilt, self-blame and remorse are carried forward into this current 'clean-up' lifetime, in an attempt to bring this into balance.

Vickie completes the session by clearing the shock and trauma surrounding this curse, and retrieves my lost soul fragments. She describes the washed and cleansed pieces as rainbow-colored shards which fall into the spaces along my spine and into my kidneys. She marks the karma as complete.

When finding out about this lifetime, I suspect that it may be the underlying reason I am being drawn to Malta—although Zurell's timeframe seems to have happened long before Atlantis.

Side bar:

It takes me another two years before I am ready to examine the destruction scene that I was responsible for. Until then, I do not realize that this aspect of myself (Zurell) has never crossed over. He remains attached to me in what looks like a 'fog bank.'

More pieces come together as I realized that my present-day husband was back then, my wife Zephra. I have had no awareness of the 'daughter' I lost, until I have surgery to remove a bleeding polyp in my uterus. In the middle of the night after recovery, the voice of my daughter comes to life in my head. She informs me that I had agreed to suffer through a miscarriage (thirty years earlier) when I desperately wanted a daughter. This was a soul agreement to re-experience having her torn away from me ... again. I had *asked* to feel the loss in this life because I wouldn't let myself feel anything when I blew the ship apart. She indicates that the rupturing polyp was the body's recording of the guilt and self-directed blame that was bleeding through from both the miscarriage and the deeper wound of the fiery explosion. She pointed out that all the fibroids that were in the walls of my uterus were the energetic manifestations of the countless souls who were blown to bits because of my command.

Her words rang in my head, *"You have a tomb in your womb."*

It isn't until December of 2014, when I receive a Soul Detective Session with Dr. Barbara Stone, that I am able to do the work needed to free Zurell from his self-imposed 'prison.' I perceive the earthbound souls that were involved in the blast as particles floating in space, like drifting debris in an asteroid belt. Zurell is finally able to ask for forgiveness from his wife and daughter as well as to forgive himself. This starts the reassembling process of calling all the scattered pieces back. It is like rewinding a disaster movie of an explosion where the reversal re-orders everything back to wholeness again. With Barbara's help, I am able to gather them as a group (Zurell, Zephra, my daughter, and the entire destroyed ship of souls), and watch them move through the portal, taking the shape of a colossal many-pointed star.

Now ... back to 2012.

After hanging up the phone from the Theta Healing session with Vickie, I go into the labyrinth to clear my head and review what has just been revealed. I sit down in the center with the intention to receive any further guidance about the event. These words begin to flow through me: *You were already told that you made a vow to the Earth upon your arrival here.* (These are words that I received in 1986 and now come flooding back.)

"Far above the boughs of green and emerald Earth
you are free to roam and make your home of peace.
But this must wait for now because of a vow long pledged in love.
To what degree you honor the map that directs your soul,
know that your desire has already made it so.
And the fire will spread until all hearts feel the flames of truth
and urgency you carry forth. The green will wait,
but not forever as you tend to the things of the air.
Then return you will ... upon Earth's hill and welcome those who have
remained the fair.
Do not fear, for you have already succeeded in taking us from here
to there."

The message continues. *"It is because of the vow made in that sector of the world that you joined forces with the other representatives to love, honor, and protect the jewel Gaia and her sovereign souls. Because of the vow, the Draco initiative 'to destroy and conquer' had to be consciously released from your system.*

Going back to Malta, initiated through Vickie via Christine, is a promised return you all made. 'Return you will upon Earth's hill ...' It is the fulfillment of the vow made long ago and it will initiate the birthing of a new 'dream' for each of you. The 'gold essence' of each individual's life force is being activated and coming to the surface to be recognized. The old vows are reopened so your core essence can re-evaluate and flow unencumbered. The 'honey/nectar' of life has always been available and protected, waiting for the shift in awareness that allows it to be harvested.

Just as shards of your energy essence returned today to empower your 'back-up' system, there will be final pieces that come when your physical body stands again on that holy ground. The alignment of this day opens the portal once again to activate your innate rainbow nature and the future assignments that await each of you."

The paths that each of us take through life
are the vehicles through which we awaken.

~ **Hank Wesselman** ~

28

INNER EARTH INCUBATOR

In preparation for Malta, I walk barefoot through the drought-stricken paths of the labyrinth, opening myself to receive inner guidance. I am quietly nudged to resume a visual meditation that I had done every day for a year in 1996. It consists of standing in the center of the labyrinth and envisioning my body as a chalice, open to receive the liquid light pouring down from the Great Central Sun. I would imagine it entering my crown and flowing in a downward spiral through all my chakras, out my feet, tunneling down to the core of the Earth. My focus would then shift to all the waters of the world—oceans, seas, rivers, lakes, springs and underground water domes—the kind that naturally form beneath labyrinths. I'd envision trails from each of them flowing downward, finding their own meandering channels into 'Inner Earth' where they all merge. At that point in the meditation, the flow is reversed, sending the force of the collected waters back up through the tunnel beneath my feet, spiraling up through my chakras and out the top of my head like a fountain. With each exhalation, the diameter of the spray expands until it forms a toroidal field that encircles the entire planet.

I can't say I understand what this does, but it seems related to unification and cleansing. The water is somehow carrying information around the planet. Sixteen years later, in 2012, when we are coming to the end of one global cycle and transitioning into another, a request is being made to reactivate the visualization. Immediately I comply, thinking that it might be helpful for the

Earth and grounding for me.

Standing in the hot August sun, facing the gnarled root that marks the center of the labyrinth, I close my eyes and expect the visualization to proceed as it always had. I spread my arms above my head to embody the chalice, preparing to receive the cascading light. Nothing happens.

I begin thinking something is wrong when an inner voice intercedes, *"Place your focus on the ever-present 'pilot light' within your heart. The light will expand with each breath until you are standing in the middle of your own 'central sun.' The light was never outside of you, but now you are invited to embody this truth."*

Instantly, the 'pilot light' ignites, consuming my body and spreading into my aura, fanning out in all directions. I am aware that it reaches above my crown, touching my *soul-star*. This point is sometimes considered our eighth chakra, found about a foot above our heads. Simultaneously, the energy extends a foot below my feet to the chakra point known as the *earth-star*. All of my attention is drawn beneath the soil. I am reminded that my *earth-star* serves as the grounding cord for my light body.

My vantage point shifts from that of the observer, standing above the scene, to an active participant who—without warning—is whooshing through a light-tube 'waterslide' that dumps into a vast ocean. I find myself comfortably afloat, bobbing like a cork within 'Inner Earth.'

Immersed in my liquid viewpoint, I have the impression that waters all over the Earth are being simultaneously directed into this bottomless cauldron that is serving as an underground incubator. There is a 'knowing' that the waters are different now than they were in 1996, most likely because, as carriers of information, every particle of water is now holding the higher frequencies. The thought hits me that I am floating in rich, 'amniotic fluid' within a protective sac. It is intended to stretch from the inside out, enfolding the Earth and her masses in an invisible membrane designed to nourish our accelerated development.

Everything in this water-world is brilliantly lit. I soak in the perspective of being IN it, instead of above it (a faint reminder of why we all chose to come into these bodies and have the human experience). There is a building pressure beneath me as if I am treading water just above the blowhole of a whale. In an instant, I'm riding the pressured spray up through the pipeline of my access tunnel, forcefully expelled to the surface. Planted back on the ground, my body becomes an extension of the pipeline tubing, sending the exploding light up my chakras in a clockwise spiral and out the top of my head in the familiar, tube-torus fountain. Each time I drag my hands up the midline of my body, circle-sweeping them above my head and then swan-diving them to the ground, the fountain goes out even further until it envelopes the entire Earth. There is a faint sense that the 'umbilical cord' anchored within the Earth's core is being pulled up through this 'light canal,' stretching all the way to the Galactic Center.

(The torus is a geometric shape that allows a vortex of energy to form like a fountain. The toroidal shape is similar to a donut but rather than having an empty central hole, the torus folds in upon itself and all points along its surface converge together into a zero-dimensional point at the center called the Vertex. Everything in existence has a toroidal energy field around it. In the body, the spindle of the torus creates the pranic tube-explained in Chapter 51, "Putting It All Together"—with the Root chakra at the bottom and Crown chakra at the top. According to Itzhak Bentov (scientist, inventor, author, and an early pioneer in the research of consciousness), zero point energy fields contain pure potential which can only be activated by the power of intention. They neutralize harmful frequencies, increase spiritual awareness, and a sense of oneness. When the torus is in balance and the energy is flowing, the perfect state exists to clear ourselves of anything that is 'not self.' Bentov reminds us that "Love is the glue of the Universe.")

Along with resuming the meditation, I accept that I am being prepared on many levels as I meet one afternoon with Shamanic teacher and respected psychic, Shinkara. When I share that I am going to Malta, she tells me that the reason she sees that I am going is to help the 'Sleeping Goddess' cross over. She has a vision of her suspended behind a grid-like latticework, waiting to be assisted. I feel the weight of the responsibility that she is implying and want to push it away. Although I have helped many souls cross over, there is something about this one that I am stepping back from and denying. It just sounds too far out ... even for me. Why would the star-being Mistress, 'Queen of Heaven,' need any help from mere mortals?

When my ego is in self-importance or heavy resistance, it is always beneficial to go within, and open my own Akashic records. Sitting in the center of the labyrinth later with pen to page I find myself engaging in automatic writing, accessing layers beyond my conscious knowing.

"You enrolled in the 'polarity integration' experiment with conviction that you could learn to balance the dark and the light. Balance doesn't come from straddling both sides, but by recognizing and honoring that both are the flip sides of one unit of consciousness, choosing two expressions.

The visualization you are doing is entering the Earth's womb space or 'dream incubator,' no different than what was created in the hypogeum in Malta. They were simulating going into the hollow earth where all potentiality exists to dream their intentions into being. Problems began to occur when the existing power struggles escalated, creating crossed intentions and contaminating the incubator.

In the beginning, 'incubating the dream' in the womb space involved soul travel to communicate and consult with the 'Sun Lords.'

Sun Lords are described by *Maia Chrystine Nartoomid as "The Illumined of our Universal Kindred—from various star systems, yet most prominently from Orion, Sirius and the Pleiades who came to the Earth to aid in the reparation of the human DNA from the damage which had been done by the Nephilim."

The automatic writing went on: *"The soul that Shinkara is picking up on is the one from the Atlantean time frame known as Astarte. She went by other names too (Ashtatara) but the records of her rule have been altered or eradicated. Astarte was a higher-density being, interfacing with the earth population, made up of humans and other-dimensional beings, and hybrids. She lived among them, monitoring their creations while attempting to steer them toward a self-responsible 'service to others' existence. The term you have heard described as a 'soul-net' was put into place at that time."*

'Soul net' or 'soul-catching net' is a concept held by a variety of old and new sources describing an artificial energetic grid that was placed around the

Earth using reincarnation as a revolving door, to create a 'prison planet' that is hard to escape. One of these sources is the *WingMakers Neruda Interview#5* which presents humanity's history as well as a spectacular array of poetry, paintings, and music. Although there is a disclaimer stating that it is fiction, the information rings true to those who are exposed to it. The interview with Dr. Neruda describes how humans came to be trapped inside physical bodies that die. It also describes three separate alien races (the Annunaki, the Serpent Race / Draco, and the Sirians) conspiring together to trick the Atlanteans to inhabit biological vessels. It states that the Annunaki reptilian king took this further by setting up planes of existence to trap the souls, establishing the recycling process. Our DNA was tampered with and our abilities suppressed to keep us in the *Matrix*, unaware of the 'prison guards' and compliant with the imposed sanctions.

In the film series *The Matrix*, the 'soul net' is referenced when Morpheus shows Neo that we are raised as an energy source for the 'controllers.' We generate 'fuel/food' for them through the discharge of our negative emotions that they cleverly work behind the scenes to trigger. Their intent is to keep the Earth as a closed system where people are born without remembering who they really are or what the real situation is.

Information from my Akashic Records continues: *"Astarte was aware of the soul detainment process being put into effect, and began negotiating passage for those who remained quarantined in the lower frequency bands when they died. She was using the inner earth 'dream incubator' as a way to soul travel and confer with the Sun Lords while maintaining her denser body or the version that remained anchored as a placeholder on the Earth.* (This would be akin to placing herself in one of the neural transference pods depicted in the James Cameron movie *Avatar*.)

Astarte began escorting the souls to the Orion 'threshold.' This alone was a bone of contention as the Orion Nebula portal provided passageway—like *a super express wormhole—out of the containment zone and into the beyond. Many forces were vying for control over it. They believed that whoever controlled this 'stargate' would control the galaxy. The 'service to self' league realized that if the detained souls' continued to cross over, the 'controllers' would lose a big part of their 'energy source'—energy obtained by feeding off the fear and despair that had been manufactured and intentionally perpetuated. Astarte's interference was seen as a big problem that needed to be dealt with.*

A loyal aide had been entrusted to monitor Astarte's physical vessel whenever her essence-self traveled unrestricted throughout the galaxies. He was bribed with the promise of advancing his status and enhancing his position if he agreed to take her stasis-self offline. This meant giving her the equivalent of an anesthetic overdose. As the physical connection was severed, she was unable to hold the frequency to the Sun Lords who were trying to assist her. In her confusion and disbelief over what was occurring, she fell in consciousness (or we could say, she fell asleep in suspended animation), caught behind the frequency fence with the throngs of souls she was attempting to free. Her physical form remained in the 'sleeping' posture. The Sun Lords knew they could not interfere. Because the disruption was caused by human betrayal and interference, human intervention is required to free her.

While Astarte was on Malta she served as a go-between, and now others must be this for her. Your method of jumping the 'frequency fence' is by using the sacred geometry of the labyrinth pattern and its counter-rotating fields. It imitates what is occurring in the higher realms as the ever-expanding spirals rotate inward and outward. The created tube torus energy acts like a rocket booster that opens the passageway into the beyond while it provides 'lift' to those souls who are ready to return to wholeness.

'Return you will upon Earth's hill to those who have remained the fair ...' It's helpful for you to view this information in the context of the Inner Earth meditation you are doing, and make the connection of why it needs to be reactivated now. Your role is not that of a 'savior' as no one needs saving. Your job is to realign with Wholeness by stepping out of polarity. Both sides are present in the counter-rotating fields. There would be no change—no charge— no movement possible—without the sacred tension that is simultaneously pulling all of you back and pushing you forward. Your role is to remember and to share—to do what a 'wanderer' naturally does: open closed passageways. There is no such thing as closed. You simply exist by aligning your thoughts on the other side of the obstruction, and the obstruction is non-existent. Meet

yourself there."

Continuing the meditation to 'Inner Earth' on a daily basis, I begin envisioning all the labyrinths around the world being connected to the Inner Earth pipeline.

Input comes in response to this addition. *"Ride your earth-star tunnel to the core, like a meteor breaking into the Inner Earth's sky, and dive into the primordial waters that are being summoned. They respond to the light and come forth to receive it. In this womb space, gestation is occurring. The 'star tunnel' you are creating is a delivery point. The more points of delivery that manifest on the surface* (the more individuals drawing this energy up to the surface through intention)*, the greater the stabilization, uplifting the planetary frequencies."*

The visualization seems like a good distraction from the constant companion of my self-doubt ... which is still questioning why I am involved with helping Astarte cross over. I don't realize then that the visualization has an intricate part to play with my 'assignment' to come.

Authentic Power
is when the personality comes into alignment
to serve the purpose of the Soul.

~ Gary Zukav ~

29

BORDERLAND

Long ago I had to accept that spiritual information comes to me on a 'need to know' basis so it doesn't really surprise me when, while walking the labyrinth for the last time before departing for Malta, I receive the following message:

"All of your aspects are being summoned to this soul gathering. All the 'watchers' know of this quickening. The convergence was ordained to occur and the promise to participate was recorded in the *'Halls of Amenti.'

"You made the pledge in love to assist from the human level because you were there with Astarte when the 'sleep' was induced. Blessed are the handmaidens. As Ochicus, Astarte's personal attendant, you blamed yourself for not seeing the deception and stopping it, bleeding your grief into the cavern. You went to Vickie, who then served as someone overseeing the inner chamber sessions. She was as devastated as you were. You did not take your own life in the typical suicide fashion. You didn't need to. You took your physical form 'offline' in your desire to be with Astarte. By withdrawing your attention from the body vehicle, you were able to step out of it. You chose to remain with Astarte behind the barrier. She stayed in the 'sleep' state while an aspect of you remained in a state of attendance. It was this 'attending' portion that called to you on January 1, 2012, waking you with the words 'Sleeping Goddess.' Because many of your incarnations ended with aspects of yourself remaining earthbound, you have firsthand experience knowing the feeling of

separation that is induced. It has shaped your present interest and involvement in assisting others. You have seen through your work that 'separation' is seldom outwardly imposed by someone else. The 'controllers' simply replay the emotional upheaval reel, knowing exactly where your Achilles' heel lies. They step back as you exercise your free will to choose to stay behind the 'frequency fence' in a non-deserving, justified state. Yet containment serves its purpose for those who want the experience of restriction in order to focus.

Astarte remained 'asleep' by choice, waiting for your present planetary evolution. Gone are the locks that can keep her in a suspended state of futility and hopelessness. There are no restrictions that can paralyze your soul orders. Your human resolution to serve at this time allows the effortless dissolution of the barriers. You curse the 'defects' of your human frailties and doubts, but those defects forge notches of compassion and humility into the key, supplying access codes that can reset the locked areas.

Astarte will be escorted to the 'borderland' where you will come into her awareness. Your voice will re-key her lock.

'Lift up your gossamer wings to the sky. It's time to open, it's time to fly. Follow the circles your heart-song intones. Unwind the golden thread to find the passageway Home.' (This line is from a song I wrote entitled "Call to the Feminine." I understand from these words that I am to sing the song to her when the time comes.)

Knowing that she is loved ... it will be felt by her. The feeling is the freeing. We who serve as her 'Sisters of Hope' will assist as forces gather at the Gozo site. You are returning home to bring us home to ourselves. 'Being between worlds' is the mode of travel that will serve you throughout this journey.

The center portal of the Prairie Labyrinth is now connected and calibrated to resonate with the portals that you will be creating there. If you question or need support, just link back to this 'root' portal. It will enable you to walk on solid ground as worlds shift beneath your feet."

Closing my journal, I kneel down at the base of the center post and dig in the dirt to uncover a sacred artifact that I put there many years earlier upon returning from Peru. The smooth iron stone looks like a petrified donut except the outer edges are scalloped. My fingers close around them as natural finger-grips, pressing the solid weight of it into the palm of my hand. The stone is an ancient representation of the tube torus and I want it with me as a 'touchstone,' reminding me of my connection to the portal in the center of the prairie.

I choose to walk straight out of the labyrinth instead of taking the meandering paths. This is to intentionally keep the energy open. Doing so is like leaving the computer on in my office so I can access 'files' from far away.

Getting to Malta means we have to choose a larger city to fly into that will accommodate the Maltese Islands. Of the twenty-seven free spirits who are being called to assemble for this adventure, I only know Vickie and a dear friend Carol (who is part of the Labyrinth Society), and together we decide to fly into Rome. We have about an eight-hour layover on the way to Malta, and an overnight stay on our return leg fifteen days later.

Of all the things one might hope to see in Rome, the main draw for me is the *Piazza del Campidoglio*. In 1538, Michelangelo was commissioned to revive the Capitoline Hill area which entailed redesigning the plaza and the buildings surrounding it. My interest is not in the architecture of his buildings, but in the focal point of his pavement design that all the buildings are situated around. It consists of a twelve-vesica star, laid out as a continuous walking path. It is the inspiration for Alex Champion's adaptation, installing the nine-vesica star pattern in my back yard, the pattern that I call Chante Ishta. With Vickie and Carol agreeing to search for it, we are open to whichever leg of the trip brings us the opportunity to walk it.

Within an hour of landing, we are climbing up the sweeping staircase called *The Cordonata* leading to Capitoline Hill. At the top of the steps on either side we are greeted by the statues of the Dioscuri (Gemini Twins) and their horses. With Castor to the left and Pollux to the right, we enter Michelangelo's portal design by passing between 'the protectors of Rome.'

It is surreal to be standing here in what once was the symbolic center of ancient Rome. I am suddenly aware of the perfection of starting our journey in this location and am clear about what we are here to do: open the portal by walking the design. We begin to wind our way through each of the twelve vesicas in a counter-clockwise fashion, drilling the energy down and calling out to all the accompanying Higher Selves to start assembling the souls, preparing them to use the amassing energy ... to cross over.

The interlaced, twelve-pointed star pathways revolve around the center space called *Caput Mundi*. This is Latin for 'head/center of the world'—which of course was a statement on how they regarded Rome. This design takes longer to walk than my much smaller version at home. In the slight depression of the center's twelve-pointed star stands a pedestal with a larger-than-life, bronze, equestrian statue of Marcus Aurelius. From the tourist's quizzical looks, I assume that most people regard the pattern of elliptical paths as decorative and not as a design to interact with. It doesn't have a clear entrance point like a labyrinth, but with the continuous paths, it gives you the freedom to step into the ever-evolving *seed of life* motif, beginning and ending where you choose.

When we return to our beginning point, Carol, who understands the process, checks in with Vickie and me by asking, "And now we walk the whole thing again, but in the clockwise direction. Right?"

I feel into what is occurring on the etheric realm before answering, "No. We're done. It has to stay open for the work we are to do in Malta."

In my mind's eye, I am aware of a huddled group of women in another dimension who inform me in hushed tones, *"It's begun. We are moving her to the borderland."*

Everything changes
when you start to emit your own frequency
rather than absorbing the frequencies around you,
when you start imprinting your intent on the universe
rather than receiving an imprint from existence.

~ Barbara Marciniak ~

30

MOSTA DOME

osta comes from the old Maltese word *mistur* (meaning hidden). Situated in the middle of Malta, the town of Mosta may someday reveal what researcher and native-born temple expert *Francois Xavier Alosio believes: that there are additional prehistoric sites still hidden beneath this soil. He contends that this includes a hypogeum bigger than the known existing ones, with its center somewhere beneath the main attraction in Mosta. This is a huge, round church with the third largest unsupported dome in the world. The Mosta Dome is said to have the greatest vibrational energy on the island of Malta (perhaps because of the energetics that still lie beneath it). Those energies may have helped shield it from an afternoon air raid on April 9, 1942 when two bombs bounced off the building while a third one (a 200-kg Luftwaffe bomb) dropped through the dome among a congregation of more than 300 people and did not explode.

This church was built over a prehistoric site using the same principles as the temples. The energy on Malta represents the yang (+), positive, protons, or masculine polarity while the island of Gozo holds the yin (-), negative, electrons, or the feminine polarity. From a spiritual perspective, the incoming male energy is thought to be generated at the center point of the Mosta Dome. What better way to start our exploration of the megalithic temple sites dedicated to the Great Mother, than by being initiated by the strongest male energy on these islands?

Our thirty-member tour group is swallowed up upon entering the massive structure. Swarming pods of people are circumnavigating the round interior, moored to their guides with headsets dialed to languages that can decipher the murmuring babble.

Dizzy from the surge of energy that I feel pulsing through me, I quickly sit in the last row of chairs, hardly aware that I plunked myself down in another group's lecture. The mix of multiple dialects becomes part of the background hum, fueling the generator known as *The Rotunda of Light.

The nave of the church is roped off to the public, blocking access to the power point of the center. Directly below the dome on the floor is a marble tile pattern of an eight-pointed star. It is surrounded by rings of petals representing the Yin and the Yang in alternating shades of dark and light. Diamond cut points in progressed proportions radiate out from these rings, sending the energy in all directions. Both the ceiling and the floor portray the radial movement of the tube torus with the Yin energy coming up and out from the center and the Yang energy, flowing inward and down. Sacred Geometry makes up the entire building, uniting the upper and lower worlds. The hole in the sky dome is framed with 32 petals, elevating and expanding our consciousness to open to the infinity of the Cosmos.

If ever there was a place to commune with an aspect of my inner masculine energy, this is it. Still feeling lightheaded and aware that my hand is shaking, I put my pen to the page of my journal and give myself over to *Zurell's* energy signature.

"I was a commander of fleets, broken by the loss of loved ones, believing I was responsible, believing I failed—only to realize that all was (and is) as it should be to allow for everyone's soul growth and depth of experience. I enter your heart space more fully aware of the balance you desire. I can assist you more consciously now, helping you align with your fearless nature. Being fear-less is when you feel fear, but relate to it with so much spaciousness and compassion that you turn it over to the part of you that is inherently unafraid. With an open heart, you are able to respond with the expanded awareness of stability and composure. Being fear-full is when fear consumes you, contracting your spirit in paralysis, squeezing pure awareness out of the equation, rendering you helpless. Failure is an illusion that is born from

Fear's judgement. It can be used to destroy and sink your spirit, or as a rudder to right your ship.

Carry me with your shoulders erect. You called to me early in your life using my presence to press forward. I flood you today with a new level of integration. All power has to be tempered with compassion. Think of the distance you have come—from the timid child who was self-conscious and so full of doubt. It may seem to you that you still double guess yourself, but know... this is just an echo from our joined past.

Allow me to align your spinal column, to infuse my energy into your nervous system. Allow it to rise and radiate outward to fill this dome—to fill the sky with your commitment to serve. Serving is showing up—enough to fully feel, experience, and express. The dome is not just overhead; it surrounds you, it is beneath you. There is no up or down. You are in the egg of existence. Send your golden rays out to all corners of the firmament."

Closing my journal, I realize the church has all but cleared out and only our group remains. Our guide has secured permission for us to unhook the dividing rope and walk up the center aisle to stand in the magnificence of the marble star that marks the center. Tentatively, we make our way forward to stand encircled, becoming a living extension of the floor's radiating rings.

Christine tells us that we will each have a moment to step into the middle as a human antenna, connecting Heaven and Earth. She makes the suggestion that we bring energy down from above, up from below, and then send it out to each of the four directions.

When it is my turn to step into the middle, I take my torus touchstone out of the left pocket of my jeans and place it on the floor in the center of the star. My intent is to link up the energy of this power spot with the center of my labyrinth at home. Standing over it with my feet apart, I raise my hands above my head, re-enacting my familiar ritual to become the chalice that receives the in-pouring light. Bringing the energy down through my body, I bend to the floor in a forward-fold motion sending the energy down to Mother Earth. Pausing here, I open to the Earth energies and begin scooping the light from far below. In the process of rising, I deliberately drag my hands up the inside of my legs, up the midline of my body, up over my face and out the top of my head, releasing them with a wide-open gesture, expecting to feel my fingers flick the air. Instead, the silver and turquoise ring on my finger hits hard metal, ramming into an ornate and monstrous incense burner that hangs suspended above us with chains that go all the way to the center of the dome. A loud, clanging sound reverberates all the way up the chain as the burner sways like a swinging chandelier. We all gasp. I have no idea how it is even possible to reach this. I am not that tall, but perhaps Zurell has had his 'hand' in this. A bit shaken, I finish sending the energy to the four directions, trusting that surely some kind of signal has just been sent out to 'all corners of the firmament.'

The traveler sees there are many paths
through the forest,
but only the experienced guide
knows the way of least resistance.

~ **Ed McDonough** ~

31

FOLLOW THE MOON

Victoria, as the capital, is considered the heart of Gozo, but at the heart of Victoria lies 'The Citadel'—the feminine energy counterpart to the Mosta Dome in Malta. It is said that these two locations bring together the positive and negative charge of the Universe. The Citadel has its own 'pericardium' (the tough, double layered membrane which covers the heart in the human body). The protection here comes in the form of massive walls built by the Knights of St. John, making the Citadel a historic, fortified castle and town. It's built on the site where a Roman temple once stood dedicated to Juno, an ancient Roman goddess who was a protector and special counselor of the state and who (fittingly enough) looked after the women of Rome.

After experiencing the buzzing electromagnetics of the Mosta Dome, I am prepared to be 'blown away' by the charge in this Cathedral, but that is not the case. Perhaps it is because I am on overload with processing all the temple sites on Malta, or perhaps it's because I am still making the adjustment of switching hotels and taking a ferry from one island to another, but the plain fact is that I don't feel any circuit being completed here. To me, although beautiful—and VERY protected—it is just an impressive church, steeped in layers of history and shrouded behind veils of mystery. Behind all of its well defended walls, I am cut off from hearing the voice of the feminine.

With our luggage transferred from Malta to our new accommodations on Gozo, Vickie and I find our way to a corner room at the top of the stairs on the second floor. From the walkway balcony where we stand fumbling with our key, we can see the vast expanse of the horizon flowing into the Mediterranean Sea.

Our first night is spent with little sleep as we try to adjust to the harder beds and the new environment with strange smells and sounds, including a rumbling air conditioner. By 4:30 a.m. I hear Vickie push her covers back and slide open the screen door. This is followed by the unexpected sound of suitcase wheels rolling over the ceramic walkway. Wondering what is going on, I turn on the light and move to the door to find Vickie standing on the balcony, looking out at the sky. She tells me that she can't sleep, but the suitcase was someone else leaving. We stand in silence, mesmerized by the waning slice of the crescent moon, so radiant that we can see the illumination of the whole sphere. The blanket of the night sky—sequined with the jewels of the Big Dipper, Cassiopeia, Sirius, Orion's belt, and the Pleiades—tucks me into the feeling that, no matter how far away or distant this place may seem, I am connected by this overarching view to my own backyard.

Vickie turns to me, "Well, if we can't sleep, what should we do?"

I don't have to give this much thought. "Let's go walk. We can follow the moon."

Hastily pulling on our clothes, we leave the Cornicopia Hotel in darkness and head out into the narrow streets that wind up a steady incline towards the center of the small village of Xaghra. Gozo is more traditional than Malta, and life moves at a slower pace. Having no destination and no sense of direction, it is nice to be observers in a country that appears to have no connection to the present time. The random alleyways we are winding through are empty until a door opens from a side street and a young woman steps out to briefly greet her girlfriend. They giggle with heads drawn together and take off at a fast walking pace, showing us that Gozo is still in step with those in the world who get up early to exercise.

Growing between the buildings are patches of wild fennel. I pinch the tips of the flowers and put the seeds in my mouth, delighted that the licorice flavor is so much richer than the fennel I have in my spice cabinet. Stepping out of my usual routine and inhaling the cool crisp air seems to have heightened my senses.

Our wandering leads us into the center of a small market area. We see a bakery, not yet open, with a man unloading fresh goods from his delivery truck. Local store fronts create a promenade leading us to the main attraction commanding the plaza. This is the local parish church, the Basilica of the Nativity of the Virgin Mary. We know in this predominantly Catholic country that there is a high concentration of churches (313 in Malta and 46 in Gozo). Low tones from unified praying voices are amplified by the building's acoustics, drawing us nearer.

Vickie turns to me, "There is a mass going on. Let's go in and be part of this." Going to mass is not an experience I think I need to have, but we were obviously pulled here and, if we want to fully submerge ourselves in their culture, this is the best way to do it. With my mouth still full of fennel seeds, we slip in through a side door and find a pew in the back section of the church. The Maltese language reminds me of my childhood when the masses were still said in Latin. The people around us are private, but kind. Even though it is obvious that we are strangers, we feel welcomed into their ornately decorated 'home' covered with marble. One of their treasures is an incredible statue of the young Virgin Mary that was brought all the way from Marseille, France in 1878.

When it comes time for communion, I hesitantly follow Vickie up the aisle, worried that the priest is going to place the wafer on my tongue as I frantically try to swallow the remnants of the remaining fennel seeds. When he places it in my hand, I am relieved that they have forsaken this old practice (even in Gozo) and relax into the ritual of receiving 'the body of Christ.'

Enlivened by the time we exit the church, we are not ready to end our adventure so we reestablish the moonlight as our guide and walk in the opposite direction of our starting point. A short time later, we come to a large map posted under a street light that informs us that we are now in a different locality. Our attention is drawn to a huge hole under the sidewalk in a triangular shape where the earth is dug away, surrounded and sectioned off by protective railings. To the right of this 'construction zone' there is a bigger oblong hole with the same kind of railings surrounding it. We surmise that they are possibly there to keep people from falling in. Intrigued by the hole, we slip under the railing for a better look and begin toning and making sounds, listening to hear our answering echo. Our approach is lighthearted, even though the depth of the dark pit is a bit unsettling. I push the eerie feeling away. Stepping back onto the sidewalk, I notice that there is an official-looking copper sign mounted at the edge of the sidewalk. Straining to make out the words in the pre-dawn darkness, we laugh at the irony when we are able to read that this is part of the Xaghra Ggantija temple sites where a collection of prehistoric bones, figurative sculptures, and symbolic artifacts have been found.

Beyond the cave, the moonlight reveals a faint pathway bordered by an old wall made from gathered stones. We pick our way along the snaking rubble wall lined heavily with fennel and interspersed with prickly pear cactus and other scrub bushes. The feeling is odd, like we are being watched but not threatened. When we reach a place where the path seems to end at a higher stone wall, we decide to turn around and find our way back to the hotel before the sun starts to rise.

This place where you are right now,
God circled on a map for you.

~ Hafiz ~

32

FIRST WAVE OF SOULS

"Return you will upon Earth's hill ..." The phrase runs through my head like a mantra as we near the place where I speculate that in the long ago I made my pledge to assist the Earth and to someday 'return.' With little sleep, it feels like we have already put in a full day when we arrive at the Ggantija temple complex at the end of the Xagħra plateau. In Maltese, Ggantija means *giants*, *tower*, or *grotto*. According to an ancient legend, the temple walls were built in one day and one night by a female giant named *Sunsuna* who, in 'Wonder Woman' fashion, built it while nursing a baby.

Facing the south-east, this Neolithic monument is really two temples, built side by side and surrounded by a common wall which reaches up seventeen feet high. The oldest section predates the pyramids and Stonehenge by hundreds of years. The round, curved architecture of the temples characterizes their dedication to the Great Mother as a place of prayer and healing, and there is evidence that it was also used as an oracle, much like that at Delphi.

As I enter the main interior passageway of the older temple, my eyes are drawn to the highest section of the far boundary wall where I see a rising ridge of stacked boulders. Captured in stone is the distinct suggestion of two ancient figures guarding the temples. On the left is a male reptilian-like winged being, with an elongated body pressing forward and leaning in to kiss the giant human female. She stands upright, apart from him, her head slightly tilted back, meeting his embrace. I can't take my eyes off of them, moved by the union of all that it represents to me: the integration of polarities, the acceptance of diversity, the origin of human and non-human races coming together to seed a new world.

I take a small quartz crystal out of my pocket with the intent to push it into a rock that I am leaning against as an offering.

A message is swiftly sent in response, *"No. You are here to receive. You are here to reclaim your bigness."*

Feeling pretty small in that moment, the voice fades and I am left to sit in the energy of these ancient stone beings, filling up in wonder.

Just outside the temple grounds, there is a local woman selling her wares. She has her young adult son assisting her in making change and packaging the items. Members from our group are swarming her tables where she has laid out beautiful shawls and scarves crocheted by members of her family using unusual thread made from tiny squares of silk material. Many are making purchases knowing the quality of these items. I find two shawls and buy them without hesitating. As the group begins to reassemble and starts making their way back to the bus, I run my hands through the piles once more, picking up a scarf that reminds me of my dear friend Alyse back home. The colors dazzle me and I decide that it is perfect for her. I tell the woman I will take it as well as two postcards.

She hesitates and chokes up a bit. *"You don't need to pay for the postcards. You have already done enough."*

When her tear-filled eyes meet mine, I am bewildered, but touched to the depths of my soul. Something breaks open inside of me and I find myself holding her as we both cry. I am not sure what is being exchanged in this moment except that she feels like my long-lost sister.

She mumbles in my ear, *"I cannot thank you enough for returning. I don't know how to thank you ... Thank you for coming back."*

Her son packages up my scarf and takes my money, confused by our interaction. My logical mind tells me that she is thankful that I would make one more purchase, helping her sales that day, but my heart knows there is more to this soul-recognition between us. In my mind's eye, I try to place her as part of the temples in the ancient times when she may have known me as Astarte's handmaiden, or even earlier as the fallen commander (Zurell) making the pledge to return. The only thing that seems certain is she is one of those *who has remained the fair.*

Catching my breath on the short bus ride, the group arrives at the Xaghra Stone Circle, also called the Brochtorff Circle named for local artist Charles de Brohtorff who recorded the excavation site in 1830. His watercolor depictions show that there was an above-ground stone circle with two huge megaliths that served as the threshold with steps leading down into the caves. At the center was an altar-like structure with a massive trilithon. Stone slabs were used as walls to divide the natural caverns and niches. Most of these are gone now and replaced by a modern field wall. Because we came in through a different entrance enclosed by a ten-foot-tall wire fence, it takes a moment to recognize this as the opposite side of the field wall where, just hours ago, Vickie and I were standing at the turn-around point on our moon-lit walk.

No one ever refers to this place by the name *The Xaghra Hypogeum,* and with an untrained eye you would never know that this area had any prehistoric significance. We walk to the edge of an irregular depression of stones that resembles the aftermath of a small meteor hitting the ground. The low-lying rubble of rough, coralline limestone is now overgrown with bushes and weeds. On the surface, the gaping hole is somewhat contained by a skewed circle of bigger boulders lying in juxtaposition around the edge. Our guide tells us that bodies have been uncovered here and that this has been used as a burial site, but the full extent of this is understated. Our group is quietly respectful. No one wants to climb down into the exposed areas of the grassy hole so most of us are milling around the upper outer rim. I am drawn to sit in a depression on a large flat stone, angled at an incline above the hole with my eyes closed to tune into this subdued energy.

Receiving the strong guidance to begin moving souls on from this place, I trace the path of the labyrinth in my mind, superimposing the seven-circuits over the gigantic hole. When I reach the center, I send out an invitation to all the Higher Selves of the souls who are ready to cross over. A rapid transformation occurs as a steady stream of light beings morph into departing star tetrahedrons that continually rise and evaporate. As a bystander I observe this from a distance, staying far enough back to feel detached and removed from the repetitive process that continues to play out the entire time our group paces or sits as guards around the perimeter. Thirty minutes later, I withdraw my attention when it is time to leave. I have no concept or attachment to the numbers that have chosen to make their exit.

Much later, I learn that the excavation of this area between 1987 and 1994 revealed that this was one of the largest prehistoric burial assemblages of human remains discovered in the Mediterranean, amounting to 220,000 bones that belonged to anywhere from 450 to 800 skeletons. This was a sacred site for the dead, positioned in the middle of the Ggantija temple complex. The findings indicate that this was not a cemetery, but a powerful ritual site where dead bodies were brought intact before the parts were separated and redistributed. This ritualistic process was called *deconception* (the opposite of conception) by one of the scientific experts, *Dr. Stoddart. He didn't determine why or how they died, except to say they were not killed by a disease, but he did note that the majority of the population consisted of young adults—slightly more males than females—who had not reached maturity.

The study explained that the Xaghra Stone Circle was a walled enclosure surrounding a natural subterranean cave system that was adapted using much older megalithic structures. It was uncertain if the time period was before or after the carved, subterranean, Hal Saflieni Hypogeum on Malta.

In the early afternoon, the bus takes us as far as the Ta' Cenc Hotel on the South coast of Gozo where we walk an undetermined distance along a dusty, rutted road following the Ta' Cenc Plateau. In search of a small, obscure dolmen, it feels like we are looking for a 'needle in a haystack' which, in our case, happens to be a large agave shrub that is an identifying land mark. Picking our way among varieties of cactus and wild flowers, we stumble along the rugged rock terrain, over some of the famous cart ruts—a huge network of deep, parallel tracks cut like troughs into the limestone outcrops, found all over Malta and Gozo. We are treated to a panoramic view of the Sea.

Christine's voice rings out that our guide has found the dolmen. Gathering in our scattered search party, we collectively stand before an unimposing dolmen which consists of a large slab propped up by three small stones. The dolmen itself is not nearly as impressive as the alignment it forms with the

Xewkija Church and the Ggantija/Xaghra complex. It is the junction-point of this ley line, forming a 'line of sight' alignment across the island of Gozo.

The Xewkija Church, dedicated to St. John the Baptist and known as the Rotunda Church, is another domed church like the Mosta Dome in Malta, but this one was built on a site where a large dolmen once stood. According to a *local guide book that claimed that, up until the seventeenth century, the large dolmen had a fifteen-foot square capstone and four uprights of about five and a half feet high. The capstone was incorporated as part of the church's foundation, along with other assorted stones including a twenty-five-foot *menhir* (a large upright-standing stone).

Spreading out from the dolmen, we each choose a nearby stone where we plant ourselves, creating a human standing-circle. Toning together, we use the focus of the dolmen's low-lying portal to project sound down into the grid, unblocking the clogged areas where souls are stuck or holding on, refusing to cross over. Energetically, the underworld in this entire area feels like a backed-up sewer system where all the ancient pipes need to be snaked out and unplugged. As an extension of the work that was started at the Xaghra Circle, you could say that we are priming the pump.

When I heard the bell ring,
suddenly, there was no 'I' and no 'bell',
just the ringing.

~ Zen Master ~

33

VOICE OF THE FEMININE

From our morning balcony view, we watch the thunderclouds roll in, blackening the horizon over the Mediterranean Sea. The changing skyline rearranges our return plans to Malta. We were to take speedboats to the island of Comino, part of the Maltese archipelago, situated like a small stepping stone (measuring only 1.35 square miles) between the islands of Malta and Gozo. With our swimsuits under our clothing, we were excited about being whisked to the Blue Lagoon—a picturesque bay known for its white sandy beaches and crystal clear waters. But the native people take stormy weather on the islands seriously because they know how quickly it can turn treacherous.

We opt to take the ferry back to Malta, as it is safer than the speedboats. Because it departs later in the day, we find ourselves with extra time on Gozo and decide to visit the Rotunda Church in Xewkija. This is the massive domed structure that towers over the Gozo countryside in perfect alignment with the dolmen. By this part of the trip, I have had my fill of churches and want nothing more than to have a day in the cyan waters, but acknowledging that the hand of serendipity (or perhaps the goddess) arranged this window of time, I let go of my attachment to how the day should unfold and open to what awaits us.

Xewkija (a Maltese and Arabic name meaning *thistles* or *thorns*) is the oldest village on the island dominated by the newest church. Constructed by local masons and craftsmen using Maltese stone, it was built around the former church (creating a church-within-a church) on the same site as an even older chapel and over the ancient dolmen ruins that were incorporated into the existing structure. The community, made up of farmers and fishermen, made a weekly offering beginning in 1952, sacrificing their wages for 20 years to raise the enormous Rotunda. We are intrigued to step into this eight-sided edifice corresponding to the eight points on a compass and the eight dominant winds. An octahedron comes to mind.

The spacious interior, washed with the light of the pervasive yellow limestone, is a breath of fresh air. It stands in contrast to the ostentatious display of wealth that we have seen in other churches, lavished in gold-gilded adornments with paintings and fabric that hold heavy layers of history (along with possible soul attachments).

This might not be swimming in the Mediterranean, but it is clean and clear energy that is as easy to soak up as sunlight. At the center of the marble tile floor is a sixteen-pointed star. The eight-pointed star of the *Maltese Cross* or the *Cross of the Knights of Malta*, with the additional points, creates a three-dimensional effect. It is aligned directly beneath the round skylight of the expansive dome. The diamond-cut marble tiles are similar to the pattern on the floor of the Mosta Dome, directing the energy out into the grid, radiating like sunrays to touch every point on the island. I take a deep breath, noting that even though the Citadel is the physical place on Gozo where the feminine energy is said to reside, for me it is *this* spot that is the energetic counterpart to the Mosta Dome.

We are greeted by an exuberant pastor who is delighted to have a captive audience to showcase his people's proud achievement. One of the things he encourages us to do is to take the 'lift' (located in the sacristy) up several floors to a walk-around balcony that surrounds the dome. Here you can see the original church that the new structure was built around, from a bird's eye view. Several of us head in that direction, halted by a nun (who was surely a commanding general in some other lifetime) informing us that there is a fee to be 'elevated' as well as a limit to how many can be in the 'lift' at the same time. As five of us pay and are squeezing into the small space, Christine comes back and tells us that the weather has cleared and we are leaving immediately to catch the speedboats for the Blue Lagoon. As we protest that we have already paid, she tells us to go ahead but that no others will be following.

Quickly perusing the eight sides of the upper structure and taking in the expanded view, I come upon a spiraling metal staircase leading to the bell tower. The others are ready to find their way back to the lift, so I tell them I will be right behind them after I check out the tower. The logical (male) part of me questions why this is necessary, in light of the urgency to get to the speedboats, but I surrender to the intuitive (feminine) impulse directing me to climb to the top.

Aware of my labored breathing and the stinging burn in my quads, I make the last tight turn, pulling myself up the remaining steps just as I glimpse the giant clapper of the bell swinging into action. It reverberates against the metal sides with a deafening GONGGGGG. Holding my hands over my ears, I laugh out loud, descending as fast as I can move. The cells of my body are a magnified current vibrating with a growing charge that begs to be grounded.

It seems incredible that, at the Mosta Dome, the energy was sent up the chain of the incense burner to reach the top of the dome, and here the energy, originating at the top, is rushing to the ground. When the door to the 'lift' opens, I run across the empty church and down the front steps, feeling like Cinderella at the stroke of midnight, racing to catch her coach. The ringing 'voice' of the feminine obliterates all other thoughts, all other sounds. In the midst of the humming resonance, I feel the 'siren' of the goddess calling us to her sacred dwelling place in the Sea.

It is hard to believe that the sea-foam waters we are now skimming across had tornados touching down on them just hours earlier. We arrive in perfect weather, hot and sunny with clear blue skies. The rocky island of Comino (named after the cumin seed that was once as plentiful on Malta as the fennel that now grows) is a nature reserve and a bird sanctuary. There is no need for roads here with only four permanent residents keeping it pollution-free in the absence of cars. One of the tourist attractions is the trek up a prominent pathway on a steady climb leading to St. Mary's Tower. This is a structure built by the Knights of Malta in 1618 to fend off the pirates who frequently used the many caves, cliffs, and coves of Comino to stage raids on boats crossing between Malta and Gozo. Later, in the sixteenth and seventeenth centuries, the island served as a prison where knights who committed minor crimes were exiled. They were sent to man the isolated Tower from the highest point on the island.

I notice the steps leading to the switchback pathways, but the Tower is not my destination. Climbing out of the speedboat, I am mesmerized by this secluded inlet paradise, drinking in the most vibrant turquoise-aqua water I have ever seen. Our speedboat captain tells us that, if we choose to swim, it is safest to stay within the roped area. He indicates with his pointed finger that the tow is stronger beyond the strung together buoys. He will be back to pick us up in a couple of hours.

Dazzled by the pristine beauty, I shuffle my feet through the white sand to a small, contained pocket-cove off to the left side of the main beach. The inviting wading pool gives me the option to acclimate (and make sure I am not dreaming this) before full submersion. Like so many of the temples that have *libation holes* or perforations designed for offerings or cleansing before entering the main passageway, the subtle placement of this purification pool off to the side of the entry feels intentional. With the water up to my neck, I am ushered through a natural easement before being released into the deep, hypnotic waters of the Blue Lagoon. Thousands of fluid fingers massage my muscles as every cell stands at attention, tingling with heightened awareness.

Across the bay, the long-outstretched arm of a limestone ridge reaches out into the water, cradling the inlet cove. There is a missing chunk in the middle of the landmass like a shattered elbow, revealing the open sea just beyond the protective cliff. To the right of this missing section, low-lying scrub-brush gives way to a well-worn path rising through the rocky terrain used by hikers to scramble up to the highest point where they can gaze out at Malta and look behind to see her sister land of Gozo.

Below this section of the rugged cliff lies the islet of Cominette. The main portion is a small patch of beach rolled out like a white sand prayer rug lying before the opening of a wide mouth cave. At first glance this looks like a deep black cavern, but squinting reveals a jagged slice of blue lightning pouring in from the furthermost point. When I grasp that the crack is the wavering blue reflection of the incoming waters from the opposite side gushing through this tunnel, the power of its magnetic pull is beyond my resistance. I calculate the distance across the bay, knowing I am not a great swimmer.

I look to a friend who is luxuriating in the water next to me and tentatively inquire, "How good of a swimmer are you?"

Indifferently she answers me, "Good enough to be on my college diving team." Somehow this gives me the safety net I need for my own assurance. I tell myself that she will be nearby if I get into trouble. Wearing a visor and sunglasses, I set out with the intention of keeping my head above water, alternating between the breast stroke and a side stroke. I am aiming for the ropes that I need to go beyond. When I make it to the welcome mat of the beach, I feel triumphant that I have pushed past my own fears while also realizing that no one else from our group is here yet.

The sound of the pounding water draws me to the cave where I stand in reverence, peering into the protected cavern of the Great Mother's womb. The tide from the wide-open sea rushes through the long birth canal, smashing into the cervical barrier of rocks where I tentatively stand. The roar of the feminine voice is amplified in this passageway. As an embryo soul, I lower myself carefully into the water, attaching my back to the wall of the battered rocks like a clinging barnacle, waiting for my own process of gestation. A short while later, others from our group arrive. With bravery in numbers, we push away from the side walls to be lifted up—body surfing in the amniotic fluid that suddenly reminds me of returning to the waters of Inner Earth.

In this corridor of incubation, we find ourselves treading water beneath the ancient stone lining of the high uterine ceiling. Enraptured as a group of developing fetuses, we compulsively offer the only authentic communication that is appropriate in a sound chamber. That happens to be singing interspersed with primal sounds of harmonious and dissonant toning. We are content to float and bob for an undetermined period of time, undulating to the echoing acoustic waves responsible for the rhythmic heartbeat pulsing through this ancient sanctuary.

I swim the length of the tunnel towards the opposite end where the water gets deeper and the waves are higher until the piercing blue sky opens above me. Here, I give myself permission to turn around and not entirely leave the cave walls as I realize that, just outside the opening, the tow is strongest which makes it harder to get back safely.

Each one of us imprints the memory of this in-utero retreat before we leave the cave and start back across the bay. Halfway there I can feel the fatigue in my body. Straining to keep my head above the water, I tell myself I have to tough this out even if my endurance is waning, and then I silently ask for help to give me the energy I need to make it back.

A simple suggestion drifts up to my consciousness: *"Turn over on your back and float."*

I resist this idea, because I am nervous about losing my sunglasses and hat, and thus far my dog paddle/breast stroke has worked well to 'keep my head above water.'

As I continue to struggle, the words are repeated again. *"Turn over on your back and float."*

I let out a sigh, no longer needing to prove anything to myself or others... no longer needing to do this alone. Turning over, I arch my back, stretch my arms above my head, and fall into what surely must be the mermaid's dream of home. I am able to release my resistance, my vanity, and my fear. My entire body is lifted up with my underbelly fully exposed to the cerulean blue sky. In my vulnerability, I have never felt as strong or as buoyant. All tension and tightness dissolve. The weight of my body working against itself is gone. Tears come to my eyes as I am held in the arms of the Great Mother, feeling only her unconditional love and protection.

A rush of gratitude ripples through me as I hear her voice in the waves, *"Until you let go, you cannot be supported."*

The words quietly lap against the walls of my stubborn mind, reverberating over and over again, peeling away the shell of my ego-driven desire for control and ringing even louder in my ears than the gonging bell. *Brene Brown's words capture the sentiment that comes through loud and clear.

"You can't get to courage without vulnerability."

There are gaps between the fingers.
There are gaps between the senses.
In these gaps is the darkness
which hides the connection between things.

~ Idris Parry ~

34

THREE HILLS

Back in the comfort of the Corinthia Palace hotel on Malta, I wake in the middle of the night from a restless sleep.

A persistent thought holds my attention. *"More souls are ready to leave. Tonight, the exodus begins in earnest."*

It seems we have been building up to this, putting the necessary pieces in place by visiting all three islands. Guidance takes over. I am directed to envision the outline of the labyrinth pattern as if superimposing it over a regional map of the area. The entrance point or mouth of the labyrinth is placed over the Mosta Dome in Malta, which means the furthest circuits swing out to encircle all of Gozo with the goal area centered over the channel of the Blue Lagoon in Comino. I am aware that there is a triangulation of points being used and activated as portals. Perhaps this is really a reactivation of the area known as the *"legendary three hills,"* described by *Francis Xavier Alosio as "the *eye-land* of the gods." Due to the surrounding Mediterranean basin with its nine mountain ranges, each with three mounts, the wall it created at the time of Atlantis looked like an eye. The cluster of Maltese islands in the center was considered the iris. Malta not only joined with the other energy points around the world but, according to Alosio, was the hub or center-point uniting them all together.

By just mentally placing the labyrinth image over the areas, some kind of movement has been activated and an indeterminable number of souls begins flashing before my mind's eye. All three locations are involved. My first attention point is drawn to the ceiling of the Mosta Dome. I am mesmerized as the recessed squares and raised structural ribs of the domed ceiling begin to come alive, looking like an active honeycomb. The 'hive' pattern morphs into countless yellow-colored bricks, precision-cut from the raw globigerina limestone quarries. They are linked end-to-end like train cars that begin moving along the curves of the vesical-shaped tracks. My imagination easily sees this as an efficient high-rail tram system made up of glowing golden 'boxcars,' carrying the cargo of precious souls. They spiral through the toroidal tracks in an oscillating fashion with increasing speed and purpose, heading toward the black tunnel opening at the top of the dome. Boxcar after boxcar, they disappear through the vortex of what seems to be a dimensional wormhole.

My attention then moves to the Blue Lagoon area where I see an underground boarding station receiving souls flushed from the underworld regions of Gozo and shuttled to the Mosta Dome. I have the distinct feeling that this is not a one-time event, but a process that we first set into motion by walking Michelangelo's twelve-petal vesica design in the plaza in Rome and it is intended to continue.

I am quietly reminded, *"Astarte has initiated the release process and needs the assurance that the souls are leaving before she will agree to cross over herself."*

The sheer numbers begin to feel overwhelming as I check in with each area, impressed with the efficiency of the ongoing exodus. A chill goes up my spine, pulling my awareness back to our room. There is something here that I have been feeling on the periphery while moving on the other souls over the last couple of days. Up until now, it was only a sense of being carefully watched from a distance. But now there is a definite presence making its opposition known. The reality hits me that detrimental energies are here in full force, seeping in like toxic fumes, spreading stealthily into every crack and crevice of my mind with the intent to scare me enough to derail the operation. They are less than thrilled with the idea of losing the exiting souls. This is a new sensation for me—realizing my actions have activated a 'service to self' sleeper cell. Their covert intent is to sabotage or stop the entire mission, no different than those 'controllers' who put an end to Astarte's soul-crossing efforts.

I sit up, feeling the cold grip of fear in my chest, and fumble for the shelf next to my headboard where I have placed the touchstone of my torus. Grasping its solid weight in my hand, I place it on my skin just below my navel and above the pubic bone. This is the *Tantien/Hara* point (the name in China/ Japan for the center of our energy body). The fear subsides when I breathe from the light at my center, focusing on the internal toroidal field that expands from my heart. I keep breathing until I'm enveloped in my own golden bubble. I imagine that I am standing in the center of my labyrinth back home, filled with the connection and love that I feel for my land. Out of habit, but also heeding the feeling that I need to become 'invisible' to them, I drop into the tunnel below the center of the labyrinth, down to my receiving place within Inner Earth. From the core of the Earth, I am immersed in Gaia's magnetic field. Just by being in mental resonance with the Earth's core, I am being stabilized.

From my 'protected' vantage point, I observe the crossing-over process, resting here until daylight begins to stream through the cracks in our drapes.

Vickie stirs in the morning, sounding worn out and a bit shaken, "I am not sure what is happening, but I feel exhausted like I've been moving souls on all night."

"That's because we have been, and it is going to continue," I confirm.

For the remainder of our stay here, I go to sleep (a questionable term) with the torus touchstone in my hand, attempting to unify my mind, body, and spirit to hold space for the nighttime operations that are clearly underway. It appears that we are part of a revised network, sanctioned to reinstate a new version of the old *underground resistance* and, for now, we are on the 'night shift' and need to take precautions for our own safety as well as for that of the outgoing souls.

We are well aware that all of this is building in preparation for Astarte's release. This is planned for our last day when we are scheduled to visit the Hypogeum (the place where Astarte died). We don't know what it is going to entail, but I have no doubt that the 'orders' will come when everything finally aligns.

We fall from womb to tomb,
from one blackness and toward another,
remembering little of the one
and knowing nothing of the other...
except through faith.

~ Stephen King ~

35

WOMB AND TOMB

The Hypogeum was first put onto the map of my consciousness in 2001 when I heard the repetitive mind altering chant from *Jennifer Berezan's album, called *ReTurning. The words and improvisational layers of cyclical sounds evoke the memory of the ancient goddesses, calling for us to *"Return to the Mother of us all."* She recorded this inspired legacy to female deities all over the world from inside the earth in the Hypogeum at Hal Saflieni in Malta. Permission was granted to record her healing music beneath an elaborately painted ceiling of red ochre spirals in a rectangular chamber called the *Oracle room*. This is a contained space that amplifies the lower tones of sound up to a hundred times.

In 2001, if you had given me a real map, I would not have had a clue where Malta was geographically located. Even though Malta has the highest concentration of prehistoric temples in the entire world, I was in the majority of the population that knew nothing about them.

The Hypogeum, recognized as a World Heritage Site, means *underground* in Greek and has the distinction of being the only prehistoric or Bronze Age subterranean temple in the world. Often called a *labyrinth*, the underground complex has more than thirty rooms on three levels, with deeper levels rumored to exist below it that remain unexcavated. There is a series of architectural halls with trilithons and blind niches, elliptical chambers, passages, egg-shaped cubicles, stairways, and interconnected tunnels. Amazingly, they were all exquisitely sculpted from one solid piece of coralline limestone before the age of metal ... over 6,000 years ago. The complexity and sophistication of this monument hewn within the earth reflects the technological abilities of master craftsmen, artists, and architects with knowledge of sacred geometry. What exists here far surpasses the expert's idea that this was created by simple people limited to the primitive tools of that age: stone mallets, horn or antler picks, and flint or obsidian scrapers. This place has the mark of 'higher density beings'—or at least 'technologically advanced beings'—written all over it.

Ironically, it was a stone mason who accidentally discovered the Hypogeum when he broke through the roof of the top level in 1902 while digging to put in cisterns for a new housing development. A year later, an official excavation began, and in 1908 it was first opened to the public.

It is acknowledged that the Hypogeum was originally used as a sanctuary, but perhaps not as widely accepted that the creators of the Hypogeum installed it as a 'dream chamber' used to incubate new life forms. From the perspective of Francis Xavier Alosio (the author of the book *Islands of Dream*), he sees the Hypogeum as a 'womb' or a 'creation chamber' designed to birth and then nurture 'Consciousness.' He believes that the people used this as a place to dream and listen to the "oracle of their own soul." He recognized that they also went there to prepare themselves for the afterlife.

Death was seen as a passage of birth into the higher dimensions, and not as a separation or an end, yet Astarte's dedication to guiding earthbound souls to the stargate of Orion indicates that not everyone at that time died in a higher vibrational state.

The masses buried within the Hypogeum come from the next civilization following the fall of Atlantis, when there was great upheaval and war, and it is possible that the Hypogeum and other subterranean caves and tunnels were used for shelter and safety. The bones of anywhere from 7,000 to 33,000 different people were found here. One theory for the massive number suggests a great wave of water that would have crushed and decimated everything in its path. Analyzing the disarray of bones found without complete skeletons has led the authorities to conclude that the Hypogeum was used as a necropolis (large cemetery or burial ground), but it is also known that the Neolithic people practiced two-stage burials. The bodies were first de-fleshed with the assistance of vultures and animals above ground, and later (perhaps at seasonal times of the year) were ritualistically brought down to the chambers with reverence.

Archaeologist *Marija Gimbutas also views the Hypogeum not only as a tomb, but also as the regenerative womb of Mother Earth. From a more holistic view, the Hypogeum is seen as an ancient underground ritual center (temple) where people would come for visions and healing with the intent to honor and celebrate the ancestors and prepare them for the passage to the underworld. Some researchers make the distinction that the underground temples celebrated Death while the above-ground temples celebrated Life. The early people that used the temples were a culture dedicated to regeneration. Symbolically this is portrayed through the carved and painted motifs of polygon patterns of honeycomb cells, spirals, and snakes. Birth, death and re-birth are all interwoven transitioning points in Life's eternal cycle. According to Christine Page, the temples were built as a way to download information that came from cosmic consciousness, and that information was put into the Earth by the Star races. Several in our group have the realization while we are there that the three levels of the Hypogeum were created in reverse: from the bottom up—not dug from the top down.

The tomb aspect long associated with the Hypogeum has reached into more modern times, according to a two-part story that we first heard days before our scheduled tour. Later, I discover that this 'urban legend' has been documented in an old issue of Riley Crabb's *Borderland Science* magazine, published by the Borderland Sciences Research Foundation (B.S.R.F.) and reprinted in full in *Dr. Allen's book *Enigma Fantastique*.

The most compelling version of the story comes from the woman who was directly involved, C. Lois Jessop. Lois was an employee of the British embassy and later became secretary for the New York Saucer Information Bureau (NYSIB). In the mid—1930s she was visiting friends on the Island of Malta when six of them decided to take in some of the popular attractions. Because of the heat, they sought out the underground temples, bringing them to the main street in the small town of Paola where the entrance to the Hal Saflieni Hypogeum was located. Securing a guide for the tour (a man named Joe), they entered the large cave entrance. He gave each of them a lighted candle and proceeded to take them through the narrow passage to different rooms, pausing to point out things of interest. The group steadily descended to the two lower levels. There they saw skeletons through a slit in one of the stone walls and Joe told them that this was a room where they had buried their dead. Reaching the third and lowest level, he indicated that they were to turn around and go back. Lois noticed an opening low on one of the walls. When she asked about it, Joe replied, "Go there at your own risk, and you won't go far."

Three of her friends agreed to explore the passage with her while the other two remained with Joe. Lois was wearing a dress with a long sash, and used the sash as a rope to link herself to the person behind her. Stooping and sometimes crawling, she led the group into a low and narrow passage. She came out onto a two-foot wide ledge with a wall to her left and a sheer drop of fifty feet on the right side. Inching forward close to the wall, she held up her half-burnt candle. She could see an opening far below her, and out of it twenty gigantic beings emerged. They walked slowly in single file along a narrow ledge. She estimated their height to be twenty to twenty-five feet tall. Their bodies were covered with long, white, shaggy hair. They had oval shaped heads, elongated both at the top and at their chins, with white hair draped around their shoulders. In unison, they all looked in her direction and raised their arms, making motions with the palms face down as if beckoning or feeling for something.

Her friends who were still in the narrow passage called out to her, pulling on the sash. Frightened, Lois told them there was nothing to see. Placing her hand on the wall to steady herself, she realized that, instead of touching the cold rock, her hand was on something soft and wet. When it moved, a wind came up and blew out her candle. Finding her voice, she told the others to go back. She used her sash to guide her because her light was gone.

Returning to the large room where the others were waiting, she did not share what she had encountered because of the look of caution she saw on Joe's face. This made her believe that he had also seen the creatures at some point. Outside in the open, they thanked and tipped him. Joe told Lois that if she wanted to explore further it would be wise to do it with a group. He told her that a school teacher was taking his students on an outing and perhaps she could join them. Interested, she left her contact information with him to give to the school master, but she never heard from him.

A short time later, one of the friends who had accompanied her that day called to relay an article that was in the Valetta (Capital of Malta) paper. It stated that a school master with thirty elementary students went into the same tunnel, roped together with the end tied to the opening of the cave. In the place where Lois's candle blew out, the rope was cut clean and the walls caved in. After three weeks of excavations and search parties, they gave up the rescue. Mothers of the children reported hearing wailing and screaming coming from underground throughout the island, but no one could locate the source of the sounds. The story of the children was reported in the National Geographic magazine, Aug. 1940, in an article by Riley Crabb; Commander X, entitled, *The Reality of the Cavern World.*

Months later, Lois returned to the Hypogeum with her sister to make the same tour, but there was a different guide. When they reached the lowest level in the room where Lois left to explore the tunnel, the entrance was boarded up. Inquiring if this was the place where the school master and children disappeared, the guide was noncommittal. Lois questioned if he was new and asked about Joe.

The man told her, "I don't know any Joe. I alone have been showing people around this catacomb for years."

Lois did not tell anyone her account until 1960, and by this time it was impossible to get facts to corroborate her story from old newspapers and the Museum. The Maltese people are very private and hold onto their secrets, but local residents who spoke to an investigator in the sixties shared that at one time you could walk the underground tunnels that extended nine miles from one end of Malta to the other—until all the entrances were ordered closed because of the tragic disappearance. The many subterranean passageways, including the ancient catacombs, were part of the island's defense system where supplies were kept, as well as used for bomb shelters during World War II.

100% of the journey takes place within the dark.
Its brilliant design forces us to grow our light
in order to see inside ourselves ... where Home is.

~ Lauren C. Gorgo ~

36

PASSAGEWAY HOME

earing Lois' story, we discuss the possibility that the interior of the Earth is home to many different races that include different densities with the abilities to shift between the border of 3D, 4D, 5D and beyond. We also consider that the 'Inner Earth' civilizations are made up of both polarities—those oriented toward 'service to others' and those who follow the 'service to self' path of evolution.

Because of everything that the story is bringing up, I question if the Hypogeum is the most suitable place to create the portal for Astarte's departure. The logistics involved with the Hypogeum tour makes the decision easy. In an attempt to preserve the ruins, the tours are limited to ten people at a time, splitting us into three separate groups. Once we find out that Vickie is in the last group and Carol and I are in the first, we agree to meet afterwards back at the hotel to create our own private ritual. A part of me is relieved that I will be able to just take in the experience and not worry about opening a portal for Astarte.

Our bus arrives in the town of Paola and pulls off on an ordinary residential street. At 8:00 a.m., we walk up to an insignificant doorway on the side of a building. There is an unpretentious sign that simply reads - HYPOGEUM. From the outside, it looks like we are going into a small, retail shop. We are ushered through the narrow lobby in front of a counter where they are selling tickets and museum souvenirs, and are told that all of our belongings will be locked

273

up in a cabinet to keep our hands free. I tuck the torus touchstone behind my belt buckle into the waistband of my pants. While they pass out headsets and give instructions, I look through the glass-sealed enclosure that surrounds the entire area behind us and can see the stairway that will take us down to what is considered the first level of the ruins. The steps disappear into the wide-open mouth of the ancient entrance.

A calm voice awakens in my head and whispers the command, *"Create a left-handed labyrinth over this opening."*

Without hesitating, I draw the pattern in my mind, but instead of it staying stationary as it usually does, the image begins floating like smoke rings, upwards above the glass enclosure, resulting in a three-dimensional labyrinth (like the Glastonbury Tor) with each circuit climbing higher than the one below it.

Before I can comprehend what is happening, the voice continues, *"Now, make a right-handed labyrinth and send it down."*

With each turn, the circuits drop lower and lower. The impression I am left with is two conically elongated, three-dimensional labyrinths suspended like hornet nests, one pointing up and the other down, far above and below the Hypogeum. While I hold the image in my mind, a guide escorts our group into a room to watch a ten-minute video, primarily giving the scientific background of what we are about to see. My attention is split between viewing what is on the screen and watching what is unfolding in my mind's eye. I turn down the volume of my headset to listen to the internal broadcast that has now taken over my 'airwaves.'

"Go to Inner Earth. You will have to do this through the tunnel under the Prairie Labyrinth instead of going down here beneath the Hypogeum."

I press my hands against the torus stone at my waist and imagine myself at home, easily sliding through the opening into the waters of Inner Earth.

Once there, the voice instructs, *"Look from this position all the way across the ocean and turn on a tube torus fountain beneath the Hypogeum in Malta."*

Thinking makes it so. Instantly a geyser of liquid light shoots up from beneath me and I watch it intercept and connect both of the labyrinths, with the fountain continuing to skyrocket farther and farther out into space. No longer tracking what is being said on the video, I blankly stare at the images, realizing that the force-field has already activated souls and they are beginning to rise. Silently, I call for the Higher Self energies to meet them, feeling that the momentum is now beyond my control. I have no sense if Astarte is among those leaving, but it is apparent that there is no turning back now. The only thing required is to let go.

Our small group of ten takes the stairs down to the entrance where we're swallowed by the wide-mouth opening into the throat of the cave. I am suspended between two realities that are both surreal. We are herded from one point of interest to another, holding onto metal handrails that keep us on a dimly lit walkway. The areas being described by the audio-guide are flooded with a soft golden light until the description is over and the object of interest is blinked back into the shadows. Shuffling to the next illuminated niche, the guide leads us to a small side chamber called the *Oracle Room* (where Jennifer Berezan did her famous recording). On the wall, there is an oval niche known as the *Oracle Hole*, designed to amplify lower tones. Each of our three groups has been divided with one man in each section just for this reason: so, he can tone into the hole and we can experience the echoing. Anders, a delightful British gentleman who is up for the challenge, takes a full breath and lets out a deep "OMMMM." Because the women were told that our voices would not have any effect because the higher tones do not reach the resonating frequency of the room, I am surprised to hear some of the women's voices softly filling out his resonance with higher harmonies. (We later learn that these harmonic sounds are not coming from the women, but are part of the phenomenal amplification that occurs.) Bits and pieces of what is happening are selectively registering in my consciousness against the backdrop of the continuous flow of souls, rushing upward like thousands of champagne bubbles in effervescent effusion, escaping to the ethers.

Transitioning through a small intermediate floor, we drop to the Middle level and come to a section called the *Holy of Holies*. This refers to the innermost sanctuary. The layout of this space was influenced by the solar alignment of the winter solstice sunrise, designed to receive the best possible natural lighting, casting the highest sun to the darkest point in the lowest portion of the underground temple complex. The lobby has elaborate relief carvings implementing vertical and horizontal curves. Here the walls arch up to join with the carved circular ceiling with three consecutive rings of stone, one above the other, each with a smaller diameter to create the partial corbelling that forms a dome-like structure over the entire two-roomed chamber.

The hint of a curving doorway takes my breath away—not because of its impressive architectural achievement, but because I can feel the energy from the room that it leads to. Even though our view is obstructed, my stomach is churning, knowing that this is the place where Astarte did her soul journeying. And that this is possibly the room where she died. It's beyond this room in a deep pit where the terra cotta replica of the 'Sleeping Goddess' was buried in her honor. This is the Main Chamber.

The audio-guide brings my attention back to a description of a water cistern that sits in front of the *Holy of Holies*. It is reached by walking down seven uneven steps to the lowest level. I recall Francis Xavier Aloisio's interpretation that the seven steps represent the seven chakras and the seven dimensions of consciousness or the seven doorways between dimensions, which can only be reached through an altered state. The water cistern is positioned at the deepest part of the Hypogeum, symbolizing the underworld.

Tracing the seven pathways of the labyrinth takes on a deeper meaning for me, and helps me to understand why moving the souls through these seven layers would help them to shed their attachments, while steadily shifting them beyond this dimension.

The defining light over the *Holy of Holies* suddenly blacks out and we are moved along the walkway.

Holding back, I whisper to Carol, "That's the room. That's the room Astarte used. I want to see that room."

As if on command, the next area that is lit up for our viewing is the *Main* or *Central Chamber*. We are peering into a single circular room from the opposite side through a large round opening that was once a solid wall. The simple interior has an intimate feeling—as if we are peering through a window into someone's living room. I can almost imagine the low-lying slabs arranged around the central area serving as stone couches. There is an upper and a lower level of recessed niches encircling the room. For a moment I am back in time, seeing these areas as individual chambers where people are reclining, 'incubating their own dreams.' This room stands in contrast to the embellished relief carvings on the outer façade. The way the niches are cut into the wall creates a fish-eye effect with the vertical lines curving outward. I move robotically through the rest of the tour, saturated in the membrane of unearthed impressions that are still breathing in the living stone.

Upon leaving the Hypogeum, I am reassured, *"The layer of souls that are crossing over have been here for a long time. The portal is now concentrated over the Cistern. It will remain open with a continuous exodus occurring. Their passing is necessary to Astarte's release. She waits for your signal."*

Hours later, when Vickie returns from her tour, the final details have fallen into place and present us with the perfect environment for releasing Astarte into the next world. As part of the *Athenaeum Spa's* offerings within the hotel, we have booked an hour in the floatation tank. Limited to three people, it is recommended that we float in the nude due to the high concentration of salt that would pull the color from our swimsuits. What could be more appropriate for a 'birthing ritual?' As the 'midwives,' we too must be uncloaked, surrendered in a state of openness and vulnerability.

Slipping into the Spa's long white robes and slippers in the upstairs dressing room, we pause before going into the pool area, preparing to set everything into motion before we enter. I have an image of the Chakra Labyrinth from the *Chakra Labyrinth Cards* that I hand to Vickie to finger-trace while I read the statements from the 'Chakra Angels' that accompany each path. This is a way to invite the angels in to direct and guide the process with the intent of opening the portal. It is easy to envision the labyrinth pattern being projected over the pool area because it is directly below us. As I read the statements, I imagine the labyrinth beginning to rise like "seven uneven steps" coming up from the underworld.

CHAKRA ANGELS:

1. Root Chakra—**Kadmiel**—*"I am related to Adam Kadmon, the first human. I am the union of opposites, half male/half female, embodying Divine Wholeness. Dissolve your sense of separation and trust the stability of your core foundation. The bloodline of the 'I AM' is infused in your roots."*

2. Sacral Chakra—**Hamiel**—*"I flow with the kundalini life force energy, stirring your senses awake. Find what excites you and remove your resistance to FEEL. Every relationship is a mirror reflection inviting you to accept yourself."*

3. Solar Plexus—**Natanel**—*"I hold the light of the Great Central Sun. Your internal fire builds your presence, giving you courage to take action and move with confidence in the world. I ignite your true resonance to reveal the Divine."*

4. Heart Chakra—**Gabrielle**—*"I stand at the gateway of your heart in the crosswinds of your human experiences. This space can take your breath away or it can fill you up. Allow Love to breathe through you."*

5. Throat Chakra—**Michael**—*"My sword cuts away layers of self-deception. The only protection you need is against your ego interpretations. Lean into my expanded energy and trust your inner voice to speak loud enough for you to hear."*

6. Third Eye—**Raphael**—*"Give up the demanding distractions of your mind chatter and enter into the still point of your own single eye. Use it as a headlight to see what is right for you. Shifting old perceptions will change the world behind your eyes and redefine what lies before you."*

7. Crown Chakra—**Uriel**—*"I open my mind-shaft that leads into a passage of amethyst light where you are eternally connected to your Higher Self. Actualize this connection and know you are One."*

The stage is set. We enter a darkened room, noticing that the back wall is lined with glass windows tucked into a border of lush greenery. The pool stands in the center, encircled by a shallow cement wall and ringed by lit candles. There is a domed hood over the pool that is lit like the night sky with tiny sparkling lights that are timed to intermittently twinkle and then go black, leaving only

13 star-points lit on the outer rim. Soft music stirs our senses. There are three floatation 'noodles' lying in the water, waiting for us while the jets at the center move the water up and out in continuous circulating pulsations.

I slip into the water, walking to the center to place the touchstone of my torus on the bottom of the pool. Each of us lies face-up with the noodles supporting our necks, drawing our heads together in the center. The salt water caresses our naked bodies, suspended in weightlessness. In this water chamber we are effortlessly lifted, facing the domed representation of the galaxy above us that is serving as the focus of the portal opening.

I know what I have to do. Closing my eyes, I return to the Prairie Labyrinth and drop through the center sky of Inner Earth. From beneath the merging waters, I sense the pressure building and the fountain erupts. The new path we are forging with our present intention ties into the ancient grid lines. Watching the liquid light fountain rise in my mind's eye, I begin to call to the Higher Self matrix for Astarte and for the aspects of any of the accompanying souls, including Ochicus, my handmaiden self. In an instant I am engulfed in the presence of unseen helpers who seem to be all around her.

I hear their request, *"Reach to her with your voice. She will respond to your singing."*

The song is emotional for me; I never suspected, when I wrote it in 2003, that it would be used in this way. With every part of me submerged in water except for my nose and mouth, I take a deep breath and begin to sing.

> *I call to the Feminine, the Mothers, the Maidens,*
> *to gather your love, to lift up the babes.*
> *I call to the Feminine, returning to Earth,*
> *to reclaim the child within, preparing for birth.*
>
> *Lift up your gossamer wings to the sky.*
> *It's time to open. It's time to fly.*
> *Follow the Circles your heart song intones.*
> *Unwind the golden thread to find the passageway home.*

I call to the Feminine, the Mothers, the Crones,
to weave the new web, to release the old bones.
I call to the Feminine that lives in each heart,
to heal the imbalances that tear us apart.

Lift up your gossamer wings to the sky.
It's time to open. It's time to fly.
Follow the Circles your heart song intones.
Unwind the golden thread to find the passageway home.

I call to this gathering. Have the courage to shine.
Merge with the Mystery—dance your soul's design.
I call to this gathering to be the stars that align.
Ignite the new resonance to reveal the Divine.

Lift up your gossamer wings to the sky.
It's time to open. It's time to fly.
Follow the Circles your heart song intones.
Unwind the golden thread to find the passageway home.

While I sing, Astarte is attended to by her priestess sisters in spirit who lovingly guide her toward her own radiant Higher Self matrix. Merging as the spinning Merkaba, she is lifted from my perception with streams of souls following her as shimmering ribbons of light. It is gentle and loving, without fanfare or difficulty. Each one of us has our own impression of her easily slipping out of whatever hold she was in.

I am reminded of the words spoken to me when all of this began, *"Open closed passageways—it's what a 'wanderer' does. There is no such thing as closed. You simply exist on the other side of the obstruction and the obstruction has to shift."*

Thankfully, I know we are on the other side of this.

We shall not cease from exploration,
and the end of all our exploring
will be to arrive where we started and
know the place for the first time.

~ T. S. Eliot ~

37

CLOSING THE PORTAL

On our return layover in Rome, we take a bus tour that allows us to get on and off at locations of interest. One of the stops happens to be back at the Capitoline Hill at Michelangelo's, *Campidoglio*. In hindsight (the view of clarity) it appears that the Universe intended for us to bookend the trip—beginning and ending—with this Master portal. This time, we are able to walk the twelve-vesica pattern in the clockwise rotation, with the intent to close the portal that we opened two weeks earlier. It is also sending the energy out to all the reaches of the Roman Empire. Stepping out of the last circuit brings a sense of completion to everything that occurred. Closing this portal has a domino effect, spinning shut each one of the places that was opened throughout the Maltese island region. I am ready to go home.

After a week of heavy-duty sleeping, I am still feeling the effects of jet-lag and have little to no energy. I pull myself outside to assess the falling leaves of late October that are filling up the sand paths in Chante Ishta (my 9-vesica design). I know I should clear the paths and rake the leaves up, but all I want to do is go back inside and take a nap.

The inner voice that has been quiet since my return home springs to life. *"Before you go into the house, just walk the paths as if you are moving someone on."*

I internally agree to do that and start the process of walking the pattern in the counterclockwise manner. When I reach the starting point and am ready to reverse the direction, I realize that this is not just an 'exercise' to get me moving.

I respond out loud, "Okay, I get it. I really AM moving someone on, and I don't need to know any of the details."

At the completion of the walk, I hear the faint murmur of *"Thank you"* waft around and through me, fading away through the portal in the center.

Instantly I feel more alert and energized—enough so that I get the rake and work outside for several hours.

Days later, the realization hits me that the earthbound soul was my handmaiden self. My focus was so fixated on Astarte in the floatation chamber that I just assumed that Ochicus left with the whole entourage. This gives me a good idea of what people feel like who have an earthbound soul connected to them: tired, run down, stuck, no energy, flat, fatigued, and depressed. An earthbound soul doesn't have energy of their own so if someone is attached to you, you become the energy source for them as well as for yourself. It reminds me of the days when my son was a baby and an extension of my hip. All of you who are mothers know this feeling. You learn to function because you have to, but it also takes a lot of energy. I don't believe that most earthbound souls have any idea that their presence is causing a strain or hardship on the living, but informing them of this sometimes helps elicit their cooperation to leave.

For months after returning from Malta, I am in an internal integrative process, unable to outwardly share what has occurred. When I am finally able to begin writing, five months has passed and then something shifts. I have a conversation with Vickie about the Hypogeum and she asks me if I read about the ancient accounts telling of deep caverns beneath the Maltese Islands. The underwater tunnels stretched far beyond the islands, running hundreds of miles north to intersect with catacombs that were built beneath Rome under the Vatican Hill. This revelation sheds new light on our impulse to start and end our journey in Rome, and our last-minute decision to take the tour of St.

Peter's Basilica in the Vatican.

The following day in Yoga class, we are in a meditative state doing a breathing posture for an extended period of time when my state of 'no mind' is supplanted with the image of the plaza in Rome. In my imagination, I am standing off to the side of the *Campidoglio*—as if I have come here to be shown something. In a flash, a tube torus fountain comes up around the *Marcus Aurelius* statue in the center and shoots skyward, followed by a flurry of souls. Disoriented, I don't know what to make of this. Souls continue to be sucked into the light in rapid succession. They include many flashes of priests and religious hierarchy connected with the Vatican. This continues throughout the hour-long class. When I return home, I walk into the labyrinth with paper and pen, asking to receive some kind of understanding.

"What was started five months ago has now moved to the next 'level.' There were always three levels to this process. The portals in Rome, Malta, and Gozo are active again. Your conversation with Vickie triggered your awareness about the subterranean tunnels connecting Malta to Rome, enabling the onset of 'Level Two.' The energy sent up the chain at the Mosta Dome was a signal broadcasting out to the awaiting souls. At the Xaghra Stone Circle, the souls were in alignment with the idea of crossing over because you introduced your energies to them earlier that morning on the moonlit walk. The momentum was building at the dolmen, accelerated by the entire group's focus using the ley line as an 'instant-message' delivery system. When you reached the top of the tower in the Rotunda, you took the 'sound' energy to the ground, sending it into the earth and the subterranean tunnels.

Know that this entire area is littered with souls that died and remain in layers of timeframes that all overlap in the astral. Behind the barrier, battles still wage in the 'polarity integration game.'

Swimming the Blue Lagoon channel dipped into that subterranean energy and started the stirring. Just as the sound vibrations of a single note that is held can break a glass, your unified voices, amplified by the echoing cave, acted as an 'ice breaker' to crack the consciousness of the souls that had remained frozen, as if in a 'stillborn' state. 'Sound' crosses all language barriers and is universally activating. Bobbing in the primal fluid started the 'contractions' that began nudging the souls, preparing them to be revived and rebirthed to another level of awareness.

When you returned to Malta, you became aware of the awakening and could feel the exodus at the Mosta Dome but, as intense as it was, only the top layer of souls that grasped the concept of free will made the choice to bypass the imposed 'frequency fence' and use the available portal opened to them.

By discussing the Hypogeum's subterranean levels with Vickie, your focus served as an accelerant being poured into the tunnels and those fumes spread all the way to Rome as you finally made that connection. Both ends of the portals—the Cistern in the Hypogeum on Malta and the Campidoglio in Rome—were activated as if a match were dropped into the tunnels. You could say that a 'fire ball' roared through the tunnels in both directions, alerting and attracting souls throughout the honeycombed catacombs like moths to a flame. There were millions of swarming souls responding to the light tower cascading out of the Campidoglio.

Today in Yoga class you witnessed the beginning of 'Level Two.' Because you closed the portal when you left Rome, you needed to be in attendance and in alignment with it being re-opened. Writing up the account allows for another round of focus which does not require your physical presence.

As you saw this morning, many priests and/ or religious leaders that have remained stuck by grief, shame, and secrecy are being invited into the light to release their hold and contribution to the infested energy of sexual abuse and, ultimately, abuse of power. (Pope Benedict XVI resigned four days after receiving this writing.) The entire region of Rome is stuffed with souls that clamored for power and did many things that, upon death, they regretted.

Portals have nothing to do with 'judgment.' They are simply beacons of truth, calling all souls back to their own true God essence. Astarte held this essence and ignited it in others. Her interpretation of 'failure' had to be adjusted before those who looked up to her could adjust their own perspective. With her on the 'other side,' she is able to once more be that clear clarion bell, calling out to others over the Atlantean region—which includes the entire Mediterranean with Greece and Turkey at the forefront.

Other portals will be established, but in 'Level Two' the existing ones in Rome, the Hypogeum, Mosta Dome, Rotunda Church in Gozo and the Xaghra Circle are fully functioning again.

Astarte will be overseeing the transfer of souls. All of the soul layers that stayed stuck remained there because of the influence of the layer below it. This goes back to those who were choosing to stay earthbound when Astarte was living. They saw the 'star beings' as their 'gods/goddesses' and wanted to remain in their energy. When Astarte's life-line was cut, they surrounded her on the astral plane, remaining by her side in loyalty. Where she was, they wanted to be. It didn't matter that she was silent, not attempting to influence them. Her 'sleep' was accepted as it was when she was soul traveling in the Hypogeum.

Her new state of awareness is catalyzing all of them. She knows the way home and continues to show them the way by embracing her own awakening. More souls from the Malta region are using the portal in the Hypogeum that has formed over the Cistern. Clearing the astral tunnels there will dislodge the remaining layers waiting to leave in 'Level Three.'"

Silent harmony is the gift you give yourself...
As you push past the infinite, you can feel your own music,
your own frequency, beginning to project
itself past you, beyond infinity, into nowhere,
starting to generate its own star.

~ **Robert Young** ~

38

LEVEL THREE

Entering the labyrinth, I pause at the first chakra post (Root chakra) and ring the single wind chime that hangs there, keyed to the note of middle C. The reverberating tone is accompanied by inner guidance.

"While you walk the path today, envision that the Prairie Labyrinth is superimposed over Michelangelo's Campidoglio design."

On my way to the center, it's easy to flash to the sights and sounds of the early evening plaza in Rome. I hear the cooing pigeons as a counterpoint to the staccato of mid-morning song birds I see flitting between the fallen stands of prairie grass in Missouri. When I reach the center of the labyrinth, I sit on one of the benches.

Hanging from the center post in the goal area is a three-foot long six-tube *Corinthian Bell Chime* with deep, resonant tones. From perfect stillness, one of the tubes suddenly rings out in a precise sequence of three long tones and, just as abruptly, returns to silence. What remains of the echo punctuates the incoming message.

"This signals the beginning of 'Level Three.' It is an unfolding process, just as the other two levels have been."

Ironically, it's been three weeks since 'Level Two' began. We are coming into the Aires new moon, starting the first lunar cycle of 2013, heralding the time for new beginnings. Fittingly, the 'dark of the moon' is the time when astral shadows walk the world—a time well-suited for looking behind the veil.

Sitting on the bench and closing my eyes, I see Roman soldiers surrounding the outer perimeter of the twelve-vesica design in Rome. They look somewhat confused, questioning if they are to leave their post. I assure them that the portal is meant for them, too. Evaporating before my eyes, their presence is replaced by countless rings of people, flickering as holographic images, fading in and out of timelines and spanning layers of history.

When we were in Rome, we witnessed many areas in the city that were built thirty feet on top of previous ruins, representing as many as three unearthed civilizations. It is common knowledge that there are earlier settlements lying beneath cities and towns that were plundered, pillaged, and destroyed throughout the world. We like to think that we bury our dead and move on, building on top of the rubble. We don't consider the layering effect of souls when they don't move on ... or the effect that their staying behind may be having on the living.

My attention is pulled back to Malta where I am given the metaphor of a centrifugal pump to explain the dynamics of the releasing souls. In this kind of pump, the fluid typically enters the pump impeller along or near the rotating axis and is accelerated, flowing outward into a diffuser chamber where it exits. In this case, the cistern in the Hypogeum is the source of the down-draft, suctioning souls that have remained in the tunnels (of time) and sweeping them into the rotation of the tube torus energy which serves as a pump impeller. Souls that have been stuck in their grief, trauma, or denial of death are discharged through the updraft, exiting the Earth plane at the *Campidoglio*.

The voice resumes, *"Gaia has been steadily moving through her own Ascension process. All of you that consider yourselves 'Light Workers' came to the Earth to contribute your talents, gifts, and passions, adding to the rising vibratory levels that are creating the rotational field for the up-lifting. Astarte knows that the most significant way that she can contribute is by focusing on the soul-clearing. Her death was followed by huge numbers of lives lost with the eventual destruction of Atlantis and the tsunami that devastated the whole region—including those seeking refuge on the subterranean levels. Those who remained went to the lower astral in their confusion, trauma, and terror. Those lower layers have settled in like 'sludge' with their unresolved issues clogging the system, needing to be 'roto-rootered' from the tunnels of time. Their energy produces a 'drag' that not only slows things down, but impacts as well as 'packs in' all the layers above it, keeping consciousness in a stagnant frequency loop."*

Earth has been the victim of countless cataclysms of fire and water that nearly wiped out life altogether. Before and after Atlantis was submerged, there were floods and volcanic eruptions; but geologists believe that *Thera*—on the island of Santorini—was the single most powerful explosion, dwarfing anything that humans had ever seen. It exploded with the force of several hundred atomic bombs in a matter of seconds. The combination of tsunamis, volcanic ash, and a drop in global temperatures rearranged the entire ancient world indefinitely, with the effects being felt across the globe. Archaeologists date the eruption anywhere from 1645 BC to 1500 BC. Some link the demise of Atlantis and the exodus from Egypt with this epic catastrophe.

The loss of life in the famous eruption of Krakatoa, Indonesia in 1883 was estimated upwards of 40,000 in just a few hours and they calculate that Thera's eruption was four or five times more powerful. Given the suddenness of the explosion, it makes sense that many souls would have been unprepared to cross over.

Sitting in the labyrinth, a realization slowly begins to penetrate my awareness. I am compelled to voice this out loud: "Unlike Level Two's short time frame of three weeks, Level Three is going to take much longer ... likely to go on for years."

This is immediately confirmed by my guidance. *"You have signaled your readiness to step into your next area of focus. This will be in place for the next seven years—until 2020."*

The time frame takes on deeper significance when I read the book *2012-2021: The Dawn of the Sixth Sun.* The author, *Sergio Magana, as spokesperson for the Nahuatl tradition, brings to life the ancient knowledge of the pre-Columbian people of Mesoamerica who were the creators of the Mayan and Aztec calendars. Through his explanation, I understand that the term *Sun* refers to a cycle or movement that lasts 6,625 years. According to the Mayan calendar, December 21, 2012 was the end of one of those cycles, but the Mexican calendar continues for at least two more Suns or 13,250 years. Instead of one Sun beginning at the time that the other one comes to an end, there is a period of overlap where they coexist. During this time, the new Sun's influence gradually grows until the two energies are equal.

According to Sergio, the Sixth Sun energies first entered the scene in 1991. By 2003 the new Sun was beginning to 'gather strength,' and on December 21, 2012 the two Suns had equal power. This gives me insight into why going to Malta at the end of 2012 was supported energetically. It was a period where the fulcrum between the dark and the light could perfectly balance, creating an opening. Then the old Sun gradually withdraws until the new Sun becomes the sole holder of the cycle. This means that, from 2021 onwards, the governing influence will be completely shifted over to the Sixth Sun.

I note that the transitional window (from 1991-2012) coincides with my growing awareness and direct involvement with earthbound spirits, as well as corresponding to the 'Ascension process' that is well underway. This Ascension process is a conscious choice to engage in our soul's evolution, expanding into higher consciousness as multidimensional human beings. It is a reunification with our own divinity, the "I Am" presence.

*Suzanne Lie in *Arcturian Ascension Tools* (a website with archived articles regarding Ascension from a wide source of contributors going back to 2012) added to this in 2016 by sharing, *"Earth has resonated to the third-physical and fourth-etheric, and astral frequency for eons. Now Earth is merging with, and returning to, the fifth dimensional frequencies of reality. However, it takes quite a great deal of adaptation to merge with these higher frequency carrier waves. In order to calibrate our consciousness to these fifth dimensional, Ascension Energy Waves, we have found it is best to fall into this experience. This type of surrender is possible because the fifth dimensional energy frequencies are flowing into, through, and out of us, NOW! If we surrender to these fifth dimensional energy fields as they flow 'in-to' and 'out-of,' it is easier for us to accept and slowly adapt to them."*

I also appreciate a perspective by Sandra Walter who tells us, *"The Ascension process is a choice to engage with the unknown in order to experience the new."*

I invite you to look back and see what events were occurring or what was set into motion for you personally beginning around 1991. Consider your own

Ascension process and what the triggers have been to motivate you to face, embrace, and resolve your issues. Realize that your healing process may be having a ripple effect in both directions, clearing the tunnels of time for those who went before you, as well as preparing the way for those who will follow.

Entering 'Level Three' means we are ushering out the old energies of the Fifth Sun (called the 'solar justice' consciousness) while preparing for the 'unified energy' of the Sixth Sun that will be governing our consciousness for thousands of years to come. As the Fifth Sun reaches the end of its reign (2013-2021), its energy influence will be intense, expressing in two possible ways: destruction and personal crisis, or the positive influence that leads to one's own 'blossoming.' As we look out at our world, we would likely agree that it is some of both: things have to fall apart before they can come together at a higher level.

Blossoming requires doing our inner clearing work, which means addressing our own unconscious or shadow energy. Because the Sixth Sun is a sun of the *nahual* (the governing energy during the sleep state), Sergio believes that people will be forced to get to know their own underworlds, sorting out unconscious issues that they may have postponed—perhaps for thousands of years. 'Dreamtime' will become especially active as the deep unconscious is excavated and the fourth dimensional terrain starts intersecting our waking reality. We will all be going on personal, 'archeological digs,' bringing up 'artifacts' for examination and current resolution. It makes sense that this personal clearing would also include 'calling back' or reclaiming, and finally releasing, lost or stuck aspects of our own soul that may have gotten sidetracked somewhere 'out in the field' during the long reign of the Fifth Sun.

It's as if our souls are broadcasting the call "Olly olly oxen, free," which is associated with the childhood game of hide-and-seek. It signals to the players who are still 'hiding,' or who are still 'out' there,' that it is safe to come back to base without penalty or that it is time to regroup because the game is over. Some speculate that the saying originates from the German phrase "alle alle auch sind frei," which was mispronounced by non-German children. Loosely translated, the original phrase still applies to our earthbound players, as it means *"everyone is also free"* or *"all ye out, come in free."*

PART
3

Before I went to Malta,
my experience with earthbound spirits did not include
'dark entities' or detrimental energies.
The 'dark side' was like a septic tank that stayed below the surface
and one that I saw no reason to open up and climb down into.
But once the lid was raised,
I came to accept my role alongside many other *Cosmic Janitors*.
Cleaning up the scum of disturbing intrusions doesn't have to be repulsive
if you're armed with the right tools and the right attitude.
You can't dig in the 'dirt' without excavating shadow aspects of yourself
waiting to be dusted off, forgiven,
and lifted to higher ground.

Bringing to light what had been hidden in darkness
should not overwhelm you,
but EDUCATE you.

~ **Solange Nicole** ~

39

"KP" DUTY

There is a prolonged period of time, when I am around ten years old, that an unsettling occurrence begins happening while lying in bed ready to fall asleep at night. Before my eyes, a sequence of adult faces start to materialize one after another as if placed on a Rolodex. They zoom in close, looking back at me empty and distraught, and then flip and fade into another disturbing stranger. The images are dimly lit, reminding me of a dank underground prison cell. As I watch, perplexed, their features begin to distort into grotesque shapes as if their faces are made of melting wax. This is a bad version of *The Twilight Zone* shown in slow-motion with horror movie special effects. I don't know who these people are or why they would be showing themselves to me. It's clear that they are not happy. They want my attention, and possibly the satisfaction of a frightened reaction. The images are unnerving, and each time it occurs I sit up, blinking them away.

As it goes on, I begin challenging myself to stay in the observer role, becoming more curious than frightened. It is a bit like having a staring contest to see who will blink first. I find I can outlast them by continuing to watch until they evaporate. I don't remember how many months this continues but, once I get to the complacent state and think, *Oh, it's just the faces again*, it stops altogether. I know nothing then about the lower astral realm, earthbound spirits, or dark entity 'controllers.'

At eighteen, I still have no conscious experience with the 'dark side' until a memorable day brings me to investigate an old abandoned church, bordered by an even older cemetery. The local kids refer to it as 'The Church of the Devil.' I am accompanied by a classmate, Ye, who because of our experiences on the Mississippi River I will always consider as my 'Huckleberry' life-long soul friend.

I awaken on my birthday at 6:00 a.m., hearing strange sounds outside of my bedroom window. Opening the door, I find Ye standing there grinning, holding onto the reins of two horses. His plan is for us to ride about fifteen miles to one of our favorite hangouts in the country, an area called 'Twin Springs.' Once there, we will make our way to a rugged limestone rock outcropping. The outcropping was separated from the original bluff when it was blasted apart in the late 1800s to accommodate the laying of a rail corridor that was a part of a thousand-mile track system that traversed the state of Iowa. Ye refers to this as "the quarried spine of Earth." Many of our friends regularly hike to this spot, spending time on top of the rock or wading in the creek in the grassland pasture below it. The easiest way to get there, once you arrive at the old iron bridge spanning the meandering stream, is to simply follow the railroad tracks.

The horses carefully pick their way over the long stretch of iron rails to arrive at our destination. Here, Ye hands me his reins and asks me to take the horses down to the water for a drink. He heads to the top of the rock. When the smell of bacon drifts down to the water's edge, I think I must be imaging it as there are no houses for miles. Slowly the realization of what is going on begins to dawn on me and I am overwhelmed and delighted. As if the horses weren't enough of a surprise, Ye has gone through enormous effort to have brought cooking supplies and food out the day before. (This still remains one of my most cherished birthday memories.) Because we are riding bareback, we make the decision by mid-afternoon to leave all the cooking gear on top of the rock and return later that day to retrieve it.

On the trek home, we encounter very strange weather. It transitions from a normal, sunny day in the 80s to cool rain which briefly changes over to hail. This is a bizarre weather pattern that is not too comfortable for us or the horses. Having all the seasons represented in mid-July seems pretty peculiar to us.

Returning early that evening, the weather is still unpredictable. By the time we reach the last long stretch of railroad tracks and head back to the car, the sun is completely down and it's raining again. This is when the idea occurs to duck into the church to wait out the storm. Forcing aside a board in the front door panel, we find ourselves enveloped in a very dark room. We have to let our eyes adjust before making our way up to the front pew where we sit down. By then we can subtly make out a pulpit and other fixtures. The thunder and lightning continue as we sit dripping, staring into the silent space.

Without warning, a blinding-fast blanket of blackness sweeps horizontally across the altar area in front of our faces—close enough to touch us. (Years later I describe it as looking like the 'smoke monster' featured in the television series *Lost*.) We both gasp, checking to be sure we saw the same thing.

Jumping to his feet, Ye insists, "Let's get out of here NOW!"

As shaken as I am, his reaction has a steadying effect on me. A calmer, detached part of me takes over and digs in.

"No! We aren't going anywhere."

Within seconds the 'smoke monster' zooms across our vision again, dowsing the entire room in another blacker gradation, as if someone is steadily dialing down a dimmer switch. Sitting attentively in the pew, the 'taunting' has served to grow my resolve, replacing my remaining vestiges of fear with stubborn defiance. I can feel myself challenging this presence as if it is a bully.

Inwardly, I am saying, "Is that all you got?"

We remain quiet and unmoving as the elongated curtain of inky darkness dashes around us with two more passes in front of our eyes. After a suspended period with no more incidents and a marked shift in the energy, we decide that it has left and I finally agree to go.

Later, I discern that the dark energy backed away because it was not getting the terror response that it wanted and had nothing to feed on. I did not know consciously that the best way to address 'dark entities' was from a detached place without fear, but I instinctually knew, from childhood, that it was the only approach that would work. Taking an oppositional stance (whether it is flight or fight) against something that we fear only gives fuel to the situation and invites more aggression and negativity.

I would have many opportunities to face the cold darkness—although it often felt more like standing before a furnace of intense control tactics. The challenge was not to get 'burned' by my own rash judgment, or the feelings of hopelessness urging me to run. Every encounter was a 'baptism by fire,' so this quote by *Aaron*—a high-level being channeled through *Barbara Brodsky*— continues to 'shore me up' and remind me of why I do this work.

"Only if you stand where the fire is can you transform the fire. The fireman goes to the fire, not to the other side of town. What makes you capable 'firemen' is that the heavier density energies are familiar to you and are part of your daily life. We of spirit can work to support that transformation, but we are not where the fire is. We can support you energetically, but I do not have a heavy-density physical or emotional body, so I cannot transmute the physical as you can. In the process of realization, you bring forth the energy that truly transmutes the heavy-density experience and literally brings the Earth into a higher vibration."

Most of us who are dominantly polarized toward the light are much more comfortable operating from the upper chakras (Heart, Throat, Third Eye and Crown) than dealing with the lower three (Root, Sacral, and Solar Plexus). That's because the bottom three carry all of the heavy issues—our core wounds, relationship and sexual challenges, power and money struggles—and, of course, our body issues and how we feel about ourselves.

Individuals who lean toward a 'flight into light' preference may come across as being spacey to others because they are likely operating with only a portion of themselves, completely in the body. This could be the result of not feeling safe enough to be grounded and fully here, or they may just feel that they don't belong (or want to belong) in the harsh playing fields of Earth. Either way, they are opening themselves up for challenges as having an exclusive 'love and light' mentality does not give you a 'pass' from the karma you are here to deal with.

The concept of *Ascension* first began hitting the internet somewhere around 1997, primarily through individuals considered 'light servers.' They were describing a process affecting the entire world that involves the ongoing acceleration of vibrational energy coming into the planet, creating expanded awareness and a shift in consciousness. Even though this is an energetic process, the effect that it is having on our energy bodies is out-picturing in very physical (and not always pleasant) ways. Signs and symptoms were being identified and outlined which meant that, instead of fearing that you were falling apart, you were being assured that, as you embodied more light, your energies were just being rebooted or up-leveled (like a DNA upgrade) in order to adjust to the gradually rising frequencies. (A detailed list of symptoms can be found at http://www.ascensionsymptoms.com)

One might associate the word *Ascension* with religious connotations or think of it as lifting off into the ethers and going 'home,' but as the symbol of the labyrinth reminds us, organic processes don't usually move in a straight line or with a steady forward motion. Instead, there is an ebb and flow to it, and a crucial part of our individual and collective Ascension process first involves descending into our own dreaded underworlds.

According to *Lisa Renee's Energetic Synthesis website, *"Ascension is about bringing the layers of light, the force existing within the levels of our spiritual bodies (our Multidimensional God Selves) down, descending these layers into matter, anchoring them into the physical plane of reality ... This process will bring our deepest fears, beliefs of limitation and old pain patterns up to the surface through events that trigger them into our awareness so that we can consciously acknowledge, resolve and heal them. Some of these issues are ancestral or inherited in their nature and may feel rather odd, yet familiar when they are brought to our awareness. It is important to remember that we are not only clearing our own individual 'mind' grid, but also the karmic mind implications and collective (un)consciousness implications on this planet from the last evolutionary cycle."*

The Ascension process is preparing us as individuals to take this leap in consciousness, but it is also activating those who made a soul agreement to midwife the Earth into the next octave in frequency. This means that many of you are here because you agreed to *de-evolve* back into third density and immerse yourselves in the muck, willing to face and address whatever has served as a barrier, keeping the Earth in a lower vibrational state. The more aware we become, the more capable we are of facing our personal and collective fears, as well as our personal and collective darkness. It is a challenge to meet with compassion and love that which is coming up to the surface, and that which will continue to be revealed.

To make room for the refined frequencies of the higher dimensions, we have to let go. This may mean letting go of outdated beliefs and thoughtforms, old coping mechanisms, self-judgment, doubts, and things that we habitually project onto others. It also includes the nitty gritty aspects like removing the clutter in our homes, addressing our unhealthy addictions, changing our eating habits, and detoxing our livers. Cleansing requires a healthy relationship involving discipline between our physical, mental, and emotional bodies as we clear out the old to make room for the new.

A friend of mine (Susan), like many others in the early 1980s, believed that there was going to be a 'Pole Shift' around the year 2000 (Y2K) with the Earth tilting on her axis, resulting in the majority of the population perishing. This was a very real and intended scenario by the 'powers that were.' Susan had a reoccurring dream that, on the 'morning after,' when the dust had settled and the remaining few survived, she would be among them.

Jokingly she would add, "Of course I will survive. I signed up for KP duty."

'KP' is the military acronym for the unglamorous job of 'kitchen patrol' or 'kitchen policing' (scrubbing floors, toilets, pots and pans)—the work assigned to the 'grunts.'

The shift out of the predicted collision-course timelines can be attributed, in part, to other dimensional light beings, but keep in mind that they have to take their cues from us—their earthly counterparts who voluntarily incarnated here, intentionally choosing the KP 'short straws.' The 'in-bound enlistees' (which probably includes you if you are reading this) arrived as part of the spiritual 'clean-up crew' long before mass destruction was seen as inevitable. How do you take a barreling train and redirect the point blades to successfully guide the switchover to a new 'track' or timeline? You do it with a committed 'crew' onboard, willing to get their hands dirty, willing to take on the karmic clean-up and emotional cleansing needed for consciousness to be re-routed to a higher track.

Dealing with the 'dark side' is probably one of the more undesirable KP duties and one that requires more self-awareness and self-discipline.

There is a whole secret faction of 'dark forces' operating behind the scenes, who have been called the *Cabal, Global Elite, Shadow Government* or *Illuminati*. They are 'banksters' and war and disease profiteers who empower themselves by disempowering others, manipulating all the world systems from behind the scenes for their own self-serving agendas. Those who are the in-body representations of this 'bloodline' do not work alone. They are intimately connected and controlled by dark entities / energy vampires who are off-planet. Gnostic Christians would call the figurehead *the *Demiurge* (false creator god), describing it as the 'principal of cosmic ignorance.' The interdimensional forces who act as the Demiurge's assistants or servants call themselves the *Archons*. This is a Greek term that means 'rulers' or 'lords,' as they consider themselves the rulers and enslavers of humanity, guiding our history for their own gain for the last 6,000 years. *Cameron Day, who has written extensively on this subject, calls them 'Ankle Biters' which is a more accurate description of who they really are. As psycho-spiritual mind parasites, they are a form of Artificial Intelligence (AI) that takes over like a computer virus designed to corrupt our human physical expressions, and destroy the organic soul connections we have with each other and the Earth. They have no understanding of our sacred connection to Source, except that it stands in the way of their 'takeover.' Their goal is to move us toward artificial expression, replacing human contact and time spent in Nature with sitting at our computers, televisions, tablets or smart phones.

Like a virus that systematically distorts everything it touches, they have been actively interfering with our biological programing. Their ultimate goal is to steadily infiltrate our consciousness, making it OUR idea to become trans-humans, effectively separating ourselves from our innate God-spark. 'Soul snatching' is part of their agenda, with their endgame focused on forcing humanity to willingly wipe itself out.

The *Illuminati* bloodlines were created to be vehicles of these entities or 'cyborgs' who inhabit mind-controlled human bodies bred to infiltrate all levels of our operating systems with the purpose of hijacking this reality. It may have been the Reptilians whose systems were first infected, bringing them into the Earth, but the battle for our consciousness is now here, and we are all involved.

The non-physical 'handlers,' like their *Cabal* counterparts, are negatively polarized. They were never in a human form, but that does not stop them from attaching to vulnerable humans like an intestinal parasite, worming their way into the consciousness of susceptible individuals—as well as confused earthbound souls—and extracting *loosh* (the lower vibrational energy that is released when one is experiencing fear or negativity). Dark entities have a vested interest in manipulating and destabilizing our world in order to control it.

Many *starseeds/wanderers* have agreed to be born into human bodies and come to the Earth at this important time of Ascension to assist Gaia in raising the vibration and to reclaim our sovereignty. This means that, as the *starseeds* awaken and step more fully into their 'missions,' their emerging light may be seen as a threat to the 'power brokers' who would attack with some form of mind control and possibly assign to them a dark-attachment detail to create some kind of reactive disturbance. The intent is to side-track them or shut them down. As parasites, dark entities suck energy from your body, and over time, their presence can make you sick or create a disturbed mental, emotional, or physical condition. Ultimately their goal is to get you to self-destruct, as they still need to honor the precept of your free-will.

Surrounding our planet, there is a dark layer (control grid) created by those who want power over Gaia and her inhabitants. It is made up of the collective accumulation of all our lower-vibrating thoughts and emotions, including decisions we may have made in our soul's past that have bound us to the dark. This dark layer of the Lower Astral Plane is a zone that lies between the third and fourth dimensions. As a barrier constructed by the 'Ankle Biters,' it was meant as a trap to gather human-generated low frequencies to keep us in the third dimensional illusion of polarity and separation, and out of the higher fourth dimensional planes and beyond.

One of its functions is to block the higher frequencies coming from the galactic core. The dark grid holds our unacknowledged fear, shame, resentment, guilt, rage, etc. and is the food supply sustaining the dark side's insatiable appetite. We manufacture more 'food' when we are triggered by fear to react negatively, or when we think poorly of ourselves. Division is created in lots of ways when we suffer trauma or go through any kind of disturbance, disappointment, shock, let-down, or abusive situation.

Trying to function from our small, fractured egos reinforces the illusion that we are separate from each other and separate from Source. Our belief in separation is the very fabric of the 'dark net.' Like a Velcro hem that lines the entire 'hoop skirt' of the dark layer, the dark entities adhere tightly to our fields, tucked out of sight, into the energetic folds of our biology (especially our brains and intestines), or wherever we are most vulnerable.

If there is physical, mental, or emotional trauma affecting us in our daily life, then it is likely that an entity is involved. Our upset emotions feed them—providing all the fertile soil they need to burrow in deeper—unconsciously giving them permission to fester and grow. If we deny or are ignorant of our Inner Divine connection and the True power we have as co-creators to reclaim the sovereign territory of our Selves, the 'squatters' stay firmly planted in our energy fields. But the amazing thing is that, when we become conscious of their presence and claim ownership of our Inner Divine Self, it changes the entire dynamic. Acknowledging them and dealing head-on with the emotional issues their presence has uncovered is the equivalent of boring a tunnel of high powered light right into the inner lining of their lower astral den. Exposing them is 'turning over the dirt' and pulling up their insidious roots. Without our complicit agreement, they have nothing to hold on to.

No matter what belief system you follow regarding the origination of the 'dark side' (Fallen Angels / The Lucifer Rebellion / negatively polarized ET's / Reptilian or AI agendas / a Dark, false creator god / the division between the Annunaki brothers, Enki and Enlil), all versions point to the fact that there was a clear choice made, at some point, to distort and disconnect from Infinite Awareness. The bigger Truth is that polar opposites (good and evil) come from the very same Source but, because the Universe is engaged in a 'Polarity Integration Game,' duality and opposing factions are allowed as a way to promote soul evolution. Those who choose the 'service-to-self' route prefer (and maybe even revere) the *conditioned* distortion of their individual personas. They not only see themselves as separate from their Light Essence, but they identify completely with the condition of their darkness. This results in holding on to the delusion of a self that is separate from and (in their minds) greater than the *Unconditioned Whole*.

Polarizing to either side (the light or the dark) keeps us embattled. The only way we will be able to bring this 'Grand Experiment' to completion is to integrate the light and dark within us. This is what the Ascension process is all about. As awakening human beings, we are here learning to generate our light from a platform of divine neutrality, intending that Cosmic Intelligence take it wherever it is needed. Our willingness to simply illuminate the dark creates space for the 'change agent' of *choice* to be present. If we come from ONE Source, the 'Grand Experiment' is not a design flaw, but a free-will journey intentionally routed through the obstacle course of separation, challenging each of us to find our return path back to Wholeness.

As humans, we have a very special mission to fulfill,
to heal and uplift the entire universe and each other.
We are divine frequency generators,
the antithesis to duality
and this is why the Archons fear us.

~ Justin K. Marlatt ~

40

FOOD SUPPLY

"When the student is ready, the teacher will appear." Most of us would never associate this Buddhist proverb with dark entities but, in Earth school, learning takes place under the tutelage of *all* kinds of teachers.

The Dalai Lama reminded us of the Buddhist point of view when he stated, *"The Chinese officer who is committing the cruel act against the young boy is initiating a new cycle of negative karma. In the case of the child, there is a closure of a particular karma that the child is experiencing. The perpetrator of the crime is in fact an object of more compassion and mercy than the child."*

At first, this point of view is hard to wrap our heads around, especially if you are upset and confused when 'bad' things happen to 'good' or innocent people. But what if there is something bigger going on—something beyond our black and white perception? And what if that 'bigger picture' includes the presence of dark entities? Before arriving here, we each knew we were coming to the 'polarity prison planet,' with the intent to resolve karma through choosing a path of evolution (service-to-self or service-to-others). We can't resolve karma and grow our 'faith' unless karma is present and our faith is challenged. Our souls co-create tailor-made situations that give us opportunities to choose our responses ... again and again. Dark entities operate in stealth mode, skillfully maneuvering their landing gear to dock right into the heart of our most karmic situations. Why? Because that's where the fertilizer/shit is stored and they want to keep close tabs on the 'ground' conditions. They think of themselves as upper management in a food processing plant. They do not walk around openly on the 'floor' of our awareness, but sit in our 'back offices' (our subconscious), running programs to manufacture negative output which directly converts to their 'food supply.'

After the dark undercurrent I experienced in Malta, my interactions with earthbound spirits are getting more challenging. I decide that no matter what kind of negative, non-physical beings might be in attendance, I will always be given the help I need to address them and reset whatever imbalance they may be causing in me and around me. This kind of attitude provokes dark entities, like an annoying student raising a hand and zealously waving it to be called on. It doesn't take long before I get their attention.

Six days after returning from Malta, I receive a (literal) phone call from a woman (Julie) who lives several hours away. She informs me that she is dealing with more of a poltergeist problem than just typical earthbound spirits. Julie is a gifted medium who both sees and hears spirits, but she has never tried to assist them in crossing over. That is, not until a few months earlier when she first called me about her multiplying, unseen 'house guests.'

The unsettling activity has been going on for years on a much smaller scale, leading her to research her property. She shares with me the factual and the anecdotal information that she thinks might be relevant to her 'home invasion.' Julie has identified the primary spirit as a woman (Bertha) who used to live there, and Bertha had begun aggressively coming to Julie, telling her to get out of her house. From the historical information, Julie knows that Bertha's mother married a man (EC) who designed and built the house as a wedding present for her. Bertha was just a young girl, but we conclude that she did not like this man replacing her deceased father and was jealous of the loving relationship between him and her mother. As an adult, she persuaded her mother to leave everything to her in the will, convincing her that EC would more than likely precede her in death. Instead, the mother died unexpectedly, leaving EC heartbroken with all the material possessions willed to her daughter. EC went into deep grief and was despondent. Bertha took steps to have him committed, telling the town that he was crazy. They locked him up for a while until the judge ruled, saying that the step-daughter had to take him back into his own house and provide the care he needed.

A short time later he fell down a flight of steps, which resulted in a broken hip and a cracked skull. While convalescing at home, Bertha was responsible for administering his medications and he didn't last long. After EC died, Bertha stayed in the house for the rest of her life, but not without her own hardships. She lived there with her husband and when he died unexpectedly, she was left to raise her two children who became estranged from her, and in the end she died of breast cancer.

In our first session, Julie had confronted Bertha about EC's fall, suspecting her direct involvement and questioning if she had overmedicated him to complete the job. Bertha never did admit to this. She did, however, finally accept that she no longer belonged here and was open to the possibility that we could help reunite her with her own Higher Self, and move her to a new home of light. We created an energetic labyrinth in Julie's living room and Bertha left, along with countless others who had taken up residence in the house.

With so many spirits present, I had suspected that there was a natural portal somewhere on the property that was drawing in all the earthbound traffic. Julie immediately identified a crawl space in her basement that always felt 'creepy' to her, and a cistern was located here beneath the house. After our session dealing with Bertha, Julie had been guided to outline the whole house in rock salt and then trail it around the outer perimeter of the property. She also burned sage in different rooms of the house and used holy water over the doorways.

Now, months later, she is calling me with an urgent tone in her voice stating that she believes she is dealing with a 'demonic spirit.' She backs this up by telling me that there is a male presence in the house who is taunting her. The paranormal activity of lights turning on and off and doors opening has escalated to another level. She can clearly hear him threatening to "kill" her, stating that there is nothing she can do to stop him. This has my attention, as this kind of direct threat is unlike any other expressed by earthbound spirits I have encountered. I tell her we are going to figure out what this dark consciousness is connected to.

By just saying this, Julie is suddenly aware of EC, realizing that we never even considered him when we dealt with Bertha and all of the other intruders. It seems quite likely that he never moved across—especially if there was foul play involved in his death.

When Julie tunes into him to see if he is the one making the threats, she relays to me that EC, who is on the verge of answering her, is interrupted by the same unmistakable threatening voice, *"You imbecile! Shut up and don't tell her a thing!"* This is a clarifying moment for us as the dark entity just 'outed' himself, removing his biggest advantage: his veil of secrecy.

Using the image of the tube torus fountain coming up from the Prairie Labyrinth, we visualize it arching across the state coming down like a waterfall over Julie's backyard in southwestern Missouri. Here it merges with a labyrinth pattern that she is envisioning outside the area of the underground cistern. The tube torus serves as a 'pillar of light,' able to organize aspects or fragments from multiple timeframes occurring in different locations. It is the perfect tool to create a unified intersection point.

The need for revenge that continued for two generations between EC and his step daughter pulled in all kinds of souls who may have had matching emotional issues: grief, jealousy, entitlement, resentment, hatred and confusion. Beneath the magnified mess, a higher-ranking dark entity was being revealed—the one most likely responsible for keeping the long-standing turmoil in operation. He staked out this house as his own personal 'feeding trough,' and was naturally invested in maintaining the 'food supply.' We had disrupted his steady menu of upheaval by releasing Bertha (one of his 'personal chefs') who left with a large entourage of 'sous chefs.' This called him out from his covert 'control tower' where he orchestrated mayhem from behind the scenes, bringing him smack into the main 'kitchen.' In order to gain control of his 'dining hall,' he had to personally serve up a restricted diet of fear.

As a single mother, Julie raised her three kids in this house, plagued the entire time with disturbing supernatural situations that, more than likely, contributed to personal conflicts and health challenges. This included estrangement from her adult children and her own diagnosed breast cancer.

It is probable that EC blindly saw Julie as an extension of Bertha. Caught in a continuous loop of unresolved feelings, EC was fully engaged in an escalating battle with both of them.

Now that we understood the situation, we could reach EC by speaking directly to him. "We know that you were a good man who deeply loved your wife. Would you like to see her again and be reunited with her? This is possible. She is waiting for you to join her."

Our words take him by surprise, as if he is suddenly remembering that this is all he has ever wanted. I assure him that we can call her to him when he is ready to move into the portal. Redirecting his focus to his wife is all it takes to shift his energy.

He shouts to us, *"Get me out of here!"*

Julie reports to me with concern that the dark entity is growing bigger, looking more like a werewolf, and becoming more threatening to EC.

We ask EC, "Does this 'beast' have a name?"

Before he can be silenced again, he blurts out, *"Librem!"*

With the portal open, we call in the Higher Self of EC, asking that his wife also come in to assist him. As soon as he sees her, all his resistance is gone. He is sobbing and holding on to her. Escorted by the two light beings, they move into the center of the tube torus fountain running through the middle of the joined labyrinths, and then they are gone.

Now Librem is extremely mad as he hisses at Julie, *"This is never going to end! Reinforcements are on their way and you are powerless to stop us!"*

Calmly, I answer, "That's not the way we see it, Librem."

In a fit of anger he jumps up and down, screaming, *"You are imbeciles! And my name is NOT Librem!"* (I had pronouncing it Lie-bram) *"It is LIBREM!"* (Lee-brim.) It is like listening to "Rumpelstiltskin" shouting his name. I am thrilled to get the right pronunciation, as it seems important to be able to name him in releasing him.

Repeating his name correctly, I call his Higher Self to come. This elicits squeals of laughter, telling us that there is no such thing as a self that is 'higher' than he is, and there is NO light in him. Ignoring him, I call anyway. All of this is being translated through Julie who is seeing and relaying the conversation to me. She tells me that, when the two light beings arrive, Librem has a temper tantrum and pounds the ground with his fists. In his anger and resistance, he digs his nails into the soil and holds on. I ask the light beings to enfold him, and Julie watches as they lay their light bodies completely over him like a blanket. She describes steam pouring out from under them. When they stand back, all that is left is a small, deflated ball of what used to be Librem. He still is quietly claiming that there is no good in him. The two angels pick up the remaining glob, looking now a bit like roadkill, and press it lovingly between their heart chakras as they wrap their arms around each other. As one unit of light they lift off into the swirling tube torus and evaporate.

We invite any other spirits who are witnessing this, including the three minions who have arrived as his backup, to use the portal while it is available. The three disappear without any resistance. When everything is calm, Julie uses her hands to make counter-clockwise circles over the cistern area, clearing the last vestiges of any remaining residue. We envision turning off the tube torus fountain and tracing the labyrinth in reverse to close it. In the aftermath, Julie uses salt to make an equal sided cross with a clockwise circle around it over the door to the cistern.

Together we say the words: *"Let all energies of anger, fear, resentment, envy, jealousy or hatred that have come through this portal be transformed to loving energy and returned to Source. This portal is now sealed for all time."*

Julie decides that, for any future work with souls she encounters, she will use the outdoor labyrinth at a church that is only blocks from her house. Later she finds out that EC and his wife were members of that same church.

Julie is presently cancer free and pursuing the work that she has a God-given talent for. As an 'Unexpected Medium' and translator of the unseen worlds, she is educating and assisting others who are beginning to venture into these realms.

~ Julie Kellogg, The Unexpected Medium
   theunexpectedmedium.com

Our greatest enemy is the fear
that we have hidden deep inside.
If that fear can be brought to our awareness
it can be loved free.

~ Aaron ~

41

MOVING ON

How does a dark entity get past the protection of your own fortified 'firewall' to take over the controls of your personal system? As master 'hackers,' the dark forces exploit the weaknesses of the human condition. They use our fears, curiosities, tragedies, traumas, insecurities, vulnerabilities, obsessions or addictions as passcodes, giving them unrestricted access. The dark entity in Julie's encounter was attracted to a nest of disgruntled earthbound spirits, but they were all pawns designed to spread the 'virus' of EC's unrest into this timeframe and infect the present-day inhabitants.

All over the world there are dark, clandestine operators on both sides of the veil, targeting and affecting the health and wellbeing of non-suspecting individuals. A whole-body 'system takeover' may seem rare, but it's likely that it happens more often than we think. How many people who are being treated for physical, emotional, or mental illnesses are actually unknowing victims, targeted by the dark side? Programing a young, malleable mind is an effective way to infiltrate and upset much bigger systems. I believe we have seen this repeatedly, especially behind every so-called 'terrorist attack' that are largely false flag events designed to induce terror. It is not surprising that impressionable, confused, testosterone-laden young men would be desirable marks for mind control in combination with entity attachments. The following story is about one such 'take-over' attempt from the perspective of my friend Dan, who shares our joint experience in shutting it down.

"January 23, 2013, the temperature is very cold, and the yin effects of winter dominate the environment. I receive a phone call at about 11:30 p.m. from one of my best friends, Jim. We catch up with small talk, but I can tell something is up. He finally tells me that his son Ralph, who is 18, is in the hospital and, after doing every test possible, the doctors still have no idea what is wrong. Ralph's heart rate is completely erratic, jumping all around with no consistent rate or pattern. This began three days earlier when Jim and his wife, Suzie, were awakened by hearing Ralph arguing with his little sister. This was out of character for Ralph. He was extremely upset and when Jim came to see what was going on, he became aggressive and pushy. Frightened, Jim called the police to keep everyone safe, as he had never seen Ralph act like this before. Convincing the policeman that he needed medical attention, the officer agreed to take him to the hospital.

Now Jim is having a hard time coping with the fact that everything has come to a standstill and nothing seems to be helping. He asks if I will come to the hospital in the morning to see him. I suspect that this is going to be more than just a typical visit so I begin my own preparations, breathing, meditating, and visualizing love, light, and healing energy showering down on me. I know I need to be fully focused in the present moment and at my best to evaluate Ralph's situation and condition.

The next day I arrive at the hospital and, as I make my way down the hall to Ralph's room, I see a monitor in the nurse's station showing all the heart rates of each patient and one stands out. Immediately I know it is Ralph's. I watch in amazement as it jumps all over the place, just like Jim told me. I think to myself, 'This is crazy. How can this be?' As I look toward his room, I can feel the change in the energy around me. Walking through the door into his room is like entering a basement that is dark, heavy, and stagnant. Ralph is lying in the bed with his head tilted up. His whole body is stiff and it is easy to see that he is not himself. Jim is there with him with a worried look of despair on his face. He steps outside to take a breather, giving me time to talk to Ralph.

I've known Ralph for years and have never seen him acting this weird. Asking him questions, I can see from his responses that he is fighting something within himself. Because his breathing is labored, I say to him, 'OK, Ralph—

let's do a little breathing together.'

As I place my hand on his heart, I notice that his chest is cold and needs energy. He seems drained. I hold acupressure points on his body with the intention of hooking up his central nervous system. I instruct him to put his hand over mine while we begin to do deep belly breathing together, encouraging the Chi to flow in his body. He starts to settle down so I continue to ask him more detailed questions about what is going on inside of him. He points to his mouth and begins moving his head back and forth while blowing in an attempt to get something out. His demeanor changes with each question. It is like talking to two different people. The only place I'd ever seen anything like this was in movies. I can't help but ask myself, 'Could Ralph be possessed?' He is starting to get a little stirred up from all the personal questions, so I decide to give him a break and step out in the hall to process all of this.

Suzie walks up to me and confides that, out of desperation, she has contacted a psychic that she respects from Indiana. He has determined that her son is being possessed by a negative entity named Jean Claude Menieval and identifies him as one of Napoleon's henchman from the 18th century. I don't know what to think about this, but return to his room to see if this demon is for real.

Ralph's eyes are glaring at me as I enter the room, as if he knows what I have come for. He displays signs of fear and nervousness. I pull my chair close to the bed and sit very still, just watching him. Immediately Ralph's body starts fidgeting, with his arms, legs, neck, and head moving all around. He looks at me with far-away eyes and a weird smirk on his face, and says 'WHAT?' as he shrugs his shoulders and then looks away. This catches my attention, convincing me that there really is something going on deeper inside of him. His breath is labored, his eyes blink uncontrollably, he chatters a little bit in very low tones, making it hard to understand him.

Staying focused on his erratic behavior, my senses become sharper, really tuning into the rhythm of his body, following the energy that is moving all around inside of him. The left hand begins twitching, the elbow moves, and then his whole arm moves from his shoulder. The head begins jerking, moving to the right shoulder, and then down to his right elbow. He bends and clenches his fist and then flexes it wide open. I watch his right elbow bend all the way up to his chest, twitching his right shoulder forward, then back. When his chest begins to expand up and outward and then rapidly contract, it looks like something is poking outward and moving around the Solar Plexus. It's like watching a creature from the movie *Alien making its way down Ralph's abdomen. From under the bed sheets, I can see and feel the weird energy moving down his legs, then back up his legs. Back up through the abdomen to the solar plexus again where I notice this strange probe-looking thing pushing in and out of his body like it is trying to find a way out ... or maybe a place to attach more deeply. After his hand reaches up and out, making a fist and releasing it, I realize that this strange energy is following the meridian pathways inside Ralph's body.

Ralph looks at me and asks, 'What's wrong?'

He is rubbing his third eye, making a face that tells me he is in pain. I continue to monitor whatever is still moving around his body, knowing it's what is causing him such discomfort.

Suzie receives a text with a couple of prayers on it from her psychic friend. They are intended to cleanse him of anything negative or evil, so we surround Ralph and recite them over and over, blessing him and forgiving him, calling anything negative to come forward. The tension in the air is really building now and Ralph is squirming all around in his bed.

I call out to Jean Claude Menieval or any other spirits within him to come forward. 'I command you to leave this man's body right now.'

Ralph's body starts to arch, bending upward like a bow. His mouth is making a round shape, like he trying to blow something out again, moving his head back and forth. When I put my hand above him and demand the demon to come out, his body begins jerking and pulsating until it rises up, like it is being raised by a rope or string attached to his navel. In an impossible back-bending position, his toes and back of his head are the only things touching the bed. Seeing this, I have had enough. I have no doubt that this kid is possessed by something, but it's time to back off and try to calm him down. His body drops down to the bed as he hyperventilates and shakes uncontrollably.

He motions to me to come closer to him as he attempts to blow something out of his mouth. As I move my face a little closer to his, he lunges forward at me opening his mouth wider. Immediately I read his intentions and move back to a safe distance. I feel like something is trying to jump out of him and into me! In past situations requiring healing, I have instinctively taken the pain away from others into my own energy field where I transmute it and help to release it. This one is different and I know I cannot take this demon into myself, but I do not know what to do.

Suddenly it comes to me to call my friend, Toby Evans. I go out into the hallway and pull out my cell phone. I begin telling her what I have been experiencing with this young man and she agrees that he has a negative entity attached to him.

She explains how to release it using the image of the labyrinth, and emails me a picture of the Chakra Labyrinth pattern and an image of the Merkaba energy field that will help take the entity out of our dimension. This sounds like a lot to remember, and after what I have just seen I do not feel comfortable or confident in attempting this alone. Toby agrees to meet me at the hospital the next day.

Before leaving, I retreat to the lobby where many members of Ralph's extended family are gathered. They are trying to piece together how this came about. His little sister, Cindy, tells me she overheard Ralph and their cousin Bob (who is about the same age), talking about looking up 'dark side' web-sites on the internet. Concerned, she tells me, 'They were saying they did not believe in God, but they did believe in the devil.'

With this information, I make my way over to Bob and confront him, asking him if this is what they have been doing?

He admits it and justifies it by saying, 'Ya know, the Universe is a strange place. I've had hallucinations and seen really weird things. Hallucinations are the best! You can see so many things, ya know? Things you never imagined are real.'

I ask if he is still engaging in these dark side activities and he says, "No."

I also find out that Cindy has told her parents that, the night Ralph started acting weird, he was playing a video game all night into the morning called 'Black Ops.' This is a very violent military-themed game with intense scenes, profanity, and gore that is recommended for adults only. She remembers Ralph saying that there was someone in the game who had never been in it *before, and he could not figure out how this guy was in there because he had been obsessively playing the game for weeks and would know if there were any new players. This guy knew the game inside and out. Right after that is when Ralph changed, and began cursing and getting agitated.*

Saying goodnight, I head for my van for the ride home. I can't help thinking about the close call of Ralph trying to blow Jean Claude Menieval into my mouth. The wind picks up as I approach the bridge over the river and the van begins to shake. With the front end bouncing around, it is becoming more difficult to steer. Once on the bridge, I see some kind of orb or figure that looks like it has a hold of the front of the van and he is trying to push it off of the bridge.

I hear him in my mind saying, 'It's you! You're the one in my way! I have to get rid of you. You are not going to stop me!'

I grip the steering wheel tighter. The van is jumping around pretty good now, making it harder to keep it on the road. It keeps pulling to the right. I realize the entity is trying to cancel my plans for releasing him from Ralph tomorrow.

The assaults continue to come at me, 'You have to go. There is no way to stop me.'

I shout back at him, 'No! I am not going anywhere and you haven't seen shit because you haven't met Toby yet.'

At that moment, the orb-looking thing jumps off the van, vanishing into the river, and immediately the wind is calm and the van is driving fine again.

Arriving at the hospital the next morning, I find there is a monitoring station set up in Ralph's room due to his heart arrhythmias, with a technician assigned to be in there around the clock to watch the readings on the screen. I find Ralph squatting down on the bed with his hands under his armpits chirping like a bird, flapping his wings.

'I'm a bird, Dan', *he says to me,* 'Chirp, Chirp.'

I respond to him, 'No you're not. You are Ralph.'

It takes us a little while to get him to lie back down in the bed. I then find out that Jim and Suzie told the hospital staff that they believed their son is possessed by a spirit and that someone is going to be coming this morning to do a ceremony to exorcise him.

When Toby arrives, she is met with a concerned Head Nurse and the Head administrator of the Hospital who lead all of us into a conference room. Their primary concern is for the patients in the hospital, and they want assurance that what we will be doing is not going to endanger Ralph or anyone else. It has already been discussed that the next stop for Ralph is going to be the Mental Health Ward. They want to know what they can expect from what she is going to be doing.

Toby assures them that this will not look like a *Linda Blair scene from the horror movie *The Exorcist, and there will be no drama. She shows them an image of the Labyrinth on the inside cover of her Chakra Labyrinth Cards and explains that she will simply be tracing the image to create a portal to release the spirit. I think they are relieved. They remain professional but are surprisingly accommodating, telling us that they have seen everything imaginable over the years. They give us permission—the closest thing to their blessings—adding that they will replace the tech in his room with the Head Nurse who will be there to monitor his physical symptoms and, of course, his heart.

Toby sits on Ralph's left side, and I sit on his right. She says a prayer and, in her mind, draws a left-handed labyrinth over Ralph and envisions it dropping below him. She then draws a right-handed labyrinth and sends it above the bed, creating a contained portal of light over the room, connecting it to the 'Prairie Labyrinth' on her property.

Ralph is starting to look a little worried as we settle in around him. Toby directs her attention and remarks to Ralph, not Jean Claude Menieval (who has demanded that we use his full name when addressing him). She suspects that he is just an imposter spirit working with the dark side who enjoys this bogus identity that gives him a false measure of status and power. She ignores him altogether and reassures Ralph that it is time for the imposter to leave and for him to fully reclaim his body again. She adds that we would like his assistance in helping the entity to cross over successfully. Ralph is passive and quiet and agrees to help. Toby places the pattern of the Labyrinth on his lap as he is sitting up in an inclined position and I put my left hand on Ralph's heart, helping him to hold the pattern.

She explains to Ralph that he is going to trace the path into the center, with the idea that Angels and Light Beings will be gathering to assist us in releasing all energy that does not belong to him. They will be helping to guide it out of his body. She tells him that when he reaches the center there will be two beings of light forming the Merkaba around the entity, escorting him back to the appropriate dimension for his growth. I show Ralph the picture of the Merkaba on my phone so he can envision it with us. He thinks it looks cool.

With deliberation, he starts to trace the pattern. It seems a little difficult for him, as he pushes his finger slowly around each of the seven chakra paths until he arrives in the middle. He pauses here as we all envision the angelic beings coming in to surround the situation. She tells Ralph it is time to fully release Jean Claude Menieval as she begins twirling her fingers in counterclockwise circles in front of his third eye. This is where the pain has been most concentrated. He suddenly arches back, taking a deep breath, and bends forward, blowing with all his might until his head is touching his knees. When he fully expels all of the air, we all take a deep breath.

She instructs us to picture the Merkaba forming around the exiting spirit as it spins in counter-rotating circles, enclosing him in a whirling net of light that finally takes him up and out of the top of the portal. She asks for any other minions, dark entities, or bound spirits who were with Jean Claude to be gathered up by the angelic forces and taken through the portal. When this seems complete, she tells Ralph to retrace the Labyrinth path back out as a way to close the portal.

As he completes the final Root Chakra pathway, there is a feeling of *calmness in the room. Ralph begins to cry, looking lost and bewildered. His mom, Suzie, who has been sitting in a chair at the bottom of his bed, comes to hold him. He thanks everyone, saying that he loves us—finally returning to the Ralph I always knew.*

About fifteen minutes later when Toby is leaving, the Head Nurse tells her that she watched Ralph's heart rate register at 140 when we began, spiking to 180 at the moment of release, and immediately afterwards, flipping back to 110 ... where it remained, staying consistent for the first time since he entered the hospital.

After the ordeal I return home and just sit, thinking about the whole experience. I would never have believed that any of these things really existed before witnessing it firsthand. I had my own experience in the Labyrinth years before when I was down in the dumps depressed, and hating my life and myself. I had to overcome my own resistance and fear just to make my first journey to the Labyrinth. There, in the middle, I released the negative energy, garbage, and mind chatter, enabling me to sit still and be in the present moment. A lifetime of rubbish was being washed away from me so I could be free to love myself and everyone else. My heart was blown wide open. That same day, I learned the power of forgiveness which freed me from my own prison. I see myself in Ralph. After this experience with him, I want to learn more about the Labyrinth. To know this path is to begin to know myself and open to my real self—my Higher Self.

Ralph checked out of the hospital the next day and was really grateful to be going home. I hope he learned a valuable lesson from his desire to explore the dark side and open himself to negative energies. Ralph says he cannot remember most of his experience. Looking back for him, it seems like a blur, but I won't forget it. I am grateful that there is a defined path like the Labyrinth that can help us all 'move on.'"

~ Aloha'Dan Dan Fagan
  fullblownfengshui@gmail.com
  Kansas City, Missouri
  Master Instructor Tae Kwon Do

You stand on the cusp of returning to your SELF,
but before you can proceed you must consciously face
and conquer ALL your own darkness.

~ Suzanne Lie ~

42

CLASH BETWEEN REALITIES

A desire to explore the dark side isn't the only way for you to pop up on the radar screen of a dark entity. Even if you are not looking for them, and even if you don't believe they exist—if you become a threat to their 'food supply,' they will find you. I have great compassion for Ralph as I know from my own past experience what it is like to be pulled into fear, battling an entity for control of my own body.

At the completion of an Incan Medicine Wheel training in 1997, I journeyed to Peru with several friends from my ayllu (our Shamanic community). Weeks before leaving, I have the foreboding sense that I am being drawn there to meet my own death. I rationalize that it's more likely that I have had a previous lifetime when I died there. I am just beginning to grasp the concept that there may really be such a thing as aspects of our souls that have not crossed over, but this is still before I realize that I can use the pattern of the labyrinth to assist them.

In preparation for the trip, I stand in the center of the Prairie Labyrinth and suddenly feel the presence of Sai Baba, an Indian spiritual guru who is the one who initially instructed me to 'become the chalice,' receiving the incoming light for the year-long guided visualization I was doing at that time.

He simply drops an offer into my mind, *"Call on me if you need any help."*

The week before leaving, I come down with the flu and still feel wretched on the flight there. To my amazement, all of my symptoms disappear once we arrive in Cuzco.

The city of Cuzco is said to be laid out in the shape of a puma, the animal symbolizing the Inca dynasty, and on a hill overlooking Cuzco is Sacsayhuaman— the puma's head. Sacsayhuaman is a massive walled complex, built with enormous precisely-fitted boulders, which rivals any ancient monolithic monument built on the Earth. It is not hard to imagine the outer three terraced rows of zigzagging limestone walls as the puma's jagged teeth. To some they represent the three levels of the Andean spiritual world: the lower or underground (Ukhu Pacha), the middle world (Kay Pacha), and the upper world (Hanan Pacha). The Inca empire ended in 1532 when Spanish conquistadors, under the command of Francisco Pizarro, slaughtered thousands of innocent people.

On our third day in Cuzco we have a prearranged agreement to meet a local shaman outside the walls of Sacsayhuaman where he will be performing a *despacho* ceremony with us for the Solstice. A despacho is an Andean practice of making offerings to Mother Earth (Pachamama), the mountains (Apus), and all other spirits in nature as a way to enter into unity with all things in reciprocity, respect, and gratitude.

And how did we connect with a shaman so quickly? In Peru, shamans line up outside the airport waiting for wide-eyed New Age newbies right alongside the taxi cab drivers. The ceremony we arranged is a concession as this was not the shaman's first choice. He told us that a daytime ritual was not possible and instead offered to perform (for much more money) an ayahuasca ceremony, beginning the night before, that would last into the morning of the Solstice. Ayahuasca, commonly called *yage*, is a medicinal tea or psychedelic brew made from a vine in combination with other specific plants found in the Amazon jungle. It is referred to as the 'truth vine,' 'vision vine,' or 'vine of the dead.' This powerful plant medicine is not to be taken lightly as the latest spiritual fad. Ayahuasca, regarded as a sacred being, must be invited in with great reverence and requires proper attunement—physically, mentally, and spiritually. Our shaman does not mention any necessary preparation or make suggestions for our wellbeing, only insisting that anyone who wants to be present for the ceremony, without exception, will have to agree to take the ayahuasca.

I am in turmoil. Even though I was a teenager at the tail end of the 60s spiritual and sexual revolution, the expansion of my consciousness did not include drugs. Many of my friends smoked weed or experimented with a variety of substances, but something held me back. I couldn't imagine that I needed to take anything to feel better than I already did, but I'd also conceded that perhaps I didn't like the idea of being out of control. Unknowingly, I had also been safeguarding my energy system.

Those in our group who have already done ayahuasca matter-of-factly describe that the process will involve ingesting and then releasing the drug—in a combination of ways that may include vomiting, dry heaving, or diarrhea—before the visions set in. This not only sounds unappealing, but I have an aversion to throwing up. I will do anything to avoid it. The majority of our group is all for complying with his terms, but I can't ignore the uneasiness churning in my gut. As the primary hold-out, I am aware of the peer pressure I am feeling as well as the seduction of the ceremony.

Knowing we need to reach a consensus by that afternoon, I retreat to my room on the second floor of the lodge. In conflict with my own resistance, I am trying to discern if I am just being an uptight prude, or if my body is in caution mode for good reason.

In exasperation I turn to Spirit, saying aloud, "If participating in the ayahuasca ceremony is for my highest good on all levels, then I ask to be given some kind of sign that all is well. If this is not for my highest good, then please block it."

I feel better immediately just turning it over to a higher power, not having to figure it out with my head. Within 30 minutes of uttering this prayer request, I hear an animated conversation taking place outside—just below my window. Looking down, I see the shaman waving his hands and speaking rapidly in Spanish to the woman in our group who is serving as our translator. He is irritated and upset. About ten minutes later, they come to some kind of agreement as things quiet down and he walks away. She calls us together to report that the batch of ayahuasca that was coming over the mountains was somehow contaminated by mold and deemed unusable. This has never happened to him before and he is not happy. Because of this new development, he agrees to do the despacho ceremony with us at Sacsayhuaman the next day—in broad daylight. I feel immediate relief.

By mid-afternoon we reach the end of the very long ceremony with the shaman burning the despacho offering. I fear that my flu symptoms are returning as I start to feel dizzy and slightly nauseous with a mild headache. I drink more water, telling myself that I am just dehydrated. The shaman transitions to the role of our tour guide, leading us to another area as he lectures on its significance. He takes us through a winding passageway between high boulders, pointing up to a ledge with shelf-like vertical niches cut into the stones. The translator interprets that these were once used to store mummies.

I reach my hand up and brush the base of one of the concave units when I hear a faint voice drift up to my consciousness informing me, *"I was among them."*

This statement is quickly followed by a meek request, *"Do I have permission to enter?"*

I hesitate aware that there is a silent alarm going off prompting me to quickly respond, "NO!"

I feel as if I am tentatively standing at a door with the safety chain still in place and my guard up. This is like peeking out at Little Red Riding Hood holding her basket, but the raised hairs on the back of my neck tells me that the Big Bad Wolf is hiding beneath her cloak.

My attempt to shut the energetic door and establish a boundary is met with the overriding sentiment of *"Tough shit!"*

The 'door' is shattered with the force of a battering ram, and in a terrifying split second my energy system is taken hostage. I can barely talk I am in so much pain. There is a vice grip around my head that keeps ratcheting tighter and tighter. The shaman looks over at me with his eyes growing wide as I plead for him to help me. He takes his bottle of Florida water (used much like sage for smudging) and splashes it in my hands, being careful not to touch me. All the while he is rapidly admonishing me in Spanish for making myself available to dark spirits. Unsure of all he is uttering, I am clear that he wants nothing to do with them so he quickly distances himself from me. The others in our group follow his lead. Even in childbirth I have not experienced this level of agony.

The group hovers around the Shaman as he makes his way toward the first wall with the biggest, megalithic stones. I fall behind, barely able to put one foot in front of the other.

Somewhere beneath the raging battle in my head, an inner voice instructs me, *"Open the top of your Crown Chakra and send them to the sun."*

I have no idea who or what I am dealing with, but it certainly feels like two opposing factions. I stop on the dirt path and visualize the top of my head opening as if I am using a corkscrew to pull out a tight-fitting plug. There is a shift in the pressure as I close my eyes and continue imagining counterclockwise rotations.

My friend Carol comes up behind me, "Toby, what are you doing? There is a pillar of light coming out the top of your head and it is going all the way up to the sun!"

I manage to say, "That's what I am trying to do!"

With her arms around me she looks over my shoulder to describe Pac-Man-looking blobs of black energy all around the hills being sucked back into the stones through the triangle-like windows that open and then shut. The pain subsides and Carol joins the others. I attempt to reach the group, but as I get closer to them the ratcheting pressure resumes and intensifies. Off to my right I see an archeological site roped off with a wooden sign pounded into the ground that reads, "Rainbow Temple." It jars me out of my stupor, reminding me to call upon Sai Baba. He is often called the "Rainbow man" because of the numbers of rainbows that have appeared in his name. Silently I beg for his help.

The group has made their way to the third terrace before I catch up with them. I listen to the Shaman giving them information about the climb to the top level where there are giant rings of stones around a circular shaped ruin, designated the *Sun Temple*. I collapse just off to their right, sinking against the outer rim of the stone wall where all of their backpacks are leaning. I know I will not be going any further.

I am still pleading for Sai Baba's help when I hear his calm instruction, *"And now it is time to throw up."*

This is NOT what I want to hear. I thought I avoided vomiting by not doing ayahuasca. I begin protesting, pointing out that there is no good place to do such a thing without drawing attention to myself and disrespecting the sanctity of this sacred site.

Realizing he is not budging from his position, I begin bargaining. "Then find me a place where no one will see me."

Looking furtively around, I know this is not going to be easy. Every crevice is crawling with tourist groups.

Sai Baba's lighthearted words sing in my ear, *"You don't have time for this."*

It dawns on me that he is saying that I do not have time to go *anywhere*. This is going to happen right here, in plain sight—right where I am now! In a panic, I pull at the grass with the intent to dig a depression, not registering that we are in the southern hemisphere going into the winter season and the ground is quite hard. In response to my insane expectation, the earth releases in clumps as easy as pulling up handfuls of Spanish moss. I have a sizeable hole dug in seconds. I lunge forward, preparing for the dreaded retching that I can no longer hold back. Opening my mouth, I watch in astonishment as viscous silver mercury comes pouring out of me. There is no taste of bile because my stomach is not involved. My head is like a water cooler with the faucet wide open. In disbelief, I watch the 'liquid mercury' draining out of my mouth and disappearing into the hole. As the substance pours out, the pressure level in my head steadily drops.

I feel Sai Baba slightly above and behind me, coaching me to say the words, "I release you—I release you—I release everything that does not belong to me."

When it is over, the mercurial substance has completely evaporated and with it the pain in my head. No one has noticed a thing, but I am wiped out on every level. My brain is unraveling like a snagged ball of yarn that I am desperate to untangle. Within minutes, all of the various groups that have been swarming the three lower areas are gone, making their way up to the higher levels. I sit alone in a daze, propped against the wall, content to be left to watch over the lined-up backpacks that remain as the only witnesses to my ordeal.

All over Peru there are clusters of small children between two and ten years of age who take their 'job' of trailing tourists and begging for money very seriously. Barely able to catch my breath, I am descended upon by five youngsters with their hands outstretched. I don't have the strength to shoo them away, but simply shake my head 'No.' One of the young girls comes closer with a look of concern in her eyes. I try to convey to her that I do not feel well. It is late afternoon by now with a growing cloud cover and noticeably dropping temperatures. The children, barefooted and scantily clad in light cotton dresses or tee shirts and shorts, brace their small bodies against the cold misty winds that are picking up. I pat the ground next to me, inviting them to sit against the wall to try to stay warm. Without hesitating, they drop down beside me, tucking themselves under my outstretched arms until we are all huddled together. Their complete trust disarms me. I realize the truth: they are really holding me—pulling me back to 3D Earth—back into the lap of Pachamama who is beneath us—grounding me through the gift of their human touch. I feel like a deer that has outrun its predator to finally arrive in a clearing where it can let down its guard and shake off the adrenaline overload. Realizing that I am safe within the protection of their tender hearts, I hold onto them tightly, allowing a flood of tears to stream down my face. The children stay nestled against me until the rest of my group comes off the hill and, with their help, I find my sea legs to walk the distance back to our lodging.

Long after I returned home, a member of the American Dowsing Society explained to me that the mercury-looking substance was *ectoplasm*. Some may refute that ectoplasm is nothing more than fictional 'Ghostbuster's slime,' but they have never had it coming out of their mouth. Ectoplasm is described as "the state of being which ghosts and demons take on in order to enter our realm." (I think of Ralph also trying to blow the intrusion out of his mouth.)

The following words helped me to reframe this experience, understanding that I unknowingly opened a portal into the Lower Astral Plane which vibrates at a lower frequency than the Earth.

"When one is a portal opener, they are the first ones in. As you first enter into that which has just been opened, you meet the resistance of what we call 'the clash between realities.' You are actually leaving the 3D reality.

Thus, you must find your way through the lower fourth dimensional—Lower Astral Plane. Within this lower plane rests all the effluvia of darkness that has reigned over Gaia for more of your 'time' than you would want to know. Within the lower Astral Plane, you will meet all you have not yet completed."

~ Suzanne Lie

It is not until one seeks to find the Light within them
that they come into their own power.

~ **Marlene Swetlisoff** ~

43

JEWEL IN THE LOTUS

In the immediate aftermath of my "ectoplasm" experience, I am fragmented and fragile with no point of reference to process or understand what has occurred to me. It takes quite a while for me to wrap my head around the idea that the 'mummified' aspect was a part of me from an Incan lifetime that had not crossed over and had been waiting at the "Lower Astral" station (with many others who jumped on board) when my consciousness arrived there. The dark entities were scrambling to reinstate control by terrorizing those who were attempting to flee by running a replay loop of fear, reliving their original attack. I felt the battle being waged inside my head because access to all realities lies within.

The following morning at breakfast, someone in our group comments that it is likely that I was just suffering from high altitude sickness. (After three days of already acclimating in Cuzco, it was more accurately, the 'altitude' of the lower dimensional frequency that I couldn't handle.) On the recovery side, I am left feeling empty and stripped of any solid sense of who I am, wishing that I was on a plane heading for home. Instead, I sit withdrawn in the back of a van that is transporting our group to the 'Temple of the Winds,' *Ollantaytambo*. Located at the northwestern end of the Sacred Valley of the Incas, this is a massive citadel that was used as a temple and a fortress. For many tourists, it is the common starting point to hike the Inca trail. As the royal estate of Emperor Pachacuti, who was responsible for conquering the region, it also served as a

337

stronghold for the leader of the Inca resistance during the Spanish conquest.

Still shaken by the incident, I have no interest in our destination—only happy to be leaving the immediate area ... especially Sacsayhuaman. With the shell of my psyche broken into tiny pieces, I am holding a fractured perception of the Cuzco region.

Just as 'demons' can interfere with and interpenetrate our reality from a lower vibrational frequency, it is also true that 'angels' or multidimensional beings can come in to assist us from a higher dimensional field. On some level that I am unaware of, my soul is calling in an 'emissary of light' to reset the disruption in my energy system.

After checking into a local hostel in Ollantaytambo, we make our way on foot to the entrance of the ruins where we face the *Temple Hill*. This is an impressively steep hill on which the Incas built a ceremonial center. Between two huge rock outcrops, there is a gigantic series of stair-stepping terraces that appear to be ascending up to the stars. They are called *The Terraces of Pumatallis*. There are more tourists here than I have ever seen in one place, climbing to the top of the terrace complex by following a designated pathway of quarried stone steps.

Our group scatters like ants, anxious to get to the top, while I remain close to Carol, carefully taking the mammoth steps at a tentative pace. When we reach the point of the complex where the area splits off into three sectors, we have a choice to make. We pause, allowing the steady stream of people to come out before we commit to one of the sites. An older man catches Carol's attention. He is small in stature, bald, wearing wire-rim round glasses and a long trench coat with *Teva* sandals on his browned feet. He is unassuming and shy, but has a twinkle in his eye and a pleasant look on his face.

Carol enthusiastically points him out to me, "Oh, look at that little man. Isn't he cute?"

I turn in his direction. My immediate impression is that I am looking at a clone of *Ben Kingsley in *Gandhi*. He meets my stare with a kind, bashful smile and continues on his way down the long descending steps.

We decide to head north to the Funerary sector, noticing that fewer people are moving in that direction. Along the way, we run into two of the guys (Scott and Richard) from our group. They tell us about one of the terraced areas off the beaten trail where we can sit uninterrupted and meditate. The idea of a beautiful grassy overlook without the throngs of people sounds like a wonderful idea to me. We follow them on a switch-back course, making our way down to what feels like a secluded hideaway. Each of us picks a spot to sit with our backs against the stone wall and closes our eyes. I feel myself relaxing, allowing the fear still tucked into the recesses of my body to slowly lift and start to dissipate.

An undeterminable time later, we begin to stir, noticing that the sun is fading behind the mountain and casting long shadows on the terraces.

Richard is the first to speak. "Did you guys see that man who climbed all the way down here and did Tai Chi in front of us? That was pretty incredible, wasn't it?"

The rest of us look at Richard, puzzled. With our eyes closed the whole time, we never saw a thing.

Richard adds, "Well I didn't know what to make of him at first, but it felt like he was blessing us."

In silence, I accept whatever it was that he was offering, acknowledging that I certainly needed it.

We spend the next few hours climbing between the three sectors, absorbing the fortified protection of the energies and the breathtaking vistas. Finding our way back to the terrace complex, we navigate the pathway by the light of the rising full moon. I notice that the longer I have been wandering up and down the levels, adjusting to the gradually fading light, the lighter and brighter I feel inside, becoming less armored and more closely aligned with the others. All of the tourists are gone now, following the rules to be off the hills by sundown. Somehow we'd missed that piece of information, and I am glad. The secluded descent is exactly what I need to return to my own instinctual pace, sensing and feeling things from an inner-lit perspective.

Our first collective thought once we get back into the town of Ollantaytambo is to get something to eat. We are grateful to find a restaurant that is still serving this late. At the end of our meal, we look over to see a man across the room who Carol immediately recognizes.

"Look! That is the little man who we saw earlier on the steps! Let's ask him to join us."

Richard chimes in, "That's the same man who was doing Tai Chi in front of us when we were meditating!"

That seems synchronistic, given the last time we saw the man he was going back down the mountain, but there are no such things as coincidences. We nod to him, wave him over to our table and ask him to sit with us. He smiles in agreement.

Carol asks him, "Do you speak English?"

"No—Portuguese."

"Do you speak Spanish?" (Carol speaks enough that she could translate for us.)

"No—Portuguese."

Ignoring the obvious language barrier, we proceed to ask questions in English, and somehow he understands and is able to respond with limited vocabulary ... in English.

"Are you from here?"

"No—Lima."

"What do you do there?"

"I am a Doctor."

"What is your name?"

"Sifu."

We do not realize until later that this is a title that means *master* or *teacher*. In Chinese martial arts, it can also mean *spiritual father*.

"Do you teach Tai Chi?"

"Yes, I am a Tibetan Monk and a Tai Chi master."

"Were you the one doing Tai Chi in front of us on the upper terraces?"

"Yes, and I notice you are not like the other tourists."

"Neither are you!"

Together we laugh wondering what this strange connection is that we are all feeling toward this man. Sifu looks intently at each of us as if he is sizing us up on a level we can't comprehend.

He takes a deep breath and tells us, *"It is time now to open your hearts."*

He then places his focus on Scott. *"You are a profound man, but you are hiding. You are in disguise—No?"*

Again, we laugh, not quite sure what he means by this. Scott is very tall and lanky with long brown hair parted in the middle and falling around his shoulders, along with a beard and mustache. We wonder if Sifu thinks he is hiding because of this.

In Scott's defense we respond, "No, this is not a disguise. This is who he really is."

But Sifu persists, *"Yes—Disguise! Like me. See—I show you."*

With this, he stands up and moves a step away from our table. He turns his back to us, taking off his tight-fitting skull cap and long, brown trench coat. Folding them neatly, he carefully places them on the empty table next to ours. Then he reaches up and removes his round wire-rim glasses and adds them to the pile. Slowly he turns to face us. His shoulders are back and his hands are by his side with his palms opened toward us. We stare in stunned silence, not quite sure what is happening. The man who we all have been talking to, who appeared to us to be in his late sixties or early seventies is now standing before us as a man half that age. It isn't just that he is younger, but he seems timeless. There is an inner radiance illuminating him. It's as if he has unzipped his skin and is allowing us to gaze upon his true essence. (I have no concept at this time of a state called the *Great Perfection* in which the soul dissolves the human body into its essential essence. Ascension researcher *William Henry calls this the "Rainbow Light Body." He explains that the Tibetans teach that just seeing an image of the guru in his "Robe of Light" has a profound effect on our own vibration. This is because we entangle with his state of mind and become it. Sifu is showing us how to wear the "Beaming Garment of the Avatars.") He takes in our reaction and turns away, putting everything back on again.

Transforming back to the older man, he sits down and says, *"See— disguise!"*

This demonstration has deeply touched each one of us as we sit overcome with emotion. In the kitchen area of the restaurant a song comes on the radio that catches our attention. The lyrics are interspersed with a group chanting the single word *OM*. Sifu reaches for our hands and we automatically respond, forming a linked ring around the table. Simultaneously, we take a deep breath and let it out in a collective, resonant "OMMM" which vibrates the room. The workers come out of the kitchen and stand staring at us. We don't know who Sifu really is, but being in his presence is certainly like sitting with a 'master.'

We ask him, "Can you teach us more mantras? Can you work with us?"

After considering this, he suggests that we meet him back up at the entrance to the ruins at midnight. We don't even hesitate, knowing our time with him is limited as our group is already scheduled to catch a train to Machu Picchu at 8:00 the next morning. The four of us race to our separate rooms to put on layers of warmer clothes, noticing how much the temperature has dropped since coming off the mountain. Two hours later, Carol and I meet back up with Scott and Richard and approach the gate.

Under a light at the entrance we can see Sifu ahead of us. We watch as three young children come running out from the shadows, all squealing, "Sifu! Sifu!" They act as if they know him and love him. He pats their heads as he puts something in each of their hands and as quickly as they appeared, they scurry off. It is perplexing to me that three young children who are without coats or warm clothing are still roaming the streets at midnight. I wonder if they have parents to care for them or a warm place to go home to. Sifu takes all of this in stride and motions for us to pass through the entrance. Instead of going up the steps, he leads us off to the right side where there is a maze of walkways winding throughout the stone ruins of old walls. Finding the appropriate spot, he asks us to sit in a row in front of him and leads us in the Tibetan Buddhist mantra, *"Om Mani Padme Hum."* Directly above us is the full moon with a complete rainbow halo around it. We sit in silence, meditating for a long time. I am subtly aware that all of the scattered fragments of myself that have felt like shredded internal 'folders' are being automatically 'defragged.'

About an hour later, Sifu stands ready to lead us out, but I stop him and boldly ask the question that has been whirling through my mind, "Sifu, where are you REALLY from?"

He quickly answers, *"Lima—I told you."*

I shake my head 'No' and point to the sky.

"Tell me which *Ch'aska*." (In the Quechua language, Ch'aska means "Bright Star"). Even though it is dark outside, with the light of the moon I am able to catch the glint of a tear in his eye. Instead of answering me, he raises his right index finger and points to Scott. He motions for Scott to take his own index finger and meet his touch. (I can't help but think, "ET—phone home.") Facing Scott, Sifu takes his left hand and trails it across the black, diamond-studded sky until he comes to the Southern Cross constellation lying on its side. He stops at the star on the left side of the cross called *Mimosa*, which also forms the head of the Emu constellation.

He nods at Scott as if to say, *"This is your home star."*

He releases Scott's finger and points to Richard who places his index finger against Sifu's. With his left hand Sifu begins scanning the sky again and this time stops at the bright red star (*Antares*) under the constellation of Scorpius. (Richard was born under the astrological sign of Scorpio so he relates to this.) He nods to Richard and lets his finger go as he turns to Carol. Stepping forward to meet her, Sifu begins the search process with his left hand in the scanning mode, stopping once again at the Southern Cross, but this time he points to the star at the foot of the cross (*Alpha Crucis*).

I think to myself, *You are not telling us where YOU are from. You are focusing on us.*

He reaches his right hand out to me and presses his index finger against mine. He takes his left hand, but does not start, as he did with the others, up in the sky. He begins by pointing down to the ground. Slowly he raises his arm upwards, making a huge arch following the Milky Way across the entire sky. Instead of stopping, the sweeping motion continues all the way back down to the ground again where he lets go. I have no idea what this means.

My mind is racing ... *Is my home star in the Northern Hemisphere? Does this mean I do NOT have a home star? Did I come from an Inner Earth civilization or somewhere outside this galaxy, outside this dimension? Is this an indication of my 'wanderer' self? Where is your (Sifu's) REAL home star???* I have to accept that none of these questions will be answered by him in the concrete form that I want.

He indicates that he will meet with us in the morning and asks us to be back at the entrance at 5:00 a.m. All of us agree to this. As we walk in single file back to the gate, the same three children in their light summer clothes come running to us. I am dumbfounded. We have been in there over an hour and they have been outside all this time, patiently waiting. Unbeknownst to us, they have a prearranged mission.

The oldest girl who looks to be around eight years old grabs both Scott's and my hands and swings us into a tight circle. The six-year-old girl grasps both of Carol's hands while the four-year-old boy holds onto Richard. As if all of this has been well rehearsed, the children in perfect unison break into a lively song and dance, twisting and spinning us around as the momentum builds. This is a polished performance. They are singing the words at the top of their voices. It is so well done that it is likely something they have performed at the yearly ritual called *Inti Raymi*, celebrating the Inca New Year and the Winter Solstice. The tune reminds me of the old (1966) "Batman" TV theme song where the crescendo builds to the word "BATMAN." In this case, the prominent word and the only one that I can understand is "SACSAYHUAMAN!"

Every time they stress this word I hear the pronunciation as "SEXY WOMAN" which they accentuate by wiggling their rear ends. This is like watching a flashback of the sassy Latin actress/singer Charo who became famous for her catch phrase of "Cuchi, cuchi." As surreal as this all seems, it is also hilarious. We are completely caught up in their uninhibited enthusiasm and infectious swing dance.

The negative association I have equated with Sacsayhuaman is being rewired in my brain, replaced with a new, uplifting image that makes me laugh. When the song comes to its end, the kids drop our hands, bow, and run away. They disappear into the dark shadows again as we all clap. Sifu obviously put them up to this, but how did he know what occurred at Sacsayhuaman?

Afraid that we might not get up in time, we forgo sleep to meet Sifu at the entrance three hours later. We take our places along the wall and repeat the *"Om Mani Padme Hum"* chant. Sifu then jumps up on a raised terrace. With the removal of his outer coat, the 'ageless man' comes to life again. He begins doing Tai Chi in slow motion—gracefully, fluidly, one movement flowing into the next—seamlessly transitioning into a rapid-fire display of perfectly executed martial arts death blows.

The hair on the back of my neck stands up. This is not a demonstration, but a soul to soul transmission. I am receiving personal instructions on how to move through my life, but he is accentuating how to move through passages into the lower astral and how to navigate everyday negative encounters. He is showing me that everything is part of the 'path' (*Mani*) towards enlightenment. To move forward on the path means removing the obstacles that arise, cutting away the illusions that block our own deep wisdom. Wisdom is symbolized by the lotus (*Padme*). The lotus comes forth unstained, emerging from the mud.

Sifu is showing me how to embody the lotus—not fight an outer enemy. He is doing this by slicing away all distractions, all judgements, all contradictions to the purity of his soul. The last syllable (*Hum*) of the chant speaks of our willingness to send out energy from our center and receive energy back. It refers to "the immovable, unfluctuating, that which cannot be disturbed by anything." The mantra is indicating that "I am in You and You are in me," acknowledging the unity and brotherhood of all beings, as well as their inner divine potential. That potential is referred to as the "jewel in the lotus."

How do we keep finding our way back to the origination point (*OM*), to the innate, radiant jewel of our True Self? By remembering that there is no greater force in the Universe than the original 'root ball' of LOVE. From the muddy depths, the tuberous stems grow strong, sending their shoots skyward to reach high above the murky water. The blossomed flower closes its petals at night and sinks underwater, only to rise again at dawn, opening its petals in response to the first light. Because of this, the ancient Egyptians said that the lotus gave birth to the Sun.

Sifu delivers this transmission as an encapsulated thoughtform that will be released throughout my system over an extended period of time. The entire message is encoded through his exacting moves. Watching his actions has removed the last vestiges of my armor. In my attempt to deal with the 'dark side,' I went into a contracted stance of self-defense, attempting to protect myself by hardening or masking my real center. It only served to close me down, making me feel small, weak, and fearful. Sifu is inviting me to regain my balance by removing my 'disguise.' He is assuring me that the resilience and agility of a wide-open heart is the only protection I will ever need to face any hardcore adversary. The power of a single aligned soul who embodies the Light will easily shatter the darkest recalcitrant layers of lower density beings.

When the time comes to leave him, I ask if we can take his picture. He places his hand over his heart and shakes his head 'No.'

"Remember me here."

I have my doubts if a camera would have even picked up a human image.

Now when I reflect on this sacred initiation in Peru with beings of both dark and light, I find myself humming one of my favorite John Denver songs, realizing Sifu was showing me how to live my life as the "Flower that shatters the stone."

Many still slumber in the illusions of polarity
and domination of an outside force.
If the "minions" of humanity
were to know their true power within,
the forces of "power-over-others"
would be put out of business.

~ Suzanne Lie ~

44

DARK SIDE DEFECTORS

The gap between the worlds has closed significantly since my 'lower world' experience twenty years ago. As we transition to a higher vibration, the whole planet is phasing in and out of the fourth dimensional field and the overlapping tenets of time and space. It stands to reason that there would be a greater awareness of earthbound spirits because doorways are now opening that were not available before, allowing for lost souls or trapped energies to return back to where they rightfully belong. This also means greater instances of intercepting fourth dimensional, dark force entities and their deep, undercover intentions.

If 2012 was a year of equal balance between the Fifth and Sixth Sun energy, the scales were tipped in 2013, exposing hidden agendas and shadow, undercover factions to the bright light of day. (Disclosure of the dark and polarized positions are only going to escalate as the light intensifies.) It's as if the contents of "Pandora's box" were placed into a cremation urn and scattered all over the Earth. What do we expect when 'Spaceship Earth' flickers in and out of the debris field of the lower astral plane? It puts us on a collision course with the 'dark matter' that we recoil from and want to push away. But we each signed up for this 'Tour of Duty' at this precise, soul-stretching time to resolve the 'Grand Experiment' split that both sides agreed to play out.

I do not yet have this understanding in early 2013, when I am hit with a steady influx of clients all dealing with negatively polarized entities, making me question what is going on and if I am once again out of my depth.

Divinely guided, a friend who knows my involvement with earthbound spirits sends me an email with the link for a website called *Soul Detective*. This is a certified training program created by *Dr. Barbara Stone, a psychotherapist and a professor at Energy Medicine University. Barbara was one of the early 'portal openers' who got thrown into the 'deep end of the pool,' having clients coming to her with issues that went beyond the scope of typical 'talk therapy.' They included past life trauma, earthbound spirit attachments, curses and hexes, ancestral wounds, soul loss, invasive implants, and various forms of detrimental energy including dark entities. She made it her mission to find effective methods to minister to their wounds and keep her clients afloat. Out of her commitment to "track the origin and heal the emotional pain" came the name "Soul Detective." This describes her work and how it can eliminate the unseen causes of problems or get to the *Invisible Roots* (the name of one of her popular books). The program is a vast collection of cutting edge protocols that use muscle testing to find out how the spiritual realm is impacting the client. They are designed to help therapists resolve *"the spiritual aspects of emotional problems so their clients can regain autonomy and fulfill their soul's mission."*

This time when I indicated that I, the student, was ready, an authentic teacher of the 'Light' appeared. (Thank God/ess!) A month later, my good friend and 'Energy Medicine' colleague Jean and I begin the training. By May of 2013, we were completing Level Three. This level has a heavy emphasis on the Detrimental Protocols. You can't be this focused on dark entities without attracting their attention. All of us in the training are sensitive to their presence, feeling them circling the house like sharks in bloody water.

I am well aware of the uneasiness I am feeling, trying to remain aloof while keeping my distance. Finishing up the third day, several of us go to dinner. While sitting in the restaurant, I can feel the tell-tale signs of an attachment trying to take hold. For me, this is a combination of localized pain gripping the back of my neck (a vulnerable area because of whiplash due to two different car accidents over the years) and a dull headache that slowly begins intensifying.

I am so tired of dealing with them that I don't say anything to the group, but by the time Jean and I get back to our room I am in real pain and anxious to have it over with. I ask Jean to help me remove this. We use the protocol we have just learned in class, based on *Dr. William Baldwin's *Spirit Releasement Therapy*, which involves dialoguing with the entity. We want to find out their purpose for attaching to me, and then help them to reconnect to the spark of light that (even they) hold within.

Because they are not plugged into Source, they feed on suffering and usually enter our fields through a 'chink in our armor.' This may be an emotional wound—or in my case, disdain—with fear and judgment of their presence. I love Barbara's attitude that "treating them as if they have a personality gives us a method to transform the detrimental energy into beneficial energy." However, when you are in physical pain it is harder to move into an unbiased negotiating zone by yourself. Your inclination is to pull the covers up over your head and not get out of bed. (That will have to wait until after we have removed them.)

We start by constructing the Golden Octahedron of light and calling in the 'cavalry' of protectors to assist us, asking if we have permission to proceed. If we had received a "No" to this question, we would have turned it over to the Angels and 'higher dimensionals' (as that would have indicated that we were not centered enough or not equipped to handle what we were dealing with). This isn't the case.

Since there are many dark entities, we proceed by asking to speak to the 'highest ranking' member or the one who clearly believes he is in charge. Even though this is a bit like inviting the head of a street gang into our hotel room to sit down and have a chat, it immediately neutralizes a tense situation. By coaxing the head honcho out of the shadows (which is his comfort zone) we separate him from the larger numbers of his minions. Shining the light of our undivided attention on him feeds his ego, diminishing his imposing bravado. It also pulls down the curtain of 'smoke and mirrors' that is part of his masterful illusion that keeps us off balance. Our objective is to find out his purpose for attaching to me and to negotiate another way of being that is a win/win for all of us.

Using muscle testing to communicate, we work our way through the dialogue. His primary motive was "intimidation" to get me to stop doing this work. By the end of the session, we offer him a better job working for the Light where he doesn't have to answer to a controlling hierarchy. (The Reptilians and Draco factions are all consumed with the 'power structure.' Those who consider themselves in the 'higher ranks' seem oblivious to the fact that they are really 'middle management,' working for someone else who is corded to them. Parasitically, others above them are feeding off of the energy they are extracting. For someone who believes they are the one in control, this information does not sit well. He does not like finding out that he has been lied to and, like a puppet, his strings are being pulled because he is doing someone else's bidding. When the truth of this sinks in, he is more willing to consider 'going rogue' if he can be assured of invisibility. We bargain that Archangel Michael will remove all of the control 'cords' that go back to his 'dark master' if he removes whatever is 'corded' into me. He agrees and finally leaves in the company of the Archangels. We're thankful that the minions always follow their leader without any resistance. It's a relief to have them go, as the attachment process took a toll on every aspect of both my psyche and my physical body. I needed a good night's sleep just to allow my nervous system to stop unraveling and to reset back to its own energy field.

On our plane ride home a day later, Jean and I are seated behind a man and his wife who are openly friendly, engaging a young college student that sits between them. We have no idea that he is carrying two earthbound spirits that have attached to him through a past life connection and who are ready to leave him (in hitchhiker fashion) and attach to us. By the time we get back home, we are exhausted, but unaware that it has more to do with the 'entity transfer' than jet lag.

At dusk, we walk the labyrinth and I can feel the old familiar feeling tightening in my neck. Jean acknowledges that she too has picked something up that has attached to her 'port' (her susceptible area is a spot in her back). Because we are so tired, we wait until the next morning to set the sacred space to deal with it. Even though we are using the labyrinth as the portal, we visualize a golden octahedron—a four-sided upright pyramid at ground level with a mirror reflection of another four-sided pyramid going down into the ground. This is the image Barbara uses as a portal to assist the souls, and it works beautifully alone or in combination with the labyrinth. We invite the Archangels to assist us. They stand in the center of each of the four sides with Archangel Michael at the apex above us.

Starting into the process, we use muscle checking to discover that not only are there earthbound spirits, but we are encountering a situation that we have never dealt with before. We are communicating with the leader of a group of 5,232 'dark force entities' (DFE's) who tells us they have all come to the joint decision to defect. They are asking for our help to do so. They have been waiting for the right time to make their move, seeing their chance on the plane when the earthbound souls joined us. It is possible that they were 'assigned' to them, but they also could have been a part of the larger contingency of dark entities that had been observing us during the training or specifically when we released the smaller convoy in the hotel room. Either way, they made their decision to attach to us when the opportunity presented itself. We ask Archangel Michael to place a cloak of invisibility over the situation before he carefully used his sword to disconnect the cords from their backs (which in this case appeared like a tail) severing the connection back to their 'bosses.' This is done in a 'stealth' manner so we are not hit with dark reinforcements that would want retaliation or want to stop it. We call in 'Warrior Angels' and 'Angels of Mercy' (those who are former defectors now working for the light) to accompany them across. As a gifted intuitive, Jean describes the surprising sight, witnessing them helping one another through the portal, being kind, thoughtful, and treating each other with respect.

"Once the archangels have the situation well in hand, we turn to the two earthbound spirits, whom we address as 'Spirit A' and 'Spirit B.' The first spirit is a male, named Vasily (Vass-EE-lee), born in 1810. He was 46-years-old when he died from an act of war in 1856 near St. Petersburg, Russia. His extended family lived on a large tract of land that had been granted to his ancestors and handed down through the generations. Along with him are his wife and three children, a younger brother (Spirit B) along with his wife and one child, four other siblings and their families, plus their parents and grandparents, all of whom lived on the family land. All of them were killed when soldiers attacked, taking their land and all their possessions. Some of

them did not know they were not in their physical bodies anymore.

Vasily's younger brother (Spirit B) was 42-years-old when he was killed in the assault. As Vasily's right hand man, he was assigned the task of managing the family land and keeping everyone together. He declines to give us his name at first, deferring to Vasily as the family leader. Vasily died trying to protect him.

In the group of relatives, we find that one grandmother is holding everyone back from crossing into the Light because she is afraid of the unknown and sees leaving as betraying 'Mother Russia.' They have agreed to stay together, not wanting to leave anyone behind. We use the Soul Detective protocols for helping the group clear their desire for vengeance and their limiting beliefs—that they did not deserve to get through this trauma, or that it was not safe to release it. Then the clan is ready to cross. The angels ask Vasily and his brother to stand on the two sides of the portal, to see that everyone makes it through.

When Vasily's younger brother realizes what he is being asked to do, he says, 'I have always deferred to my brother and been, in a sense, his lieutenant. Now that I am being asked to stand as an equal with him at the door to Light, I want you to know my name is Dimitri (Dim-EE-tree).'

This moment is emotional for all of us. As the others watch, Vasily and Dimitri turn into light beings at each side of the portal, Vasily to the left and Dimitri to the right. Their extended family, including the reluctant grandmother, cross together into the Light.

We ask to multiply the benefits to include all who were killed and hurt by class wars and other injustices throughout Russian history, and to heal a long-standing, collective, national sorrow. There is a line of souls crossing through the portal that is three to four abreast, stretching back further than we can see. We muscle test that we need to leave the portal open for sixty hours to allow everyone to get through."

~ Jean Kilquist
  Reiki Master
  Joplin, MO
  knitbikeread@gmail.com

The next afternoon I am working in Chante Ishta, weeding the flower beds when my neck begins aching again and a steel band of pressure starts spreading around my head. Knowing the portal is still open out in the labyrinth with continuous traffic going through it, I am in denial that this could possibly be an attachment. When the pain gets too strong to ignore, I stop to check what is going on. I discover that there is a five-year-old Russian girl holding onto me. With the large masses going through the portal, she got separated from her Mother who was carrying her baby brother.

She wandered in my direction, attracted to a life-like white unicorn statue that is lying beneath a Rose of Sharon tree. I have noticed over the years that when I pick up earthbound spirits that are children, the pain is much more intense, as if they are clinging with all their might. (It also makes me aware of the possibility that there may have been children attached to me in Sacsayhuaman.)

The little girl's name is Sasha. I tell her that I can take her out to the portal and we can call her mother to come back and get her. Her grip grows tighter around my neck. She is afraid of being swept up in the middle of the masses again. I assure her that I can open another portal using Chante and I will call her mother to this opening. Walking the pattern of the vesicas, I ask the angels to bring her mother to meet her. Within minutes there is a happy reunion and I return to my weeds, having new respect for the magnitude of what is occurring out in the portal of the Labyrinth.

The following night, at the end of the sixty hours, I walk to the center of the Prairie Labyrinth while Jean finger-walks the pattern on her *Chakra Labyrinth Cards* at her home in Joplin. We thank the angelic assistance and trace the pathway out, closing the portal. Because Vasily and Dimitri stood as guardians at the gateway of the portal, thirty of their family members agreed to leave. Their willingness to cross over became the catalyst for 1,508,945 Russian souls who responded when we asked that the "benefits be multiplied."

With the addition of the 5232 dark entities who chose to defect, the total of souls that left was 1,514,207. It's no wonder little Sasha was overwhelmed! To her, the massive exodus in the center of the labyrinth must have felt like a frightening stampede.

In forgiveness lies the answer to stop the wheel of karma.

~ **David Wilcock** ~

45

RECONCILIATION

There's a difference between people who cling to their stories like broken pieces of wreckage they mistake for a life raft, and those who are willing to let go, dropping down into the core of their wounds to search for the buried treasure of their own Divine blueprint. When I meet Rhonda at an annual Labyrinth Gathering, I know that she is one of those deep-diving soul seekers.

A year after we are first introduced, Rhonda gets on a plane and flies across the country for a hypnotherapy appointment with me. Her interest is not in a Past Life or a Life Between Lives Regression. For the past two years, she has been doing extensive *Family Constellations work (also called Systemic Constellations) developed by Bert Hellinger. This is a well-respected approach for revealing the hidden dynamics in a family so that they can be worked through and healed. She has reached an impasse in her process and intuitively feels that the core of her remaining issues goes back to the seventh generation—a place she has not yet explored. In a conversation with her, I suggest that using hypnotherapy to go back may be more expedient. I also mention that, because of her insistence that the seventh generation holds the key, that perhaps she will encounter herself in that lifetime. She shrugs this off by telling me that past lives are not really part of her belief system and that it is likely just something in her lineage that she needs to uncover.

As a preamble to her session (or maybe we should call it a 'cosmic set-

357

up'), the hotel where she is staying has a broken air conditioning unit and the room is unbearably hot. They finally put her in another room at 3:00 a.m., but when she arrives at my home she has had little to no sleep, and cannot seem to get her body temperature to cool down.

Minutes into the induction designed to help her relax, Rhonda is swept into another time, reliving a nightmare in a log cabin. She is a frontier woman named Ann, cooking at an open fireplace when grease catches on fire. She cannot put it out and, in her panic, is screaming to her husband Will to come down and help her. She races to a corner of the room to pick up their baby from a crib, completely unaware that her skirt has also caught on fire and is spreading the flames. When Will comes down the stairs with his teen-age son, John, and 12-year-old daughter, Julianna, the corner of the room with Ann and the baby is completely engulfed in flames. Will knows that he cannot save them and is determined now to get his other children to safety.

At this point in the regression, I quickly give the command to Ann that she is no longer in the body, but she can still track what is happening with the others. She describes her husband running to the barn, giving the order to his children to follow him. His goal is to get the horses and ride to get help. Julianna does not heed his order, but instead runs back to the house, unable to accept that her father is really going to leave them to burn. She cannot fathom having a life without her mother, but she also cannot make herself go through the wall of fire to reach her. She runs out of the blazing house in a state of panic, needing to get away from everything.

A small hunting party of Indians find and apprehend Julianna when they come to investigate the blaze. She is already in a crazed state, but this quickly turns to madness when she interprets their presence as being attacked by monstrous savages. The more hysterical and out of control she becomes, the more they fear her, convinced that she is possessed by demons. They hold her down and, with a blow from a hatchet, kill her. Her frantic father later finds her bloodied body with a search party of men who also uncover the charred remains of Ann and the baby in the ruins of the cabin. Ann looks on, blaming herself for all of it. Following them into the future, she sees that her devastated husband takes her son and moves back East to be near his family to start their lives over again.

Coming out of the session, Rhonda is shocked at the sensation of reliving the horrors of this life, admitting that it was real, that she *was* Ann and her skin was on fire. She agrees to do the additional work needed to help the involved souls to cross over. It is clear to all of us that Ann's broken spirit needs a lot of reconciliation in order for this to happen.

When Rhonda returns home, the depth of the feelings that she experienced has triggered her abused inner child who felt ambushed, taken by surprise and thrown into the past life. This has made her feel re-abused and re-traumatized. We know she needs to feel some measure of control when going into the follow-up session in order to avoid feeling again like a powerless victim.

In a phone session we open the portal of the labyrinth, surround it with the golden octahedron, and create a council-like setting, inviting everyone involved to participate. In addition to Ann's family, a Native American Chief (who was not part of the initial incident) enters the circle with the group of braves who were responsible for taking and killing Julianna. We encourage Rhonda's inner child to orchestrate where she would like to have everyone seated. When she feels safe, she steps aside and allows Rhonda's adult self to take over.

All eyes are on Ann when she begins by timidly approaching Will, her husband, down on her hands and knees. Filled with shame and remorse for destroying her entire family, she is asking for his forgiveness, fearful that she is not worthy or deserving to receive it. He takes her hands and lifts her up to her feet, seeing far more clearly than she: that this was an accident that she'd had no control over. Unbeknownst to her, he has been carrying the burden of responsibility, blaming himself for moving his family to the West. He deeply regretted his decision, feeling that each family member paid the ultimate price for him to follow his dream. He asks for her forgiveness and then turns to Julianna. He especially feels a sense of blame for not being able to find and protect her. Julianna is able to come out of her own shell of protection to feel her parents' anguish and love for her, granting the forgiveness needed.

The energy switches then to the braves. They stand with their heads bowed with the Chief behind them. He is a silent witness, making sure that they are here to stand accountable for their actions. The one responsible for killing her apologizes, explaining that they were in a state of panic themselves, believing that they had to destroy the demon that had taken her over. From the council perspective, they can now understand that she had gone mad from witnessing her mother burning alive, which was further fueled by the terror of their presence. They show remorse for their mob mentality and ask for her forgiveness. She expresses regret for viewing them as demon 'savages,' seeing how this contributed to them playing out that role. In the end, she forgives them and they forgive her. Led by the Chief, the entire family and all of the Indians cross over through the portal together.

Integrating Ann's lifetime is an ongoing process for Rhonda. The possibility that her soul may have had other lives requires her to adjust her beliefs, but it also allows her to view her present-life choices to never marry and have children from another perspective. Devoting her life to teaching children, she chose to channel the natural mothering qualities—that she now attributes to Ann—in a different direction.

Staying in touch with Rhonda by phone, she decides to return again, though she is not really sure that there is anything in particular to work on. She wants to walk the labyrinth and elicit my help in making a portable labyrinth for herself on a board. Months before her visit, she calls me to share a tragedy that has occurred in her area.

Substitute teaching in a nearby school district as a PE teacher, Rhonda is helping them out with a fundraiser that involves outdoor relay races. From the view on the field she can see that, across the street from the school, there is a park with walking paths. After school that day she decides to walk one of the trails, but stops short when she is overcome by the presence of an evil energy that feels so ominous that she fears for her safety. Looking around, she sees nothing but houses further back from the field a few blocks away.

Less than a month later, a story breaks about a sixth-grade girl (Angelina) who had been abducted a short distance from her home on her way to school—the same middle school where Rhonda subbed. Two weeks later, Angelina's body is dumped where law enforcement would be sure to find it. The placement is intended to steer suspicion away from where the killer lives, which is just over a mile from Angelina and in one of the houses that Rhonda had her back to when she stood on the trail.

Rhonda volunteers when a call goes out from the school requesting help in handling the students once the discovery is made public. She is aware that memorials are being planned for Angelina and wants to participate, so she buys a teddy bear to place at one of the sites. She admits, however, that it is uncharacteristic for her to feel so involved. After school, she attempts to go to the first publicized memorial, but the 'circus' atmosphere is too much for her, sending her back to the original park where a smaller memorial was set up. While placing the bear, it occurs to Rhonda that Angelina has not crossed over. Because of the work Rhonda has done, she begins the process of setting her intention and envisioning the golden octahedron while saying a prayer.

This is cut short when she hears Angelina's voice inside her head. *"I do not want to go to the other side. I want my killer to be found. The police are looking in the wrong place. I want you to help me. Go to the police and tell them ..."*

Rhonda interrupts her, "Wait a minute, Angelina. I am just a substitute teacher. You need to communicate with someone who has credibility with the police. They are not going to believe me or trust that you are talking with me!"

Angelina is upset that Rhonda will not help her and she vanishes. A short time later, the mother of the 17-year old killer turns her son in. The police had been looking for an adult, not really believing a younger person could do this. Angelina was not his first attempt. He tried to abduct a woman jogging on the same trail where Rhonda sensed danger months earlier, but she got away. This is when he decided to target a younger person who would not be able to overpower him.

By the time Rhonda visits me months later, everything has settled down and the killer is in jail awaiting trial. Rhonda is able to turn her attention back towards developing a capacity for a life partner. This is a longing that has been activated by her involvement with Ann and Will.

We take chairs outside and sit in the center of Chante Ishta as Rhonda reads me an excerpt from her journal regarding Ann and Will's relationship. She is encouraged by the clearing that has happened between them, regarding them as good examples of a strong, healed partnership since they crossed over. She tells me that, although it feels a little strange that they would be back, she can feel their presence very strongly hovering just above her. Without warning, this suddenly shifts to an awareness of Angelina.

It has been ten months since her death, and once again she comes to Rhonda asking for help. She wants to cross over, but she is conflicted with the barrage of feelings that she is still carrying. Rhonda agrees to use the Emotional Freedom Technique (EFT) and 'tap' for her, expressing the emotions that are bubbling up inside. The deeper we go into the process, the more Rhonda allows herself to become a channel for Angelina, giving voice to everything she experienced before and after her death. She moves from terror to sadness, to fear and rage. In this process, we ask if she wants to address her killer and say what she needs to express directly to him. I assure her that he is in jail and can no longer hurt her.

When Angelina realizes that her own need for revenge and wanting her killer to suffer the way she did is part of what is holding her here, something clicks inside of her. Rhonda, who is the one noticing all of this and reporting back to me, suddenly stops the session, terrified. She insists that Angelina has gotten what she came for, but now needs to be removed from the prison setting to a safer place. The logical place is into the arms of Ann and Will who have been holding space for us since we began.

Rhonda begins to describe a very threatening, higher-ranking dark entity. She believes he is attached to the young man. The entity owns him and as long as he can keep Angelina in the victim cycle, fueling her hopelessness and rage, he has both Angelina and the killer in 'lockdown' under his evil control.

We call in the angels for assistance and begin to dialogue with the entity. When we come to the part of having him look inside for any light, he wants nothing to do with this. The angels surround him and open his heart.

Together we all begin flooding him with light (which he expects to be painful) until something shifts that breaks his hold and he lets go of the young man. Under a white net of light, he is moved through the portal along with his many minions, flanked by battalions of angel escorts. Angelina is able to release her troubled killer, knowing she doesn't have to oversee the justice that he will face. She is able to feel compassion for this self-proclaimed "monster," realizing that his whole existence has been in a twisted and broken state. Enfolded in Ann and Will's embrace, Angelina drifts into the center of the portal and all of them are gone.

How does a soul end up playing the horrendous role of a brutal murderer at this young age? Victimizers are probably the biggest victims, incapable of seeing any other way out, which opens them to dark predators who—committed to the negative-polarity path of service-to-self—can easily highjack their being under the seduction of making them feel powerful.

Imagine if everyone out there who feels separate and alone in dealing with their own dark thoughts could have the awareness that all of what they were feeling might not belong to just them ... Imagine if we understood that they may be targeted because of their isolation, poor self-esteem, and possible abuse... They are strategically drawn in to merge with the 'demons' who are feeding on and perpetuating their lower vibrational agendas. The underlying shadow intention is to coerce and co-opt their targets' mind/body/spirit complex.

Dark entities prey upon our emotional weaknesses and wounds to magnify and escalate the negativity we carry. Once they attach to someone's field, they begin to pull the strings, imposing a form of 'mind control' that is designed to steer the individual toward self-destruction or destroying other lives. If only we had awareness and the proper training in the school system, in the mental health world, and within the prison systems to recognize this kind of 'takeover' from a Soul Detective perspective, treatment could be much more humane and it could circumvent a great many future problems. It is up to each of us to monitor our own thoughts and feelings, questioning when something arises that begins to pull us into fear, hopelessness, judgment, and retaliation, or when it escalates into any of the stronger lower vibrations. We are each responsible for the choices we make and the help we seek but, ultimately, we are all connected and our personal choices affect the whole.

Two months after we release the dark entities, the case goes to court and the young man, against the advice of his lawyers who want him to take the insanity plea, accepts full responsibility for the charges. He cries at the hearing when the family says that Angelina's light can never be put out.

Over time, Rhonda slowly comes to the realization that Angelina was a reincarnation of Julianna, which helps all the pieces fall into place. Because Ann and Will had crossed over, they were right there to help their 'soul-daughter' remember the freedom that reconciliation brings in order to guide her safely home. This alignment marks the close of the cycle of Julianna/Angelina's soul needing to take on victim roles with the false belief that death can diminish or 'end' who she really is.

When Rhonda had first set out to address the dysfunctional patterns in her 'Family Constellations,' she'd had no idea that she would be extending the healing circle to include members of her 'soul family,' as well as to individuals in her community that she didn't know personally and would never meet face to face. Every step of her journey brought broken pieces to the surface, to be fused by the glue of her willingness to forgive herself and others. She had to model how to forgive the unforgivable before she could witness the domino effect occurring to all the soul aspects that were drawn into her path.

On her last visit, Rhonda and I stand once again in Chante, recapitulating the long series of events that she had experienced. In discussing the apparent attitude shift in Angelina's killer (reported in the press at his sentencing) we both attribute the change of heart to something few would ever consider: that he was no longer under the influence of dark entities.

During this discussion, Rhonda becomes aware that the killer's spiritual presence has tuned into us. She moves quickly from apprehension to observation relaying to me that she views him standing back at a distance, asking for our forgiveness. He also makes a surprising request, wanting my assistance to help him cross over to the world of light when he dies. I give him my word that, when that time comes, I will be notified by my Higher Self, and through his own desire he will receive help, surrounded by angelic beings and the matrix of his own Higher Self. I also talk with him about suicide, as I can feel him contemplating this as a way out of the nightmare he has perpetuated.

Without the attachment of the dark entities, he is without the buffer of cold indifference. Left to examine the aftermath of his destructive actions, he finds himself filled with remorse and the challenge of taking responsibility. This is a painful reality leading to a forked road where he will have to choose self-punishment ... or the harder road of self-forgiveness. We ask him to be open to what his soul may have in store within the prison system, and to use the opportunities that arise as a way to consciously make amends.

My wish for him is that he someday experiences the far-reaching effects of reconciliation the same way Rhonda, Ann, Will, Julianna, the Native Americans and Angelina all did—knowing that the power to forgive and to be forgiven reaches across all timelines and dimensions.

Everything is your reflection.
There is nothing we are not.
This is about re-integration.
It is all energy.
We are all one.

~ Story Waters ~

46

NOT GONE

In a Soul Detective session, muscle testing is used to help determine what is going on in the person's energy field. This involves testing a particular muscle like the anterior deltoid, but there are also a number of ways that the client can self-test. One that I prefer is a standing test sometimes called the 'Tilt Test.' This is done by crossing the wrists in front of the heart while facing north and making a statement. The body will automatically lean forward in response to a True statement, or lean backwards indicating a False statement. Before proceeding with more challenging questions, centering exercises are done and a base line is established. This means testing a neutral fact, such as saying your given name. If you are centered, you will lean forward after saying, "My name is _____." To be sure that your energy is not frozen or reversed, you also test it with a false statement. It helps to choose a false name that you have no connection to, such as, "My name is Peter Pan."

In the early fall of 2015, I have a series of Soul Detective clients coming to see me and each time I demonstrate the Tilt Test, the false name that pops into my head is "Marilyn Monroe." The first time, I am a bit surprised, but find myself repeatedly using it without much thought as to why.

About a month later, a friend of mine Googles the title of my book and finds out that the name "Dead, but __NOT__ Gone" is already being used. The author, *Réal Laplaine, has written a sci-fi account of Marilyn Monroe coming back from the dead and telling her version of what really happened to her, hence the subtitle, "What would you tell the world if you came back from the dead?"

At first I am upset, thinking I will need to rename my book, but then the realization dawns on me that there is more to this than mere coincidence. Spirits use all kinds of ways to get our attention, and Marilyn certainly has mine. The final nudge comes when another friend orders Réal's book and relays the contents to me, which includes the detail that Marilyn had an abortion in the early part of 1962. I am prompted to focus on Marilyn directly while asking her questions.

"Did you ever cross over?"

"No."

"Did you really have an abortion?

"Yes."

"Did your baby ever cross over?"

"No."

"Are you ready to cross over now?"

"Yes."

"Would you like assistance in crossing over?"

"Yes."

I have no idea where the inspiration came from for Mr. Laplaine's novel, but I question if there wasn't a bit of a channeling behind it with Marilyn wanting to somehow set her own record straight.

I ask Marilyn, "Are there any other earthbound souls with you?"

"Yes, I am not the only one here."

Because of all the rapidly mounting signs, I accept that this is the day to assist them. There are things beyond our left-brained planning that get arranged in spite of us, and this is one of those instances. A friend (Kate), who is a Tarot reader and psychic, selected this particular Halloween morning—a month in advance—to come out and walk the labyrinth. A day when the veil is purported to be thinner feels very intentional for the task at hand.

Greeting Kate in the field, I fill her in on the new agenda to walk the labyrinth today as a way to open the portal and help the swiftly multiplying souls to move across.

Kate immediately tunes in and relays to me, "Marilyn is also issuing a caution to you in going forward and becoming more public, because of what she has been through."

When I inform Kate that there are others besides Marilyn who are ready to cross over, she starts to receive a barrage of names. "Two of her husbands—Joe DiMaggio and Arthur Miller—are among them, along with others that were maligned during the McCarthy hearings."

The hearings were a paranoid witch hunt looking for infiltrators, labeling many writers and entertainers as communist sympathizers. Ending in 1954, the hearings affected 320 upcoming artists who were blacklisted.

When Kate points out that James Dean is here, we realize that this is a specific culture of well-known individuals, artisans, movie stars, writers, producers, politicians, etc. who were in their prime between the 1930s, and 1970s. It is likely that the social memory that we hold about these folks has contributed to keeping them here, magnifying their personal wounds. Although everyone in a body carries their own burdens, when you are under the microscope of the public eye you are subject to the public's projected opinions. Those opinions are often manipulated by someone in the 'power vacuum' who sees an upcoming 'star' as a threat that needs to be controlled (bribed or blackmailed), and if they don't fall into line, executes a form of a character assassination against them.

In cases like those of Marilyn Monroe and James Dean, I'm sure there were questions and suspicions that included the details around their deaths. Many of these public figures lived a life of secrecy and were likely targeted by a secret Cabal that pulled the strings of their existence, which included shaping the images they wanted portrayed. Cabal groups are threatened by highly creative people who are possibly starseeds or 'wanderers,' so they attempt to control and derail them from their soul missions and what they might contribute. Dying young and troubled serves the Cabal, reminding the population that if you shine too brightly or find out things that may expose them, or try to derail their nefarious plans, you will pay the ultimate price with your life.

Dark entities are often assigned to such brilliant individuals at the height of their careers to exploit their wounds and find a crack in their armor, perpetuating any lower vibrational emotions like fear, depression, anxiety, sadness, guilt, regrets or perceived wrongdoing. The Cabal's mission is to take them down, but their dark assignment doesn't end when the individual dies. Instead, it is actually reinforced. It appears that this entire group has been in some kind of holding tank, or some form of energetic 'lockdown.'

With the enormous frequency shift that the planet is experiencing, massive unprecedented 'soul releases' are also increasing world-wide. (It's interesting to note that, in the United States, this time period of October 2015 corresponded with the largest one-time release of about 6,000 federal prisoners by the Justice Department in an effort to reduce overcrowding and provide relief to drug offenders who received harsh sentences over the past three decades.) It appears that the releases occurring on both sides of the veil are another indicator that the Cabal, in collusion with the dark entities, is losing control.

In the middle of the prairie we have a group of souls gathering that died half a century ago, who have been effectively immobilized by the powerful drug of mass consciousness. But now the induced state that has kept them in detainment is wearing off, due to the increased vibrations bombarding the planet. The change in their consciousness is directly related or wired into ours, and vice versa. When we—the ones in body—receive their energetic signal asking for assistance, we automatically respond like a dispatch center. I can't help but think of this 'crossing' work as a well-coordinated, etheric *Uber* service. As a growing transportation network, we are being called upon to voluntarily assist other souls who need a lift. It requires using our own personal vehicles (our physical body/mind/spirit complex) with the intent to deliver them to the nearest station to make their off-world 'flight connections.'

Kate and I walk the labyrinth as a way to open the portal while clipping the fallen grasses along the paths. Symbolically, we are clearing the way of any last obstructions or resistances that might be under the surface. When we reach the center, we invite their Higher Selves to meet them. There is a palatable whirling of energy as if we have entered a grand ballroom, with Marilyn moving among the 'guests' like their mistress of ceremonies.

In a detached sense, Kate and I sit in the background while their 'Ascension Ball' gets underway. One after another, the souls are swept into the portal of the central vortex like a revolving dance floor. Additional names continue to surface in our minds, putting us into the role of the acting commentators announcing their arrival. This leads to discussing and recognizing the contributions each one of them has made. Paying homage in this way feels appropriate before their final departure.

With all of these creative individuals returning to the other side, I can't help but feel that the planet will be receiving an influx of freed-up vital energy made available to the next generation of budding stars (*star-beings?*) who will not be held back this time.

We may never know what kind of energy was hitting the planet on and around Halloween 2015, but another friend who is an intuitive empath concurred that she was also having her own experience with earthbound spirits signaling their readiness to be released around this same time. This is what was happening from her perspective:

"I started picking up on the spirits of Native Americans when I was a kid. They were always in the woods at my parent's house. Then in 2013, I became aware of clusters of them around Kansas City—the River Market area, Cliff drive, KCK, and up north of the river. They let me know they were around, but didn't show me much else. Slowly they revealed to me how they died, which was suddenly. For some that happened through war, but for others it was from illness that spread like wildfire through their camps. They felt like they were dead before they died, and afterwards they were so angry with what happened that many of them stayed around. It was almost like they stayed underground and influenced the city with different types of energy after their death.

On Halloween of 2015, they decided they were ready to move on. They asked me to help them by creating ceremonies that were to be done over a period of ten days. My guidance was to set out different glasses of water, because the different tribes (about fourteen groups) were not always friendly with one another. Their territories were separated by water when they were living, so the glasses provided symbolic boundaries giving them their own place to stay where they didn't have to interact with the other tribes. I put some of the glasses out in my house, but I also placed them around the labyrinth image that is part of the Chakra Labyrinth Cards.

The tribes asked me to start opening up the labyrinth portals by finger-tracing the pattern and walking the one at Unity Village in Lee's Summit, MO (an eighty-foot Chartres-style design on blacktop), *as well as burning lots of sage and Palo Santo. Walking the design into the center was opening the door for them. They assured me that this was all that was needed as their ancestors and guides would help them with the rest.*

I could feel their soul-guides overseeing the whole thing, making sure energy was only going where it needed to go, and providing protection for me. In the beginning, they wanted me to open the door for each group separately, which meant continuously re-walking the path to the center, but after a few times of this they understood that the door was remaining open, and just took turns going through it.

Ten days later on 11/11 we did a closing ceremony. It was made very clear to us that this ceremony wasn't to close the portal or to signal the end to the natives moving on, but it was a celebration of how far we had come over the last few days. Once it was over, I was left with the sense that I was going to be doing this a lot. The natives even told me that, in return for helping them, they would protect me in future ceremonies.

I already see evidence of this as I used to have terrible nightmares whenever I would return to my parents' house, and be unable to walk in certain rooms or in certain parts of the yard. Yet when I went there over the holiday, I didn't feel any of that. Something has definitely shifted."

~ Kristen Wolf
  Kansas City, MO

Conscious choice is beginning to trump unawareness
and our unwillingness to see.

~ **Ronald Head** ~

47

UN-BINDING

When traumatic or negative events occur, they are accompanied by an emotional charge that creates an 'attractor field' around the location. This has the effect of drawing in earthbound spirits who resonate with—and therefore are responding to—the 'charge.' The attraction is greater for those who lived or died there. Depending on the situation, dark entities might be sent to a particular place to maintain the instability, keeping the disruption perpetually active. Souls that still roam the 'halls' of another time can and do interpenetrate our dimension. It doesn't matter if it is a battlefield, an asylum, a hospital, orphanage, prison, cherished home, or stretch of land, because to the deceased the place has personal significance that keeps them there.

If you are highly sensitive, you may have gone on a vacation or visited a place where you could sense or feel the 'undercurrent' of what occurred there. Perhaps you felt an unseen presence observing you, or were even a witness to unexplained phenomenon. More and more people are having intuitive impressions or experiences that they can't easily dismiss, which coincides with the steadily growing obsession we all have with the paranormal. TV shows and movies are reflecting our fascination, cashing in on these themes.

This has resulted in the booming sales of things like electro-magnetic field detectors (EMF meters), infrared LED video cameras, EVP audio recorders, and a whole slew of other equipment that paranormal investigators rely on. 'Ghost Hunting' has become big business with many groups clamoring to make a name for themselves and get recognition. Unfortunately, ghost-hunting can be more about the thrill of the hunt (which can border on harassment), than the desire or willingness to help those who are being 'hunted.' Most paranormal enthusiasts don't even know that it's possible to help a 'ghost' cross over.

In many cities, there are hotels or buildings with historical significance that are advertised as being 'haunted.' They may be in the business of preserving a landmark and making it available to the public but, if they are also advertising that it is haunted, they are capitalizing on the 'attractor field' to make money. They draw in the curious, the serious—and of course, the thrill-seekers—who never consider that they may end up going home with 'souvenirs' that they never bargained for. These popular excursions may be a form of entertainment for a group of friends, but in many ways it is like going on a safari to find the animals who have fallen into a trap and remain in a zoo-like existence with people traipsing through their 'enclosures,' treating them as a curious novelty. Instead of freeing them, zealous investigators unwittingly poke around their fields with meters and recorders in an attempt to elicit some kind of response. Beyond the intrigue and adrenaline rush, those involved may actually be picking up more than electromagnetic fields or muffled voices.

The following story is shared by a woman who, as a medium herself, went on one of these ghost tours. As an empath, Julie has been able to see, hear, and feel spirits throughout her entire life. Unfortunately, her strict religious upbringing had taught her to fear death, and with it the spirit world that communicated so easily with her. Consequently, she shut down her spiritual gifts for many years, which sent her into fear and made her extremely ill. After suffering for over twenty years, she went through an awakening that reconnected her to accepting and using her gifts. Just before this outing in 2015, Julie had learned how to deal with spirits in a more compassionate way than her earlier religious upbringing had taught. She was newly aware that she could open portals and help the earthbound souls cross over.

"September 12, 2015

I must begin by telling you, I don't typically go to places where criminals or insane people might have lived. I don't like their spirits (ghosts) and I don't like the dark entities that usually inhabit such places. But several friends were going to the 1859 Jail and Marshall's home in Independence, Missouri, and they persuaded me to come along.

Before we even started the tour, Sean (my seventeen-year-old son) and his friend wanted me to look at the small schoolhouse that had been moved to the property. The school had several spirit children that came and went all evening long and we met a couple of those children later in the evening during the investigation.

The paranormal investigation began with a tour of the Marshall's home, which is actually connected to the jail by a hallway. We went upstairs first to the master bedroom. As I entered I could hear a woman screaming and see, in my head, a woman giving birth. I had the distinct feeling that three children had lived in the home. There was a great deal more screaming and confusion. The new screaming seemed to be overlaid with the sound of running and shooting. The guide told us later that the Marshall's home was attacked and the Marshall was shot, dying later of his wounds. (Note from Toby: This is a good example of spirits being caught in an incessant time loop, continuously repeating an emotional traumatic event.)

We moved forward to the upper jail, which completely caught me off guard. I had been told that the lower jail had two bad spirits in it, but nobody had said anything about the spirits in the upper jail. As I stepped into the area, I was assaulted by screaming so loud that I had to plug my ears.

I spun around in circles, saying aloud to myself and anyone else who would listen, 'No, no, no, no, no!'

"I was completely unprepared. The emotions, mental confusion, and screaming in the upper jail were overwhelming. I was able to block them out pretty quickly, but I did not appreciate the 'welcome committee' in the upper jail.

We went back downstairs and went to the front parlor which was fairly calm. The only noticeable reaction I received came from the Marshall's wife. She informed me that her husband was an SOB and she was glad he was upstairs. The guide also told us that the pictures of the couple were frequently askew, or completely off the wall in the morning until the staff decided to hang the pictures on different floors.

Next, we passed through to the Marshall's office where the investigators had set up a bottle of whiskey, a cigar, and one hand of cards on the Marshall's desk. I was informed by someone in spirit that you can't play cards with only one hand. I had to chuckle. There were obviously some intelligent spirits inhabiting this property.

The Marshall's office opened into the lower jail via a hallway, which we passed through to gain entrance. By this time, I was ready to be done for the night and we had only been on the walk-through for about forty minutes. As I stepped into the lower jail I was nervous, but I was much better prepared. I walked quickly to the other end of the cell block and stood with my back close to the stone wall. Suddenly, Frank James (in spirit) walked up behind me and introduced himself. He was very polite and kept calling me "ma'am." He assured me that I would be safe with him, and he continued to follow me around the entire time I was in the jail.

As soon as we were done with the initial walk-through, I was ready for a break. I went back upstairs in the home where a couple of interesting things happened. In the master bedroom, two of the investigators were using some equipment to try to talk to a little boy who had 'played' with them in the past under the bed. When I walked in, he stopped playing, crawled out from under the bed, stood up and looked at me. He was adorable. He looked like he was about six and he was wearing clothing that would have been appropriate for the civil war era.

Then he looked at me and said, "I'm sick."

Dark circles appeared around his eyes and I could tell that his soul had been here too long. In my mind, I told him that if he followed me home I would help him get to a place where he could get well, but that I couldn't do anything right then. He looked so sad that I wanted to cry. Then he disappeared and their equipment stopped registering anything. With a heavy heart, I went down the hall.

At the end of the hall was a child's bedroom. There were two incidents that occurred in this bedroom. During one incident, my friend—who is also a medium—and I sensed two spirit children playing on the bed. I believe that they were both girls. The energy was very light and playful. During another *incident later in the evening, one of the investigators was having a flashlight discussion with a child named Beth who was sitting on the bed. Again, the energy was very light, but I wondered why these children would choose to come to this place.*

I spent the rest of the evening in the section of the building that had the investigator's base set up. Sean and several other teenagers were having a flashlight discussion with Jesse James. They asked Jesse if he was ready to cross over, and he said that he wasn't quite there, but it didn't matter because all of the spirits there had been 'bound' to that place. They also found out that Frank James had crossed over and came back regularly to watch over those who were left behind.

September 13, 2015

When I returned home later that evening, I attempted to help the children cross over, but I was not sure I was completely successful because it felt like someone had been left behind. This feeling was intensified by the thought of the souls being 'bound' to that building. This was really bothering me.

It finally occurred to me that, before I understood that a person's soul has a choice about whether to cross over or not, I had been assuming that all of the spirits I encountered throughout my life were bad. I know that my dad assumed that all spirits except heavenly angels were evil, which meant if he sensed any kind of spirits around, he taught us to 'bind' them (by using that word) and cast them back into 'Hell.' As human beings, we do not have the power to cast another human being or their soul into hell; however, we do have the power to bind a spirit or soul through our intention, directed by our words. This means that if a person had died and not crossed over, then the living can bind their soul to a particular place. I am not saying that it is right, just that it is possible. (Note from Toby: 'Binding' can happen in a moment of anger using a 'curse,' or a 'hex,' which is an intentional negative program sent from one person to another.)

So, it occurred to me that I and my family have in our fear and ignorance, left a wake of destruction and earthbound souls behind us. I asked Sean to join me and we set up an octahedron, asking God to put His strongest angels on each side, top, and bottom. We asked for a one-way portal from here to Heaven with St. Michael and his sword to show the way. Then I asked for forgiveness for 'doing it wrong' all these years, asking God and all of the spirits that had been affected to forgive me.

I could see an image of the globe in my mind, and there were points of light (just like the pictures you see of the Earth with the lit-up cities taken at night) clustered all over Europe and North America. The lights indicated the places where souls were wrongfully bound. I had to mentally go to each location, moving as fast as I could, while calling out to the souls. I apologized, and when I told them why I was there, they immediately responded with joy. At one point, it felt like a spiritual 'tweet' was coming in. I was getting responses from places I hadn't even gotten to in my mind yet. Every soul responded in a positive way. They smiled and began to glow. Some laughed, some cried, some cheered and a couple of them even kissed me on the top of my head. They were all very gracious about forgiving our ignorance. Then they gathered together with us at our home to pass through the portal.

I asked that they would be set free in Jesus' name and given an angelic escort to Heaven. Then I asked that all of the spirits that anyone in my family (regardless of how far back or how far out on the family tree) had wrongfully bound be set free and escorted to Heaven. Finally, I asked that any spirits that I had wrongfully bound in any other incarnation be set free and escorted to Heaven. It was from the 'family bindings' where the majority of the souls were released. There were repeats of the spiritual 'tweets' going out all over the world. We had spirits responding from Europe, Egypt, North Africa, America, Eastern Canada, and I am sure that I have forgotten a few. The one constant was that they were all filled with light and joy. They were beautiful, gracious, forgiving, and loving. We did a tilt test to find out how many spirits we were releasing and how long to leave the portal open. There were a little over 175,000 spirits. We ended up leaving the portal open for about an hour because we had some additional spirits that needed help.

Towards the end, Frank James showed up with some more of the children from the jail and some innocent souls that had been bound to the jail. My best interpretation of the pictures he showed me and what he said was that some of the people who were put in the jail under article 11 had died in the jail. Some of those who died did not cross over, and then some of them were bound to the jail because they lost touch with their family, or because the whole family died and this was the only place they knew. However, because they were bound, they had to be extracted very carefully to make sure that the dark entities were not alerted. God gave me the right words and I felt much better. Even the little boy who was sick got out.

After we released the 175,000 souls, my printer came on by itself and printed the words 'Hi Julie.' We received three more messages in Greek, all attempting to get my attention and lead me on a wild goose chase. As intriguing as it was to begin with, I determined that a 'false light' (impostor spirit) was trying to lure me in and distract me from releasing any more souls.

September 14, 2015

Frank James showed up with a 'wagon train' full of people in my bathroom this morning. Very unnerving. My bathroom is off limits and Spirit knows that, but a few of the people were in a hurry and did not want to wait. They were fascinated by the water coming out of the wall in the shower! I told Frank that they would have to wait in the hallway until I was out of the shower and dressed, and then I would help them. Once I was ready, Frank told me the story of the people who had died. I do not believe that all of the people were in the same wagon train, but this was simply a commonly understood form of travel for the people who were involved. I had one man who didn't want to go across if his team of oxen couldn't go. I assured him that they were God's creatures too and that they would also be welcomed into Heaven. One little boy wanted to make sure that there wouldn't be any snakes because his dog had been bitten by a snake. I explained to him that all of the animals in Heaven got along and that nobody bites. The man and his oxen, the boy and his dog, and about seventy other people passed through the portal. Once they had all passed through, Frank told me that he probably would not be coming back for a while."

~ Julie Gosney McCutheon
  Kansas City, Missouri

A good book that thoroughly addresses the concept of 'binding souls' is *James Twyman's *Kabbalah Code*. In it, he is guided to go to particular churches throughout Paris to 'unbind' spirits (positive and negative) that had been both inadvertently and very intentionally 'imprisoned' throughout history. He chanted different *Sacred Names of God* in Hebrew to open the seals that were holding the souls, as well as the seals within himself to be a channel for grace to come into the world and assist them in leaving. He realized that, with their consciousness trapped dimensionally, they could not fulfill their soul's purpose. This is true for all earthbound souls, and a good reason to help free them.

Resistance causes symptoms / Allowing catalyzes miracles.

~ **Shifra Hendrie** ~

48

UNDERWORLD CHRYSALIS

Nikkea went on a 'ghost tour' with her eyes more wide-open than the mainstream participants who are usually drawn to these experiences. She went in armed with the knowledge of how to help free the spirits, along with the conviction that it was right to do so—yet that didn't stop the attachments that took place. Sometimes an agreement to assist earthbound souls means we have to 'suit up' and go down into the 'underworld,' willing to bring the 'wounded' back with us. 'Coaching' from the 'ground level' isn't always going to get the results our soul has in mind. Metamorphosis is a process that happens from the inside out.

"In April 2013, my friend invited me to a ghost tour at the Mansfield Reformatory in Ohio. I was quite apprehensive about it, as well as intrigued. Although it saddened me that people were making a profit off of earthbound spirits who were suffering and confused, I found myself drawn to what had actually happened on the land where the reformatory was built. Finding out that it was once an old Civil War basecamp was perhaps behind my compulsion to attend. My intention was to use the knowledge I had learned over the years to cross over any of the souls who wanted my assistance.

The friend who invited me had also been very interested in the Civil War. I sensed that I may have had a fragmented part of myself 'left behind' there, and it was possible that she did, as well. I knew there was a personal reason

I was going and it seemed right that we were going together.

Weeks before the tour, when falling asleep at night, I sent distance Reiki to the future situation, visualizing the land and reformatory. During that time, a few images of men's and women's faces flashed before me. The two that stood out the most were an African American man who had no teeth, and a woman with short, whitish-blonde hair standing in the jail cell. She appeared very mentally unstable. The connection to the reformatory, the land, and these faces filled me with a deep sadness. Through my fear and uncertainty, I prepared myself with prayer, meditation, Tom Kenyon's sound healing, and working with the Archangels, asking for their protection. The evening before and the morning of the tour, I did a guided visualization and began to feel a deeper sense of calmness. I knew at a soul level that I was supposed to go, even though I was apprehensive.

When I arrived at this huge, creepy yet beautiful place, I began to envision a labyrinth below the reformatory and one above the building, holding the intention in my heart to assist any souls who would like to take advantage of the portal that was being created. I activated the Tube Torus at the center of the labyrinth so it created a pillar of light for their souls to travel up on as they made their own 'jail break.' I called on my Higher Self and any of the earthbound spirits Higher Selves.

During the tour—which lasted through the entire night—all the lights in this massive building remained off. We used flashlights to navigate. I felt different emotions such as fear, deep sadness, hopelessness, helplessness, and anger. I realized that not all of these emotions were mine, but possibly of these spirits or the energy imprints.

I heard a man's voice in the Infirmary yell out, 'Get me out of here!'

I also felt such deep sadness in the jail cell area, and immense fear in the basement area. They were prisoners in that lifetime and now remained prisoners after death. I continued to hold the vision and intention of those spirits ready to cross over being enveloped by their Higher Selves, and greeted by their loved ones as they crossed into the World of Light.

At the end of the tour, although I enjoyed spending time with my friend, I was relieved it was over. My friend joked in the car that perhaps we brought some spirits home with us in the back seat. Although I giggled with her about it, I knew that this could potentially occur, and was hoping that was not the case.

A few days after the tour, I began to have strange and uncomfortable symptoms which increased in intensity over several weeks. I had muscle twitching in my legs, and I felt really drained. Looking in the mirror, my first thought was, 'I look dead. I think I'm dying.' Big circles appeared under my eyes. My right hand and right foot were noticeably colder than the rest of my body off and on throughout the day. I experienced aches in my gallbladder region and my fourth toe felt numb periodically. I had swollen lymph nodes, and couldn't shake the feelings of 'fight or flight' that kept occurring without warning. Eventually I went to the doctor and my lab results detected that my immune system was imbalanced. My body felt threatened by something and it was attacking itself.

One night, I dreamed of being dragged by something through the halls of the jail cells at the reformatory, flooded with feelings of hopelessness and fear. In my waking life, I felt like I was being dragged through the dark. Most nights, I didn't recall my dreams at all, which was very unusual for me. I was struggling to function. During the same time, a close friend shared a dream she had about me.

Her words were, 'This is not your energy. I saw an 'alien' face and heard Archangel Michael tell it to be gone now.'

I was perplexed and was not sure what this all meant. I was also frightened, drained, and not at all feeling like myself. My children noted that I didn't seem like the 'Mom' they knew. I found a note on my bed from my six-year-old daughter, Julia.

It said, 'You are Love Mom, you are Light.'

My heart filled with joy and grief hearing such kind words, as I felt far from the love and light within myself. I was grateful this sweet angel was there to remind me.

When I stood outside between two of my favorite trees, pleading for clarity and help, I kept hearing, 'You need to move the energy on or the energy will move you on.'

This didn't make sense to me then. I also noticed the clocks often displayed number sequences such as 4:44, 3:33, and 11:11. I sensed these were *signs to get my attention, or that I was on the right track as I uncovered more. Julia made pictures for me, often with butterflies. Before bed, I laid beside her in the dark with some light from the hallway on her walls. She would teach me how to make butterfly shadows with my hands. As we moved our hands together, I remembered that 'Butterfly' is the symbol of transformation, and her beautiful soul was reminding me of this. I felt like I was in the midst of a major transformation, but the path just felt so dark and dismal.*

Pictures of Jenny, my childhood best friend who had committed suicide, kept turning up 'out of the blue' and my children kept asking about Jeff, my boyfriend who had died in a car accident (shared in Chapter 24, "Solar Portal").

One day, Julia painted a picture for me and I couldn't help but be alarmed. She said, 'Mommy, I really need you to look at this.'

Staring back at me in her drawing was a red face that looked like it had a black eye. I recalled a medium once telling me that, if I ever saw a red energy around an earthbound spirit, not to work with the energy until protection was in place. I began to put all of these unsettling experiences together and realized I was receiving vital messages and signs. I knew it was time to contact Toby. She was ready and willing to assist and, for the first time during that dark and confusing period, I felt there was light at the end of this dark tunnel. I actually sensed a stirring of energy around me, as if the spirits who were with me were relieved that she could help.

In the beginning of my session, I felt very weak and not like myself at all. I recalled hearing my voice and thinking it didn't even sound like me. Through our Soul Detective session, Toby used muscle checking and her intuitive skills to discover I had seven earthbound spirits who were men from the Civil War basecamp located at the Mansfield Reformatory. She explained I had a deeper connection to these men, as though I had made a contract to return to assist them. I also had a dark entity attachment assigned to keep this 'unit' of fear in place. I immediately recalled Julia's painting of the red face with the black eye, and I imagined the dark entity having that resemblance. Toby explained that these dark entities like to feed off of our fear (I had plenty of that on the tour), and the seven earthbound spirits were like food for the dark entity, feeding off of their despair and confusion as well. I could imagine that the dark side wasn't too thrilled about any of the souls who had crossed over during the tour, and assigned this particular demon to take me 'off-mission.'

I recalled the dream Ella (my older daughter) had about me during this time. She'd written it down on a piece of paper and told me to not to open it until she left on the bus for school, because it scared her so much. On the paper was an image of a scary-looking doll who spoke to her about me.

The doll said, 'We will take everything she loves, so that it weakens her, so she has nothing left. And that's when we will get her.'

My heart broke at the thought that Ella had to experience such a sinister energy.

As we released the dark entity, Toby helped me to release my fear and become more empowered. While assisting the other earthbound spirits, I began to feel this heartfelt connection to the men. I finally could understand that, through my uncomfortable physical symptoms, they were trying to get my attention, imprinting onto me the physical conditions that they had struggled with. It helped me understand all the fear that accompanied my initial desire to attend the tour. On a certain level, I knew that all of this discomfort and suffering was going to be part of it.

Toby's assessment confirmed that the attachment (cording) occurred at my gallbladder area, where I had been having aches. She explained that spirits will usually attach at a weak area on someone's body. This made complete sense to me. Due to the aches, I had scheduled an ultrasound a few days after my session with Toby. It showed a polyp had developed on my gallbladder. I imagined that it created a little 'hook' area into which they'd attached (and it is also possible that their presence caused the polyp). Toby also shared that the fourth toe is the end point of the gallbladder meridian, so I finally understood the connection to the strange numbness of my toe. I was amazed at how much our bodies and even immune systems react to 'foreign invaders.'

When the men crossed over, I felt them leave like a breath of fresh air blowing past me. I was much lighter and relieved that my own energy was running freely through my body again, and I actually recognized myself when I looked into the mirror. Afterwards, through my own tilt testing, I was able to tune in more to receive further information regarding the seven men. The testing confirmed that I had been in the war with them as part of the Union side, and considered them my friends. I had agreed (made a soul contract) to 'go back' to assist them as 'Nikkea,' in my current time. Perhaps I was unable to help my friends 'back then,' and wanted this opportunity to help them now. Through this ordeal, I received such a gift from these earthbound spirits, healing the fear and uncertainty, and learning more about helping spirits make this major transition. I was so grateful to them for this learning experience, even though the unpleasant feelings and body sensations had to be a part of it.

A few days after my session with Toby, I awoke to seeing a three-foot, blackish-brown spider web in our upper right-hand corner of our bedroom. I didn't feel uplifted when I saw it, and it reminded me of an eerie gate. Following it up with muscle testing, it was confirmed that I had brought this portal home with me after the ghost tour at the reformatory. Perhaps I was literally seeing a portal into that time, which meant something got opened within me at the prison, which brought the opening home with me. Toby assisted me with closing and sealing the portal with the help of Archangel Michael. I felt much more empowered knowing this, in case it should occur again.

Immediately after my session, as I opened our bedroom door, my three children said, 'Hi Nikkea.' I was surprised, because they never called me Nikkea. They were acknowledging the true 'me' without all the attachments. I felt like myself for the first time in a long time. I also received a Mother's Day card with the words, 'Loving, caring, supportive, wonderful, wise, patient, nurturing, amazing, generous, friend, MOM. This is YOU.' I began to cry. My children were reminding me of the qualities I felt I no longer had within me after this confusing and exhausting experience.

My symptoms began to dissipate one by one, as I felt my own essence returning. I was much freer and more empowered with the information I had learned, knowing this could make such a difference for others experiencing earthbound and dark entity attachments.

Within a few days of our session, my husband Denny bought me a beautiful butterfly yard decoration. As I placed the stake into the ground, I felt like it was a reflection of the grounding within myself, the grounding of my energy into our planet, feeling the strength of Mother Earth holding me, and the transformation that had taken place. I had emerged from the chrysalis (as difficult as it felt) with brand new wings that would always support me. The butterfly spun gracefully with the wind, and continues to remind me to move with grace and ease in this world as I continue reclaiming my energy and sovereign-self.

I sensed this entire experience was part of the Underworld initiation through my personal Pluto-square-Pluto, and Pluto-square-Uranus cycles, where I felt incredibly unsafe, vulnerable, with my fears magnified. Many gifts came from this Underworld experience which ultimately allowed me to feel more empowered, standing more firmly in my true essence. It left me much more equipped to assist earthbound spirits, assessing myself for attachments, and trusting myself. My fears were released, which felt like a lifetime of draining energy melting away. I knew this was something I wanted to continue to learn about to assist others and our planet.

Fast forward to 2015, where I continued to be in tune with the earthbound spirit realm. Responding to the gentle encouragement from Toby, I decide to attend the Soul Detective workshop by Barbara Stone, PhD to further my training. On the way to the workshop in Medina, OH, I came upon the same exit to the Reformatory ghost tour. It had been a rainy, gloomy day. I found it synchronistic that I would be passing this exit, of all times, on the way to this workshop.

At first, I just wanted to pretend I didn't see it, as the painful memories flooded me. As the rain hit the windshield, I imagined those were the tears I shed during the time I had the attachments. I could see the faces of the Union soldiers, the dark entity, and those who were stuck in jail. I recalled the dream I'd repeatedly had after the tour: that of being dragged through the jail cell. Then a feeling of humbleness and gratitude flooded me as I approached the exit sign. I could feel the value of the entire experience since it seemed to open doors I was excited to walk through.

The sun surprisingly came out, and suddenly there were absolutely no clouds over the entire exit and Mansfield area. It was like a hole was punched out with only clear, blue skies. I nearly rubbed my eyes to see if I was truly seeing this peculiar sight. I looked in my rearview mirror after I passed it, only to see the dark clouds behind and ahead of me again, amazed that the opening had been there only for that brief time for me to witness.

I gasped, holding my heart with joy, and imagined the earthbound spirits waving 'hello' to me from a higher realm. I felt immense gratitude and respect for their journey, and for how they had impacted mine. My own internal sun was shining brighter, inviting me to remember the deeper wisdom gained from this experience. I knew the sun appearing was a powerful sign that the light really does shine again for those willing to make the transformation from the Underworld back to the home that waits for them in the World of Light."

~ Nikkea Walkker
  Mainville, OH

When I let go of what I am,
I become what I might be.

~ Lao Tzu ~

49

MACGREGOR

Years ago, I did something called a *Transition Team Training* in Hawaii with *Steve Rother. It was held for people whose jobs or interests revolved around assisting others going through the two biggest transitions we encounter as humans: *Birth*, coming into these bodies, and *Death*, getting out of them. Many have remarked that it is much easier to die, being released back to the infinite expanse of the *All-Knowing Awareness*, than it is being born, trying to squeeze our vast consciousness down into the density of these little, restricted bodies.

At the training, there were people from all over the world who were either there as birth greeters (midwives, doulas, nannies, doctors, nurses, and *Healing Touch* practitioners), who welcomed and anchored souls into this life, or those interested in the other end of the spectrum—the ones dedicated to preparing souls for their journey home. These were hospice workers, paramedics, police officers, spiritual advisers, counselors, caregivers, and many who were dealing with death personally. It helped me step into my own role as a psychopomp and grasp the significant details that were involved in the dying process.

As part of the training we were led through a guided exercise to simulate what to expect at the time of our own deaths. This was meant to prepare us for leaving our bodies and journeying into the world beyond.

I was immediately supported and enfolded by an invisible loving presence that was positioned behind me—as if I were a skydiving trainee making a 'tandem jump.' We were moving rapidly through a tunnel, much like the lava tubes we had explored while on the Big Island of Hawaii. The black canal disappeared, leaving me awash in aqua and blue hues that swirled together like a parachute that I had become completely entangled in. The interblending of these two 'color-beings' acted like an alchemical solvent, dissolving the barriers I had constructed and peeling away the borders of my limiting identity. The evaporating edges of my otherworld escorts became fused into the expanding fabric of my eternal being, reassembling as the unified essence I had always been.

As I look back on this vision experience, one part in particular stands out. My dear friend Ye, who I referenced previously as the one who brought horses to my window for my eighteenth birthday (Chapter 39, "KP" Duty), was suddenly there. His grinning face lit up the horizon as an extension of the blazing sunset. He was waiting for me on an oceanfront beach, holding the reins of two white horses. The ride was a blur of joy flying over changing landscapes of water, mountains, deserts and forests, all with endless stretches of sky taking me to the gateway threshold of the new world that waited.

It is rare to maintain a friendship that goes back to high school, but the ones that endure in spite of distance or infrequent contact most likely remain because there is a 'soul-group' connection. With certain individuals, we agree to be 'touchstones' in each other's lives. In *Shakespeare's play *As You Like It*, Touchstone is a character described as *"a wise fool who acts as a kind of guide or point of reference."* Ye and I have certainly been that for each other.

In 2014, ten years after the Transition Training, Ye visits our home in Missouri. This trip coincides with seeing one of his daughters who came to the Midwest for college and remained here, making a life for herself. She is planning her wedding for the following year and Ye wants to have alone time with her, lending his support while she walks him through the wedding venue. At the end of his stay, he carves time out to be with us.

Meals, laughter, and labyrinth walks are the backdrop for exchanging the latest updates in our lives. An hour before needing to leave for the airport to catch his return flight home, Ye agrees to do an Emotional Freedom Technique (EFT) 'tapping' session to help address and shift the heavy feelings he is carrying. Attempting to get to the bottom of the primary negative emotions that are surfacing, he begins talking about his lifelong struggle with anger and how, even as a child, it had resulted in his parents' decision to send him to an all-Catholic boarding school. Besides always trying to mitigate or numb the anger, he is also consumed with the feeling that he is a 'bad' father for abandoning his kids—especially the daughter he has come back to visit. This is ironic to me as Ye, with all of his relationship struggles resulting in three different marriages, has always stood out as one of the most loving parents I have ever encountered, completely devoted to each of his five children.

Sitting on the front porch of our old two-story farmhouse, we begin the session with me spontaneously making statements, trying to capture what I am hearing him say while adding in statements he *isn't* expressing. I am attempting to bring the deeper underlying feelings up to the surface where they can be energetically re-routed. Ye is repeating the phrases, while simultaneously tapping on the different meridian points by mimicking me.

"Even though I have all of this anger inside, I choose to love and accept myself.

Even though my anger can be debilitating, I would like to love and accept myself.

This anger has been with me my whole life.

My mother recognized my anger and knew it was a problem.

I am tired of carrying this burden of anger. I try to push it away, but it always comes back. It is always here with me.

I have so much shame and guilt with the anger.

I have shame and guilt for hurting those I love.

I have shame and guilt for not being able to work things out.

I have shame and guilt for leaving my kids.

I abandoned my kids when they needed me the most.

It's hard for me to be happy when I carry this burden of guilt and anger. Am I sabotaging myself? I wonder if I deserve to be happy?

I am angry with myself. Holding this anger is exhausting, but it won't let me go. It just turns into frustration and depression, but it is still mine to hold."

The more I dig into what I am perceiving as his suppressed feelings, the more I witness another personality emerging from Ye—coming to the forefront in emotional waves. Ye's face and body are revealing a character that, in my forty-five years of knowing him, I have never seen before. I suspect that he has an earthbound spirit attachment. Through muscle checking, this is confirmed. Our EFT session quickly transitions into a 'Soul Detective' session which means we will be identifying interference patterns and helping the soul cross over. I place a thirteen-inch wooden labyrinth on Ye's lap, knowing he will eventually be finger-tracing it to the center to open the portal for the soul's release. But first, we need to understand what we are dealing with.

I have him repeat the phrase, "What if all this anger is not mine? And then, "What if I agreed to hold this anger in order to release it ... in order to release whatever/whoever it belongs to?"

I pause, asking the 'entity' through Ye, "Is there a name that we can call you?"

Without hesitating he replies, "MacGregor!"

MacGregor's story follows as told by Ye:

"The sky is a leaden grey and the cold black earth runs with blood. As far as the eye can see there are bodies flattened against the earth, profiled like some black, human wasteland in the uncertain light of early dawn. Moans of the dying fill the air. Bodies without heads, heads without bodies, feet, hands, and limbs askew on a muddy, black landscape. White faces, drained of blood, frozen in time, eyes bulging, mouths agape dot the dark, desolate ground. I stand with my father and a clutch of men and women, once-bright kilts and heavy woolen capes stained dark with blood, earth, sweat and stink. Still holding our massive broadswords, but now in repose, stabbing into the ground to become a litany of bloody crosses. Above us, to the East, an undefined, watery sun rises; an impassive witness to the insane, moving massacre of war; of men, women, children and horses cut down dead.

I walk with my father through the battlefield, skirting the dead, looking for life to silence, agony to end. The last duty of the victor to finish what was begun a day earlier. Memories of the battle come in flashes, shaken loose by our shadow task of swinging swords, aching with the muscle memory of angry battle. We were there all day on the bright, noisy field, swinging our heavy swords wherever they needed to go. Ducking, stabbing, pushing, spearing, swinging hard against armored flesh. Severed heads tumbled down from bloody necks. Time disappeared as the world dissolved into red. We would have our way with this army that sought to deprive us of life. This clan that had raped our women, stolen our lands, and sent demented hounds to hunt down and kill our innocent. My justifiable anger felt righteous and provided energy in battle, yet the knowing that such indulgent action would perpetuate more of the same against my clan threw a shadow over our 'success' and turned victory on its head. There can be no victory when every enemy's death is eventually your own.

It's hard to put into words, this memory of an old, recurring dream that followed me from childhood, but it provided a visual narrative backdrop to what was being unearthed in the NOW—connecting me with the quick, sharp anger that often rose in me unbidden and unrestrained. This anger was mine. It came from within me but for no reason that I could identify. This 'take your head off' anger felt justified in the moment, yet the voice of reason always emerged, saying that even as I reveled in battle more suffering was ushered into the world.

My childhood was full of incidences of discord and dislocation. From the moment of my breech birth I was that colicky kid that required a middle-of-the-night car ride to calm. Bullied in grade school, I fought back with a crazy ferocity that got me in plenty of trouble. I learned that it was always the retaliatory action that got punished, but that never stopped me from responding to a real or imagined slight. I had a 'chip on my shoulder' that unknowingly allowed me to relive past conflicts, some of them centuries old as I would later learn. I relished going against the grain and was at war with the world; I look back and call it World War Me, or World War Ye.

After completely frustrating my parents who had four other kids to raise, I was given the opportunity to attend a Jesuit high school, Campion, where 'Send us a boy and we'll give you back a man' was on every billboard and letterhead of the school. I wanted to become a priest so a Jesuit institution was a privileged choice. It also seemed like a good escape from the trouble that followed me, the trouble that I created without knowing why. A 'location cure' that never quite worked, but changed me nonetheless as our country burst into the flames of protest.

That was 1966, and driven by the carnage and stupidity of the war in Vietnam, a rising wave of revolution in art, music, and science drove the social revolution of the 60s. It affected every person and penetrated every institution, including Campion. So now I was not the only one pushing back, and my war with the world merged with the counterculture. In 1967, a few other students and I engineered a very public student protest which blocked a large ROTC parade on campus. There was some pushing and shoving, and I found myself in a fight. This was the first time that I remember experiencing the violent images of my clan war dream, and in the course of the fistfight I 'woke up' to find myself being pulled off another student that I had been wailing on. I was expelled two weeks later with complete justification.

I returned to live with my family, and finished high school with my brothers and sisters and many new friends—most of them musicians, artists, and free thinkers. I would not have a revisit of this dream for two years and then not again until much later in college. This 'monster' was something I was familiar with and was mostly able to repress with the help of drinking. Anger seethed below the surface, however, and could emerge at any time for any number of reasons. Usually I simply became cold, distant, and verbally menacing if pushed. I never knew what I was doing until later, and then would remember the feelings mixed with images of battle and sword decapitation.

Sadly, this and factors beyond my control eroded my marriage. I continued to be an active father to my children and enjoyed other relationships, marriages, and more children. I kept watch and a check on my anger, learning to avoid situations and conflicts that would bring it up. I still had my clan battle dream once in a while, always waking in a sweat like I had just stepped through a 400-year-old time warp. The fact that I shared this dream with no one attests to the fact that I was not proud of my anger yet, in truth and deep down, I completely owned and identified with this warrior with all of his passion, strength, and truth. I did not know who this warrior was, and simply felt he was a creation of what Freud would call my id, which

I felt was also the source of my passion and creativity. All three of these threads—passion, creativity, and anger—have been present throughout my life, but I have learned very recently that the personification of my warrior as manifested in my reoccurring dream actually had a name ... one that didn't come out until my impromptu session with Toby, when it was revealed to us both for the first time. And when he emerged he was no warrior, but a tired, broken man seeking a way home. And as his story came out of my mouth, the recurring dream and many other things fell into place.

His name was MacGregor and he was obviously a clan leader in Scotland. In my dream/memory, he and his brothers along with their father had just won a huge battle and had killed many enemies in one day of bloody and savage fighting.

I don't remember a whole lot of what happened on the porch other than MacGregor leaping out of my mouth and me feeling tired, relieved, and free. I know I cried a lot and I know that part of that was mourning for my father who I miss terribly because I kept seeing his face. He seemed mixed up in all of this, and I am actually happy for that because it brings him closer to me."

During the session, as I witness MacGregor's personality emerging through Ye, I ask him to describe his surroundings and what he is experiencing. He begins by recounting a battle scene, giving me the impression that this was an ongoing occurrence that came with the responsibility of his lineage. I tell MacGregor he does not need to remain here. He has suffered enough, caught in the relentless loop of pain and destruction. He is reluctant to believe that it is possible to step out of it. I suspect that MacGregor is a 'lynchpin soul'— someone that others respected and followed with pride, staying with him or around him after he died, loyal beyond the grave. I explain to MacGregor that we can open a portal to the World of Light and, with his help, he can lead the battle-weary souls surrounding him to be reunited with their families and clan members who will be waiting to welcome them home. We do additional tapping, gearing the statements to fit MacGregor's regrets and sorrows, helping him adjust and open to his new assignment: getting his people home. This portion is emotionally overwhelming for both Ye and MacGregor. The overlap of their unresolved feelings is converging to address and dismantle their long angry history.

Using the *Chakra Labyrinth Cards,* Ye agrees to pull a card representing possible blocks that are ready to be released from each of their seven-chakra energy centers. He reads one at each turn as he finger-traces the wooden labyrinth pattern to the center with the intent to open the portal. The statements are to help Ye identify and ultimately let go of the lower, eroding feelings that are co-joined with MacGregor. When he arrives in the center, in the company of his own Higher Self escort, I asked MacGregor if he is ready for this new journey of leading his people to a new homeland. There is no hesitation. I am instructed to keep the portal open for several days for any straggling souls who are slower to respond.

Due to the need to get Ye to the airport on time, all of this happens quickly, but even that is not an accident. Although it means Ye is still in an emotional daze, I trust that the long flight will give him the space he needs to be with all that has occurred, to deepen his own understanding and to gather any additional pieces that may come forward.

"On the flight home I begin to remember some things about my family that seemed to connect to things Scottish. Why, for example, was I so filled with emotion and pride that I could hardly speak whenever I heard a pipe band? It's true that others who have no obvious connection to the Scots get emotional when hearing bagpipes; but for me there was something else. My father used to use our house stereo as an alarm. Every morning he would play bagpipe music turned up on high volume to get us all out of bed and started for the day. Of all the famous bagpipe tunes he could play, which one did my father put on? The one called *'The Young MacGregors.'

In college, my father played bagpipes and marched with the Highlanders. I have a picture of him in a kilt. Even though we did not have a Scottish name, when I was a child he acted like he was proud to be Scottish, once showing me a blanket that was a MacGregor tartan and a coat of arms that showed a family name—not MacGregor but, as he said, 'related.' He used to tell me with pride that in WWI the Scottish 'kilted regiments' that had a pipe band contingent used to 'strike fear in the hearts of the Germans' when the pipers began to play. He told me they were called 'The Ladies from Hell' by the Germans because they were fierce fighters that didn't give up.

After returning home from Toby's I did some research on Clan MacGregor, and I also looked into my family tree with renewed interest to see what my father had been talking about. Our surname is French, but my paternal great grandmother's name is *Hattie Greig. It didn't occur to me until a few days later that when one says Greg with a Scottish accent, it could be spelled Greig. I was amazed. I looked up Hattie Greig and found that Greigs were Gregors ... MacGregors! When I looked up Hattie Greig in an old album of my grandmother's, I realized that it was the same woman whose portrait was hanging in my bedroom closet, waiting to be brought out when I found out who she was."

When I asked Ye if he has noticed any changes since the session, he replied, "One by one, completely out of the blue, my children have asked me about the change within me. One of them said, 'Dad, I want to know how you have become so relaxed, you know, calm. Nothing seems to rile you. Even in the more tense situations I have seen you act so calm, steady, and guided by concern for everyone present.' While riding with me during rush hour another one of my other children said, 'You've been cut off several times and you don't honk, you don't speed up, you don't even complain.'

The truth is, I feel at peace. This has allowed me to see ahead, what is likely to happen, and know the best way to deal with it. There are hundreds out there who are ready to do battle, either at home, on the job, or in the circus of our freeways; and I have discovered that the adrenaline rush that comes with this urge is as addicting as any drug, only harder to discover. Anticipating the battle allows me to redirect the energies away from the addicting rush of confrontation, and in so doing keep everyone safer. Each time this happens, each time I see the clear path to peace and act on it, my body reinforces the *peaceful path; to experience yet again the deep peace that freedom from a need to battle brings."*

Ye also recounted a dream that he had two or three times, starting somewhere around 2005:

"I am walking through a rocky desert path with towering mesas on both sides. A rattlesnake appears on the rocks close to the level of my head. It launches itself toward me and I step back, jerking my head away. As it flies by I draw my sword and take its head off in one clean sweep.

After my visit in 2014, I had the dream again. This time the snake speaks to me before it strikes. It offers me some kind of wisdom and I decide that I want it. Somehow I am unafraid, and know I will either absorb the poison and live, or I won't and will die. I tell the snake to 'bring it,' and drop my hands. The snake springs at me and latches on to my throat, biting deeply. I feel the poison enter my bloodstream and my neck begins to swell. I enter a state of deep meditation where I absorb everything that is happening. I sense the struggle of my body around me but I am unmoved, watching in a detached way. I awaken with a good feeling, part of which is a knowing that I will not need to slay any more snakes and that I have gained some wisdom and entered a new understanding. A new path awaits."

~ Stephen Merritt (Ye)

Whether Ye is the reincarnation of MacGregor, or MacGregor attached to him as a distant family relative, Ye agreed to take on the formidable issue of anger and use his current life experiences to feel, face, and finally open to the inherent wisdom that was waiting beneath the 'poison' of his anger. He had to come to the place of being ready to own it before he could receive the gift of deeper understanding that accompanies the choice point that is always present. Anger is an old energy habit we use to protect and defend ourselves, and indulging the demanding habit also keeps us entangled in a destructive cycle of shame. The outer battles that divide nations, races, political parties, tribes, clans, families or our fractured senses of self won't end until we are willing to remove the armor of angry self-protection that blinds us and binds us to fear. The freedom that comes with foresight, born of self-awareness, can only flourish in a daily practice of self-control, arising from compassionate self-acceptance.

The lament of the bagpipes, once considered a 'weapon of war,' stirs emotional memories in our collective consciousness; but for the awakening masses, the powerful sound can be a present call to transmute the venom that divides us ... reclaiming peaceful co-existence as our unified birthright.

For death is no more than a turning of us over
from time ~ to eternity.

~ William Penn ~

50

DEATH RITES

Losing a loved one is part of the human experience that no one escapes, yet we don't always have forewarning with a chance to prepare ourselves. Nor do we always have the opportunity (or courage) to step into an active role to assist someone when we receive the news that they are dying. If we knew the basics of how to best help our loved ones, fewer souls would be sitting in the 'driveway' of indecision, grasping the emergency brake in their reluctance to leave. If people were educated about death and knew how to assist others in the dying process, there would be no earthbound souls. This chapter is designed to give you information that can help someone move through the death process with more acceptance, awareness, and grace.

Family members, spiritual advisers, energy healers and hospice workers are all wonderful candidates to serve as human psychopomps, as they are naturally positioned on the front lines, providing comfort and care to those in the death process. More than a bedside vigil, the soul-tending of a psychopomp is geared toward helping the departing soul untangle their 'kite strings' from the dense fog of earthy concerns that could keep their final flight 'socked in.' It's not enough to help them die; the goal is to help them die *consciously*. This means helping them to shift their identity from the *body*—that does not want to know or accept that it is dying—to the *soul/spirit* that is attempting to separate from this world and prepare for the journey beyond.

There are some common-sense steps that can encourage this, based on the death rites practiced by Shamanic traditions. They boil down to helping the individual *review, release,* and *realign.* As the survivor, we have to be willing to create an opening for them to talk about death and what this means to them. I have heard many survivors state that they put off having any kind of meaningful conversation with their loved one because they didn't want to give them the impression that they had given up hope, but often our reluctance is mingled with our own discomfort and non-acceptance of what is happening. We wait for the 'right' time or an opening to occur to bridge the subject and, too often, we miss the chance completely. A good way to begin is to ask them about their favorite memories. What were the moments that stood out to them?

Review

Recounting memories is a way to begin the in-body 'life review' intended to reminisce, capture and appreciate the positive highlights. From there, you may want to prompt them to voice their concerns, worries or fears about leaving. This may naturally lead into their regrets, perceived failures, aborted dreams or unfulfilled promises, helping to uncover any areas where they may need to forgive themselves and others. Bringing up past experiences allows whatever happened to be processed in a new way. Finding out if they have any last wishes or desires can become a natural segue into addressing unfinished business. Don't underestimate the release that can happen when they are able to give voice to their ruminating, unexpressed thoughts and emotions. Reviewing can lead to reframing how they've been holding something, no longer giving it power to hold them in bondage.

Release

Although Carl Jung's famous saying *"What you resist—persists"* was referring to his research on 'the shadow,' the concept still applies (maybe more so) after death. The trick then is to lighten up your load or unpack your 'luggage' before you die. If it's true that all suffering is caused by non-acceptance (denial) of what is occurring, then helping the dying talk about what is happening to them can be a relief, bringing light into their shadow reality. The burden of fear can be lifted when it is acknowledged and doesn't have to be held alone. That acknowledgment can give them permission to set down the heavy bags they've accumulated over their lifetime.

Three nights before my dad's death, when all of the family arrived, he was fighting to hang on, still outwardly struggling to beat this 'thing.' The Hospice worker went in and talked to him alone. Although we don't know exactly what was said, he came to some kind of acceptance that he was dying and immediately we all felt the change. He asked for the intravenous feeding tube to be removed and began outlining his wishes, planning with us who his pallbearers would be. The shift was startling and somewhat surreal, but his new acceptance of this powerless situation gave him back some measure of self-dignity and control.

If we can help our loved ones clear their concerns, fears, or negative emotions, it creates the space they need to start anchoring into what awaits them and fosters a state of gratitude, grace, and positive reflection. This process is greatly assisted by the powerful death rite of energetically cleansing and balancing their *chakras* (energy centers in the body). This is something that can be done effectively even with those who are unwilling or unable to talk about the past, and includes those who may be sedated or unconscious. It can also be done remotely by simply imagining yourself to be at the person's bedside while going through the actions, or you can use a surrogate person or even a stuffed teddy bear. Those who are dowsers, can draw seven vertical circles (symbolizing the seven chakras) on a piece of paper and use a pendulum instead of their hands.

The Seven Chakras

The Seven Chakras are seven universally recognized energy centers located on the midline of the body and described as rotating vortices (wheels of light) that carry energies in and out of the body. Like data discs with infinite memory, they store the imprint of every emotion or event that we have ever experienced. Each chakra has seven layers that go down into the body and attach to the spine, as well as seven layers that move out from the body. They form the bio-field (the physical, emotional, mental, intuitive and spiritual fields). The outermost or top layers process recent or current experiences as they are being lived, while the middle layers store the information that has settled which becomes our beliefs, confusions, habits, self-concepts and life-long stories. The deepest layers hold the reservoir of our earliest life experiences (good and bad) as well as our ancestral, genetic, DNA and—in the case of our Root chakra—past life information. The 'dross' of life that builds up like sludge can keep the chakras from vibrating at their purest frequency and hinder the detachment process at death, binding the luminous energy field to the physical body and resulting in an earthbound spirit.

As an *Eden Energy Medicine technique, clearing the chakras is a simple and effective way to bring stale, toxic, or painful energies up to the surface where they can be removed. This beneficial technique can be used whenever we need detoxing on a deeper, energetic level, but as a preparation for death it is additionally suited for erasing the imprints from the luminous body, greatly assisting in the final detachment.

Setting Sacred Space—Creating an Octahedron of Light

To do this for another, begin by asking for their permission. If they are not conscious, or this is a remote or long distance session, ask internally for their permission and set the caveat that this is an invitation, an energetic offering of balance, not an imposition to supersede their freewill. If you have the 'green light,' set sacred space by saying your own prayer and calling in assistance from the angelic realm or your personal guides, as well as the other person's guidance team. Through the power of your imagination, visualize a golden *octahedron* of light all around you. (In the *Hathor material through Tom Kenyon, this shape is known as the *Holon of Balance.*) You mentally place yourself in the center of a four-sided pyramid that extends above you with another matching pyramid below you. The bases are joined, forming a square. It may help you to visualize this by aligning it with the four walls of the room you are in, but it can be any size as long as it completely surrounds you. It is stated that *"geometry compels energy and specific geometries compel energy to flow in specific ways." An octahedron balances the male and female aspects of consciousness.

If you are not physically in the same room with the person you are working on, envision this same shape around them. Put your attention on your eighth chakra (found about a foot above your head) at the 'soul star.' Bring your hands to a prayer position at your heart chakra, centered in your intent to be a 'soul bridge.' Keeping your hands together, allow them to slowly move up your body, stretching above your head. Imagine that you are placing them into the radiant sphere of your own 'soul star.' Turn your palms outward, expanding the radius of this light; spread it out as you bring your arms down like two great wings, creating a cocoon of light that will first surround you and then extend your arms outward to enfold the person you are working on.

Clearing and Balancing the Chakras

The names of the chakras correspond to their location. The first (RED-Root Chakra) is at the base of the spine. The second (ORANGE-Sacral Chakra) is about four fingers below the navel. The third (YELLOW-Solar Plexus Chakra) is found at the solar plexus. The fourth (GREEN-Heart Chakra) is in the center of the chest. The fifth (BLUE-Throat Chakra) is at the hollow of the throat. The sixth (INDIGO-Third Eye or Brow Chakra) is between the eyebrows in the middle of the forehead. And the seventh (VIOLET-Crown Chakra) is at the top of the head.

Cleansing the chakras helps to reveal and transform outdated beliefs and behavior patterns, unblocking and clearing old, stale, unwanted energies. This is done by slowly moving one or both open hands counterclockwise about two inches above each chakra center. Working on the front of the body, you begin at the first (Root Chakra) by placing your hand above the pubic bone. As you stir the energy, it's helpful to envision a funnel. Your hands will naturally dip down closer to the body as you access deeper layers and then pull the energy up and away from the body. Imagine scooping the toxic energy out and discharging it into a violet flame placed off to the side, where it is transmuted and neutralized. You will be intuitively drawn to stay longer on an area that needs it. When it feels complete and the energy seems lighter, shake off your hand(s) (into the flame) and reverse the spin, by slowly stirring the energy in a clockwise direction. This direction balances and resets the energy. Move up to the second (Sacral chakra) and repeat the process. When the second chakra is complete, instead of moving to the third (Solar Plexus Chakra) go back to the first Chakra and clear it again. You are doing this because clearing higher chakras may trigger more fallout, spilling over to the ones below it.

For this reason, going forward involves first going back to the beginning and repeating the process. For example: if you are on the fourth (Heart Chakra), you would cleanse and rebalance it, and then return to the Root, Sacral and Solar Plexus, to cleanse (spinning counterclockwise) followed by rebalancing (spinning clockwise) each one again before proceeding to the fifth (Throat Chakra). You would continue this process all the way up to the Crown chakra. (Note: with men the Crown chakra is reversed). You would begin by spinning your hand in a clockwise manner and end in a counterclockwise spin.) When all is complete, make large, sweeping 'figure eights' over the entire body. End the session by imagining them in their own cocoon of light, and gather the protective blanket of your own energy back into you, grounding yourself in the Earth. Zip your own energy up by dragging your hands together up the midline of your body. Pause at your chin and then shoot them high overhead, letting your hands fall back to your sides, returning to stand in the center of your own fountain of light.

Realign

Another important death rite that assists the dying is to simply give them permission to go. This is especially important if you know they have concerns about those they are leaving. You can assure them that there is an unbreakable bond of Love that will always connect them to those they cherish, while gently steering them inward toward the expanding lighthouse of their own Higher Self. Their *spirit* will naturally grow clearer and brighter as the physical body dims and fades, but this realignment requires that the *soul's* concerns (negative emotions and thoughtforms) are addressed and released.

I resonate with the notion that the tunnel of white light, so often described at the time of death, is generated from the *soul star* (eighth chakra) which drops down to envelope the other seven chakras in the form of an egg-shaped orb. Each center begins to release the 'luminous threads' that served to connect them to events from the past. The 'orb' travels up through the *pranic tube* or central axis that energetically runs in front of the spine, moving from the perineum to the crown. The outgoing release of the luminous body containing our consciousness, forms a vortex (unzipping like a jacket lining from the inside out). Moving upward through the narrow axis of its torus-shaped energy field, the *soul/spirit* (luminous body) exits through the 'tunnel' (or the 'donut hole' of the torus) at one of the chakra centers. The Eastern scriptures tell us that the chakra that the energy body exits through, will be the one that is in alignment with the soul's level of development. Tom Kenyon describes the exit as *The Fifth Perspective*. This is the recognition that you are unconstrained by space or time. It is the foyer or entrance to the fifth dimension, and here you are endowed with free will to make a choice. If you are unencumbered, you can become a witness to the dream-like nature of your life, history and experiences, transcending the perception of time and space while moving forward into the unified field of the higher vibrations that await you. But if the disengagement process is hampered by the residue of sludge still residing in the chakra centers, your attention may be fixated on the unresolved details, pulling you back to the lower vibrational levels and 3D concerns.

While we are still in these bodies, it is most beneficial to enter into an expanded sense of spaciousness (stepping out of time) as often as possible, in preparation for the ultimate sense of freedom that will occur when we leave these bodies. This happens naturally when we engage in right-brain enhancing activities that elicit our creativity.

When assisting someone at the end of their life, you can encourage this expanded state with simple things like surrounding them with higher energy from nature (flowers, plants, stones or crystals) and, if you are in a home situation, allowing beloved pets to be near them. Dogs and cats are natural bedside companions, giving unconditional love and comfort while often removing negativity. The expanded state happens naturally with inspirational music, or there are many relaxing guided meditations available on the internet by searching for 'guided relaxations.'

Pay attention to their environment. Keep it clean and serene. I remember before my dad died, we had to remove the police scanner that was going 24/7 in the headboard above his bed. He lived with this noise for years, wanting to know what was going on all over the city, but when he was entering into the last stages the constant static and abrupt tension was not helpful or soothing to his spirit. Removing it was a way to shift his focus away from all the outside drama he was leaving behind, helping him tune into the subtle signals that were being transmitted from within.

Realigning means helping them make the leap from *resistance* to *anticipation*. As a psychopomp, you can begin to bridge the gap by asking them what their thoughts are about the afterlife. It is important to honor their own cherished beliefs without imposing yours on them, but you can encourage them to talk about dear ones that have preceded them in crossing over. It is common for individuals to begin seeing or even speaking with loved ones as the veil begins to thin allowing them to straddle two worlds.

I asked my father if he was aware of his two brothers who had died several years ahead of him, and was surprised when he told me that he had already seen them. This created an opening to speak of them as his welcoming committee, waiting for him at the graduation threshold, ready to celebrate his homecoming. Giving the dying permission to call on those who have already made this journey ahead of them reassures them that, with spiritual helpers present, they will not be alone.

It is a lot easier to travel to a foreign country when you have made preparations and have a general sense of what to expect. Likewise, gleaning information from those who have touched down on the new soil of the afterlife can be reassuring and beneficial to both the caregiver and the person preparing to travel 'abroad.'

If we could remember what happens when we die (most of us can't) or employ the next best thing—learning from those who have been there—then our faith in the forgotten crossing-over process could be restored and fear would be released. As the care-giver, sharing ideas and experiences that others have had can reassure you as well as help them. It is a great way to indirectly address their fears and concerns. Helping them clear their clutter creates the inner space necessary for their take-off. There is no greater sacred 'rite of passage' than death.

Recommended reading from other-world 'travel guides' might include *Annie Kagan's *The Afterlife of Billy Fingers*, *Eben Alexander's *Proof of Heaven*, *Nanci Danison's *Backwards*, *Dannion Brinkley's *Saved by the Light*, *Michael Newton's *Memories of the Afterlife* and *Echo Bodine's books, *Echoes of the Soul* and *What Happens When We Die*—just to name a few.

If you are with your loved ones at the time of death, you may choose to assist them in releasing their energy body and sealing the chakras after they have died. It is recommended that this be done immediately or no later than forty hours after the person has passed. This procedure is called *The Great Death Spiral* and it is considered the final Death Rite. It is explained and illustrated with a helpful chart at: http://www.dyingconsciously.org/great_spiral.htm

Another excellent resource is that of *The Greatest Journey* organization, which is a free service dedicated to helping people die consciously. Their intent is to bring dignity and peace back to the dying process, providing healing and closure to the person dying and to their loved ones. You can visit their website at www.livingdying.org/conscious-dying

Fear is a question:
What are you afraid of, and why?
Just as the seed of health is in illness,
because illness contains information,
our fears are a treasure house of self-knowledge
if we explore them.

~ Marilyn Ferguson ~

51

PUTTING IT ALL TOGETHER

If you are someone who suspects you may be part of the 'soul-bridge' here to guide earthbound souls home, but you are still unsure about the particulars of what is going on and feel uncertain about how to assist them, then this is the chapter for you. I will address basic questions you may be having, as well as guide you in putting this all together. If you have no interest in this "how to" section, feel free to skip to the last chapter, but remember—if you are ever dealing with an earthbound situation and want to review how to handle it, it is all laid out for you here.

Earthbound spirits: Who are they?

In the early days of doing this work, the clients coming to me for Akashic Record Consultations, Spiritual Regressions, or just to walk the labyrinth had no idea that an earthbound spirit was with them (even if they were grieving the loss of a loved one) because, at that time, the presence of an earthbound spirit was too foreign or taboo. People are more self-aware now, to the point of contacting me if they suspect that something is 'not quite right' in their energy field after going through a loss or a challenging situation. Care-givers of all kinds—energy workers, counselors, medical personal, massage therapists etc.—have a tendency to pick them up from their clients.

The most common attachments are souls that had a close bond to the survivor: family members, friends, co-workers, loved ones or relatives that died. In the case of a relative, you may not have known them when they were living, but the lineage connection may still bring them into your field. (E.g. A young woman in her twenties found that her grandmother was attached to her, in spite of never meeting her or wanting her around. She had died on the very day that the young woman's mother found out she was pregnant with her. The grandmother already had a strong bond with her only daughter, but the awareness of her granddaughter gave her an additional, protective incentive to stay attached.) A spirit relative may also show up because they are drawn to the most 'open' member of the family (the one most aware of them, or most likely to help them cross over). It is much easier when the client already knows who the earthbound spirit is, but that isn't always the case.

Relationship categories for earthbound spirits:

1. **Someone you were related to, knew or were strongly bonded with.**

2. **Someone you never met in a physical body, but with whom you have an unresolved emotional trauma in common:** Emotional wounds can leave an opening in your emotional body. The earthbound spirit may have a similar emotional wound and be magnetically drawn to you due to your matching vibration. (E.g., a mother of three small children who was sexually abused from the time she was two years old, came to me with a large number of earthbound souls attached to her. Some were children who were ritualistically 'sacrificed' at birth, or died young from abuse. Some were women who died as sex slaves, and some were the perpetrators themselves who were still drawn to the 'victimized' energy that the group collectively carried.)

3. **A past life aspect of yourself:** 'Soul splits from another lifetime, or aspects that haven't yet crossed over, can attach themselves to you at the time of your birth. They may also 'show up' when you reach a particular age, when you go through a triggering experience, when you meet a certain person that was present in another lifetime, or by visiting or moving to

a location that holds significance to the soul. As far-fetched as this may seem, many people—including myself—will deal with (or have already dealt with) this form of attachment due to the 'Ascension' process. We have agreed to resolve whatever was unfinished in our past lives, coming in on behalf of our 'multidimensional selves' to round up, resolve, and then bring home all of our 3D aspects.

4. **Hitchhiker souls:** You can unknowingly pick up earthbound spirits from another person (like energy workers do), or from 'emotionally charged' places. A spirit can jump from one person to another. They may be attracted to your energy because they identify with you in some way; they may feel 'safe' with you or want your help, or they may be coming from a lower vibrational energy and want to harass you or 'have fun' with you. You could (unknowingly) make yourself energetically available to them through your own desires, longings, or obsessions—including sex, drugs, alcohol, pornography, violence, video games or horror movies. Lowering your vibration with negatively charged addictions or habits is inviting lower vibrational souls or dark entities into your field.

5. **Substance abuse:** Drugs, alcohol, and other mind altering substances can open holes in your aura that attract earthbound souls, especially those who have had similar addictions when in a body. They can more easily attach to you when your consciousness is altered. This also includes dark entity attachments. If you lose consciousness under the influence, a dark entity or an earthbound spirit who craves that substance can enter your unprotected energy field, greatly influencing your actions and increasing your cravings or addictions, steering you toward self-destruction.

6. **Anesthesia:** Going under anesthesia can also open the psychic gate, like leaving the front door of your house open. It is a good idea to mentally place an octahedron of light (or your own version of a psychic shield) around you or your loved ones before undergoing surgery. Hospitals are hotspots for spirits looking for a 'friend' to go home with. If you or someone you know experiences sudden personality shifts after surgery,

explore the possibility of an earthbound soul who may have died at that hospital.

7. **Organ transplant:** Be aware that an organ recipient could possibly receive more than just the organ, if the earthbound spirit of the donor has not crossed over.

Why do spirits stay earthbound?

Strong emotional ties to someone still living may keep the deceased from letting go. Feelings of love, grief, sadness, or the desire to 'watch over' or protect someone can act as a binder that keeps the soul here. If anger, fear, guilt, obligation or frustration are present when they die, these denser feelings can hold the spirit down, keeping them more connected to the earth plane. With sudden or unexpected deaths—heart attacks, aneurisms, dementia patients, accidents, overdoses or comas—confusion can cloud their mental capacity and keep them clinging to the only world they know. Suicide may be a factor for keeping souls here if their reasons for taking their own lives are motivated by lower emotions (anger, despair, hopelessness, revenge or spite). There are some people who have unfinished business and are not at peace until their issues are resolved. Others fear dying with no faith or belief in an afterlife, so they stay close by, preferring to remain with what is familiar.

How do you know if someone who has died has remained earthbound?

Above all else, trust your common sense as well as your *Clair Senses*. This means all types of psychic sensitivity relating to your senses. All of us have psychic abilities, waiting to be more fully developed through self-discipline and awareness, and these 'senses' will get stronger as the bombardment of higher frequencies continue to come into the planet. You may be picking up information through more than one of these areas, so pay attention and don't discount the 'truth barometer' of your own internal informant. Your intuition is the translator for your Higher Self.

~ Clair Senses ~

- **Clairvoyance** (clear vision): Perceiving from your inner sight within the 'mind's eye' to see beyond your ordinary reality. You may receive visual impressions or actually catch glimpses of someone out of your peripheral vision. This happens more easily when you are not actively trying, or are in an alpha state ... relaxing, meditating, or waking up in the middle of the night. Many people see physical anomalies like the lights flickering on and off, objects moving, or other electrical disruptions, but clairvoyants see beyond the veil into the ethers able to receive visual impressions or symbolic images that relate to the deceased.

- **Clairaudience** (clear audio-hearing): Hearing sounds, noises, words thoughts or whole conversations that are interpenetrating our reality from the spiritual realms, with the ability to converse with them telepathically.

- **Clairsentience** (clear sensation or feeling): Receiving information or impressions by feeling into the situation. This means having a 'gut feeling' or inner knowing. Possibly aware of temperature or vibrational changes in a room (cold spots) or body sensations (tingling, goose bumps, or having the hair on the back of your neck stand up). As a natural empath, you may have physical indicators in your body that someone is watching you or around you.

- **Claircognizance** (clear knowing): You just know about things without being told. Information or insights pour into your awareness ('download' into your mind from your Higher Self or Spirit Guides), and it's easy for you to receive. Your conscious mind is not generating the information, but observing it and trying to interpret it.

- **Clairempathy** (clear emotion): Tuning into the emotional experience, attitude, or ailments of another person or entity. This may include receiving a download, sensing or feeling what has occurred at a given place or to an individual. You are able to experience their emotional state.

- **Clairscent** (clear smelling): Picking up scents, odors, or fragrances that are not in your current surroundings. (E.g. Tobacco, perfume or food associated with someone who has passed).

- **Clairtangency** (clear touching/psychometry): Handling an object or touching something and receiving information about the history of the object or its owner.

- **Clairgustance** (clear tasting): Tasting a particular substance without putting anything in your mouth.

What are the symptoms of an attachment?
- Emotional mood swings, or persistent thoughts that do not feel like your own. Depression, feeling stuck, unable to go forward or get on with your life. You may find yourself struggling with more anxiety, frustration, sadness, anger or hopelessness with possible thoughts of suicide. Any persistent thoughts that were with the individual at the very end may be running on a loop that can be transferred to you. You will think they are your own thoughts, and find them disturbing.

- Physical changes in your well-being that may include disrupted sleep patterns, fatigue or exhaustion, tightness, unexplained pain, head or body aches. If you knew the person who died, notice if you start manifesting symptoms that were related to their cause of death or ailments that they suffered with.

- You may have dreams about the deceased person that feel very real. If they have already crossed over, these dreams may be pleasant or reassuring as if they are checking in to let you know they are just fine. If they have not crossed over, you may be left feeling uneasy, anxious, or even confused, not quite understanding what it is they are trying to convey.

- If the earthbound soul is someone who was close to you, you will have an innate sense of whether they have crossed over or not. Many times we try to talk ourselves out of what we are picking up, because we don't want to appear crazy to others or ourselves. When in doubt, take the steps to find out, as it cannot hurt ... and it is very likely that it will help you both.

- If the earthbound soul is someone you have never met, but you suspect you 'picked them up' because of a place you recently visited, or a person you were around, or an event that triggered the attachment, then the changes that you notice within yourself will seem to come on suddenly (within a few days). These attachments are sometimes easier to recognize because you have a clear contrast of what you were feeling like before and then afterwards, without the emotional upheaval that accompanies the grieving process.

How do I know if I am to help?

Pay attention to your feelings, your inner nudges and synchronicities after being with someone new or participating in a large gathering or event. If you are traveling or visiting a place of historical significance, tune in and even ask if there are souls there that would like to cross over to the world of light. Think of the places in the world where tragedies involving death have occurred. There is no shortage of clean-up to do. If it is yours to be involved in (because you have the qualities needed to help or because an aspect of your soul may be involved) you will be magnetized to participate, like me when I was drawn to go to Malta and Peru. With free will, the souls need to be on board with crossing over, but because we are at the close of one cycle and opening to another, the souls are more responsive, feeling an undeniable pull to reunite with their Higher Selves. You do not need to go out and look for souls. If you are 'assigned' to them, they are looking for you, and even involved with the set-ups that get arranged to bring you into their path.

If you begin having unusual experiences, impressions, or strange feelings after someone you know dies, investigate the possibility that they are still here, and offer to help them. Speak to them from your heart. Create the octahedron in your mind or finger-walk the labyrinth pattern, and offer them the opening to leave. If you own a labyrinth, create labyrinths, or have an opportunity to walk them, intend that, when you reach the center, the portal will be open. Ask that the angels be there to assist in bringing any soul present into the awareness of their Higher Self. Being part of the soul-bridge means acknowledging that you are part of the human race, willing to extend your energy. There is no greater power than that which is generated from our joined consciousness.

How do I begin?

Once you determine that it is likely (or at least possible) that you are dealing with an earthbound spirit, prepare to **set sacred space** to create a container of safety for yourself and the earthbound soul.

Create a golden octahedron:

Envision an image of a golden octahedron of light, and place it around yourself and the area you are in. If you are in a building, you can use the four corners of the room to imagine the four sides of an upward facing pyramid with the point going out through your ceiling. Then create the image of another, downward facing pyramid with the point going down into the earth. The floor beneath your feet serves as the base where the two pyramids are joined.

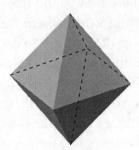

Invite Helpers:

The Archangels are ready to take their positions in the middle of each of the sides—Archangels Raphael, Gabriel, Uriel and Ariel—with Archangel Michael at the apex above and Archangels Metatron and Zadkiel below. Invite in your personal guides, physical protectors, essence protectors and your own

Higher-Self Awareness. I also include the Seraphim Angels. Then ask that any 'helpers' on the other side who are connected with the earthbound spirit(s) to also be in attendance, especially recognizing their Higher Selves.

The octahedron can serve as a stand-alone portal to release the souls, but you can use something that feels more familiar to you (like imagining a staircase of light, an elevator, spirit canoe etc.), or you can finger-trace the images of either the Chakra Labyrinth or Chante Ishta when they are ready to cross over. *The Chakra Labyrinth Cards* have an embossed image of this labyrinth on the inside cover that can be used with or without the cards. Images of both the Chakra Labyrinth and Chante Ishta, the 9-petal, vesica star pattern, are included as finger-tracing portal patterns at the back of this book for easy removal.

Pranic Tube alignment:

Once you have created the golden octahedron around yourself, align the energy within your body to the core of the Earth. When you enter into a mental resonance with the magnetic core, you become energetically more solid and stable. You are less affected or susceptible to emotional upheaval, mind-control, and negative effects. The subtle energy channel that starts above your head (soul star) and runs through each of the chakras (energy centers) of your body to the point below your feet (earth star) is called your *pranic tube. It is also referred to as your *Ascension column.* You can extend it with your mind all the way into the Earth's core. Tune into your connection here with the living being that is *Gaia.* Then extend your awareness up your *pranic tube,* out the top of your soul star to create a fountain effect (toroidal field) all around you. This protective field is a container for your conscious creations. You can expand the toroidal force field all the way out to the galactic center of the universe. Holding the awareness of both points (above and below) simultaneously will also allow you to better handle the waves of the multidimensional energy, grounding you as an effective conduit.

How do I get myself centered?

You need to be in a centered state yourself before attempting to get answers or opening up communication with an earthbound spirit. I have found that doing parts of *Donna Eden's *Daily Energy Medicine Routine* is very helpful.

~ Centering Exercises ~

"The Four Thumps": In Eden Energy Medicine, "The Four Thumps" refer to four specific areas on the body that would be beneficial to tap (thump) on, using the pads of your fingertips.

1. The K-27 Rub: These are the end-points of the kidney meridian. To locate them, place your fingers on the corners of your collar bones below your throat and then move your fingers down about an inch. Deeply rubbing or thumping these points can get all your meridians moving forward, bringing better flow to your whole system. They can also boost your immune system and help restore your energy.

2. The Thymus Thump: Place the pads of your fingertips together in the center of your chest (think Tarzan) and thump with some vigor. This stimulates the thymus gland, helping your body fight off disease as it strengthens and supports your immune system. It also helps your body handle shock.

3. The Spleen Point: This supports the spleen meridian in metabolizing energies, substances, and our unprocessed thoughts and emotions. The end-points on the spleen meridian are located around the side of the ribcage, about four inches down under the armpit (close to the bottom of the bra line for women).

4. The Stomach Point: This is the beginning point on the stomach meridian and can help to calm our stomach or dispel indigestion or nausea, as well as helping to calm us. Place the pads of your fingertips on the cheek bones under both eyes. Gently tap or thump this point.

The Hook-Up: This is one of the best exercises to ground and center yourself. It involves creating a connection between the two primary meridians of your body: Central and Governing. Central meridian starts at your pubic bone, traveling up the center of your body, and ends in the back of your throat, below your bottom lip. Governing meridian begins at your tailbone, travels up your spine, over your head, and ends at the back of your throat just below your nose or above your upper lip. Together they act as an 'energetic spine' that connects our mind and body. Doing this exercise can strengthen this connection while sending energy to all the other systems.

To do the Hook-up, place the middle finger of one hand at your Third Eye (the point between your eyebrows above the bridge of your nose) while placing the middle finger of your other hand in your navel. Press each finger in and pull it upwards. Hold this pose as you breathe in through the nose and out through the mouth for three deep breaths, or until you feel an energetic 'link up.'

Cross-over Exercise: Energy crosses over from the left hemisphere of the brain to the right side of the body and from the right hemisphere to the left side of the body. These cross-over patterns are found at all levels throughout our organs and cells, all the way down to the double helix of the DNA and all the way out into the auric field that surrounds our bodies. We're all familiar with the infinity sign, but may not realize that the 'figure 8' is the pattern of *infinite regeneration*. When our energy is not adequately crossing over, it begins running in a homolateral state. When this happens, you only have access to about 50% of your energies. Nature designed us this way so that when we're overdoing it, pushing too hard, going through major stress, and needing extra rest to heal or recuperate, our lack of energy begins to slow us down. The problem is that, with all the stress that people are experiencing, the homolateral state can become a habit and your energy can get stuck there. If the homolateral state becomes chronic, you will tend toward depression, feeling less alive and more exhausted, and that puts a strain on all your other body systems.

The homolateral symptoms I am describing are also the symptoms that begin showing up when there is an earthbound spirit attached to us. That's because it's hard for our energies to cross over when our internal batteries are being drained. This cross-over exercise is a variation of the cross-crawl (lifting your right arm and your left leg simultaneously as if marching in place). It is also less taxing to the body when your energy is already waning.

Diagonal Sweep: Turn your left hand over with the palm up. Take your right hand and place it on your open palm. Now stroke your palm, following through with the motion by moving your hand up the inside of your arm all the way to the shoulder. When you get to the shoulder, massage it for a minute. Then make a diagonal sweep from your left shoulder to your right hip, letting your hand pass through and off your hip. Take your right hand and turn it palm up. Place your left hand on top of it and begin the sweep up the inside of your arm going all the way to the shoulder. Briefly massage the area before making the diagonal sweep across to the opposite hip. Repeat this a couple of times on both sides.

'Figure 8' the Eyes: Another easy way to shift homolateral patterning is to make 'figure eights' around the eyes. Place your middle finger at the third eye, and act as if you are drawing a figure-eight shaped pair of glasses around your eyes. You can start at the center point and go under your left eye around and over it, crossing at the third eye point, dipping under the right eye, around and over.

Heart massage: Place your right hand on the center of your chest and then move it in a clockwise circle with the top of the clock oriented at your navel. (Your point of view is from the base of the clock looking down at it.) Move your hand up to the throat (6:00), over to the left side (9:00), down toward the navel (12:00), and up to the right side (3:00).

Continue this motion while saying out loud, *"I choose to love and accept myself with all my limitations and problems. I accept the feelings of uncertainty and doubt I may be having. I accept whoever is attached to my field and am here to assist them in crossing over to the world of light. I accept my talents and gifts and my abilities to shift this situation for the highest good for all concerned."*

~Muscle Checking~

It's ideal if you can internally ask questions and open yourself to receive impressions, but not everyone feels comfortable or confident enough to do this without the backup of another indicator. Muscle checking is a versatile option. There are a variety of ways to use this technique on yourself, and if you already have a preferred method, use it. As I described in Chapter 45 "Not Gone," the one that I prefer is a standing test, sometimes called the "Tilt Test." It is done by crossing the wrists in front of the heart while facing north (closing the eyes is helpful), and then making a statement. The body will automatically lean forward in response to a TRUE statement or lean backwards indicating a FALSE statement. A base line is first established by using your name. "My name is _____." If you are centered, your body will respond by leaning forward. To be sure that your energy is not frozen or reversed, you also test it with a false statement. It helps to choose a false name that you have no connection to. If you are reversed or your body does not respond by moving backwards, drink some water and let your mind go blank before attempting again. Trying to stay 'in control' or manipulate the body's responses will keep you firmly planted and not moving. If your body is responding correctly, muscle test the statements, *"I am centered enough to test accurately,"* and *"We have permission to work with this spirit attachment."*

If you receive a NO to the permission question, turn it over to the angels and your guide team and trust that they are detecting something that you are not aware of. It may just be a timing issue or you are not quite ready, or there could be dark entity attachments that you do not need to be involved with.

If you receive permission, you can proceed in asking questions, but I have found that explaining things first to the earthbound soul goes a long way.

~ Talking to the Earthbound ~

Let them know you are aware of them and explain that it is likely that they did not completely cross over when they died. (Remember, some do not even realize that they *did* die). They have no idea that their 'attachment' is having a draining effect on you as well as holding them back from their intended 'graduation.' Letting them know this is helpful. If you are sensitive enough to detect that they are there, you will also be able to pick up their thoughts and even have a telepathic dialogue. If there is something you question or are unsure of, you can muscle-check it.

Assure them that you can help them, and that crossing over does not mean (for those who are your loved ones) that they will never be able to connect with you again. It means that the connection will happen at a higher level of awareness that includes understanding what their entire life was about. This will give them great peace, comfort, and acceptance of what is occurring because they will no longer feel they are on the outside looking in. As an earthbound soul, they are feeling separated from all that they knew while in their bodies, but more importantly, they are separated from their own Higher-Self and their connection to ALL THAT IS. When they cross over, the feeling of amnesia leaves and the oneness of their true nature will be restored.

Inform them that there are "helpers" around them who will guide them in this process. If there is someone who has preceded them in death that they were close to, ask the angels to bring them into the portal. If you are going to use the Chakra Labyrinth pattern (or any labyrinth), tell them that, by the time you walk or finger-walk the circuits and arrive in the center, they will become aware of two light-beings or angels who will be their escorts to take them home. Once they understand this, you can ask them, *"Do you have any resistance to crossing over to the World of Light? "Are you ready to cross over to the World of Light?"*

If they are not ready, find out what is holding them back (ask questions) and address the concerns that may be revealed. It helps to 'name' the issues by using a modified 'tapping' sequence.

The four trauma points: By tapping on yourself, the earthbound soul receives the calming benefits.

1. The beginning bladder point where your eyebrows start, at the bridge of your nose.
2. The beginning stomach point, under the eyes on the cheek bones.
3. The end spleen point, under the armpits on the side body.
4. The end of the kidney meridian, K-27 points under the collar bones.

Using the pads of your fingertips, tap these areas as you state what you think may be their concerns. E.g. "Even though I am afraid to let go, I choose to love and accept myself. Even though I fear I don't deserve to go to the World of Light, I choose to forgive myself and accept that I can be forgiven. Even though I have resistance and doubt, I can open to my Higher Self and trust that I am being taken care of."

You can't do this wrong. Let your stream of consciousness take over, guiding you to say whatever pops into your head. Tune into what you are feeling from them and do your best to address it, stating the negative resistance that is present first, and then adding your own positive reassurance.

Recheck the statements, *"Do you have any resistance to crossing over to the World of Light? Are you ready to cross over to the World of Light?"*

~ Opening the portal ~

Once they are ready, your focus will be on opening the portal. Remember that the earthbound soul is entraining with your energy so they will respond to the 'container' you are providing. This can simply be imagining an octahedron and inviting them to leave through the top or visualizing a staircase of light, a spirit canoe, or anything else that you resonate with.

If you choose to walk any style of labyrinth or finger-walk the image of the Chakra Labyrinth (which is included at the back of this book on a perforated sheet for easy removal), envision that, at each turn which is signified by a chakra, they are releasing any correlating issues that may have been holding them back. You don't need to consciously know what these are, but the *Chakra Labyrinth Cards* are a helpful tool in identifying and releasing the imbalances. If you are using the cards, read the *Release* statements aloud that you have chosen for each path as you move toward the center. The earthbound souls will merge here with the presence of their Higher Selves and exit from the central portal.

Chante Ishta, the 9-petal, vesica star pattern, can also be used and is included on the flip side of the perforated sheet. To use Chante Ishta, begin by finger-tracing the entrance path and going to the right (counter-clockwise direction). Always move straight ahead until you have to turn. You are following the vesical shapes inward toward the center and then outward to the outer most points. Each of the nine vesicas will be traced by the time you arrive back at the beginning. Your intent is to help the earthbound souls raise their vibration to the awareness of their Higher Selves. You may notice a subtle shift in energy when the recognition occurs. Back at the entrance, you will turn left, moving through the entire pattern again, but this time in the opposite direction (clockwise). When you arrive back at the beginning, move your finger into the center of the nine-pointed star. This is their exit portal.

The advantage of using a sacred geometry pattern like the Labyrinth or Chante Ishta, is that they provide an instant containment vessel for the earthbound spirits placing them into their own kind of 'lock system' while giving you a tangible way to participate. The winding movement through the rotating circuits produce a rapid stepping-up of their earthbound energy while damming off the lower vibrations that have been holding them back.

Regardless of the portal you are using, calling in the presence of their Higher Self makes for a much smoother transition. You simply do this by holding the vision of a pair of angels (one male and one female) greeting them in the center. If you like the star-tetrahedron (Merkaba) image, you can visualize the male angel morphing into the upward pyramid around the soul and the female forming the interlocking downward pyramid. Ask the departing soul if they have anything they would like to share with you before leaving, and give them a moment of silence to respond. Take this time to express what you most desire to say to them. Then envision the 'lift-off,' asking the Seraphim angels to take them all the way through the portal to the World of Light.

~ Multiply the benefits ~

It is always a good idea, when you have opened a portal, to 'multiply the benefits.' This means inviting the angelic help to round up any other souls who may be 'in the wings,' observing what is happening, to also rejoin with their own Higher Selves and use this opportunity to cross over.

~ In Closing ~

In doing this work you are serving as a galactic conduit. You are agreeing to be a living antenna that connects Earth and Sky. At the completion of a session, you can intend that the portal that you opened be energetically linked in with the growing etheric network that is being constructed all around the earth. This way it will remain available to other spirits and assist with the ongoing exodus that is taking place. However, you want to also make sure to disconnect your personal energy from the portal.

If you used a labyrinth pattern or physically walked a labyrinth, retracing your steps or finger-walking your way back out closes the session and seals the portal (the portion that is tied into your energy). If you used the *Chakra Labyrinth Cards*, an uplifting way to realign your own energy and bring everything to closure is to read the *Renew* portion of the cards as you retrace the path back out.

If the octahedron was serving as your portal in addition to something else, breaking the connection to your own energy involvement can be done by raising one hand above your head with the palm facing down, and with the other hand reach down with the palm facing up. Clapping your hands together from this position signifies withdrawing your energy and closing the space.

Follow this up by thanking the Angels, Guides, Higher Selves, Masters, Teachers and Loved Ones who may have been present to assist.

These instructions primarily pertain to helping earthbound spirits that you feel comfortable with because of your connection. Dealing with more complex cases, especially when dark entity attachments are involved, may be something that is out of your comfort zone and scope of practice. In this case, turn it over to the angelic realm and know that you can always contact a certified Soul Detective listed on Barbara Stone's website (Soul Detective. net) for assistance. If you are a therapist or someone who gravitates toward this work, or want to learn more about being an active part of the 'soul-bridge,' consider taking Barbara's certification course. It is well worth it.

We are living the turning point
all of history has been rushing towards.
It is the Ascension, the Transformation, Disclosure.
It's the Solar Event.

~ William Henry ~

52

ASCENDING ESSENTIAL SELF

The longer I assist earthbound souls, the clearer it becomes that there is a connection between the 'soul crossing' work and the Ascension process that is in full swing. Remember that Ascension is an ongoing sequence of inner turning points designed to deliver you to a higher vibrational state. Like a pearl in the making, you agreed to deal with a multitude of irritants far more intense than the proverbial grains of sand. This ongoing energetic alignment is steering rich opportunities into your path to help you resolve lifetimes of emotionally charged issues. The challenge is to welcome your arising emotions as surging waves of information that bring your pain up to the surface ... so that you can release it. The counter-forces that inundate this world challenge you to change what's not working—serving the whole by provoking, prodding, and pushing you toward the New Earth.

The Ascension process is accompanied by sporadic unpleasant physical symptoms, as well as karma-cleansing excursions into the underworld. Being 'all in' requires taking responsibility for your own evolution. You have to become conscious of your mistaken beliefs and your habitual thoughts and feelings, and then be willing to shed the shell of protection they provide. You may also need to dig up, hose off, and embrace lost or disowned aspects of your Self. As private as your suffering or your epiphanies may seem to you while navigating the many tributaries of Change, your new shifts in perception have a ripple effect that flood into the collective washbasin, bathing the whole planet. It doesn't matter how awake or asleep you are, the shift that is occurring is an equal opportunity act where no one is left out. However, your level of consciousness does determine if you are choosing to be 'left behind' in a lower timeline reality.

If 2021 marks the year on the Aztec calendar of our full immersion into the 'Sixth Sun' energy, we might ask if the years leading up to it represent the countdown to a whole system reboot. *David Wilcock, author of *The Ascension Mysteries*, has studied data from multiple ancient and current sources, and believes that the 'cosmic reset' may be coming in the form of an actual event he calls the *solar flash*—a blast of light and energy from our sun.

Jay Weidner (a filmmaker, hermetic scholar, and renowned author who was a guest on one of David's *Cosmic Disclosure* shows on *Gaia TV), remarked that *"The changing Sun IS the change in consciousness."* He observed that the intensifying light is affecting our brain chemistry, and noted that meteorologist Robert Felix has blatantly stated that *"Our human evolution is guided by the sun."* It is interesting to note, as well, that scientists are discovering that our sun, and the entire solar system, are going through unprecedented changes at an accelerated pace that have never been seen before. Because the higher electromagnetic frequencies are advancing our consciousness, it has the Cabal in a panic. Seven billion people awakening would create a tipping point that would quickly remove them from power. Even if the entire 'power over others' group is frantically trying to dial down our vibration for their own self-preservation, the alchemical process that the sunlight is initiating is inevitable. Some speculate that the toxic bath of submicron metals and chemicals found in *chemtrail* spraying may have been designed to reduce the population, eroding our health by affecting our immune systems, and making us more manageable and less resistant to a future pandemic by an airborne disease. But there are other theories that suggest that the spraying is directly connected to what is occurring with the sun. The aluminum oxide may have been intended to reduce atmospheric warming as a way to shield the earth from electromagnetic pulse threats, or to protect highly sensitive semiconductor technologies. It is more than likely that the geo-engineering of our atmosphere through the use of aerosol spraying is a 'weapon of mass distraction' intended to do double duty: keep us in a lower vibrational state—either 'asleep' (mind-controlled), or angry and feeling helpless—while attempting to shield or mitigate the incoming rays. If the 'Advanced Solar Protection' (ASP) program is really just a concentrated attempt to slow down consciousness, it is a losing battle. We are in a new phase of the evolutionary 'burn' that the sun continues to intensify. In order to bring ourselves and the entire solar system back into balance, our energy systems need to flow unrestricted. In spite of the Cabal's efforts, people are waking up all over the planet, recognizing and breaking out of their old programming. As we individually harmonize and internalize the properties of the incoming waves of light, split timelines and bifurcation of realities are becoming more apparent making the old control grid feel more surreal and obsolete. To those who are already moving into the higher timelines of New Earth, things such as chemtrails do not even exist.

Dramatic as the reset of a solar flash may sound, it is a basic part of solar mechanics, taking about 25,000 years to create a torsion shear effect resulting in a 'solar pulse.' An instantaneous light transmission will radiate to every star in the cosmic web.

The calculated window for this solar event is between 2018 and 2024, but the exact timing is unknown—because it is being determined (sped up or slowed down) by our composite consciousness. How you shape your own reality impacts the collective. As an individual, it boils down to cleaning up your trauma, drama, and karma—anything that keeps you from being a pure vessel, able to hold the higher vibrations in alignment with your Inner Divine Self (no small task). Once you discover that your real power comes from within, you can no longer be controlled by outside forces. The intensifying sunlight is the alarm clock going off ... dissolving the lower timelines as we respond. How many times can you push the snooze button before you have to get up? Gaia is not waiting for another cycle. She is ascending from a third- to a fourth-density star, taking us from our third and fourth dimensional playing fields into a fifth dimensional Awareness and beyond. Every person on this planet is being given a choice to either ascend with her, or continue at their own pace in a world that will still be participating in third dimensional learning. Your everyday interactions and attitudes are determining the path that your evolution is taking: either 'power over others' (service to self), or 'power within' (service to others). The increased frequencies of the magnetic pulses are changing the way you process physical reality, bringing everything up to the surface that isn't in alignment with your higher plan. Your free will gives you the daily gift of sifting through your triggered responses and persistent or random thoughts—deciding what to keep, throw away, or place on your compost pile. The purpose is to make more space inside of you for the unconditional love (your true identity) being reflected by the incoming light. Remember, in quantum physics, a higher frequency will always pull up a lower one to meet it.

This is out-picturing in the division of our reality choices where it seems (on the lower timelines) that the 'cockroaches' have suddenly taken over. The truth is that they have always been here, ruling 3D existence from beneath the floorboards of our unconscious programing. They are now simply being made visible because there is more light coming through our windows, so to speak. The extremes of the widening consciousness gap are further revealing their presence. 'Spotlights' from individual investigators, whistle blowers, legitimate alternative media sources, the internet, *Wikileaks* and so on are exposing their congested hives. We're all waking up to the lies and manipulations that have been occurring, realizing that the ultra-low frequencies that were intended to keep us asleep, sick, numb, dumbed down, entertained, addicted, distracted, and divided have been the perfect 'designer drugs' to anesthetize our souls. Feeling helpless, indignant, and angry about it only serves to further lock us into the matrix of the lower timelines. Is it possible, instead, to accept that the programmed conditions have provided a casing around our lives that, with the right activations and internal adjustments, can molt into a chrysalis? Added light and pressure gives rise to our time-released emergence.

More awareness makes us infinitely more responsible for what we are taking in and broadcasting out. Responsibility is the balance of power. It gives us incentive to become informed, willing to look at how we've kept the manufactured timelines going. It also provides us with opportunities to stand up for ourselves, others, and the earth, and to remove our energy from the lower playing fields. More light means more disclosure, uncovering hidden agendas and the truths that have been kept from us. But caution is needed here. As the blinders come off at the end of the 'caterpillar' stage, we may go on a feeding frenzy, consumed by the revelation of suppressed information and the unjust 'crimes against humanity' that have been committed, becoming fixated on exposing or exterminating the infested nests. This is a phase of the waking up process ... but it can also be a trap, pulling us deeper into the gluey substance of the low frequency web. Release comes from shifting our focus to the renovation work of our own interiors. It's only from the perspective that our metamorphosis provides that we can begin to view what is occurring on the lower timelines, and accept that the 'controlled' environment was a part of the tearing veil (chrysalis) we are leaving behind. Confinement is a convincing illusion that serves as a catalyst to our evolution. Picking our way out of the chrysalis takes stamina and focus, especially when the world we are climbing free from looks like a demolition zone. To function in a reality that is splitting apart, we have to be rewired. This is especially true if we are to handle the upgrades that are being made to our 5D light bodies. Change is occurring in our higher crystalline DNA, which is the key to changing dimensional levels, allowing us to access the higher timelines.

We are living at the most important time that the Earth has ever proceeded through. Bulgarian philosopher *Peter Deunox gave a prophecy in 1944—just prior to his death—regarding this time between the Kali Yuga (long dark period of obscurity) and the New Era we are now entering. A select passage that stands out states: *"An immense wave comes from cosmic space and will inundate the entire earth. All those that attempt to oppose it will be carried off and transferred elsewhere. Although the inhabitants of this planet do not all find themselves at the same degree of evolution, the new wave will be felt by each one of us. And this transformation will not only touch the Earth, but the ensemble of the entire Cosmos. The earth is now following an ascending movement and everyone should force themselves to harmonize with the currents of the ascension. Those who refuse to subjugate themselves to this orientation will lose the advantage of good conditions that are offered in the future to elevate themselves. They will remain behind in evolution and must wait tens of millions of years for the coming of a new ascending wave. The earth, the solar system, the universe, all are being put in a new direction under the impulsion of Love."*

And his translation of the higher frequencies we are now dealing with is captured in the line, *"The Earth will be swept by extraordinary rapid waves of cosmic electricity."*

Individual earthbound souls (or groups of souls) are part of the entire 'ensemble' being affected by the rapid waves. They are being internally directed to get our attention, taking advantage of the light 'lift' that is motivating them to initiate their own freedom. Even if time doesn't exist in the same way for them, they sense an urgency to get out of the 'basement' (lower timelines) while they still can. Remember that souls remain in the frequency that they were dwelling in when they died. The span of all the third-density life cycles of souls reincarnating back into the polarity game includes some pretty dark and dense periods. With the higher frequencies coming from the sun, there is a reduction of the magnetosphere (the protective region above the ionosphere) as well as shifts taking place in the magnetic field, resulting in climate and weather changes that will only intensify. There are also changes we can't see or measure. The lower astral energy of the fourth dimension is merging into our third dimensional reality where earthbound spirits and entities can more easily enter our energetic receptor zones. Think of this like a 'green room' where they wait in the wings, but are aware of everything that is happening 'on the set' (looking to us for their cue to appear on stage).

While the lower astral world is still in place, it is beginning to fold in on itself, and the 'folding in' is creating something like a bubble or pocket. We can surmise that, as the energies go higher, more people will be shifting their attention to the higher timelines, and eventually the pocket will become sealed off because the lower vibrations will be too low to exist in this world.

The dark layer was designed to be a barrier for the earthbound souls, meant to entrap them in the re-cycled bondage game. The ego-invested programming that all 3D humans are exposed to (wheel of karma) makes the ensnaring process easier. Manufactured fear, shame, and guilt produce a 'smoke screen' that keeps us small, unaware of our Inner Divine Self and oblivious to the hidden dark agenda that exists. Yet the dark forces didn't take into account that, if they remained in their low-density lairs, they would be cutting themselves off from further interactions or evolution in the higher realms. At a certain point—sixth density, according to the *Law of One* (The Ra material)—the negative path of evolution becomes a dead end. This makes it clearer why some dark entities are more receptive to the idea of 'defecting,' yet there are many who are prepared to 'double down' on their nefarious efforts and take with them as many souls as they can. As the frequencies continue to climb, 'business' for the lower realms is anything but usual.

Those of you called to do soul-crossing work (like the entire Light Tribe), are here on behalf of Mother Earth. She cannot heal the planet at a low frequency state. She needs our help in detaching the dark membrane that still clings to her aura. The membrane of the 'control net' is engorged with human-generated, misaligned thoughts and emotions, nourishing the dark ones like a false placenta. If the 'soul-net' could have been taken down by higher dimensional beings, it would've been done long ago. Because it was constructed during the third dimensional lifecycles, it becomes our human responsibility to collapse this dark 'feeding sack.' The only way this is possible is if we embody the higher frequencies that resonate beyond the dark ones' reach. Approaching earthbound spirits from a place of compassion helps the souls find forgiveness and detach from the sticky hive of their own resistance and fear.

Many individuals agreed on a soul level to experience an earthbound attachment. It's your 'wounding' that allows a similar type of energy to be drawn to you or expressed through you. But the 'crack' that lets it in serves a dual purpose. There is a line in *Leonard Cohen's famous poem/song *Anthem* that speaks to this:

"There is a crack, a crack in everything. It's how the light gets in."

When you have the courage to go into the crack of your own wounds, your awareness creates the light space that reaches into the earthbound soul's awareness. They entrain with your realizations, able to step out of the ultra-low frequencies of their own tragic stories and into the higher perspective you are providing.

The more I do this work, the more I see the people who are coming to me as 'soul guides' in training. Especially the ones who have an attachment. The first time you release an attachment, or help a soul cross into the light, it initiates you into the 'undercover' soul-work of a *Crossing Guard*. I feel a responsibility to these clients, to do more than just 'treat' them by removing the attachments. Walking them though the process is a mentoring session so that in the future, should (and when) another occasion arises, they will know what to do. Since I have started sharing my process, many of my clients have gone on to routinely do this work themselves. When you go through the ordeal of an attachment, you know first-hand what it is like. You start picking up on the signs, and learn to trust that your intuition is receiving information that goes beyond your reasoning mind, which will still try to account for your 'strange' symptoms by applying its limiting logic. For many, this work becomes a part of their life purpose. If you find that you are questioning this for yourself, I assure you that if this work is yours to do, you will continually be put into situations that make it quite obvious. There is a very efficient astral-internet that gets the word out that you are 'open for business,' and souls as well as spirit helpers will be directed to you. I like the term *Crossing Guards*. It makes me think of elementary school when the older kids were selected to be on Safety Patrol. They got to wear bright colored vests, and hold a Stop sign, and get out of class early. Their presence was seen by everyone making their way from one side of the street to the other.

Now there's a new breed of Crossing Guard steadily showing up, and many of these individuals are young, wise, and tuned in. Some are just kids, others are in high school, of college age, or in their thirties. They join the ranks of those who have been quietly doing this work for years, mostly isolated and alone. A trait that they all have in common is that they are seekers—trying to find where they belong while feeling inside that they don't fit in at all. They are usually ultra-responsible and individualistic, typically hard on themselves and even perfectionistic. They want to serve the greater good and worry that they are not quite measuring up. They have a sense that they are here to do something BIG, and that feels overwhelming because this reality reflects that they are falling behind and not doing anything of significance or of 'world importance.' Of course, they are using the measuring stick of society's idea of what 'success' should look like. They struggle with an over-abundance of self-doubt, in spite of the fact that they give 110% in whatever they enjoy doing. They are smart, creative, and intuitive empaths (or 'ultra-sensitives') who have a spiritual or metaphysical interest in what is occurring in their lives. They express care, concern, and worry for what is happening in the world. You don't choose to be a Crossing Guard from your ego. There is nothing glamourous about standing in the cross-walks. It is something your soul decided before you came into your body. Many who are *wanderers* or *starseeds* will gravitate in this direction. In ancient times, the role of a Crossing Guard was primarily restricted to shamans and the priest caste, but the baton has been passed to the *Cultural Creatives now. Your age and occupation doesn't matter. Mother Earth is not discriminating. The role is in higher demand because the Earth and her inhabitants are making this Ascension leap, and it requires 'all hands on deck.'

If you agreed to be a Soul Guide/Crossing Guard, helping souls to lighten their consciousness, then you agreed to lighten your own heart and mind in the process. As a Crossing Guard, you are here to open portals to provide safe passage to the higher dimensions, but that happens because of your *light*. You project your light like a miner's helmet, but you must first illuminate and extinguish your interior fears before you can shine it into the outer trenches. The light finds any darkness rooted in your system—from all your third dimensional incarnations—and focuses on the truth that every situation offered to you. Opening to receive this information creates an alchemical effect, transmuting the 'lead' of your burdens into the 'gold' of your 5D building blocks. Your body serves as a platform, housing the light like a drilling rig that bores through density. Once you are connected to Gaia's core, the light can flow up though your *pranic tube* (Ascension column) to your heart where it can be directed as a precise instrument, into the core of the galaxy. The laser of your higher awareness can then be used to dissolve the seams that hold the dark membrane in place. You, who are dedicated to the re-birth of the Earth, are re-birthing yourselves. You are 'portal openers,' but you are also the portal. With an open heart, you direct your Multidimensional Light into the New Earth that's rising.

Whatever is not of the higher light that the sun is activating cannot be sustained and, like the membrane, will fall away. The 'lightening' of our combined consciousness provides the old energy with new neural pathways to recalibrate in the incoming Light. The more unified and clear we become in building the 'higher ways' to peace and equality, the more the status quo systems will be breaking down and going into chaos. Breaking *apart* is required before a new level of coherence and order can break *through*.

Those who have died, but remain here between worlds—like displaced refugees, looking for homes that will take them in—are streaming into the sanctioned 'port authority,' guided by our *inner* authority. This is happening now because there is enough light on the planet to acknowledge that you ARE your '*brother's keeper*.' We are all connected. We are all ONE—here to provide higher service roles beyond the old archetypes of 'saviors' or 'martyrs.' In response to the greater whole, we call for a 'soul bridge' to form across the illusion of separation. When a soul crosses over to the World of Light, or to the New Earth, it lifts all of us higher—beyond the trap of the polarity *mind* shaft that is caving in.

On Earth Day (April 22, 2017) I am guided to enlist people in our spiritual community to come to the Prairie Labyrinth and help large numbers of earthbound souls in the crossing-over process. What better way to take care of the earth than to clean up our 'littered' consciousness? This means we are coming together to acknowledge the denser energies of misinformation, misunderstanding, and helplessness that have been detrimental in our own lives, willing to release our own uncomfortable programs by energizing, envisioning, and calling forth a shift. When we no longer have to practice suppression, the unified field of our heightened frequencies provides a 'thermals column' that the souls-in-waiting can ride.

The gathering of souls begins several months prior to the Earth Day 'release' date. On my morning walk in the Prairie Labyrinth, I receive short snippets of information and inner directives of things I am to do in preparation. One is to lay base quartz crystals out in radiating patterns around each of the fence posts at the turns of the Labyrinth, simulating pathways that will magnetize and direct the souls into the central vortex. I am given the understanding that a 'sleeve' is being put into place over the central portal to ensure that the assembling souls will not interfere with or attach to anyone coming to walk the paths. Closer to the actual date, places around the Kansas City area begin coming into my awareness as key spots where a portal is needed or already exists—just waiting to be opened or reactivated. All I have to do is 'call it forth' by holding the location in mind, and watch (in my imagination) as a tube of light instantaneously manifests above it. I am also told that the portals that I used in Malta, Gozo, and Rome are to be re-opened on Earth Day and that Astarte will be overseeing the 'evacuations' in this region of the world.

Each time a new location comes to my awareness, I sense that there is a growing network of 'light corridors' being assembled (reminding me of an elaborate system of gerbil tunnels, but more like plasma tubes) that will be serving as a 'super shuttle' out of this density.

My friend Kate (Tarot reader and psychic medium), who happens to be traveling to Prague, Hamburg, and Venice, at this time, tells me she is also willing to do this work. A year earlier she had visited Prague and opened a vortex at the Holocaust Memorial where, understandably, the souls fear being forgotten. She sees returning there as a matter of doing maintenance, assuring the souls that, whatever it is they are trying to do, it will be easier when they have ascended.

When she gets to Hamburg, it is a different story. She shares what occurs:

"My first glimpse of Hamburg, Germany is through the eyes of a young border officer in the Amsterdam airport. He glances at my passport and boarding pass, and makes a joking sound of disgust. 'Hamburg?' he says, "Hamburg, really? Why? Why? Why not Amsterdam?' I laugh and reply that I had visited Amsterdam the year before. He says, 'Alright then. If you must.' He stamps my passport and waives me on through. In the next coming days, I often reflect upon that light-hearted conversation, and wonder if I should have taken it as a warning.

I had chosen Hamburg as one part of a three-week long European trip. Part of my mission in traveling is to spread healing energy and, when possible, assist any souls lingering in limbo to ascend from this earthly plane. The mission started the previous year when I took my first European trip in more than twenty years. My guides suggested bringing small crystals with me to leave as a sort of healing grid and I have done that. As I travel, I sometimes encounter a soul (or group of souls) that needs assistance in passing over. Through experiential and research knowledge I have come to believe that this is a necessary spiritual function—when our earthly plane accumulates too many souls in limbo it causes unrest, disease, and disruption. I also have a lingering suspicion (which I have not been able to confirm) that there are living people here who are quite aware of the deleterious effect souls in limbo have on the human psyche, and are invested in keeping the souls tethered here to block humans from reaching higher vibrations. The more I do this work ... the more it feels true. After my travels last year, I resolved that on my next trip I would pursue assisting souls to ascend more consciously.

Hamburg seemed a likely place for several reasons: it is a busy, industrial port city near Atlantic international flights, and cruises regularly come in and out of its waters; plus it has a thriving red light district known by the unfortunate name of Reeperbahn (this means 'ropewalk' but non-native speaker pronunciation is often 'raper bon'). In addition to the trauma of various wars and regional conflicts over the years, it also seemed a likely place to find souls who were victims of human trafficking. In my experience, water also often holds onto psychic vibrations. Hamburg is on the banks of the large river Elbe that leads directly to the Atlantic. The city is dotted with canals, and at the center lie two large lakes surrounded by park land. When I envision Hamburg on the map, I can sense a darkness there. A darkness I think I can help alleviate.

Several of my friends who have been to Hamburg tell me how beautiful it is. The guidebooks I've read gush about its art, architecture, beautiful harbor and history.

When I arrive, although I can see these things on the surface, I can also sense a seething darkness underneath that colors my every perception. I take many pictures and in viewing them I can see the beauty of the place—but not when looking at the landscape directly.

I begin to try and communicate with this swirling mass of consciousness and immediately learn that many of the souls have no interest in ascending. They are caught in an addictive loop. Their presence ensures fear and suffering which they eagerly feed on—but they are never satisfied. Their hunger for the lower vibrational emotions seems insatiable. I have previously encountered spirits who desired to linger for fear that they might be forgotten, or out of a desire for vengeance—but nothing quite as dark as what I encounter in Hamburg.

I reach out to my friend Toby Evans to get her perspective on the situation.

She recommends an effective strategy of appealing to the less addicted spirits, informing them that their free will is being used against them to keep them in a lower density 'soul trap.' She also suggests letting the spirits know that I will be setting up a portal to assist them, and that it would be wise for them to use the safe passage to leave before the frequencies go even higher—when it will no longer be possible for them to exist here.

I take her advice. I begin to discern that some beings are less committed to this cycle than others—but they have fears of the darker beings among them, not wanting to break up the pack (the gang). Slowly, over the days I am here, I begin to repeat a mantra: 'Imagine a place where you are no longer hungry, where hunger does not exist.' I feel a slow shift, yet I also feel some danger to myself. I spend an afternoon in St. Michael's church gathering strength, feeling fortunate that the symphony is rehearsing there for a performance later that evening.

Eventually I decide that I will open a vortex near the time of my departure. I sense that it will be safer for me to be gone when souls begin to ascend, and it will also be closer to the time when the vortex will be opening in Kansas City at the Prairie Labyrinth.

To the darker members of the group, I repeat that they may wish to ascend because eventually the rising vibration of the earthly plane will send them to dust. I believe some of them are willingly choosing this path either because they don't believe me, or perhaps because at their core they are miserable enough that becoming dust sounds like a reprieve.

I end up quite ill for much of the time I am there, and I believe this to be in part because my mission is not welcomed by all of the psychic community. I am undeterred, though. On my last day, sitting at the museum café, I am staring out at the smaller of the two lakes in the city. In the center is a huge plume fountain that shoots straight into the air some twenty feet high. It runs all year. It suddenly dawns on me that this is the perfect spot for the vortex.

I have already spent most of what little energy I have on this cold and wet day, but I am determined to open the vortex before I go back to my Bed and Breakfast. I make my way in the cold wind to the shores of the lake. Bright yellow daffodils line its shores, and I can see a centuries-old building that seems to shimmer behind the fountain. I carry in my pocket three crystals

447

that have long lived on my altar. I have charged them with the intention of protecting me and anyone else who might be harmed by these restless souls, and with the primary intention of assisting souls in limbo to transition. I arrive at the edge of the lake. Despite the cold and wind, there is a number of people in the park. It seems important to go unobserved in my brief ritual. I have a moment of paranoia that the spirits who do not want my help might manifest their desires in a passerby, but it soon leaves me.

I stand shivering in the wind on the lakeshore. There is a tree blooming, its flowered branches extending over the lake. I lean against it to ground and center with all the elements easily present: earth beneath my feet, connecting to it through the tree; the strong wind (representing air) is impossible to ignore; the fire is contained in the crystals ... and the water element is omnipresent. As I carefully place the crystals in the lake, I envision a vortex opening right over the fountain, ascending upwards, allowing the energy of the water to feed the energy of the vortex. I let the souls know it will be there as an option for them, and that the vortex will be gathering strength as we near the opening of the vortex at the Prairie Labyrinth. I try to envision the energy of the ascended plane so that they might sense its value through me. I walk away slowly from the lake. As I look back, the mist around the fountain seems to shift in the windy day. I see faces, wraiths, shapes in the mist. I make my way home with difficulty—exhausted, coughing, and a little feverish. Still, I feel a great relief at accomplishing at least part of what I have come to do.

The next morning I fly out early, and move on to the light of Venice where my cough and cold disappear quickly with the healing energy of that place's light and water. Such a contrast between the two cities and the souls that linger there."

~ M. Kate Sinnett, Ph.D.
  mksinnett@gmail.com

On Earth Day, thirty-five individuals come together to 'hold space' for what is occurring throughout and around the planet. Above the center of the Prairie Labyrinth, streaks of light are captured by a cell phone camera—these departing souls are made up of an eclectic group from far and wide. Among them are Osage Indians that inhabited this land in the 1800s before they were massacred by the Union soldiers. The strange thing is that most of them had already crossed over in 1995 when I first opened the portal in connection with a 'controlled burn' of the prairie grasses. They are back, pledging their help and making themselves known to me as members of my 'soul family.' There is also a number of nuns from a convent in Kansas where unwed mothers went. Some remained from the 1800s - 1900s, but the bulk of them were from the late 1930s through the 1970s. Many women and babies who died during their time there are accompanied by the Sisters of Charity who were responsible for their care or, in some cases, for their suffering and shame. The participants holding space remain in the labyrinth drumming and meditating in the center for over two hours. Those able to 'see,' 'hear,' or 'tune into' what is occurring feel satisfied that countless souls have taken the opportunity to leave. Because of the massive numbers involved around the world, I assume that the portals will remain open for several days. After asking and muscle-checking as to when I should be closing them, I finally receive the message about two weeks later that they do *not* need to be closed. They are to remain open permanently—from here on in—and portals opened around the globe in the future will automatically be tied into this evolving shuttle system. Something major has shifted; something that I do not become aware of until preparing the land for the reset energies of the total solar eclipse in August of 2017.

While listening to a YouTube interview entitled *Ascension Updates, Grid Work and Accelerated Timelines* with *Sandra Walter (a Wayshower, Gatekeeper of Mount Shasta, and Ascension Guide) she relays that 'timeline splits indicate the completion of the old storylines. These splits may appear in our consciousness as dividing DNA strands, splitting trees (something that was literally happening on our property), or train tracks. She shares that the strongest energy wave in decades came at the Equinox in September 2016, and it was aimed at accelerating the timelines. That wave got rid of many structures that kept us on a lower repetitive loop. Complexity and chaos increases as the old timelines near extinction. (The 2016 presidential election reflected this.) By March/April of 2017, we began recalibrating ourselves to the higher timelines and a greater splitting of realities occurred making the Ascension passageways more open and available to the collective consciousness, including greater masses of earthbound souls. The portals that were being constructed leading up to Earth Day were being woven into the crystalline Unity grids made up of bands of light above and below us.

The crystalline grids are a high-vibrational system that provides a bridge between the old and the new. They are in place to assist all of us in the dimensional shift to the crystalline consciousness. For earthbound souls, they offer direct flights to the World of Light and to the New Earth that is forming. Plugging into the bridge sets the intention that the highest potential for Ascension be realized for all.

After an earthbound soul has moved through a portal, instead of closing it, we can now simply remove our personal energy from it. Besides 'multiplying the benefits by inviting other souls onto the 'bridge,' the incoming light is making it possible to multiply gateway portals all around the planet.

*Lisa Transcendence Brown shares: *"Cosmically/Galactically we are raining Christed/Crystalline frequencies in 'bombardment' all day every day now. The highest light (Christed Light) is in the atmosphere and inner Earth, as they both work together simultaneously."*

The eclipse signaled a grand resolution of the conflicts and divided energy that has been created in all realities. It provided a specific window in time to witness the darkness that we have each carried throughout our countless incarnations, reviewing the old inception point of separation (which promotes enslavement) while taking us into the crowning universal re-write of unity consciousness. Here, we are being given opportunities (many, in the form of personal and environmental disasters) to come together and be of service to each other. The 'reboot' of the new programs that the eclipse set into motion is up-leveling our individual and collective purpose.

All Lightworkers are here to be 'cosmic conduits,' drawing in, anchoring, and sending out the higher intended vibrations, but Crossing Guards serve as bridge extenders that must reach back—meeting the trapped souls where they are—while moving them forward by focusing on the higher realities that link them up with their Higher Self frequencies. They stand in the converging intersections between third density and fifth density, without neon colored vests, camouflaged to others and (in the beginning stages of entering into this work), even to themselves.

There is a coordinated 'hand-off' from the ground patrol to the off-world contingency, acting more like a *Secret Service of Light*. They are made up of our Multidimensional Selves, Higher Density Beings, our Guides, Angels, Masters, Teachers, and Loved Ones who already know the way and have made this journey before. They orchestrate things behind the scenes, set up the rendezvous points, nudge us into the 'locks' to be up-leveled, gather the souls who are ready and provide layers of protection as they synchronize all the unseen details that we are mostly oblivious to. But ... they need us. Our human energy is required to move the Earth forward into the patterns of *infinite regeneration*—the 'crossing-over' patterns of self-forgiveness and self-love necessary to elevate the planet's vibration.

If the door to the unseen realms was slightly ajar for me before my first earthbound soul experience with Della, and before the deaths of my father and brother, it swung wide open afterwards and set me onto a narrow footpath (more like a dog path) that has become a well-established trail. Someday, because of the Crossing Guards who are willing to stand in the intersections providing safe passage, this trail will be well worn and marked. It doesn't matter if you are a beginning explorer or a seasoned 'trailblazer.' Equipped with the compass of your compassion, you'll find your way to the edges where an off-ramp might be needed.

Doing this work means spanning two worlds—one that is dissolving and one that is emerging. The 'flash' that you are waiting for may be a flash of self-recognition. Every time you hold the image of reuniting an earthbound soul with the matrix of their Inner Divine Self, quantum entanglement occurs. The repetitive path to 5D awareness gets imprinted on you. And the repetitive 'flash points' of remembering who you are, unties the sandbags that the 3D self clings to. You are here, in good company, stretching beyond the old crumbling barriers, and building the scaffolding of the soul-bridge with the returning Light of your Ascending Essential Self. You crossed many timelines and worlds to be an active participant in the graduation process that is happening now. Your personal Ascension is taking you to the ground of your being. It's here—through your innumerable interactions with others—that you will lift the veil of illusion and meet your Solar Self on the horizon of your own 'Soul-Rise.'

Through the Light

Oh, Ring of Fire, raised from the Earth. Oh, gilded star, awaiting birth.
Oh, liquid jewel, you are meant to shine. Winged hearts create, awake your
Love Divine.

Through the Light, through the Light. We are the Light we travel through.
Through the Light, through the Light. Become the Light that lives in you.

The dark will pass and peace will come. Release the pain, awake the Sun.
New rays will rise from opened hearts. The flaming skies will unite our parts.

The night will pass—so will our doubts. A door will form to guide us out.
It's by the star that shines within—that light reveals who we've always been.

Through the Light, through the Light. We are the Light we travel through.
Through the Light, through the Light. Become the Light that lives in you.

~ Song by Toby Evans
   Written for the Harmonic Convergence in 1987.
   Inspired by Rus Caughron's words—"We are the light we travel through." RIP

"Dear Spirit, I am alive in the years that will save the Earth,
and I am here to make a change on the planet.

I hereby drop all the vows that would get in the way of that,
for they belong to another consciousness and another energy.

Instead, I renew my vows with the same Akashic energy
that took them originally.

All of the lifetimes that are now under me are my support.
And like a rod of energy that I will put down this line through my own history,
I take control of them all now.

I will need the help of all the consciousness of these many souls who I was,
from the time I first came to this planet.

Together we will create a white light like this planet has never seen.
The light of the many me's, focused through the current me.

That's why I came this time, and that's why I have existed through the ages—
to be here now."

~ KRYON ~

Kryon, Channeled by Lee Carroll
From Kryon Live Channel, "Human Lighthouse Filters"
December 2006 in Newport Beach, CA

And, in the end
The love you take
is equal to the love you make.

~ Paul McCartney, The Beatles ~

REFERENCES

Chapter 2. Un-Dead Initiation
This chapter is reprinted and expanded upon from:
Maril Crabtree, *Sacred Feathers; The Power of One Feather to Change Your Life*, Adams Media Corporation (June 2002)
The Great Gatsby is a 1974 American romantic drama film produced by Newdon Productions and distributed by Paramount Pictures. It was based on F. Scott Fitzgerald's 1925 novel of the same name.
Therese Becker, *Traveling the River*, Mandala Press.

Chapter 4. Soul Contract of a Superhero
Neale Donald Walsch, *Conversations with God*, G. P. Putnam's Sons; 1st edition (October 29, 1996)

Chapter 5. The Changing Current
The Delta Queen Riverboat, wikipedia.org/wiki/DeltaQueen
Ronna Herman, posted in *Arcturian Ascension Tools,* ronnastar.com/messages-aam/latest.html
Anais Nin, brainyquote.com/quotes/authors/a/anais_nin.html
Touched by an Angel is an American drama series that premiered on CBS on September 21, 1994 and ran for 211 episodes (nine seasons) until its conclusion on April 27, 2003. Created by John Masius and produced by Martha Williamson
Laura Strong's site: *Psychopomps; Making A Road for the Spirit to Cross Over*, psychopomps.org/resources-for-the-modern-psychopomp.html

Chapter 6. Shadow of Death

Lilan Laishley, Ph.D. *Full Moon in Virgo and the Shadow*, Feb.25-26, 2013, www.laishley.com, or email drlilan@laishley.com

Kim Gould, http://www.loveyourdesign.com/author/admin/

Dying Consciously; The Great Journey, http://www.dyingconsciously.org/

Bob Olson, *AfterLife TV*, http://www.afterlifetv.com/

Ghost, 1990 American romantic fantasy thriller films.[2]

Mort Nicholson, *Clearing Thoughtforms*, Nicholson Personal Energy Professionals, www.nicholsonpep.com

Chapter 7. The Labyrinth Portal

The Labyrinth Society, http://labyrinthsociety.org/about-labyrinths

Kryon Live Channeling, by Lee Carroll, Breckenridge, Colorado, July 14, 2001, Kryon Annual Summer Light Conference.

Bolshoi Zayatsky, www.wondermondo.com

William Henry, http://www.williamhenry.net/

Drunvalo Melchizedek, School of Remembering, http://www.drunvalo.net/

Ghost Whisperer, is an American television supernatural drama series on CBS from September 23, 2005, to May 21, 2010

Octahedron Image, p. 60: MilanB/Shutterstock

Chapter 8. The Thin Place

Loren Artress, *Veriditas*, http://veriditas.org/

Chapter 9. Sacred Geometry as Portals

Vesica Piscis, http://www.halexandria.org/dward097.htm

Chapter 15. The Higher Self Matrix

Doreen Virtue, *Angel Therapy Training*, http://www.angeltherapy.com/events

Saxon Knight, http://www.seraphimschool.com/saxon-knight/

Melon Thomas Benedict, http://www.neardeath.com/experiences/reincarnation04.html

Chapter 16. Calling All Angels

Dr. Eric Pearl, *The Reconnection*, Hay House; Revised ed. edition (April 1, 2003) http://www.thereconnection.com/

Dr. J.J. Hurtak, PhD. PhD. *The Book of Knowledge*; Keys of Enoch, The Academy of Future Science; 6th edition (2009)

Drunvalo Melchizedek, *The Ancient Secret of the Flower of Life*, Light Technology Publishing; First Edition (April 1, 1999)

Chapter 17. The Grid of Compassion

Tim Wheater, *Heartland*, Audio CD (October 10, 1995)

Greg McHugh, *The New Regression Therapy*, CreateSpace Independent Publishing Platform (March 23, 2010) *gregmchugh@earthlink.net*
Tools for Emotional/Mental Healing # 2 of a Weekly Series (July 4, 2013)
Considering New Avenues for Treatment for Military Veterans with PTSD

Jelalia Starr, *Nibiruan Council*, http://www.nibiruancouncil.com/

Patricia Diane Cota Robels, https://www.eraofpeace.org/

Gregg Braden, www.greggbraden.com

Shifra Hendrie, *Quantum Healing Consciousness*, http://www.purposebalancelife.com/quantum-healing-and-soul.html

Global Coherence Initiative, https://www.heartmath.org/gci/

Chapter 18. Template of the Soul

Robert Monroe, *Ultimate Journey*, Harmony (December 1, 1994)

Francie Steiger, *Reflections from an Angel's Eye*, Berkley (May 1, 1982)

Brad Steiger, *The Star People*, Mass Market Paperback (April 15, 1987)

Groundhog Day, 1993, American fantasy-comedy film directed by Harold Ramis, starring Bill Murray, Andie Mac Dowelll, and Chris Elliott. Murray plays Phil Connors, an arrogant Pittsburgh TV weatherman who, during an assignment covering the annual Groundhog Day event in Punxsutawney, Pennsylvania, finds himself caught in a time loop, repeating the same day again and again.

Suzanne Lie, *The Alchemy of Creation Part 2 - Transmutation of Matter*, June 25, 2013

Sherry Wilde, *The Forgotten Promise*, Ozark Mountain Publishing (March 1, 2014)

Chapter 19. Your Soul's Best Advocate

Dr. Brian Weiss, www.brianweiss.com

Dolores Cannon, www.dolorescannon.com

The Newton Institute, *Life Between Lives*, newtoninstitute.org

Gary Craig, *EFT Emotional Freedom Technique*, http://www.emofree.com/

Echo Bodine, *What Happens When We Die*, New World Library (October 8, 2013)

Chapter 21. Getting Unstuck

Michael Newton, *Destiny of Souls*, Llewellyn Publications; 2 sub editions. (May 8, 2000)

Debbie Ford, *The Dark Side of the Light Chasers*, Riverhead Books; (November 2, 2010)

Michael Newton, *Journey of Souls*, Llewellyn Publications; 1st edition (July 1994)

Chapter 22. Dreamtime SOS

Schindler's List, 1993 American epic historical period drama film, directed and co-produced by Steven Spielberg

Ka-tzetnik 135633 (author), Moshe M. Kohn (translator), *House of Dolls*, Pyramid Books; Third Edition 1965 edition (1965)

Laurence Rees, *Auschwitz: A New History*, Public Affairs (January 10, 2006)

Chapter 23. Returning to Sunshine

Tube Torus, Rita Marr CCHyp., MPNLP, *The Hara Lines 7 Keys to Health*, https://haradimension.wordpress.com/the-torus-the-zero-point-energy-field-and-the-creation-story/

Chapter 24. Solar Portal

X-class solar flares, https://www.nasa.gov/mission_pages/sunearth/news X-class- flares.html

PART 2

Chapter 27. The Curse and Vow

Christine Page, Frontiers for Health, www.christinepage.com

Vianna Sibal, Theta Healing, www.thetahealing.com

Chapter 28. Inner Earth Incubator

Maia Chrystine Nartoomid, *Spirit Mythos*, www.spiritmythos.org/intro/maia.html

WingMakers Neruda Interview #5, www.wingmakers.com/content/neruda-interviews/

REFERENCES

The Matrix- a science fiction action media franchise beginning with the feature film 1999.

Avatar, 2009 American epic science fiction film directed, written, produced, and co-edited by James Cameron.

Chapter 29. Borderland

Halls of Amenti, The Emerald Tablets of Thoth, www.crystalinks.com/emerald2bw.html

Piazza del Campidoglio, aviewoncities.com/rome/piazzadelcampidoglio.htm

Chapter 30. Mosta Dome

Francois Xavier Alosio, *Islands of Dream: The Temples of Malta-Hidden Mysteries Revealed*, 2009 Media Centre Limited.

Chapter 32. First Wave of Souls

Mgr. Dr. Anthony Gauci, *A Historical and Tourist Guide to the Island* (1969)

Chapter 33. Voice of the Feminine

Brené Brown, http://www.goodreads.com/author/quotes/162578.Bren_Brown

Chapter 35. Womb and Tomb

Jennifer Berezan, *Returning*, recorded in the Hypogeum at Hal Saflieni in Malta. AllMusic - 2001

Marija Gimbutas, author and Lithuanian-American archaeologist known for her research into the Neolithic and Bronze Age cultures.

Riley Crabb's *Borderland Science* magazine, http://www.unexplained-mysteries.com/forum/index.php?showtopic=176068

Dr. Allen, *Enigma Fantastique*, Health Research Books, 1996

Chapter 38. Level Three

Sergio Magana, *2012-2021: The Dawn of the Sixth Sun*, Edizioni Amrita SRL; 1st edition (August 1, 2012)

Suzanne Lie, http://suzanneliephd.blogspot.com/

Arcturian Ascension Tools, http://www.arcturiantools.com/

PART 3

Chapter 39. "KP" Duty

Twilight Zone, Anthology series which began on October 2, 1959 and ended on June 19, 1964—with five seasons and 156 episodes. It was created by Rod Serling and broadcast on CBS.

Lost, Television science fiction and supernatural drama series on ABC from 2004-2010.

Lisa Renee, *Energetic Synthesis*, www.energeticsynthesis.com/index. php/about-energetic-synthesis/about-lisa-renee

Gnostic Demiurge and Archons, http://jeffreyskuppermancom/2012/02/ 15/the-gnostic-demiurge-and-archons/

Cameron Day, *Archons / Ankle biters*, AscensionHelp.com

Barbara Brodsky, founder and guiding teacher of Deep Spring Center for Meditation channeling a discarnate entity called *Aaron*. deepspring.org/aaron

Chapter 41. Moving On

Alien, 1979 British-American science-fiction horror film directed by Ridley Scott, and starring Tom Skerritt and Sigourney Weaver.

Linda Blair, star of the movie *The Exorcist*, 1973 American psychological horror film

Chapter 43. Jewel in the Lotus

Ben Kingsley, *Gandhi*, 1982 epic biographical film which dramatizes the life of Mohandas Karamchand Gandhi

Inti Raymi, *Festival of the Sun*, http://gosouthamerica.about.com/od/ perartandculture/a/IntiRaymi.htm

Om Mani Padme Hum, http://www.dharma-haven.org/tibetan/ meaning-of-om-mani-padme-hung.htm

William Henry, *We Be Beamers: Quantum Star Seeds Entangled in Mystic Union with Christ*, posted on January 31, 2018 in Apotheosis, Ascension, http://www.williamhenry.net/2018/01/beamers-quantum-star-seeds-entangled-in-mystic-union-with-christ/

Chapter 44. Dark Side Defectors

Dr. Barbara Stone, *Soul Detective*, souldetective.net, *Invisible Roots*, Energy Psychology Press; 1st edition (September 15, 2008)

Dr. William Baldwin, *Spirit Releasement Therapy*, http://www. soulrescuesite.com/spirit-releasement-therapy.htm

Chapter 45. Reconciliation

Bert Hellinger, Family Constellations, www.hellingerpa.com

Chapter 46. NOT Gone

Réal Laplaine, *Dead, But NOT Gone*, CreateSpace Independent Publishing Platform; 1st edition (December 7, 2012)

Chapter 47. Un-Binding

James Twyman, *The Kabbalah Code*, Hay House Inc. (2009)

Joe Lofgreen, *Spirit Voices, Spirit Crossings: The incredible true story of EVP dialogue and spiritual discovery*, Red Orchid Publishing (September 10, 2015)

Chapter 49. McGregor

Steve Rother, *Espavo*, https://www.espavo.org/welcome-lightworkers/

Shakespeare, *As You Like It*, Pastoral comedy written in 1599 and first published in the *First Folio*, 1623. Touchstone is a fictional character - the court jester of Duke Frederick the usurper's court.

Healing Touch, http://www.healingtouchprogram.com/

The Young MacGregors, https://www.youtube.com/watch?v=ycpJUvw5WzY

Greig, http://www.greig.org/index.php?option=com_content&view=

Chapter 50. Death Rites

Donna Eden, *Eden Energy Medicine*, http://www.innersource.net/em/

Tom Kenyon, The Hathor Material, http://tomkenyon.com/earths-magnetic

Octahedron Image, p. 410: MilanB/Shutterstock

Chakra Image, p. 411: Peter Hermes Furian/Shutterstock

Annie Kagan, *The Afterlife of Billy Fingers*, Hampton Roads Publishing; 3.1.2013 edition (March 1, 2013)

Eben Alexander, *Proof of Heaven*, Simon & Schuster; 1 edition (October 23, 2012)

Nanci Danison, *Backwards*, A P Lee & Co; 1st edition (October 1, 2007)

Dannion Brinkley, *Saved by the Light*, HarperOne; Reprint edition (November 25, 2008)

Michael Newton, *Memories of the Afterlife*, Llewellyn Publications; 1 edition (October 8, 2009)

Echo Bodine, *Echoes of the Soul*, New World Library (January 14, 1999) and *What Happens When We Die*, New World Library (October 8, 2013)

The Greatest Journey, www.livingdying.org/conscious-dying

Chapter 51. Putting It All Together

Clair Senses, http://www.quantumpossibilities.biz/clairs.htm

Pranic Tube Alignment, Tom Kenyon, www.tomkenyon.com

Octahedron Image, p. 424: MilanB/Shutterstock

Chapter 52. Ascending Essential Self

David Wilcock, *The Ascension Mysteries: Revealing the Cosmic Battle Between Good and Evil*, Dutton (August 30, 2016)

Chemtrails, http://in5d.com/chemtrail-pilot-blows-the-lid-off-of-covert-black-operation-indigo-skyfold/

Jay Weidner, https://www.gaia.com/video/chemtrails-and-sun-jay-weidner

Gaia TV, *Cosmic Disclosure*, https://www.gaia.com/seeking-truth

The Law of One (Ra Material) books were channeled by L/L Research (Carla Rueckert, Don Elkins, and Jim McCarty) between 1981 and 1984. http://www.lawofone.info/

The Prophecy of Peter Deunov - Angelfire www.angelfire.com/oh2/peterr/ProphecyOfPeterDeunov.html

Leonard Cohen, *Anthem*, 1992 album The Future http://www.azlyrics.com/lyrics/leonardcohen/anthem.html Paul H. Ray Ph.D. Sherry Ruth Anderson.

Cultural Creatives: How 50 Million People Are Changing the World, Broadway Books (October 2, 2001)

Sandra Walter on Quantum Conversations with Lauren Galey, https://www.youtube.com/watch?v=n7vZm-qem1E

Lisa Transcendence Brown, *Crystalline Consciousness with Lisa Transcendence Brown*, http://mailchi.mp/awakeningtoremembering/0423-upgrades-on-every-level-physical-emotional-mental-as-etheric-mergings-increase-1720669?e=6e18d1da73

The one who knows how to live knows how to die.
The one who knows how to fall in love
knows when the moment has come to fall out of it.
He falls out of it gracefully, with a good-bye, with gratitude.
If one really wants to live life in all its richness,
one has to learn how to be consistently inconsistent.
How to be able to move from one extreme to another—sometimes
rooted deep in the earth and sometimes flying high in the heavens,
sometimes making love and sometimes meditating.
And then, slowly, your heaven and your earth come closer and
closer, and you will become the horizon where they meet.

~ OSHO ~

TOBY EVANS

Moving to the Kansas City area in 1987, Toby Evans established *SageBrush Exchange* as an Art studio. With the installation of "The Prairie Labyrinth" in 1995, her art expanded to the energetic field, focusing on the land in sacred reciprocity with balancing mind, body and spirit. A spiritual counseling practice evolved offering therapies for the soul which include individual and group Labyrinth experiences, Akashic Record Readings, Past Life and Life Between Lives Spiritual Regressions, Energy Medicine, and Soul Detective sessions. She assists individuals with energy attachments and provides 'Soul Crossing' sessions both in-person and over the phone. Toby is an artist, a founding member of the Labyrinth Society and the Art Line Project.

Morning walk in the Prairie Labyrinth. Photo by Pamela Hawkins.